Shattered World

Shattered World

Adaptation and Survival among
Vietnam's Highland Peoples
during the Vietnam War

Gerald Cannon Hickey

UNIVERSITY OF PENNSYLVANIA PRESS   Philadelphia

Copyright © 1993 by the University of Pennsylvania Press
Printed in the United States of America

Library of Congress Cataloging-in-Publication Data
Hickey, Gerald Cannon, 1925–
   Shattered world: adaptation and survival among Vietnam's highland peoples during the Vietnam War / Gerald Cannon Hickey.
      p.   cm.
   Includes bibliographical references and index.
   ISBN 0-8122-3172-4 (cloth). — ISBN 0-8122-1417-X (paper)
   1. Indigenous peoples—Vietnam—Central Highlands.   2. Kinship—Vietnam—Central Highlands.   3. Material culture—Vietnam—Central Highlands.
4. Insurgency—Vietnam—Central Highlands—History.   5. Vietnamese Conflict, 1961–1975.   6. Central Highlands (Vietnam)—History.   7. Central Highlands (Vietnam)—Social life and customs.   I. Title.
GN635.V5H53   1993
306'.089'9592—dc20   92-45143
                                                                                                                        CIP

Contents

Illustrations

Figures

Photographs

Unless otherwise indicated in the captions, photographs were taken by the author.

Maps

Chart

Abbreviations Used in Notes

BEFEO	*Bulletin de l'Ecole Française d'Extrême-Orient*
BSEI	*Bulletin de la Société des Etudes Indochinoises*
FBIS	Foreign Broadcast Information Service (U. S. government)
IIEH	*Institut Indochinois pour l'Etude de l'Homme*
JPRS—SEA	Joint Publication Research Service (U. S. government), South East Asia section
SA	*Southeast Asia*

Acknowledgments

During fieldwork conducted in the central highlands of Vietnam between 1956 and 1973, people too numerous to mention lent assistance. They include highland villagers, Vietnamese and highlander officials, American civilians and military personnel, priests of the Missions Etrangères de Paris, and members of the Christian and Missionary Alliance. Certain individuals provided a great deal of help in gathering ethnographic data. In the case of the Rhadé they include Y Thih Eban, Y Yok Ayun, Michael Benge, Y Bling Buon Krong Pang, Katouilly-Plowatt, and Y Dhuat Nie Kdam. Touneh Han Tho was responsible for most of the data gathered on the Chru. I would particularly like to thank Summer Institute of Linguistics (SIL) researchers and their assistants for their role in fieldwork among the Roglai (Ernest Lee and Max Cobbey and Rim), Stieng (Ralph and Lorraine Haupers and Bi), Bru (John and Caroline Miller and Mondo), Pacoh (Richard Watson and Cubuat), and Halang (James and Nancy Cooper, Dinh and Luoi). Reverend Gordon Smith and his wife Laura helped gather information on the Katu as did SIL linguist Nancy Costello and her assistant, Kmeet, and informants Vien and Kithem. Similarly, Kenneth Smith of the SIL and his assistant, Hmou, as well as informants Tua and Leon Wit contributed to Sedang ethnography. Work on the Jeh was facilitated by SIL linguists Pat and Nancy Cohen and Dwight Gradin, as well as their assistants, Brol and Suai, and informants Grandmother of Aning, Cho, and Yun. Marilyn Gregerson and David Thomas of the SIL supplied linguistic and ethnographic literature.

I would like to express my appreciation to a number of individuals and organizations for their assistance in the preparation of the book. They are Douglas Murray, A. Thomas Kirsch, Mattiebelle Gittinger, May Ebihara, A. Terry Rambo, Norton Ginsburg, Susan Peterson, Matt Franjola, Hugh Mulligan, Reverend Ray Stubbe, my sister Catherine, and my niece Judy Walsh. Reverend Stan Sloan did ink drawings for Figures 4, 14, and 15 while Nguyen Van Tam did the remaining seventeen. Margaret Hemma prepared the Bu Kroai Kin Network chart. The Meadows Museum of Art in Shreveport, Louisiana, kindly permitted reproduction of the pen drawing of two Rhadé girls by Jean Despujols.

A National Endowment for the Humanities Fellowship for Independent Study and Research provided support for preparation of the manuscript. Manuscript preparation also was assisted by a grant from the Joint Committee on Southeast Asia of the Social Science Research Council and the American Council of Learned Societies with funds provided by the Ford Foundation and the National Endowment for the Humanities. A subvention for publication was kindly given by the Albert Kunstadter Family Foundation of New York.

For their roles in realizing the final product—the book—I would especially like to thank Patricia Smith, Carl Gross, Kathleen Moore, and Mindy Brown of the University of Pennsylvania Press for their professional guidance, and Trudie Calvert for her editorial assistance.

Finally, I would like to express my deepest gratitude to the people of the central highlands for their kindness and generosity, and for all I learned from them, not only about their world, but also about the meaning of courage, dignity, hope, and survival.

Introduction

Visible to the west from almost any place along the central coastal plain of Vietnam are the lofty mountains that form the southern portion of the Annam Cordillera. (The French call this range the Chaine Annamitique; the Vietnamese know it as the Trường Sơn, or "Long Mountains.") These uplands are the abode of people who not long ago lived in a world that they themselves evolved and sustained. Differentiated into ethnic groups, they speak languages either of the Mon Khmer or Austronesian (Malayopolynesian) stocks. Physically they resemble other Southeast Asians such as the Indonesians, Malays, and Cambodians, who also speak languages of these stocks. This book describes ten highland groups. Rhadé, Roglai, and Chru languages are of the Austronesian stock while the Stieng, Katu, Bru, Pacoh, Sedang, Jeh, and Halang speak Mon Khmer languages.

For the highlanders, man and society are embedded in nature and dependent upon cosmic forces. In the highlanders' green milieu of forested mountains, sweeping, undulating plateaus, and valleys through which brown rivers flow, each ethnic group over time worked out its adaptation to nature and shaped its society so that its members could survive, reproduce, and readapt to whatever changes man, nature, and the cosmic forces might impinge upon it. This evolutionary process resulted in some social-structural differences, but at the same time, adaptation to the mountain country created among them physical and ideational bonds that have given rise to a common culture, a highlander world.

It is a world centered on small communities where kinship is primary and resources are shared by all. The people respect the integrity of their natural surroundings, and each society has leaders who serve as stewards in preserving it. Villagers farm slopes and bottomland within the never-ending cycle of rainy seasons followed by dry seasons, of fields planted or fallowing. In the nearby streams they draw water, wash clothes, bathe, and fish. The surrounding forests supply them with game, wild fruits and vegetables, and firewood as well as hardwood, bamboo, and rattan for their houses, artifacts, and wood carvings. Although their religious pantheons vary, all of the highland people try to keep in harmony with their deities by observing religious prescriptions. Cosmic forces have revealed sets of sanctions, taboos, omens, and signs, and they mandate certain individuals to serve as stewards of religious prescriptions. These stewards also are guardians of moral order expressed in systems of justice wherein respect for individual rights provides a counterpoint to the prevailing concern for group survival. Finally, throughout the highland world there are expressions of beauty in art, architecture, music, and dance, all of which take on symbolic meaning within the context of religious prescriptions.

Historically the highlanders remained relatively aloof from the Chinese great tradition that molded the society of the Vietnamese and also from Indian influences diffusing eastward that brought civilization to the Cham, Khmer, and Lao. Cham rulers had tributary relations with some highland leaders, and Cham, Lao, Khmer, and Vietnamese traded with highland groups. But lowlanders by and large regarded the mountain country as a remote and forbidding place, populated by backward, often bellicose, tribes. In their historical advance southward along the coastal plain, the Vietnamese were content to remain in their orderly lowland villages surrounded by paddy fields. They believed that the wild mountains harbored evil spirits, "savages" capable of dark magic, and "poisoned water" that caused deadly fevers. Kingdoms and dynasties among the Cham, Khmer, Lao, and Vietnamese flourished and crumbled, monumental cities were sacked and abandoned, and populations shifted. All the while in the background, the mountains, their peaks shrouded in mists, were silent and seemingly immutable.

The highland people could have endured without "civilized" outsiders, but that was not to be. In the late nineteenth century the mountain country came under the colonial rule of the French, and in 1955 it became part of the Republic of Vietnam (South Vietnam). During the 1960s and early 1970s, the Vietnamese (from both the North and the South) and the Americans inflicted devastating modern warfare that engulfed the region. The end of the Vietnam War in 1975 brought Communist rule, the harshest yet imposed upon the highland people.

This book seeks to provide a picture of the highland world that existed before 1960. It also attempts to trace as much as possible the effects of the Vietnam War on that world. As the violence and destruction of the war spread and intensified, the most graphic (and observable) effect was the ever-increasing number of highland refugees who, in order to preserve the harmony among man, nature, and cosmos, had to devise a series of readaptational strategies. Another goal of this book is to assess, on the basis of the ethnographies and the course of events thus far, the impact of Communist "development" policy and programs on the highland world.

The Approach

Ethnographic research for this book began with a broad study that examined the role of the highlanders in the history of Indochina. The two resulting volumes, *Sons of the Mountains: Ethnohistory of the Vietnamese Central Highlands to 1954* and *Free in the Forest: Ethnohistory of the Vietnamese Central Highlands, 1954–1976*, present this historical picture.[1] They also analyze the combined social, economic, political, and geographic factors that fueled the rise of a pan-highlander leadership and ethnic identity. The first volume analyzes ethnic boundaries defined by Fredrik Barth as "social boundaries," which are "maintained by a limited set of cultural features."[2] This research included many discussions with highland informants, examination of ethnic differentiation in French and Vietnamese sources, and consultation with researchers of the Summer Institute of Linguistics (SIL). These data also provided the basis for the analyses of ethnic differentiation in the present work.

Between 1956 and 1973 ethnographic research was conducted among most of the highland groups. Ethnic groups described here were selected because they embody adaptational strategies found in the highlands, and they also reflect the range of readaptations that highlanders devised to cope with the disruptions of the Vietnam War. They also represent highland linguistic affiliations. Isidore Dyen groups the languages of the Rhadé, Chru, and Roglai (the latter of which has three dialects—Northern Roglai, Southern Roglai, and Cac Gia) in the Chamic group of the Austronesian stock. He notes that "a somewhat rough lexicostatistical count for Rade [Rhadé], Jarai, Chru, Cham, and Roglai indicates beyond question that these languages are at least very closely related and in some cases may even be dialects of the same language."[3] On the basis of lexicostatistical evidence, Dyen places the Chamic languages in the West Indonesian language group so their nearest relatives are the languages of Borneo, Sumatra, Java, and Bali.

David Thomas and R. K. Headley divide the Mon Khmer languages

1. Gerald Cannon Hickey, *Sons of the Mountains: Ethnohistory of the Vietnamese Central Highlands to 1954* (New Haven: Yale University Press, 1982); Hickey, *Free in the Forest: Ethnohistory of the Vietnamese Central Highlands, 1954–1976* (New Haven: Yale University Press, 1982).

2. Fredrik Barth, ed., *Ethnic Groups and Boundaries: The Social Organization of Culture Difference* (Boston: Little, Brown, 1969), pp. 15, 38.

3. Isadore Dyen, "The Chamic Languages," in *Current Trends in Linguistics,* ed. E. Sebeok (The Hague: Mouton, 1971), 8:200–210.

into nine branches: Pearic, Khmer, Bahnaric, Katuic, Khmuic, Monic, Palaungic, Khasi, and Viet-Muong.[4] Mon Khmer languages spoken by the highlanders belong either to the Bahnaric or Katuic branches. Thomas reports that within the Bahnaric branch, the North Bahnaric subgrouping contains Bahnar, Rengao, Sedang, Jeh, Halang, Monom, Kayong, Hre, Cua, Takua, and Todrah. The South Bahnaric subgrouping includes Stieng, Central Mnong (Gar, Chil, Kuanh, Rolom), Koho, and Chrau. The Katuic branch contains seventeen languages, five of which are spoken in the central highlands. These are Katu, Kantu (High Katu), Phuang, Bru, and Pacoh.

Ethnographic fieldwork between 1964 and 1973 was conducted under conditions of a war that eventually left no place in the highlands untouched. One result was that avenues of inquiry were often blocked, and at times villages and whole ethnic groups became inaccessible. Danger lurked after dark when ground attacks usually occurred (a set of notes on the Katu was burned in one such 1964 attack) and towns were shelled. Daytime dangers included Communist ambushes on roads and sudden aerial attacks on villages by American and South Vietnamese jet bombers. Finally, large-scale military operations periodically necessitated engaging in refugee-relief efforts (which did afford opportunities to observe the refugees' readaptations) to the exclusion of everything else. The limitations of wartime field research and the fragmentary data reported by other investigators have rendered variable the amount of ethnographic information from group to group. Nevertheless, it is possible to present for each one a social system that reveals functional relationships among religious beliefs and practices, settlement patterns, house types, kinship, economic activities, and village leadership.

A. Thomas Kirsch observes that "the upland peoples of Southeast Asia have developed a sociocultural system which is optimally adapted to their ecological situation. They see this ecological niche as a place in which a *total* style of life—including religious, political and economic dimensions—[has] been worked out and can be maintained." He adds, "But this culture does not define a *single* 'society.' Rather, it defines a *range* of social systems, and this range might be treated analytically as forming a single 'type,' e.g., 'hill tribes society.'" Kirsch's list of characteristics which upland people share includes two related to physical adaptation: "their ecological niche, the mountain slopes of Southeast Asia," and "their mode of adapting to that ecological niche, swidden ('shifting') cultivation." They also share "common features of the re-

4. David Thomas and R. K. Headley, Jr., "More on Mon-Khmer Subgroupings," *Lingua* 25, no. 4 (1970): 398–418; David Thomas, "A Note on the Branches of Mon-Khmer," *Mon-Khmer Studies IV,* Language Series no. 2, Center for Vietnamese Studies and Summer Institute of Linguistics (Saigon, 1973), pp. 138–41.

ligious system." Finally, Kirsch sees in all Southeast Asian upland societies "an apparent 'oscillation' between two extreme forms of organization characterized as 'democratic' and 'autocratic.' "[5]

Despite variations among their societies, the highlanders have a common culture that shares a great many characteristics of the Southeast
Asian upland culture described by Kirsch. Sheer physical adaptation to
the mountain country has lent to all highland economies a similar cast
that constitutes a strong common bond among the highland people. The
economy links the physical wants and needs of the society to the physical
environment, and the wants and needs of all the highland people have
been much the same. Despite variations in highland landscapes, the ways
in which they have gone about satisfying these needs in the general
upland setting have resulted in similar patterns in farming, hunting,
fishing, foraging, house building, textile weaving, alcohol preparation,
and fabrication of artifacts.

In describing that part of the highlands within the former borders of
South Vietnam, F. R. Moormann identifies three types of relief: excessive, rolling, and undulating.[6] Excessive relief is characterized by
strongly eroded plateaus and true mountains over 1,000 meters (3,280
feet). Ngoc Linh, the highest peak, rises 2,598 meters (8,523 feet).
Associated with this relief is a complex of mountainous soils, mostly red
and yellow podzolic and lithosolic soils that support local swidden farming. Such soils predominate in the territories of the Roglai, Katu, Bru,
Pacoh, Sedang, Jeh, and Halang. The main forest reserve of Vietnam is
in this zone, but Moormann observes that the zone has low agricultural
potential because of strong relief and predominantly poor, shallow soils.
Undulating and rolling reliefs are found in the southern and western
parts of the highlands. Rolling relief is associated with strongly eroded
plateaus, notably the expansive Darlac plateau, heart of the Rhadé
country, where reddish brown latosols, the "terres rouges," prompted
the French to establish coffee and rubber estates. The southern portion
of the highlands, where the Stieng are located, forms a terrace zone,
transitional between the mountains and the flat, low-elevation Mekong
River delta. Topography is plane to undulating with predominantly gray
podzolic soils.

Life in highland villages has seasonal rhythms revolving around two
monsoons that annually sweep the mountain country. Beginning in late
April or early May, the southwest monsoon brings its heaviest precipita-

5. A. Thomas Kirsch, *Feasting and Social Oscillation: A Working Paper on Religion and
Society in Upland Southeast Asia,* Department of Southeast Asian Studies, Cornell University, Southeast Asia Data Paper no. 92 (Ithaca, N.Y., 1973), pp. 5–6, 11, 36.

6. F. R. Moormann, *The Soils of the Republic of Vietnam* (Saigon: Republic of Vietnam,
Ministry of Agriculture, 1961), pp. 2, 16–20, 24, and General Soil Map.

tion to the windward western slopes, diminishing in September and ending in early October. C. Schutz reported in 1967 that the weather station at Ya Puch on the western Jarai plateau area at 715.06 meters (2,346 feet) recorded a monthly average of 22.5 inches during this monsoon. Farther northeast at 772.06 meters (2,533 feet) the station at Pleiku town recorded 16.4 inches. Moving eastward to the zone in the middle of the mountain range, the average dropped to between 5 and 10 inches and to 5 inches or less for the eastern slope. The northeast monsoon usually begins in late October and subsides by the end of March. Between December and February it brings heavy rains along with periods of persistent fog and drizzle to the northern part of the central highlands, where the Bru and Pacoh are located. At Bana Mountain, which soars 1,467.15 meters (4,843 feet) above the northeastern edge of the Katu country, the rain averages 24.9 inches monthly at the peak of the season. Moving southward there is markedly less rainfall. Very infrequently typhoons strike central Vietnam, usually during October and November.[7] R. Champsoloix reports that in the terrace region the temperatures are similar to those in Saigon (Ho Chi Minh City) with an annual mean of 27.5° C (81.5° F) while at higher elevations it is cooler, averaging 24.0° C (75.2° F) at Kontum, 22.4° C (72.3° F) at Pleiku, 24.6° C (76.3° F) at Ban Me Thuot, and 19.1° C (66.4° F) at Dalat.[8]

All of the groups studied in this book practice swidden farming to grow upland rain-fed rice (the Chru and some Rhadé also have wet-rice farming, which represents historical change discussed below) as well as maize and a variety of secondary field and garden crops. Research in recent years has revealed the efficacy of swidden farming under certain conditions. In discussing advantages of swidden and small-plot farming, David Harris points out that shifting (swidden) farming and small, fixed-plot horticulture involve "manipulation rather than transformation" of the natural environment, "altering selected components without fundamentally modifying its overall structure."[9] They involve substituting wild species with certain preferred domesticated species that occupy equivalent ecological niches. A. Terry Rambo observes that swidden farming has ecological advantages under tropical environmental conditions: "It

7. C. Schutz, "Monsoonal Influences on Wind, Rain, and Cloud Throughout Southeast Asia: A Study Covering the Peninsula and the Archipelago (Santa Monica, Calif.: Rand Corporation, 1967), pp. 17–29.

8. R. Champsoloix, *Rapport sur les forêts des P.M.S.* (Saigon: République du Viet-Nam, Ministère de la Réforme Agraire et de Développement en Agriculture et Pêcherie, 1952), p. 15.

9. David R. Harris, "Agricultural Systems, Ecosystems, and the Origin of Agriculture," in *The Domestication and Exploitation of Plants and Animals,* ed. Peter J. Ucko and G. W. Dimbley (Chicago: Aldine-Atherton, 1969), pp. 4–8.

gives reliable yields with minimum population density, it causes little long-term degradation of the productive capacity of the environment." Beneficial effects of burning include clearance of unwanted vegetation from the field, alteration of soil structure making planting easier, enhancement of soil fertility by ashes, and decrease in soil acidity. Burning increases availability of soil nutrients and causes sterilization of soil and reduction of microbial, insect, and weed populations. Rambo warns, however, that population increase can easily exhaust the available supplies of biomass energy, leading to shortening of the fallow period essential for forest renewal.[10]

The ethnographies in this book reveal the highlanders' fund of practical knowledge about weather, soils, drainage, and the care of plants. They also reflect concern for maintaining the integrity of the natural environment and describe leaders who act to preserve it. In carrying out farming activities, all of the groups have ways of supervising land use. Highlanders also have become very knowledgeable about which crops will grow on which soils. Swidden sizes are based on food-consumption needs and availability of labor. When clearing, large trees often are left standing, and roots of felled trees always remain in the soil. Wood is allowed to dry, gathered in piles, and set ablaze. Commonly a swidden is farmed for three years, but in some areas very fertile soils enable longer cultivation periods. Most swiddens are allowed to fallow for between seven and ten years. A wet-rice adaptation necessitates the same body of knowledge in addition to requiring water-management skills to deal with such problems as water-pressure inflow and outflow in planning dike and dam construction and orientation of channels.

In gardens and swiddens villagers grow secondary crops, the most common of which are maize, manioc, yams, pineapples, eggplant, onions, melons, gourds, pumpkins, beans, chili peppers, sugarcane, squash, taro, tobacco, and cotton. Banana, papaya, and jack fruit trees are cultivated in gardens and around swiddens. Coconut, mango, and kapok trees can be found in most villages, while less common tree crops are areca nuts, oranges, limes, and grapefruit. Chickens, pigs, and dogs forage around farmsteads, goats are common, and buffalo are signs of wealth. Elephants serve as draft animals in a few groups.

The ethnographies reflect common patterns in the general division of labor. Throughout the year women typically rise at dawn and stir fires in open hearths to heat leftover rice for breakfast. They release chickens

---

10. A. Terry Rambo, "No Free Lunch," in *An Introduction to Human Ecology Research on Agricultural Systems in Southeast Asia,* ed. A. Terry Rambo and Percy E. Sajise (Laguna, Philippines: University of the Philippines at Los Baños Publication Program, 1984), pp. 155–58.

from coops to scamper about in search of food. Other members of the family then awaken to take their first meal of the day. With back-baskets full of clothes and empty gourds and babies nestled in slings across their breasts, women gather at the nearby stream or river. There is lively chatter as they wash clothes and fill gourds with water. Females tend gardens, and every few days groups of them enter the forests to fetch firewood and forage for wild fruits and vegetables. In the afternoon or early evening women and young girls using back-tension looms sit on the floor of the main room to weave textiles. Upland textiles are woven for use in flat, untailored costume elements such as blankets, women's skirts, loincloths, mantles, and slings for carrying infants and also for tailored garments, including women's blouses and men's shirts. Rich shades of red, blue, and yellow are combined with black and white in intricate, elegant motifs. These textiles tend to be patterned primarily with warp stripes. Among some groups these stripes may be augmented with bands patterned with supplementary wefts. Anytime during the day it is common to see a female husking rice by pounding it, using a long pestle and a carved-wood mortar. The big family meal is at sunset. Women move around open hearths to stir pots of rice and vegetables and turn roasting fish and perhaps some chunks of meat.

Women and men share many tasks during planting season. When clearing a swidden, women cut brush while men fell trees. Men make holes with dibble sticks, and women follow to sow. Everyone helps with harvesting. In wet-rice farming men plow using buffalo, after which women broadcast the seeds. Men's tasks change somewhat in the annual dry season. They have more time for fishing and hunting, which require considerable knowledge of fauna and aquatic life. Wildlife abounds in the mountain country, and informants have provided the names of much of the game they hunt and trap. Another source is a work on hunting and game in Indochina by H. de Monestrol, who lists many of the Latin zoological names.[11] An assortment of birds also is hunted. Highland men

11. H. de Monestrol, *Chasses et faune d'Indochine* (Saigon: Edition A. Portail, 1952), pp. 135–40. The game includes elephants, tapirs, and several varieties of rhinoceroses (*Rhinoceros sondaicus* and *Rhinoceros sumatrensis*), although no rhinoceroses have been seen since the early 1940s and they are thought to be extinct in the highlands. There are tigers; leopards; and panthers (*Felis uncia* and *Felis nebulosus*); several kinds of wild oxen, including gaurs and koupreys; various types of bear, among them the black bear and honey bear. Deer are plentiful and include small musk deer and barking deer. Other common game are wild boars, porcupines, jackals, otters, mongooses, hares, skunks, and squirrels, including flying squirrels. Traps are placed near granaries to catch rats, which are roasted and eaten. There are many different kinds of wildcats, and among them are three types of civet—Madagascar civets, binturongs, and palm civets. There also are the common Rhesus monkey and langurs (*Semnopithecus Franciosi, Semnopithecus polyocephalus, Semnopithicus nigripses,* and *Semnopithecus nemoeus*), macaques (*Macacus cynomolgus, Mac-*

forage to the extent of cutting and carrying home wild fruit they happen upon in the forest. In the still of the dry season men take on numerous other tasks. Male artifact production and house construction display not only adaptational practicality and inventiveness in their application of basic engineering principles but also very often concepts of beauty. Serviceability and simplicity of form are demonstrated in the highly utile bush scythe and ax (see Figures 1 and 2), found throughout the highlands. The same can be said of the farm and carpentry tools described in the ethnographies. Talent is required to carve a good crossbow (Figure 3) that is at once a work of art in its graceful form and an efficient weapon with almost perfect balance. Men weave sleeping mats and apply principles of stress and strain in weaving an array of serviceable baskets whose forms follow their functions. Principles of mobility using air currents or moving water are combined with artistry to fashion noisemakers and scarecrows to keep predatory birds from the fields. Adornment is part of daily life, and villagers wear bracelets, necklaces, ivory ear plugs, and metal combs. Individual artistic expression finds free rein in stylized pipes smoked by men and women. Men make musical instruments, and specialists do wood carvings (Figure 4).

Another shared aspect of highland physical adaptation is house types. Constructed by kinsmen and neighbors entirely of locally available materials such as hardwood, bamboo, rattan, and thatching grasses, houses are built using engineering principles of tension and compression to realize sturdy structures capable of withstanding high monsoon winds and lashing rains. With the exception of one type of Chru house and some Jeh abodes, all houses are on piling, although many Stieng were forced by the Vietnamese government to build on the ground. The area under the house provides storage space for forest products and artifacts and a place to pen animals. Lifting the house off the ground protects residents from incursions by wild animals, snakes, and scorpions. It also permits air to circulate and keeps floors dry in the rainy season. A 1960 article by Jacques May based on earlier epidemiological research in Vietnam reveals that building houses on piling allows residents to escape frequent contact with the malaria-vector *Anopheles minimus* mosquitoes that breed in the clear, moving, sunlit water of mountain streams and normally fly within one meter off ground level.[12] Mosquitoes that do enter the house are likely to be repelled by acrid smoke from open-

---

acus earths, and *Macacus Harmandii*), and gibbons (*Hylobates leucogenys* and *Hylobates pileatus*). Crocodiles are found on the edges of some lakes and rivers, and other reptiles include several kinds of lizard, pythons (*Python molurus, Python reticulatus,* and *Python curtus*), and cobras.

12. Jacques May, "The Ecology of Human Disease," in *Studies in Human Ecology,* ed. L. Krader and A. Palerm (Washington, D.C.: Pan American Union), pp. 92, 97.

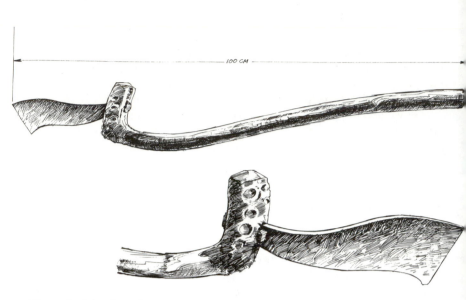

Figure 1. A bush scythe.

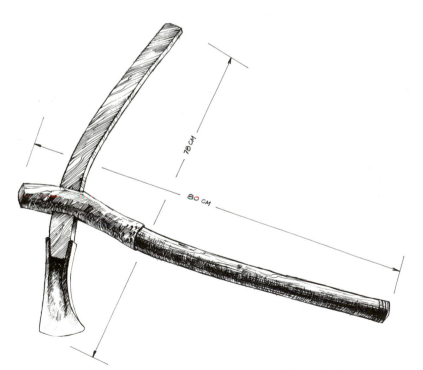

Figure 2. An ax.

Figure 3. A crossbow.

Figure 4. Wood carving for a tomb.

hearth fires. Finally, buffalo and pigs penned either under or near the house offer alternate targets for mosquitoes. Epidemiological research (summarized in Appendix C) conducted in 1967 on the Rhadé, Stieng, and Sedang suggests a relationship among house types, malaria, and frequency of hemoglobin E.

The highlanders also share ideational bonds manifest in religious prescriptions. Henri Frankfort and Henriette A. Frankfort tell us that the ancients of the Near East, like the modern primitives, had the view that man and his society are embedded in nature and dependent upon cosmic forces. Man and nature did not stand in opposition and "did not therefore have to be apprehended by different modes of cognition." "For modern scientific man the phenomenal world is primarily an 'It'; for ancient—and also for primitive—man it is a 'Thou.' " "Thou" is not only contemplated or understood, it is experienced emotionally "as life confronting life."[13] For the highlanders, cosmic forces are the prime movers of nature, and they control fertility. Although the relationship between nature and cosmic forces is dyadic and intrinsically constant, man's relationship with them is not, so his behavior can be disruptive. Disharmony between man and the nature-cosmos dyad has numerous dire consequences, one of the worst being loss of fertility. Therefore, every highland religious belief system contains definitions of the nature-cosmos dyad and prescriptions (which touch upon every aspect of society) for man to maintain harmonious relations with it. It is little wonder therefore that the highlander is as enveloped by his religious beliefs as by the dense mountain forest with its great trunks, massive foliage, vines, fronds, flowers, roots, and carpets of moss.

So people will avoid any daily activities that might be profane infringements on the nature-cosmos domain, the cosmic forces reveal taboos, signs, and omens to guide human behavior. There also are prescribed religious rituals, which have the mixed goals of gaining the sanction of cosmic forces to use nature while at the same time propitiating them and imploring their beneficence. It is incumbent upon all members of the society to honor religious prescriptions, a responsibility that colors the highlanders' activities and weighs heavily in a great many of their decisions. Every village contains stewards of prescriptions—village leaders, kin-group heads, shamans, midwives, and in some situations ordinary villagers. They are identified and validated as stewards by the key roles they play in rituals. All of the groups make ritual offerings of sacrificial

13. Henri Frankfort and Henriette A. Frankfort, "Myth and Reality," in *Before Philosophy: The Intellectual Adventure of Ancient Man,* ed. Henri Frankfort, Henriette A. Frankfort, John A. Wilson, and Thorkil Jacobsen, 6th ed. (Baltimore: Penguin Books, 1961), pp. 11–36.

domestic animals (products of animal husbandry) and rice along with rice alcohol (fruits of farming). The Katu are unique in offering human blood.

Kirsch sees political, economic, kinship, and other structures and functions in the relatively undifferentiated hill tribe societies submerged in a diffuse religious complex. Some common features include "ideas concerning human 'potency' and how it is acquired or manifested, and ritual activities which must be performed to gain 'prestige' in this life as well as in a hereafter." Using an economic metaphor, he suggests that "hill tribes society is oriented to maximizing 'potency,' 'fertility,' or some such quality." This quality is attributed to persons localized in household units or to larger units such as lineages and clans. "Each householder is conceived to be a 'religious entrepreneur,' trying to maximize his 'potency' in relation to—but not necessarily at the expense of—other householders. In the functioning of this system which might be thought of as manufacturing 'fertility,' some units will inevitably be more successful then other units." Kirsch sees "religious feasting," as a principal means among the hill tribes for manifesting potency. The successful feaster demonstrates "innate virtue" and shows "internal potency," to reflect "enhanced ritual status," "increased control of ritual rights," and therefore his edge in engendering fertility. Success in farming is equated with potency and fertility, as is "success in hunting, daring in warfare or raiding, sexual prowess, etc." Regarding the resulting dichotomy between rich-successful and poor-unsuccessful, Kirsch observes that "one way of characterizing the hill tribes beliefs with regard to individuals is to say that they have a theory of 'unequal souls.' "[14]

Within the context of the man-nature-cosmos triad, fertility and potency are intertwining themes that flow through all aspects of highland life (the Rhadé, Roglai, Sedang, Jeh, and Halang have explicit terms for potency). The fertility theme reflects concern with sustaining the group in the face of many threats to life in the mountains and the uncertainty of farming upland tropical soils under unpredictable weather conditions. Potency, a gift of cosmic forces, enables people to maximize fertility. The ethnographies reveal that in all of the groups the most striking demonstrations of potency are lavish rituals marked by sacrifices of prestigious offerings such as buffalo and pigs, accompanied by copious feasting and imbibing from rows of jars of rice alcohol. Wealth derived from successful farming is equated with wisdom and innate virtue, signs that the well-to-do are ordained by cosmic forces to be stewards of religious prescriptions and to exercise authority. The ethnographies document numerous occasions for such rituals and feasting, including observances in the

14. Kirsch, *Feasting,* pp. 5–8.

planting cycle and rites of passage (notably marriages and funerals) as well as in coping with life crises. The ethnographies also suggest that payment of costly bride-prices is an additional means of displaying potency.

Demonstrated potency enables village leaders to act as stewards in preserving moral order, which rests on harmony among man, nature, and the cosmos. They are recognized as higher authorities in dealing with conflicts unresolved by kin-group heads. They determine guilt in cases of more serious breaches such as murder and theft, often by means of ordeal trials in which cosmic forces participate, and they mete out punishments. Village leaders' potency is particularly brought to bear in situations involving dark forces. There are in all of the groups sorcerers, witches, or both, who in league with evil deities mock religious prescriptions to create disharmony between man and the nature-cosmos dyad. They are in effect the stewards' shadow counterparts, who manifest potency bestowed by patron spirits but are antifertility in creating such disharmony. A. D. J. Macfarlane draws a useful distinction between witchcraft and sorcery: "Contrasting means to end, 'witchcraft' is predominantly the pursuit of harmful ends by implicit internal means. 'Sorcery' combines harmful ends with explicit means."[15]

Additional types of potency are associated with other social roles, but none ordain individuals to any villagewide authority. Pacoh, Sedang, and Jeh rice-spirit cults, based on mystical links between female fecundity and soil-rice fertility, create special relationships between rice deities and designated women who play vital ritual roles in farming. But the potency is intrinsic to the roles rather than to the women themselves (they can be replaced if crops fail). The Rhadé female guardian of clan land has a mystical tie with ancestral spirits, performing rituals to engender fertility and exercising authority in the use of the territory. Shamans found in all groups manifest potency by communicating with cosmic forces, in most cases serving as intermediaries between sick people and spirits with whom they are out of phase. Some midwives have potency in being able to communicate with spirits but only in dealing with pregnancy and childbirth.

Traditional knowledge about religious prescriptions is preserved within highland families, passed down from one generation to another (generational continuity is expressed in teknonymy) and reiterated in kin-group rituals marking rites of passage, livelihood activities, and life crises. Within this context the household head serves as steward, and in

15. A. D. J. Macfarlane, "Definitions of Witchcraft," in *Witchcraft and Sorcery*, 2d ed., ed. M. Marwick, Penguin Modern Sociology Readings (Middlesex, England: C. Nicholls & Company, 1972), pp. 41–44.

rituals and feasting he demonstrates potency. It is he who organizes family ritual observances and invokes the host of spirits, which invariably include the ancestors, who are symbolically linked to soil fertility. Ancestral spirits have personal ties with descendants, protecting them when pleased with their conformity to kin-behavior prescriptions (in such areas as properly observing rites of passage) and punishing them (by rendering the soil infertile) when affronted by such actions as violating incest taboos. Household heads often perform divination rituals (which do not necessarily entail ritual offerings) seeking approval of cosmic forces in making decisions.

Finally, still looking at the ethnographies through an ideational lens, we see that within the context of religious prescriptions, many elements of material culture take on symbolic significance and are enveloped in a certain mystique. This is true of rice, rice alcohol, buffalo, pigs, chickens, gongs, jars, baskets, wood carvings, ornaments (beads, bracelets, and ear plugs), weapons (spears and crossbows), tools (bush scythes and rakes), granaries, and houses. Rhadé ethnography describes prescriptions for longhouse construction, from selecting the house site through gathering of materials in the forest and various building phases, to inauguration of the main hearth. The completed longhouse stands as a symbol of man-nature-cosmos harmony.

The Historical Setting

Archaeological research on the Phung Nguyen sites in the Red River delta indicates that around 2000 B.C., people moved out of the mountains to settle in open areas along rivers. They farmed swiddens, built houses on piling for extended families, had domesticated animals, hunted and fished, wove textiles, and produced pots, along with ornaments such as beads and bracelets.[16] In documenting historical highland-lowland contact, *Sons of the Mountains* notes that Chinese accounts describe later delta dwellers, the Lac Viet, antecedents of the Vietnamese, as having crossbows and poisoned arrows, tatooing, teeth-blackening, betel-areca chewing, the levirate, special deities associated with agriculture, and communal houses (*đình*) on piling. *Sons of the Mountains* also describes similar culture traits found among Mon Khmer-speaking highland groups and notes that lexicostatistical research concludes that the Vietnamese language belongs to the Mon Khmer stock.[17] This link attests to the longevity of Mon Khmer–speaking groups in the highlands, and it raises

16. Nguyen Ba Khoach, "Phung Nguyen," *Asian Perspectives* 23, no. 1 (1980): 44–47.

17. Hickey, *Sons of the Mountains,* pp. 2–3, 5–7, 24, 33–43, 49–53, 59–63, 70–71, 75–76, 83, 89–120, 160, 168, 179, 185–88, 210–11, 220–21, 240, 263–97, 447–48.

the possibility that at one time these groups shared common cultural features such as swidden farming and patrilineal descent that later were altered by outside influences.

Sons of the Mountains and the ethnographies reveal that the strongest outside historical influence was that of the Cham, who had matrilineal descent and sophisticated paddy farming. At the present time the Vietnamese, Katu, Bru, Pacoh, Hre, and Cua have patrilineal descent while farther south the cluster of Bahnar, Rengao, Sedang, Jeh, and Halang have bilateral descent. Still farther south the Sre, Mnong, and Lat have matrilineal descent, and the Stieng and Maa have patrilineal descent. All of the Austronesian speakers, the Jarai, Rhadé, Roglai, and Chru, have matrilineal descent. Wet-rice farming has long been predominant among the Chru, Sre, Lat, and Mnong Rlam but has been secondary among the Rhadé Kpa and Bih, Jarai Hodrung and Arap, Bahnar Jolong and Golar, Monom, Maa, and Mnong Chil. All of these groups are located within the area of Cham hegemony (which began in the twelfth century) and are marked by their vestiges. A Maa legend describes how some Maa subgroups submitted to Cham vassalage, but their elite patrilineages crumbled as authority passed through male or female lines haphazardly whereas Maa subgroups that resisted Cham rule retained their patrilineages and swidden farming. The legend also relates that Cham fleeing the final incursions of the Vietnamese settled in the highlands and married Roglai and other Koho-speakers. These refugees brought with them the Cham wet-rice adaptation and a sophisticated water-management system. The Chru and Roglai ethnographies reiterate this readaptation and shed light on changes it wrought in the society. It is interesting that the Sre, neighbors of the Maa, along with the Mnong Rlam and Lat, accepted Cham rule and have wet-rice farming and matrilineal descent. To the west the relatively isolated Stieng kept patrilineal descent and swiddening.

Another source of Cham influence was trade. There was a trade network among the Roglai, Mnong Chil, Lat, Sre, and Maa (eventually including the Chru), reflected in the Koho lingua franca that incorporates vocabularies of these groups. Cham traded with this network, exchanging forest products (including valuable items sent as tribute to the Chinese court) for salt, alcohol jars, and gongs. Cham influence also is detectable in the widespread practice of identifying some deities as *yang* or a cognate term thereof (evidence indicates that the word is of Austronesian origin) and in the use of the titles *potao* and *h'bia* for great leaders and their wives. Finally, there also are designations of Cham origin for shamans among Austronesian and some Mon Khmer-speakers.

The historical picture and the ethnographies also raise the possibility that Lao and/or Khmer influences resulted in bilateral descent among the

Bahnar, Sedang, Jeh, Halang, and Rengao as well as paddy farming among some Bahnar. All of these groups had contacts with Lao and Khmer through the slave trade, and the ethnographies of the Sedang, Jeh, and Halang describe Lao contact and influences. Finally, the Mon Khmer-speaking Hre and Cua (who have patrilineal descent), located adjacent to the coastal plain, borrowed wet-rice farming technology from the Vietnamese.

In trade with the lowlanders the highland villagers sought a variety of goods, the most common of which were salt, ceramic rice-alcohol jars, and metal gongs. Rhadé report that in the past their best gongs came from Laos, Cambodia, and Burma. According to French sources, the highlanders on the eastern slope of the mountains valued gongs from China and also from Hanoi and Nam Dinh foundries. In more recent times gongs were manufactured in the lowlands of Vietnam, but they are considered inferior in strength and sound. At every ritual the offerings include at least one jar of rice alcohol, which also provides libations in the feasting. Generally the older jars are of greatest value, and many are said to date "from the time of the ancestors." Most of these have a worn dark brown or black glaze, and some would surely command a good price in the world antique market. Newer jars of Vietnamese manufacture have a light brown glaze and are shipped to the highlands in trucks.

Kirsch sees upland Southeast Asian groups as "developing along an analytical continuum from a 'democratic' to an 'autocratic' type of system."[18] Within this continuum each group is in a state of constant oscillation which affects the function of potency and expressions of fertility. Historical data in *Sons of the Mountains* and the ethnographies shed light on the relatively "democratic" or "autocratic" character of some groups. They also tell of oscillations to which French colonial rule contributed by asserting control over traditional chiefs. French authority replaced the autocratic rule of the chiefs, thereby moving some groups in the direction of becoming more democratic, but at the local level the elites that had wealth survived. In the colonial government's attempts to create a pro-French elite during the Indochina War (1945–54), sons of the chiefs were drawn to the new College Sabatier in Ban Me Thuot, where they forged bonds that led to intermarriage and the emergence of a sociopolitical network that eventually would include Bru, Sedang, Bahnar, Rengao, Jarai, Rhadé, Chru, Mnong Rlam, Sre, and Lat. Among them were Christians from the French Catholic and American Protestant missions.

Free in the Forest and the ethnographies describe changes that swept the highlands between 1954 and 1980.[19] In 1955 the highlands came for

18. Kirsch, *Feasting,* pp. 24–37.
19. Hickey, *Free in the Forest,* passim.

the first time under Vietnamese rule. The forced-assimilation policy of the Ngo Dinh Diem government reflected Vietnamese ethnocentrism and nationalism. To introduce lowland adaptation and culture, the unsuccessful 1957 Land Development Program brought thousands of Vietnamese settlers into the region with no regard for highlanders' land claims. Bitter resentment by highland leaders (most of them from the intergroup elite) gave rise to their first ethnonationalist movement, Bajaraka, a name derived from the key letters of Bahnar, Jarai, Rhadé, and Koho, the groups from which most of the organizers came. Their resistance to the Vietnamese government demonstrated potency, and President Diem's attempts to suppress the movement were futile.

By the early 1960s, infiltration through Laos and Cambodia of Communist regroupees (including highlanders), who had gone north after 1954, put the Bru, Pacoh, Katu, Jeh, Halang, Sedang, Rhadé, and Stieng in the path of insurgency that soon spread to the Roglai but spared the Chru. As the sights and sounds of conflict came closer, villagers huddled in their bunkers hoping that the violence, like monsoon downpours, would pass. Leaving their villages was always the last resort, and the ethnographies record readaptation strategies that the highlanders devised in their attempts to survive as refugees. Kin and village groups stayed together as best they could. Typically a woman would cram a blanket or two, a small cooking pot, a bag of rice, some maize, a gourd of water, and often her back-tension loom into her back-basket. Men also carried bags of rice and blankets along with bush scythes, knives, a crossbow and arrows, pipes, tobacco, and chickens in baskets. In the early 1960s many packed gongs and rice-alcohol jars on their draft animals. The common strategy was for refugees to move into other villages, preferably those where they had kin or friends. In these situations they could participate in the existing social systems, and readaptations were not too painful. But as refugees continued to move into more secure areas, the shortage of land for swidden farming led to readaptations in which refugees and local residents used fertilizers to farm fields longer, shortening fallowing periods, and, where possible, turning to paddy farming. More highlanders began cash cropping and opening small shops. These readaptation strategies attest to the resilience of people who for long have lived in a relatively traditional, slow-changing mode.

But war is not just a matter of opposing forces engaged in killing and destroying. It sets off a vast array of changes that spread and deepen as the conflict intensifies. In time, one way or another, willingly or unwillingly, everyone participates. The ethnographies document social, political, and economic changes that the Vietnam War brought to highland societies. There was, for example, in 1964 the sudden appearance during an armed revolt of the movement called the Front Unifié des

Races Opprimées (United Struggle Front for the Oppressed Races), known by the acronym FULRO, which helped spread a pan-highlander ethnic identity. There also was the emergence of a leadership (whose members were of the intergroup elite) clustered in the Ministry for Ethnic Minorities' Development. Minister Nay Luett (Jarai), Touneh Han Tho (Chru), Pierre K'briuh (Sre), and their colleagues formulated new programs to give the highland people a place in the national framework while preserving their common culture.

The worst effects of the Vietnam War came in the late 1960s and early 1970s, when the ever-increasing violence engulfed highlanders who became victims of American and South Vietnamese bombing and use of herbicides and the Communists' shelling, rocketing, and nocturnal assaults on villages. Ethnographies of the Bru, Katu, Sedang, Halang, Jeh, and Stieng tell how, in the face of the mounting destruction from the world beyond the mountains, the highland people strove unceasingly to maintain the harmony among man, nature, and cosmic forces so vital to their survival. Readaptations became more drastic and wrenching as they fled with bare essentials, taking refuge in forests and other alien physical environments. A great many ended up in refugee camps, where these normally self-sufficient people became dependent upon outside agencies for everything. In all of these readaptations, which did not allow for farming, hunting, fishing, or foraging, concern with fertility was overshadowed by concern for survival. With everyone reduced to poverty, no demonstrations of potency were possible. Potency preserved by leaders at the ministry disappeared with their 1975 imprisonment by the Communists. When the Vietnam War ended, of the approximately 1 million highlanders (see Appendix A), somewhere between 200,000 and 220,000 civilians and military personnel had died. Around 85 percent of their villages had either been destroyed or were abandoned. Potency, however, was preserved in the FULRO leadership (now called the Dega-FULRO), which from forest havens has continued to resist Communist rule.

There was the possibility that the surviving highlanders, who had demonstrated resourcefulness during the war, might rebuild their villages and try to restore the traditional harmony between man, nature, and the cosmos and their common culture. But this did not fit into the plans of the Communist government. *Free in the Forest* describes how Hanoi approached the central highlands and its people with the same nationalism and ethnocentrism of the Diem administration, but submerged in Marxist-Leninist ideology. Hanoi's "development" plan, which has been implemented since 1975, calls for a new "socialist" (that is, Vietnamese) adaptation and culture in the mountain country. To this end, massive numbers of lowlanders have been moved into the region to bring

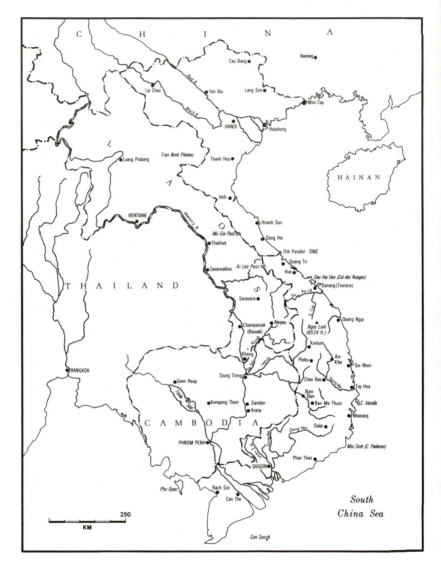

Map 1. Pre-1975 Indochina.

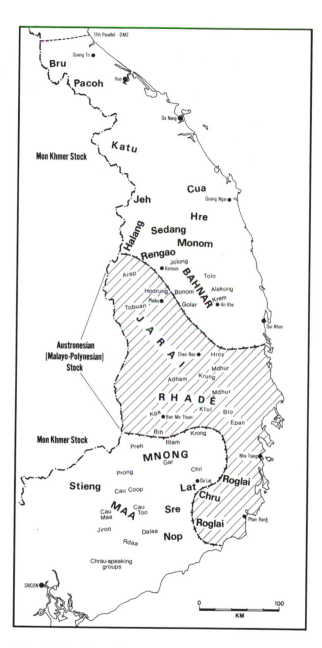

Map 2. Ethnolinguistic groups.

their lowland adaptation and culture, both alien to the highlands. Swidden farming has been banned as "destructive," reflecting the tendency to blame highlanders for the vast deforestation since 1975. In the name of "sedentarization" and "transition to socialism," highlanders in large numbers have been forced to leave their houses and villages to move into Vietnamese-style settlements. Highlanders' religious prescriptions are scorned as "superstitions" and their rites of passage as "backward." Given what the ethnographies have to tell us, Communist policy casts a shadow not only on the highland world but also on the mountain environment and the ultimate fate of Vietnamese settlers.

Chapter 1
Rhadé

The heart of the Rhadé country is the sweeping Darlac plateau with its dense forests, undulating savannas, and still swamps. The Rhadé call themselves "Êdê," taken from Anak H'Dê or "Children of H'Dê," a designation derived from a legend identifying H'Dê as ancestress of the Rhadé. Informants point out that the neighboring Jarai refer to them as Rodé, from which the French took the name Rhadé, the term most commonly used in the literature (and sometimes transcribed as Rade or Raday). The Vietnamese have long called them Êdê.

As if reflecting the expansiveness of the Darlac plateau, the Rhadé, one of the largest highland groups, are divided into far-flung subgroups (see Map 2). In his unpublished study of Rhadé customs, Y Dhuat Nie Kdam describes the Êdê-Kpă as the group living in the vicinity of Ban Me Thuot and to the south are the Bih.[1] Northwest of the town are the Adham. To the east are the Ktŭl (also called the Dliê-ruê), the Blô, Epan, and Mdhŭr. In 1967 the Rhadé population was estimated at around 100,000, and the 1989 Vietnamese population census reported 194,710 Ê-dê (see Appendix A).

The Rhadé strategy for preserving the man-nature-cosmos harmony includes interweaving male and female themes manifest in both physical and ideational sides of their adaptation. Their belief that they are descended from the ancestress H'dê signals women's central role, rooted in a mystical link between female fecundity and soil/rice fertility. Descent is reckoned through the female line (matrilineal descent), which determines membership in the longhouse extended family, the basic social and economic unit of Rhadé society. Matrilineal descent also determines

---

1. Y Dhuat Nie Kdam, "Customs of the Rhadé Highlanders in Darlac Province" (translation from Rhadé), pp. 1–3.

membership in exogamous clans (grouped into two phratries) identified by names and in some cases by food taboos. Cross-cousin marriage is preferred, predominantly marriage with the mother's brother's daughter (matrilineal cross-cousin), and residence is matrilocal. Women own all of the family property such as the longhouse, domestic animals (including elephants), and fruits of the harvest. A senior female of the subclan is the steward (*pô lăn*) of clan land, preventing abuses to the physical environment and moral profanations of the soil, affronts to the ancestors.[2] At the same time, certain individuals, particularly males, have a special potency bestowed by a spirit named Yang Rong and are destined (*dhut*) to leadership (*knuih-kŏhŭm*).

Pre-1960

According to Rhadé oral history, before the arrival of the French at the end of the nineteenth century, villages were autonomous, and from time to time a leader in one village who manifested *knuih-kŏhŭm* potency would gain ascendancy over several neighboring villages, forcing them to supply him with warriors. In many instances the leader reinforced his authority by having his wife serve as guardian of large tracts of ancestral land. One such leader was the legendary Kdam Yi of the classic Rhadé poem *Le chant épique de Kdam Yi*. In his introduction to the 1955 version of this poem, Georges Condominas notes that Kdam Yi was a robust nonconformist, who by his personal strength and bravery rose to leadership.[3] Successful in battle, he took not only his opponent's belongings but also the villagers he ruled, reducing them to serfdom. The poem tells how a ruling class of chiefs reinforced its position by intermarriage, and each marriage alliance was further guaranteed by the sororate and levirate.

Sons of the Mountains documents the great chiefs of the nineteenth century so well remembered in Rhadé lore.[4] In midcentury, Ama Bloi ("Father of Bloi") permitted the Lao to establish a trading post in the western Rhadé country at Ban Don, which by the 1880s, under the rule of a Mnong-Lao chief named Khunjanob, developed into a center for the elephant trade. Around 1887 Ama Trang Guh, a Bih chief, mustered a force of between seven and eight hundred warriors to defeat an invading

2. A depth study of Rhadé kinship within the context of village society can be found in Anne de Hauteclocque-Howe, *Les Rhadés: Une société de droit maternel* (Paris: Editions du Centre National de la Recherche Scientifique, 1987).

3. Georges Condominas, "Introduction to 'Chant épique de Kdam Yi' by F.-P. Antoine," *BEFEO* 47 (1955): 555–66.

4. Gerald Cannon Hickey, *Sons of the Mountains: Ethnohistory of the Vietnamese Central Highlands to 1954* (New Haven: Yale University Press, 1982), pp. 224, 240, 249–63, 270, 276, 323–24, 331–32, 363–66, 379, 388, 413–25.

force of Burmese, Lao, and Mnong led by a chief named Kham Leu (his Tai name would suggest that he was a Shan). In 1900, Ama Trang Guh opposed a French pacification unit, but its superior arms forced him to retreat into the mountains. Another noted chief of this era was the fearsome Ama Jhao, a Ktul, who spread terror in the eastern Rhadé country, raiding villages and selling captives into slavery. Around 1880 he worked out an accommodation with the coastal Vietnamese mandarins and merchants, allowing their convoys to proceed to Ban Don unharmed.

At the end of the century, Ama Thuot, a Kpa chief (and son of Ama Bloi), led resistance against the French, but his friend Khunjanob convinced him to allow the French to create on 2 November 1899 the autonomous "montagnard" province of Darlac (a deformation of the Rhadé name Dak Lak). The administrative center was established at the chief's village of Buon Ama Thuot (which became known by the Lao designation, Ban Me Thuot). Subsequently, when Ama Ual, the Adham chief, M'drak, and Ae Bung ("Grandfather of Bung"), who ruled the Mdhur, Blo, and Epan, submitted to the French, the entire Rhadé country passed under colonial rule. Although the autocratic power the chiefs had enjoyed was now ended, their families nonetheless continued to be recognized as local elites.

The tenure of Léopold Sabatier as *résident* in Darlac between 1914 and 1926 brought changes to the Rhadé Kpa in the vicinity of Ban Me Thuot. Road construction, telephone and telegraph service, and an airstrip opened their country to the outside. The villagers, however, were very resentful of the corvée imposed on them to provide labor for these projects. Rhadé were drawn into the new primary school education and training for civil service and work in the administration. This training led to the emergence of a new type of Rhadé Kpa leader, one familiar with French language and culture but still tied to the traditional world of his village. Sabatier also encouraged the creation of a Rhadé alphabet and codification of Rhadé customs preserved in the oral *duê*, a litany intoned on appropriate occasions. In 1923 a Rhadé law court was opened with Khunjanob, assisted by an elderly Rhadé, as judge.

The development of Darlac and the lure of the laterite "terres rouges" amenable to production of coffee and rubber attracted the attention of French commercial interests in Saigon. Anticipating a land rush, Sabatier in 1925 recommended that only ninety-nine-year leases (*bail emphythéotique*) be given the concessionaires so as to protect the Rhadé land tenure system. Sabatier's opposition to the forces of commerce led to his removal from office in 1929 when a decree granted 30,175 hectares in commercial leases, stipulating that labor would be recruited among the Rhadé and coastal Vietnamese. Ban Me Thuot developed into a market center with largely Chinese and Vietnamese merchants, which served as a window to the outside world. Also, the Franco-Rhadé primary school increased its enrollment to over five hundred, and the new American Protestant mission brought Christianity and the English language to Ban Me Thuot. During World War II, the Decoux administration improved education in Ban Me Thuot, adding secondary education and a normal school, both of which attracted students from elite families of many ethnic groups. Instruction was in French, but Rhadé fast became the students' lingua franca.

In the Indochina War between 1945 and 1954, some Rhadé joined the Viet Minh while others supported the French. In 1947 the College Sabatier in Ban Me Thuot began offering a two-year program in advanced education, which attracted students from elite families who forged a network of friendships and engendered a new spirit of highland ethnonationalism. Among them were Rhadé from villages close to the town, and their families intermarried (just as the elite families of the past had done). *Free in the Forest* describes how at the end of the Indochina War in July 1954, some Rhadé (the number was never clear) who had followed the Viet Minh moved to North Vietnam, where many received training in preparation for their return to South Vietnam as insurgents.[5] The Vietnamization policy of the Ngo Dinh Diem government and its land grabbing for the 1957 Land Development Program prompted young educated Rhadé Kpa from the Ban Me Thuot area to form the Bajaraka movement and in 1958 to organize a general strike. In response, the government jailed many Rhadé leaders, forcing the movement to go underground. This marked the beginning of Rhadé participation in Vietnamese national politics.

Religion

Rhadé religious beliefs are expressed in myths, rituals, and everyday observances of taboos and sanctions. Much is revealed in chanted prayers (*ngă yang*), which contain entreaties to supernatural beings, thereby identifying their essential roles and functions as well as their general characteristics. All are associated with the physical world and the forces of nature, and the prayers are one means by which the Rhadé maintain balance with nature and the cosmos.

Various French sources and Rhadé informants describe the creator and master of the universe, Aê Diê, the eternal and benevolent supreme deity, depicted in legends as a tall, husky, imposing male invisible to the

5. Gerald Cannon Hickey, *Free in the Forest: Ethnohistory of the Vietnamese Central Highlands, 1954–1976* (New Haven: Yale University Press, 1982), pp. 16–21, 34–36, 47–60, 65–66.

human eye.[6] Y Yok Ayun pointed out that this deity is invoked in almost all chants of the Rhadé, who look to him for all of their needs, particularly successful rice crops. He inhabits the heavenly firmament with his wife, who is never mentioned in the prayers. Aê Diê's sister's husband, Aê Du, serves as intermediary between him and the Rhadé. Entreated in most chants, Aê Du controls heat, cold, wind, storms, and the night, all of which he uses to benefit mankind. His wife, H'bia Dung Day, portrayed as having very ample and elongated breasts, is associated with rice and small children. She also is the protector of those who die young. H'bia Klu is Aê Du's sister, who aids her husband, M'tao Kla, the chief par excellence of agriculture. Another deity associated with rice farming is M'tao Sri ("the handsome, good prince"). H'bia Bao is the protector of millet. Yang Hruê is the male sun deity, and Yang Mlan is the female moon deity. Rhadé villagers explained that in longhouses a crescent and female breasts, symbols of Yang Mlan, are carved on entrance stairs and on support columns.

The beneficence of both Aê Diê and Aê Du is sometimes countervailed by the evil Yang Liê, who is associated with lightning, thunder, and violent winds that break branches, uproot trees, and destroy crops. Yang Liê is subject to Aê Diê, but when the master is not looking, the evil one foists his wickedness upon the Rhadé. H'jua, the wife of Yang Liê, is invoked in prayers, but her role is not defined. Yang Briêng, a particularly malevolent deity under Yang Liê, is chief of the spirits of those who have died in accidents such as drowning and attacks by wild animals. He appears at childbirth, ominously predicting an accidental death for the newborn, which puts him in constant conflict with the Yang M'nut Hra, good deities of destiny, who inhabit banyan trees. Y Yok Ayun explained that offering a dog or a goat to Yang Briêng can prevent accidents.

Some deities live on the earth itself. Two benign figures are Aê Mghi and his brother, Mghăn Tơ Làn, who are invoked in appeals for abundant harvests. The Spirit of Čữ-Ju (Black Mountain) and the Spirit of H'mu Mountain (called La Mère et l'Enfant by the French), the highest peaks in the Rhadé country, figure in an annual ritual in which they are implored to release the imprisoned Rice Soul so that it can return to the rice plants, enabling them to bud. Yang Mdiê, the Rice Spirit (distinct from the Rice Soul), inhabits the plant itself and is under the orders of M'tao Kla (chief of agriculture). Similarly, other plants such as maize,

6. Dr. B. Y. Jouin, *La mort et le tombe: L'abandon de la tombe* (Paris: Institut d'Ethnologie, 1949), pp. 47–18; Jouin, "Grossesse et naissance en pays Rhadé," *BSEI* 34, no. 3 (1959): 3–77; Albert Maurice and Georges Proux, "L'âme du riz," *BSEI* 29, nos. 2–3 (1954): 47–48.

indigo, and cotton have spirits. Every Rhadé has a personal protector spirit, *yang amĭ bă ama bă.*

There are special spirits associated with destiny (*pô thiê*), protection (*pô kriê*), and fecundity (*pô bă mâo anak*). *Pô dhar* regulate work, *pô dlang* observe everyone, and *pô brei* lead the Rhadé. Under the orders of Yang Liê, *k'sŏk* are malevolent spirits who live unseen in Rhadé villages and in dense forests. They sometimes appear as a person who has died, or they take the form of a rush of air, a flame, a monkey, an elephant, or a pumpkin, striking fear into the heart of anyone who encounters them.

A group of deities is associated with the subterranean world, where villages of the dead are located. *Yang čŭ* are the spirits of the mountains, *yang troh trôk* are valley spirits, and *yang ala buôn* are spirits of the village site. *Yang eâ* linger at the depths of water sources, and *yang pin eâ* live on river bottoms. *Yang k'mrŏng* are spirits of great forests. Yang Grăm, the Thunder Spirit, is associated with Yang Liê and with stone axes often found in the Rhadé country and believed to have been sent to the earth via lightning bolts. Planting banana trees during the rainy season will incur the wrath of Yang Grăm, as will cooking mushrooms with meat, particularly fatty pork. An amiable deity of this group is Aê Ayut, who, with his cohorts, Aê Biut and Aê Êsa, brings beneficial rains. M'tao Tlŭa and his brother, Kbuă Lăn, control plant growth, protecting roots from pests and worms. They are entreated in rituals during times of drought and in the ritual performed by the steward of clan land to propitiate the ancestors in cases of incest.

Origin Legend

According to Dr. B. Y. Jouin, Rhadé ritual chants describe the origin of the world in five periods, the first four marked by cataclysms and the last by the appearance of the Rhadé in the central highlands.[7] During the first period, "the earth was consumed by fire," after which there was a cooling that led to the second period, characterized by the total absence of life on the globe. In the third period life returned with the appearance of the first humans (including the ancestors of the Rhadé), but they were threatened by a great drought. Using Aê Dut (the Toad Spirit) as intermediary, the Rhadé appealed to Aê Diê for rain. When it was forthcoming, Aê Dut complained that it was insufficient, so Aê Diê sent a good deal more, inundating the land. The sole survivors were a man and his wife, who floated in a large drum to which were attached other drums containing male and female dogs, pigs, chickens, and cattle.

At Aê Diê's behest, the waters receded and the surviving couple

7. Dr. B. Y. Jouin, "Les traditions Rhadé," *BSEI* 25, no. 1 (1950): 89–109.

produced a large number of offspring, all of whom dispersed in search of food. This period ended with a convulsive earthquake that crumpled everything except the most prominent mountains. Human populations survived in small, scattered pockets of arable land. As populations increased, this land proved inadequate, forcing migration. Jouin notes that at this point in the chant there are references to a "distant land" and an "isle in the sea," from which the Rhadé forebears departed in rafts (*ki*). This is particularly interesting in view of the lexicostatistical evidence linking their language with those of Java, Sumatra, and Bali.

In the fifth period the Rhadé emerged from the legendary Băng Adrêñ hole, said still to exist near Buon Cue, south of Ban Me Thuot. Y Thih Eban related in 1969 that in the popular version of the legend, the Rhadé lived in an underground world. When Aê Diê saw that they had no idea how to make good use of the available food, he sent Y Rim to teach them how to prepare it properly and how to make rice alcohol in a jar ("to keep themselves healthy and joyful"). Everyone, however, drank too much and became ill. Blaming Y Rim, two young men, Y Tong and Y Tang, armed with knives and accompanied by their dog, chased him. They happened upon the Băng Adrêñ hole, and passing through it found themselves in a spectacular green land resplendent with fruit, vegetables, wild game, and fish. Hurrying back to the underground world, they described this wondrous place to their chief, who accompanied them back through the hole. When he saw the beauty and abundance, he immediately decided that all of the Rhadé should migrate there. The chief, a member of the Ayun clan, was the first to lead his kin through the Băng Adrêñ hole, and for one hundred days, members of the Eban, Hdrue, Mlo-Duon-Du, H'mok, Knul, and Nie-Kdam clans followed. On the hundred and first day, Y Rit (who figures in other Rhadé legends) was taking his two-headed buffalo through the hole when it became stuck and could not budge. This prevented the departure of pretty Rhadé girls, who had remained to fix their hair. They stayed in the underground world, and this, the Rhadé say jokingly, is why there are no pretty girls among them. Y Thih added that the Băng Adrêñ hole has narrowed considerably over time, but it is still guarded by the Hdrue clan.

Settlements and Longhouses

Villages usually have between twenty and thirty longhouses built on piling, and they tend to be oriented in the same direction. Rhadé Kpa longhouses in the vicinity of Ban Me Thuot have their main entrances facing north while east of the town along Route 21 houses face south. Houses vary in length, depending on the number of residents. Y Yok Ayun reported that in his natal village of Buon Brieng some old houses are around one hundred meters long and have up to one hundred residents. There is ample space between houses to guard against fires and to allow for kitchen gardens, which usually are surrounded by bamboo fences. Clustered nearby are granaries of bamboo and thatch, built on piling. Near Rhadé Kpa houses there are open latrines hidden by greenery, a modern innovation.

The mixed profusion of trees (including ancient banyans and hardwood trees) and plants on carpets of grass (grazed by tethered cattle and buffalo) conveys the impression of a lush park. In the background are splendid stands of bamboo in groves, which are taboo to enter or disturb. Paths lead to swiddens and to the watercourse. In the evening the villagers bathe, males downstream from the females. Even farther downstream elephants immerse themselves, their trunks spraying water into the air.

Rhadé villages have about them a certain grandeur that derives largely from their longhouses (*sang*), which are elevated on piling, with splendid hardwood frames, and topped by lofty, thickly thatched roofs. Traditionally they were derived entirely from nature with all building materials provided by the physical surroundings. A house should be constructed on well-drained land that is not too shaded. It is preferable to build a new house on or very near the site of the old house unless it had been the scene of accident, a murder, or an inordinate number of deaths. Before demolishing the old house, the family performs a ritual to inform the various deities associated with the house so as to gain their assent and avoid their wrath. The offerings include either a sterile sow or a chicken along with a jar of rice alcohol, tobacco, a pipe, and a gourd of water. At Buon Kosier in 1966, a longhouse built in 1953 was demolished to make way for a new one. Male kin and neighbors pitched in, and the host provided them with food and jars of alcohol. Gongs played while the house was dismantled. The workers carefully inspected the hardwood columns, scraping away dirt to determine if they had rotted during the thirteen years the house had stood. Usable wood was set aside, and the rest was carted away for kindling.

When selecting a site for a new house, it is well to avoid banyan trees (the abode of spirits) as well as the confluence of two streams (where spirits associated with each stream converge) and waterfalls (wherein dwell particularly malevolent spirits). Albert Maurice reports that when going to a newly selected house site one must be wary of dire signs, such as encountering a tiger, a serpent, a red monkey, a tortoise with its head tilted toward the east (the symbol of a tomb), holes of porcupines or moles, and the cries of certain birds.[8] Dreams also presage the fate of a

8. Albert Maurice, "L'habitation Rhadé: Rites et techniques," *IIEH* 5 (1942): 90–95.

Photo 1. A Rhadé longhouse (1956).

family in its new home. A dream motif involving a flood is a warning that fire will destroy the house. Rice-alcohol jars are signs of death, as is a large fish. Teeth symbolize members of the family, so to dream of broken teeth heralds the death of a kinsman. Domestic animals such as dogs or goats bode badly, but a catch of small fish is favorable.

Rhadé informants report that should the new house site be in another village, the husband of the senior female first clears a small area, and in the center of it he places three stones to symbolize the new main hearth (*kpur gah*), after which he buries seven rice grains wrapped in a leaf. He then pours a mixture of rice alcohol and chicken blood on the ground while chanting a prayer to the spirits asking for the well-being of the family in its new dwelling. Before gathering new construction materials, the family offers a castrated pig or a chicken along with a jar of alcohol to the Spirits of the Mountain and Spirits of the Forest. In addition, the officiant calls upon the spirits associated with swamps, flowing water, various kinds of reeds, and grasses used for thatching "to listen and to understand." If elephants are to be used in the gathering and construction, there is a small ritual offering of a chicken, an egg, and a jar of alcohol to entreat the animals' guardian spirits to protect them from accidents. Going into the forest with their bush scythes (*kgă*) and axes (*jông*) (see Figures 1 and 2), the men first seek good hardwood for the structural frame. The great hardwood tree called *ana egiêr* in Rhadé (which is *sao* in Vietnamese, identified by Pham Hoang Ho as *Hopea sp.: Dipterocarpus*[9]) is considered powerful, and so it cannot be felled. Any tree on which a certain type of orchid believed to harbor spirits of those who died sinister deaths must be avoided. A tree with a broken crown warns of the eventual collapse of the house in which its wood is used. If, with the first blows of the ax, a dry, cracking sound is heard or if water runs (the symbol of a soul fleeing the body at death), the tree is left standing. A tree that when cut does not fall straight to the ground but leans on other trees suggests a dying person leaning against a wall for support and is abandoned. Logs are carried to the village and set out to dry.

The next phase is to gather reeds and bamboo. According to Y Yok Ayun, *kram,* the thickest and strongest bamboo, is good for flooring, as are the somewhat thinner *drao* and *jut,* both of which are also suitable for walls. *Mŏ* can be used for walls, and because of its large, hollow center, it is used at hillside springs as a conduit. *Alê* and *edê* of varying thickness are employed in the roof frame. During the gathering period, it is taboo for the workers to sing or play musical instruments because to do so would invite music for a funeral in the near future. Hunting is permitted, but the meat cannot be consumed in the forest. Should the gatherers come upon meat left by a tiger, they dare not touch it.

In every Rhadé village there are adept wood carvers (in 1967, Buon Kram had twenty), and they cooperate in house building, for which the family provides them with an animal sacrifice and jars of alcohol. Some of them explained that, using bush scythes and axes, they hew logs that will serve as the main support columns (*kmeh*) and notch them at the top to hold in place the longitudinal roof beams (*êyông*) that run the length of the house. An indentation is carved at the lower portion of the *kmeh* column to accommodate the lateral floor beams (*êdê*) (see Figures 5, 6, and 7). Female breasts (symbol of Yang Mlan, the female moon deity) and elephant tusks are carved on the column located at the compartment occupied by the senior female and her family. Lateral tie beams (*êda*) for the roof are fashioned so that they will rest securely on *êyông* beams (Figure 6).

On the first day of construction of a longhouse in Buon Ko Sier in 1965, the husband of the senior female offered a chicken, several jars of alcohol, hoes, and axes to the ancestors, the spirits of the east and west, and a host of spirits associated with rice, cotton, ramie, water, sand,

9. Phạm Hoàng Hộ, *Cây-Cỏ Miền Nam Việt-Nam* (Flora of South Vietnam) (Saigon: Bộ Văn-Hóa Giáo-Dục và Thanh-Niên [Ministry of Culture, Education, and Youth], 1970), pp. 312–14.

marshes, trees, streams, and waterfalls. Then, men dug holes for the main columns using axes and long green bamboo poles split on the end to remove the soil. Gongs played as the columns and beams were carried to the site. On the second day the workers carefully inspected the holes for frogs or turtles, signs that they cannot be used. As gongs played and alcohol jars were prepared, workers hoisted a column into a hole, and while it was held in place by other men using bamboo poles, they pounded the column into the soft earth. The hole was filled, but the soil was left loose. This process was repeated with the other columns. The next step was to set the lateral *êdê* beams that support the floor in the indentations of the columns and tie them with rattan cord (see Figure 5). This procedure steadied the columns so the soil was tamped. The longitudinal *êyông* beams were then lifted on to the top of the columns, and the *êda* tie beams were placed on the *êyông* beams. If at any time during this phase it had rained or a crow had landed on the structure, work would have halted immediately, to be resumed the following day.

Maurice describes the use of male and female bamboo during roof construction.[10] Female bamboo is used for the king posts (*mbŭng gŏng*) that are affixed to the *êdê* lateral cross beams at either end of the house and also to the *êda* tie beams to support the *ana čuôr* bamboo ridgepole (see Figure 7). Male bamboo poles provide the rafters (*giê kal*) that are attached to the *ana čuôr* ridgepole at the top and to the *êyông* longitudinal beam at the bottom. Female bamboo longitudinal poles (*rôč*) are affixed to the *giê kal* rafters. A stress technique is used to hold the thatching in place. Thin lateral poles (*êmăl*) are set on the *rôč* longitudinal poles, and then bamboo laths (*kpĭ êmăl*) are arranged perpendicularly over the *êmăl*. The top portion of a bunch of thatching is bent over the lath and forced between it and the *rôč* pole, creating a thrust that holds the thatching in place. According to Y Yok Ayun, thatching is *halang,* an imperata grass. It is gathered in bunches, and a very long house will require as many as a thousand bunches.

Next is the floor, the main supports of which, according to Y Thih Eban, are the aforementioned lateral *êdê* logs affixed to the columns (Figures 7 and 8). On top of these logs are set hewn hardwood longitudinal logs (*êgap*), and over them female bamboo poles of the sturdy *kram* variety are affixed with rattan cord to provide lateral supports (*adrung*). The next layer is longitudinal bamboo laths (*ênê*), which are tied to the lateral supports. Finally, mats of split bamboo (*trêa*) are laid over the laths and attached with rattan cord. The veranda (*adring*) at the main entrance is constructed entirely of hardwood logs set close together on

10. Maurice, "L'habitation," pp. 99–102.

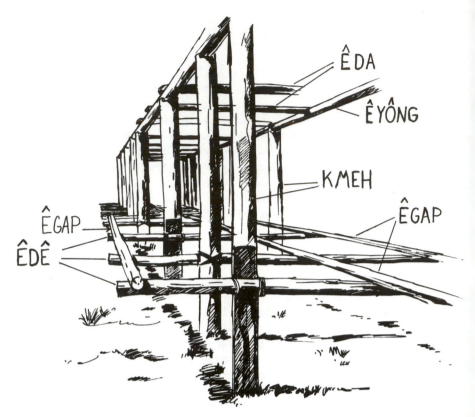

Figure 5. Rhadé longhouse structural frame.

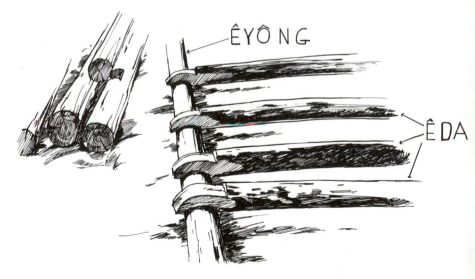

Figure 6. Carved tie beams for Rhadé longhouse roof.

Figure 7. Partially completed Rhadé longhouse.

the support beams. It is reached by stairs (*êñan*) carved in either a log or a wood plank on which female breasts, symbol of Yang Mlang, the moon deity, are carved.

For the outer wall a male bamboo log (*mbông*) is set longitudinally on the edge of the floor and is tied to the *êgap* beam that supports the floor (see Figure 8). Holes are cut in the log about five inches apart to accommodate thin bamboo poles (*msŏng*) that are attached to a longitudinal beam in the roof. Panels of reed and split bamboo (*mtih*) are then affixed to the poles, held in place by long bamboo laths both inside and out. There are windows in the walls of the main room and along the side of the house where family cooking hearths (*kpur*) will be installed (see Figure 9). Bamboo and reed sliding blinds are added later (their omission is a sign to the spirits that the house has not yet been inaugurated). When the house is three-fourths complete, the husband of the senior female performs the *ktah êdê gap* ritual, dabbing a mixture of pig blood and rice alcohol on the columns, beams, and rafters while calling upon the spirits associated with these structural features and also the Spirit of the Floor and Spirit of the Hearth to partake of the offerings and bring well-being

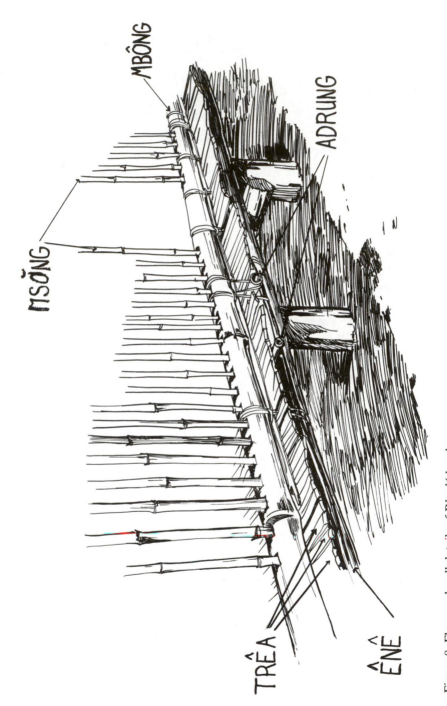

Figure 8. Floor and wall details of Rhadé longhouse.

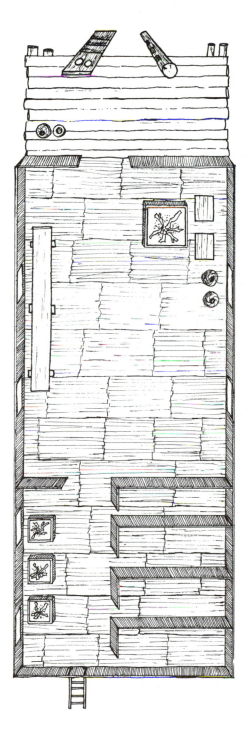

Figure 9. Rhadé longhouse floor plan.

to the inhabitants. During construction thus far, it is taboo to become drunk or to have sexual intercourse in the house. Clothes must not be hung there, and workers cannot eat mushrooms on the site. Should a death occur in the village, all work must cease until after the burial.

Now the primary hearth is installed in the main room. The sturdy hardwood frame is set in the prescribed place and is filled with earth, which is packed. Three curved stones (*boh tâo kan*) are placed in the center. A castrated pig or a chicken along with a jar of alcohol is offered to the Spirit of the Hearth, the Spirit of the Tâng Tree, and the Spirit of the Soil. Maurice reports that as he lights the first fire the officiant cries, "O fire, if you fall on the bamboo floor, if you spread to lick at the frame of the house, do not inflame wildly, do not devour, do not consume, do not renew yourself." After a brief pause, he continues, "If the chickens scratch in the ashes, if dogs trod on the hearth, inflame not with violence, inflame not the bundles of fagots nor consume them if the hearth is not well tended." Then there is an invocation to the Spirit of Water: "And you, Water, pass over the stones, and stay beautiful and clear." The chant ends with a request to the Spirit of the Hearth to remain in the house with the hearth, the three curved stones ("on which one puts the pots"), and the stairway to bring health and happiness.[11] Bamboo and reed doors and internal partitions are put in place. In the main room the poles to which alcohol jars are staked are affixed to a beam. Window blinds are installed, the final act of construction.

Y Yok explained that most inauguration celebrations last three days and reflect the family's means. Kettles, calabashes (water containers), mats, back-baskets, rice-alcohol jars, gongs, and weapons are brought into the house in that order. Two rituals honor the Spirit of the Hearth, ancestors, and spirits associated with trees, bamboo, the forest, mountains, and water. The initial offering calls for either a male buffalo and seven jars of alcohol or a pig and three jars. To the music of gongs and a large drum, the animal's head, some tobacco, a bowl of rice alcohol, and a gourd of water are placed in the main room. The husband of the senior female pours water and alcohol on the floor, invoking deities to partake of the offerings and bring good fortune to the family. He and his wife drink from the jar, followed by her kinswomen and male kin. A subsequent ritual resembles closely that of the earlier construction observance in which the columns and other physical features of the house were anointed with a mixture of blood and rice alcohol.

The house is now completed. It will serve not only as an abode but also as a place for rituals, all of which are part of the family's stewardship in preserving the man-nature-cosmos harmony. No matter how well they

11. Ibid., pp. 103–5.

meet this responsibility, there is no guarantee that the spirits associated with the house will be placated. In 1966, for example, the wife of Y Bham Nie, headman of Buon Kram, attended a sacrifice at a neighboring house and subsequently fell ill. Everyone agreed that the spirits of the house had caused the sickness, and so the house was taboo for her. At a 1967 celebration at the house, she remained outside while inside the guests drank from the jars, passing glasses of rice alcohol to her through a window.

Family

As Appendix B1 indicates, in Ego's generation, sex and age differentiation are reflected in sibling terminology, using a combination of nuclear terms and modifiers. Sibling terms are extended to cousins, who are age-graded relative to Ego. In addition, with collateral kin there are special terms for cross-cousins of the same sex. For male Ego, male cross-cousins (sons of the mother's brother or father's sister) are *dăm knai*. *Knai* is a modifier sometimes used to identify male kin on the father's side, and it also is an expression of familiarity for males of different clans and a term for a younger sister's husband. *Juk* (or *juk tô*) is the term a female Ego uses to identify female cross-cousins, and it is a familiar term used between women of different clans. Distinguishing cross-cousins of the same sex appears to be related to the Rhadé preference for cross-cousin marriage because those who employ these terms are potential brothers-in-law and sisters-in-law.

In the first ascending generation, matrilineal and nonmatrilineal kin are distinguished, but *amĭ neh* is the common term for mother's and father's younger sisters. Only matrilineal kin are recognized in higher generations. In the first descending generation, *anak* is the nuclear term for children and also the first and last born identified by modifiers. In this generation a distinction is made between clan and nonclan collateral kin with *anak* for nonclan and *amuôn* for clan members. The same distinction is made for cousins' children. For the second and third descending generations the modifier *găp djuê* is used to identify clan members. Only kin of the female line—*rông re rông rai* ("same roots")—in the fourth descending generation are recognized.

A visitor to a longhouse ascends the stairs to the veranda, where such items as chicken baskets and large, circular, flat baskets used to sun paddy, maize, coconut husks, roots, and bark are stored. The husband of the senior female of the house comes forth to greet the visitor and invite him or her to enter. Immediately inside the entrance is the *bhôk-gah*, where visitors are expected to leave their weapons. Beyond is a sizable room that at first seems dark and gloomy, the air heavy with the smoke from many open hearths. When blinds on the windows are slid back, however, light pours in, revealing an interesting and important part of the longhouse that serves at once as a family gathering place, ritual center, general work area, reception room, and storage space. Over the years the smoke has given walls, floor, columns, beams, and carved hardwood benches and stools a rich burnished brown patina. Just past the *bhôk-gah* is the *tung-gah,* the main feature of which is a large open hearth, the heart of the longhouse where everyone gathers. On either side of it are low carved-wood tables and stools. Visitors are invited to sit away from the hearth on newly woven mats spread on the floor. During rituals the hearth is the focal center for offerings and for preparing food served at the celebration. Parts of the sacrificial animals are mixed with vegetables in a black metal kettle with an enlarged bottom (*kbŭng*); these kettles are highly prized family heirlooms. According to Y Yok Ayun, some are worth five buffalo. A smaller kettle (*kbe*) may be used similarly, but the smallest kettle (*gŏ kăng*) is exclusively for cooking vegetables.

Along the wall opposite the hearth is a long bench (*k'pan*) carved from a single hardwood log to accommodate gong players during celebrations. Gongs are prized possessions, and because old ones bespeak lineage longevity, they are never sold or traded. In the past, *čing lao,* gongs made in Laos, produced the most resonant sounds; those made in Cambodia (*čing kur*) were judged second best. Least valuable were the gongs produced by the Vietnamese (*čing yuăn*). There is a set of three gongs (*sa rĭng cĭng*)—*ana čing,* the largest, *mdu čing,* the middle size, and *mŏng čing,* the smallest. All have circular indentations in the center which are struck by a wooden hammer. Y Yok recalled that when he was young, his father made a special trip to coastal Nhatrang to purchase a valuable set of gongs. Then there is a set of six flat gongs (*sa rĭng knah*), all of which have special names. Y Yok pointed out that usually these are very old, and a good set would command a price of fifty buffalo. *Čing kbuăn* is a single, almost white gong with a circular indentation in the center. *Čhar* is the very large flat gong suspended from rafters in the main room of every longhouse. The Rhadé have only vague ideas about their origin, and legend has it that they were found long ago in forest lakes, the abode of many spirits. Suspended from the rafters above the long bench is a very large drum (*hgòr*), which is played in accompaniment to the gongs. Y Yok explained that the drum is made of a wooden form over which female oxen skin has been stretched, and he added that most are from "the time of the ancestors."

In the center of the main room, *tung mnăm,* on ritual occasions rice-alcohol jars (*čeh k'piê*) are tied to bamboo poles affixed to the rafters. Old jars with worn brown or black glazes are prestigious heirlooms.

Myth describes how in remote times they were live swamp animals and upon being struck by arrows were transformed into jars. Behind the *tung mnăm* there usually is a carved-wood table used by the older members of the household. The area at the rear of the main room serves variously as a dormitory for unmarried males of the family and as a gathering place for household women during celebrations. A corridor leads from the main room to a series of compartments (*adŭ*), family quarters. Measuring around six or seven feet square, each has a small open hearth for heat.

The household group consists of those related through the female line and males who have married into the family. The rear compartment is for the senior female, mistress of the household. When widowed or elderly, she is expected to relinquish the role to her eldest daughter, but she will continue to keep the compartment. Other quarters are occupied by females and their families. Women usually receive their female guests in the compartment nearest the main room, and it serves as a dormitory for unmarried girls. Each nuclear family may have its own hearth (*kpur*) in the corridor to prepare its "rice pot" (*sa-boh-gŏ*) or several may share a hearth. At the rear of the house is a small door used exclusively by family members.

The exogamous matrilineal clans are organized into two exogamous phratries, Niê and Eban. According to Y Thih Eban, in the Niê phratry, two clans, Niê Mơô and Niê Alê, are named for species of bamboo. Two pregnant women who founded these clans were working in the swiddens when labor pains prompted them to creep under different clumps of bamboo, where they gave birth. The names of the respective bamboo specie became their clan designations. The founder of the Niê Buôn Dap clan was an orphan girl, who was brought up by the people of Buon Dap, so the village name was adopted by the clan. The ancestress of the Niê Buôn Rĭt clan was an orphan (*erĭt* is "orphan") who had been cared for by her grandmother, so "Rĭt" was applied to the girl's line. One day, the male ancestor of the Niê Sièng clan prepared midmorning rice to share with his younger brother, who took most of it. Infuriated, the elder brother threw his flat rice dish at his brother, using a gesture described by the word *sièng*, which became his descendants' name. The Rhadé word for salt is *hra*, and the Niê Hra clan gained its name because its members are "of all tastes," with the reputation of being lax in observance of taboos, even violating those concerning marriage.

Other Niê clans are the Niê Kdam, Niê Suk, Niê Blo, Niê Buôn-Yă, Niê Eñûôl, Niê Kriêng, Niê Buôn Kmriêk, Niê Adrơng, Niê Briêng, Niê Ksơr, Niê Ktla, Niê Hwing, Niê Kpơr, Niê Buôn Kdŏng, Niê Ktŭl, Niê Hrah, Niê Hlŏng, Niê Ktrei, and Niê Kmăn. Also within the Niê phratry are the Ečam and Buôn-Tô clans. Ečam clan members are forbidden to eat beef because their motherless ancestress was suckled by a cow. Forebears of the Buôn-Tô clan were "people of the forest" with long hair, who lived a hunting-gathering existence. One day, men of the Mlô Duôn Du clan (in the Eban phratry) were checking fish traps they had set in a stream when they came upon a woman and her daughter poaching fish from a trap. Outraged, they shot the woman dead with crossbows and carried the girl back to the village. She was extremely beautiful, but her fingers were joined with a membranous web in the manner of a duck's foot so they cut the webbing with a *dhŏng tô* knife. The child became known as Dhŏng-Tô, which evolved into Buôn-Tô. She learned to eat rice and lived as a member of the Mlô Duôn Du clan. Later she sacrificed a buffalo for the Niê Kdam, who accepted her into the Niê phratry, but her descendants were forbidden to marry anyone from the Mlô Duôn Du clan in the Eban phratry. Other Eban clans are the Eban, Eban Buôn Kang, Eban Buôn Sŭt, Eban Rahlan, Eban Kăt Hla Juê, Eban Duôn Kang, Hmŏk, Ayŭn, Hdruê, Buôn Krông (some are called Buôn Krông Păng), Hdŏk, Mlô (one branch of which is Mlô Duôn Du), Kbuôr, Kdoh, Knul, and Hwing. In the vicinity of Ban Me Thuot, the pattern is for males of the Eban clans to wed Niê Kdam females.

The exogamy rule appears to be stronger for the Niê phratry than for the Eban. Marriages between members of clans that contain the name "Eban" are strictly forbidden, but those between members of the other clans do take place, although the marriage is invariably preceded by a ritual offering to the ancestors as propitiation. Marriage between members of the same clan within a village is grave incest, which can render the soil infertile. There are cases of clan members from different villages marrying, and though it is incestuous, there are prescribed ritual offerings to propitiate the spirits, notably ancestors. The Rhadé prefer to marry cross-cousins, and the dominant pattern appears to be marriage with the matrilateral cross-cousin (mother's brother's daughter). The levirate is obligatory, but the sororate is not.

In the traditional courting pattern the couple meets in the evening to sing poetic songs. Premarital sexual relations are frowned upon. The girl's family initiates marriage arrangements through an intermediary, usually an older male friend. He negotiates the dowry, which must include a large gong. Well-to-do families sacrifice a buffalo for the boy's mother and pigs for his sisters and his mother's sisters, while poor families offer chickens. The wedding takes place in the girl's longhouse accompanied by animal sacrifices, drinking from the alcohol jars, and a large meal. The bride and groom exchange bracelets, sacrifice an animal, and, sharing a bamboo tube, drink from the same jar. They reside at the bride's house, where they are given their own compartment. Mother-in-law avoidance is rigidly observed, and should a boy violate this taboo he must sacrifice a pig. Joking between household or clan members (with the exception of children and the elderly) must be avoided.

Pregnancy causes a shift in the woman's place within the harmonious man-nature-cosmos arrangement of Rhadé society, putting her in a situation fraught with latent dangers. Dr. B. Y. Jouin observes that when a woman becomes pregnant, she is "contagious" in that she is highly susceptible to the influences of evil spirits, notably the fearsome Yang Brieng, who causes accidental deaths. According to Jouin, when signs of pregnancy appear, the family summons a midwife (*buê*), who in most cases is the daughter of a midwife. The midwife commands respect, but because she is in contact with evil spirits, she cannot have anything to do with caring for the sick or with organizing sacrifices. She examines the patient to determine how long (in lunar months) she has been pregnant and when birth is due. Afterward the family summons the shaman (*mjâo*) to offer evil spirits a dog and a jar of alcohol in the *kih klei k'kiêng* ritual. The woman must then remain in her compartment for three days, after which she bathes to purify herself.[12]

By the fifth month, the woman stays home, restricting her activities to cooking and weaving textiles. When served rice, she must consume it immediately and do her chores without hesitation lest the birth be long and difficult and the child retarded. She should avoid fruit because the baby may fall out of the womb as fruit falls from a tree. Consuming bananas that are joined will result in twins, a disaster because Rhadé women cannot physically nurse two babies. When labor pains start, the midwife is again summoned, and if she declares that birth is imminent, the family quickly conducts the *phat atâo* ritual. A mat is spread immediately inside the main entrance on which a small jar of alcohol, a cooked young male rooster, and a pipe are placed. Facing the entrance while squatting, the officiant calls upon the ancestors to partake of the offering and bring the successful birth of a beautiful child, preferably a girl. The husband sits nearby, and when the chant is finished he pours some alcohol to give his wife. Meanwhile, household women arrange in the corridor by the private compartments a small chamber of bamboo and mats (*adŭ k'kiêng*) for the birth. The husband fetches water from the nearby spring to wash mother and baby, and he also fashions from bamboo a knife (*k'sal*) to cut the umbilical cord.

Alone with the midwife, the woman sits on a low carved stool and grips a rope attached to roof beams to give birth. The infant's first cry is *êwa*, "breath of life," a sign that *yun* has entered the body and will become *mngăh*, the primary soul. At death, *mngăh* becomes *yun*, a spirit that wanders in search of a pregnant woman whose body it can enter. Another

12. Jouin, "Grossesse," pp. 3–72.

soul is *tlang hêă* (often depicted on coffins as a large soaring gray bird), which at death becomes dew. In an isolated place in the forest the husband and midwife bury a calabash containing the bamboo knife, placenta, and other products of birth. The mother rests on a mat near a hearth, and her body is rubbed with ginger.

The following day the midwife purifies herself at the spring, washing her hair with rice water to fend off any lingering evil spirits, particularly Yang Brieng. She also gathers dew in a copper cup to be served along with chicken, vegetables, and rice at a meal (*bi hôă buê*) during which she will name the child. Arranging the dishes near the mother, the midwife takes the infant, and, rubbing dew on its tongue, she pronounces the name she has chosen. If the infant registers contentment it is a sign that ancestors approve. While the mother partakes of food, the midwife chews a bit of chicken liver and rice, which she feeds to the baby. The child is suckled for two years. If at the time pregnancy was diagnosed the family had the midwife promise good deities (notably H'bia Dung Day) a billy goat sacrifice (*klêi k'kaih*) for an easy birth, it is made after the naming ritual (it is the only time a billy goat is the offering).

The most important postnatal ritual is *prap yun* in which a shaman invokes *yang amĭ bă ama bă* (the child's guardian spirit) while offering a chicken or pig and rice alcohol to mark the voyage of the *yun* from a person who has died to a newborn, in whose body it becomes *mngăh.* If at the time of birth there has been a death in the vicinity, that person is identified as the *pô yun* that has entered the newborn via the bluish "Mongolian spot" at the base of the spine found on Rhadé babies. For the first year the child is called *anak mda,* and then until the age of five it is *anak diêt.* At the end of that crucial period, the child is known by its given name.

A young Rhadé boy's mother's brother plays an important role in teaching the boy how to hunt, fish, and tend buffalo and in chastising him for any misbehavior. Y Thih Eban recalled that his hero was Y Plo Eban, a young leader and kinsman of his mother. Although not her brother, Y Thih nonetheless addressed him by the kin term for mother's brother. If the father should die, the maternal uncle assumes responsibility for his nephew, even paying fines he may incur. Traditionally both boys and girls undergo a severe puberty ritual marking the passage to adulthood. The child is conditioned not to display any pain and to remain stoic while kinsmen, using stones and sharp instruments, file the four front teeth. A chicken is sacrificed, and jars are opened for the occasion. Since the 1950s this practice has been fading among the Rhadé Kpa, but it has continued in more remote areas. In the past, both men and women had long hair arranged in a chignon, but among the men near towns this custom has been diminishing, as has the women's mode of being bare above the waist.

A common sight in the main room of a house is a woman or girl sitting on the floor weaving textiles on a back-tension loom tied to one of the columns. Y Yok Ayun reported that in the past the Rhadé grew cotton that was spun into thread by women who also produced their own dyes. Tree barks were used to make red and yellow dyes. For black dye a certain bark was pestled, after which it was boiled for two days and then immersed in mud for several days. Allowed to dry, the bark was rubbed with crushed white rice kernels and stretched on a bamboo rack (*hnar*), where it was brushed with bristles of stiff hairs from the back of a wild boar. The bark was then spread out to sun. Most dyed threads now are purchased in the markets, although wild indigo still is gathered by men (who also gathered the barks) and is cultivated in swiddens and along rivers. Women continue to weave textiles for blankets, slings for carrying infants, and traditional clothes such as blouses (*ao mkĕ*), skirts (*mŏiêng êlah*), shirts, and loincloths.[13]

In the dry season men may be seen in the main room weaving baskets and making tools and weapons. They also make musical instruments such as the bagpipelike *dĭng năm* (Figure 10) fashioned from a gourd (*giêt*) into which are inserted six bamboo pipes (*dĭng*), each of which has a hole (*băng*) on the side and a single-reed vibrator (*elah buôt*) inside the gourd. Air enters the mouthpiece (*kuôp iŭ*) at the end of the gourd, and the player puts his finger on the holes to play tunes. In well-to-do families, men see that the elephants have a daily bath in the stream and time to feed in the forest. Y Yok Ayun noted that in the past there was a pig sacrifice to mark the cutting of tusks, which were then sold at Ban Don. Periodically men prepare batches of rice alcohol. Although any kind of rice can be used, a red rice called *asan* is particularly good. The first step is to prepare a ferment (*k'piê*) consisting of rice flour, wild ginger root, and crushed bark from two different trees. These ingredients are ground

13. Mattiebelle Gittinger, research associate for Southeast Asian Textiles at the Textile Museum, Washington, D.C., did the following analysis of two Rhadé loincloths: "This Rhadé loincloth is one continuous panel visually organized into a centerfield, lateral margins, and decorative end borders. The centerfield is indigo-dyed, handspun cotton worked in a warp-faced plain weave. The lateral margins, from a rust-red machine-spun cotton, carry a decorative white stripe. This is a simple weave with alternate warps interlacing as in a 2/2 twill. Indigo-dyed, handspun cotton forms the weft. Both fringe ends carry a border of weft twining approximately 5 cm deep. Here designs of crosses and lozenge patterns, which show only on one face, are created by the interlacing of rust and white yarns. A line of Job's Tears beads is inserted in the warp after the twined border and secured by additional twined wefts. The fringes are lightly plied. Total dimensions 428 × 22 cm" (Textile Museum TD 389.1).

Figure 10. A Rhadé musical instrument.

to a powder to which water is added, producing a paste that is rolled into thumb-size balls that are dried on a shelf over a cooking hearth. Husked and partially husked rice is boiled and spread to dry on a large, flat, circular basket on the veranda. Some of the ferment is powdered and mixed with the rice. One ball of ferment will do for a small jar of alcohol and three for a large jar. In the next step, a mixture of rice bran and broken husks is placed on the bottom of a deep basket, and the mash of cooked rice and ferment is poured over it. The remainder of the basket is filled with more bran and husks. After one day the contents are put into a jar which is sealed with banana leaves and left standing for at least a week. On a ceremonial occasion the jar is tied to a stake, the seal is removed, fresh green leaves are stuffed into it, some water is poured to the brim, and a bamboo drinking tube is inserted. Those invited to drink must consume a specified amount, which in the past was measured by a buffalo horn. As the drinker sips, water is poured from the horn to maintain the brim level. The quality of the rice alcohol varies. "Good jars" have a sharp sweetness combined with a smokey flavor whereas "bad jars" are sour. In September 1967, Y Bham Enuol's wife declared that she did not plan to attend the funeral at a neighbor's longhouse because an old man tottering down the path reported to her that he had been imbibing from the jars, which he judged to be "sour and smelly."

Illness is caused by malevolent spirits, so the family seeks the services of a *mjâo*, a shaman-healer, who can be male or female, although most are the latter. Shamanistic powers, bestowed by the Python Spirit, are manifest in certain signs and dreams, which prompt the person to become an apprentice to a practicing shaman. In the main room of the longhouse the shaman performs a ritual to ascertain which spirit is causing the malady and what it desires in the way of propitiation. If the ailing person worsens, the family is likely to conclude that he is the victim of a *mtâo*, a sorcerer who in league with the evil *k'sŏk* is empowered to eject his stomach and intestines and have them lodge in the body of the victim to devour his primary soul, causing sickness and death. The sorcerer also can conjure up a dusty cloud that condenses fatally in the victim's innards.

Amid the firewood and pigsties under many longhouses there are coffins (*bŏng*), reminders of death. Y Sok Eban recalled that when he was a boy one of his chores during the dry season was to help his kinsmen carry hardwood logs to the farmstead, where with axes and bush scythes they fashioned coffins. At death, the soul becomes one of the ancestors who live in the domain of the dead but who return to the longhouse on ritual occasions. *Atâo mdriêng* are souls of those who have died in accidents, but they cannot enter a house so offerings are made to them through windows.

The body is dressed in ceremonial garb and, along with personal possessions such as clothes, crossbows, bracelets, and pipes, is placed in the coffin. According to Y Yok Ayun, the wealthy have two coffins. One is a simple box of wood planks (*bŏng mlŭn*) in which the body is placed, and this in turn is put in a much larger hardwood coffin (*bŏng prŏng*). Normally for between two and seven days kin and friends gather in the main room of the house, where, to the sound of gongs, drums, and the *dĭng nǎm* (see Figure 10), kin and friends perform animal sacrifices and drink from jars. The wealthy have a longer mourning period, and Y Yok recalled that in Buon Brieng, the dead were sometimes kept in the house for three months.

Tombs (*msat*) also reflect economic status in the village. For a well-to-do villager's tomb a large, square, shallow excavation is dug and an enclosure built around it. The coffin is placed in the center, and jars are staked at the head and foot. Gong players position themselves on either side while mourners gather around. While music sounds, kinsmen call on the spirits, notably the ancestors, to partake of the offerings, which consist of pigs, buffalo, rice, and jars. Michael Benge recalled that at a 1967 funeral at Buon Kram girls played an unusual wind instrument consisting of bamboo tubes containing water at varying levels to produce different notes. Ordinary villagers have simpler tombs and sacrifice chickens for the spirits.

Albert Maurice and George Proux recorded a funeral ritual prayer invoking Mtao Kla (chief of agriculture) and his wife, H'Bia Klu; Aê Du (intermediary between Aê Diê and humans) and his wife, H'bia Dung Day (protector of rice); the evil Yang Liê and his wife, H'jua; and the Spirit of the Krong Bong River. The officiant implored them to "raise the seed millet and the family of rice," reminding them that "the other evening I brought rice to the deceased, I prepared rice alcohol for the deceased, and I brought rice for the funeral." He added, "Be not unhappy . . . remain calm as swamp water, be not volatile, and do not become startled . . . henceforth when man takes rice, may it continue to be abundant, always as stable and fixed as a slab of rock."[14]

According to Y Yok, after the funeral ritual, earth is piled on the coffin, forming a high mound on top of which a small model of a longhouse (*sang yang*) is placed. For a period of up to thirty days, offerings of meat, rice, and alcohol are put in the house for the spirits. The wealthy also have a monthly pig or buffalo sacrifice and obtain the services of a wood carver to produce depictions of animals (monkeys are a common theme) and birds (usually peacocks and egrets), which are placed around the enclosure. Carvers are inspired by contemporary motifs, and sculptures done in the 1950s portray French soldiers. After anytime from two to seven years the tomb is abandoned. Families save so they can sacrifice a buffalo or at least pigs and chickens. Those who have died in accidents or childbirth are buried hurriedly in a simple forest grave with little ceremony. Bodies of soldiers killed away from the village cannot be returned, and some of their belongings are placed in a carved-wood container on a post in an isolated place.

The Land Guardian

The role of land guardian (*pô lăn*) reflects the mystical link between female fecundity and rice-soil fertility that is so much at the heart of the Rhadé adaptation. This role gives her jural authority to oversee use of clan land, preventing abuses of the physical environment. It also makes her steward of religious prescriptions related to the land, which include ritual observances and meting out punishments for moral infractions. Dominique Antomarchi recorded a story told him in Buon Jung by H'bi Ayun, a woman who was guardian of Ayun clan land in the vicinity. It

14. Maurice and Proux, "L'âme du riz," pp. 299–300.

told how, as the clans emerged from the Băng Adrêñ hole, one after another staked claims to the abundant flora. When the Niê Kdam emerged, they found that all of the flora had already been claimed so they declared themselves owners of the land. It soon became apparent to everyone that some compromise was called for so two sisters of the Niê Kdam clan and two of the Ayun clan arranged exchanges of land and flora, witnessed by their brothers. This marked the beginning of a system wherein women became guardians of clan land (Figure 11).[15]

The rights and responsibilities of the guardians have been preserved in Rhadé oral tradition and in the written codes prepared under the direction of Sabatier and Antomarchi. The passage, "if the aunt dies, the niece succeeds her, and if the grandmother dies, the granddaughter succeeds her," emphasizes female succession to the role, although not necessarily mother to daughter. The guardian is advised to know well the boundaries, marked by old trees with names, streams, hillocks, and waterfalls. The code also directs the guardian to protect the ecological integrity of the territory and "not leave the land like a goat without a master or a buffalo without a guard." Villagers are free to gather bamboo, grass, and reeds for building houses, but anyone desiring to farm or hunt there must have her approval. She should visit the Băng Adrêñ hole and every seven years walk the boundaries of the land at least once during the dry season so that "the soil will always be renewed, the waters run limpidly, and the banana trees and sugarcane thrive." On this occasion she must offer a male buffalo and five jars for "the back of the ancestors" (a metaphor for the land) and a castrated pig for herself.[16]

Maurice and Proux report that at this ritual the accompanying chant begins with invocations to the supreme being, Aê Diê; his assistant, Aê Du; M'tao Tlŭa (King of the Soil) and his brother, Kbuă Lăn; and Aê Mghi and his brother, Mghăn Tơ Làn, both associated with good harvests.[17] The guardian then invites the spirit of the stream that runs through the valley and the spirits of the water flowing from the mountain "to eat with the Spirit of the Mountain and to drink with the Spirit of the Land." Pouring water on the ground, she expresses hope that the "back of the ancestors" and two types of basket used by women in farming (which appears to be a metaphor for the link between female fecundity and soil fertility) "will not suffer from the heat." She adds, "I pour water to moisten the soil, I pour water to purify it so that if I plant banana trees

15. Dominique Antomarchi, "La légende de la terre," *Indochine*, no. 17 (1941): 13–15; no. 20 (1941): 23–25.

16. Dominique Antomarchi and Léopold Sabatier, *Recueil des coutumes Rhadées du Darlac* (Hanoi: Imprimerie d'Extrême-Orient, 1940), pp. 279–86.

17. Maurice and Proux, "L'âme du riz," pp. 212–16.

Figure 11. Jean Despujols (French-American, 1886–1965), *Little Rade Girls with Back-baskets,* pen drawing washed in color, 1937 (Indochina Collection, Meadows Museum of Art, Centenary College of Louisiana). Drawing depicts Rhadé women in traditional clothes and hats with back-baskets for carrying firewood and gourds of water.

and sugarcane they will grow and not wither and die." The code also calls for the guardian to make the same offerings in an annual postharvest ritual at the stairway to the headman's longhouse.[18]

The guardian has the duty to mete out punishment for profanations of the soil which threaten the man-nature-cosmos harmony. Maurice and Proux note that the gravest is incest, and the moral code distinguishes between *klei agam,* involving distant kin, and the more serious *klei hlăm,* implicating parent and child, household members, or clan members. She must be on guard "lest the mango trees and bamboo fail to flourish out of fear that young men and women who are brothers and sisters take pleasure together." She must be alert for dire signs—"if the watercress droops in the stream and taro wilts in the marsh, it is because young men and women who are brothers and sisters take pleasure together." Should such signs appear, the code advises the guardian to address the village chief, who "will condemn the guilty." The guardian and headman preside over an expiation ritual in which the guilty pair must make sacrifices to purify the soil and propitiate appropriate deities and ancestors. For incest between distant kin, a jar of alcohol is offered, and gifts of bracelets and neckpieces are given to the guardian. For more serious incest, the guilty woman must offer a pig and a jar for the *pô lăn* while the man offers the same for the headman. The pair then presents the guardian with a skirt, a man's mantle, a hoe for digging ginger root, a hand ax, a spear, and a platter of meat. A buffalo is slain while the guardian invites M'tao Tlŭa and Kbŭa Lăn, "who created water and planted the trees," Aê Mghi, and Mghăn Tơ Làn to partake of the offerings. She also invokes the female farming baskets and the "back of the ancestors." Naming the couple, she directs them to "bless the soil so that the trees may grow, the mangoes may thrive, and boys and girls may live in peace." As they prick their fingers, allowing blood to flow, and then wash their heads, the *pô-lăn* calls upon Aê Du to bring rain and the deities to bear witness to these acts that erase the incest. In her final chant she entreats the Spirit of the Valley Stream and the Spirit of the Mountain to join the Water Spirit, the Thunder Spirit, the Termite-Nest Spirit, and the Spirit of the Soil in drinking from the jars and consuming sacrificial meat.[19]

Another profane act is to bury cold cooked rice in a swidden because "the land will not be renewed, the water sources will dry up, bananas and sugarcane will not grow, and rice and millet will not bud." The code directs the village headman to find the guilty party and have him present the guardian with a pig and other offerings in expiation. It is equally profane to build a tomb on a fallowing swidden. The culpable party must

18. Antomarchi and Sabatier, *Recueil,* pp. 286–87.
19. Maurice and Proux, "L'âme du riz," pp. 207–16.

give the farmer the equivalent of the yield that normally would have been realized and sacrifice a pig. Pig sacrifices also purify the land polluted by blood spilled in the course of a violent death (such as being caught in an animal trap or being mauled by a tiger). Droughts are an indication that some undetected grave profanation of the soil has occurred, calling for a village propitiation ritual at which a local guardian offers a white pig, a white goat, a white buffalo, and jars of alcohol. As gongs sound, the guardian pours a mixture of animal blood and alcohol over the sacrificial animals while entreating the deities to bring "great rains each month and rains every day."[20]

Maurice and Proux observe that between 1940 and 1950, in the course of their research, some of these traditional practices had faded. Villagers were clearing new swiddens without the consent of the guardians. The seven-year visits were not made as rigorously as before. Despite efforts by Sabatier in the 1920s to protect Rhadé land claims, the French administration ignored them. In February 1971, H'won Enuol of Buon Ea Bong lamented that her clan territory of thirty-five hectares had been taken in the 1920s without compensation for construction of the Ban Me Thuot airstrip. H'ring Enuol of Buon Kosier produced a map signed by Sabatier to validate her claim to nine hectares of clan land. She also had a letter to the administration dated 1941 in which she had registered a complaint against the Compagnie des Hauts Plateaux Indochinois for taking land to expand its coffee estate. Her efforts were to no avail, and in 1971 the French company sold the land to a Chinese businessman to construct a new market. In *Free in the Forest* it is noted that in 1957 the Rhadé leaders emphasized the importance of the *pô lăn* system when the Diem administration seized land for Vietnamese settlers in the Land Development Program.[21] The first Land Development Center was established that year on land whose guardian, H'deo Eban of Buon Kroa, was never consulted. This act provoked deep resentment among the Rhadé Kpa and helped lead to the formation of Bajaraka.

Economic Activities

In the heat of the March dry season, sunlight on the Darlac plateau is veiled by smoke billowing from forested areas, signaling the burning that is part of the swidden-farming cycle around which Rhadé livelihood activities are centered (where there is relatively flat, well-watered land, some farmers have arranged paddy fields). In addition to the common garden produce, there is a plant villagers identified by the French word

20. Ibid., pp. 215–16.
21. Hickey, *Free in the Forest,* pp. 42–45, 226.

pissenlit ("dandelion") that is chopped and mixed with raw meat and animal blood to "refresh the heart." Around Ban Me Thuot the French introduced avocado and coffee trees. The Rhadé also forage for wild fruits and vegetables, notably watercress in stream shallows.

In 1967, Katoully-Plowatt, a Rhadé who had worked in the provincial agricultural service since the time of the French, reported that when selecting a swidden site, farmers look for black soil in forested areas and brown soil in brush country. Certain trees indicate great soil fertility, but they should never be felled. One, *Pentaciamea siamensis,* called "arbre aux abeilles," is venerated by villagers (Pham Hoang Ho identifies a variety of upland dipterocarpus as *Pentacem siamensis Kurz*[22]). A swidden is never cleared in the vicinity of a tomb that has not been abandoned. To dream of an alcohol jar, a roe deer, a stag, a wild boar, a tiger, panthers, pigs, a goat, or a monkey augers badly for the crops. Dreams about chickens or birds means that the rice grains will be devoured on the plants. Motifs that involve childbirth or acquisition of jars or buffalo portend an abundant harvest. A snake on a path to the field is a good omen.

Villagers observed that a farmer never discusses his choice of a new swidden site because it would draw the attention of malevolent spirits. The farmer does, however, mark the boundaries with staffs of split wood on which bits of thatch or bark have been tied. If the site is in the deep forest, he buries two dried goat's feet in the soil. Those who share the same "rice pot" make up the work group that in December will begin clearing a new swidden. Steady easterly winds dry the wood which men and women gathered into piles that are set ablaze in mid-March. Women use rakes (*hwar*) (Figure 12) to gather small pieces of wood and spread ashes that fertilize the soil and keep pests at bay.

Rhadé farmers describe a brief postburning ritual in which three bamboo tubes of water are offered to the spirits to slake thirst brought on by the fires. The prayer asks the spirits to take heed of the newly cleared field and the swidden hut (*pưk jhû*) that will be built as resting place and shelter for those guarding the field during the growing season. A chant entreats M'tao Tlŭa and his brother Kbŭa Lăn for rain and soil fertility and Aê Mghi for an abundant harvest. There are two more dry-season rituals. *Kăm angin* (meaning "prevent the wind") requests various deities to allow rain by holding back the wind, which is likened to a powerful elephant in need of restraint. The ritual takes place east of the village at an altar containing a shackle resembling that used to constrain elephants, a reed on which a bloom has appeared, and a figure of evil Yang Brieng crudely depicted with a large head and a tail. At the entrance to each

---

22. Phạm, *Cây-cỏ*, p. 317.

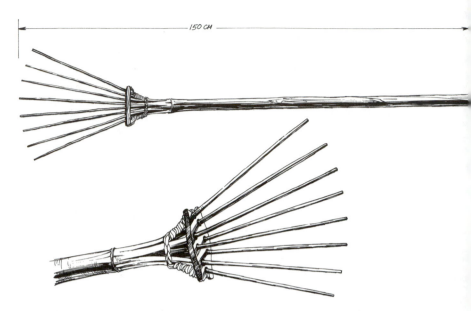

150 CM

Figure 12. A Rhadé rake.

longhouse a bracelet of bamboo fibers and a chicken plume are displayed to indicate that the family has observed the wind ritual. *Kăm hwar* (*hwar* is a rake) is held east of the village, where a bush, symbolizing a type of hardwood tree that is venerated, is planted. Offerings to the spirits include a back-basket, gongs fashioned from dried gourds, and softwood carvings of rhinoceros horns and elephant tusks.

Following this ritual, the family work group removes stones, roots, and bushes. Young men and women hoe, stopping to drink from the alcohol jars, and when finished they bathe in the river. When the April rains come, women with bamboo tubes (*drao*) filled with kernels sow maize either in rows throughout the swidden or in a separate garden nearby. To mark this event, they stick in the soil a bamboo staff on which a bit of cotton has been affixed.

Katoully-Plowatt and other Rhadé reported that the major village farming ritual is *ngă yang kăm mah* (or *kăm buh*). The headman and the *pô riu yang,* a shaman who specializes in farming rituals, select a site to clear a swidden symbolizing all of the villagers' fields. In the middle they construct a miniature granary, and along the borders they place every kind of Rhadé hunting trap. Seven jars of alcohol are tied to stakes. Gathering at the headman's house, all villagers form a single-file procession. The headman and shaman lead while behind them young men carry carved figures of Aê Diê, the supreme deity, his wife, and evil Yang Liê, depicted with his neck in a cangue, one foot encased in a block of wood, and an ax embedded in his head. One man carries a calabash of water, which is periodically sprinkled on the figures and those in the procession. Many of the villagers carry figures representing wild animals and birds that destroy crops. At the swidden the figures of Aê Diê and his wife are put in the little granary while the Yang Liê figure is placed under it. As drums and gongs sound, a pig is sacrificed, and the shaman takes some of its flesh and a bowl of boiled chicken to the granary, where he intones prayers three times calling upon Aê Diê and Yang Liê to partake of the offerings. Sprinkling a handful of earth to simulate broadcasting of seeds, he implores Aê Diê and other deities for permission to farm the soil. When he is finished, villagers move on to the field, either destroying the figures of animals and birds or putting them in the traps. The figures of Aê Diê and his wife are left in the granary to protect the crops and prevent any devilment by Yang Liê. *M'năm buh* is the family ceremony to initiate rice planting, and the shaman again officiates. Facing east, he invokes the same deities as well as the ancestors and spirits of ravines, valleys, and mountains to whom he offers pork and alcohol.

According to Katoully-Plowatt, the three varieties of upland rice (*mdiê*) most cultivated by the Rhadé Kpa are *hdrô*, early rice that matures in four months and is grown between April and September; *bla*, another four-month rice grown between April and October; and *mkĭt*, a late, five-month rice farmed between April and December. *Diŏ* is a popular five-month glutinous rice valued for feeding children, for snacking, and for making alcohol. *Asăn* is a red rice also used for alcohol production. Y Dhuat Niê Kdam reported that in Buon Ea Kmat the farmers plant the three common varieties and the less common *viêt* and *ke* the first year because these varieties need very fertile soil. *Ana*, a five-month, late rice, is planted the second year, and a similar variety, *hliê*, is sown the third year. The traditional cropping pattern is to divide the swidden into two or more sections, each planted in varieties with different maturation periods to allow effective use of available labor. A Buon Ale farmer explained that using this method he and his wife could farm a one-hectare swidden. In Buon Kram, Y Bham Nie, an innovative farmer, planted papaya, jack fruit, bananas, and guava along with rice in a swidden during the third year. The trees were too young to shade the rice, and the next year they produced fruit.

On the morning that planting actually begins, there is a brief ritual offering of a chicken and a jar of alcohol in the field to placate Yang Grăm, the Thunder Spirit, so that no workers will be struck by lightning. Jars of alcohol are staked nearby in the shade, and as gongs play, young men with dibble sticks move rhythmically, making holes in rows, followed by women with bamboo tubes containing rice seeds, releasing four or five in each hole. From time to time the workers stop to drink from the jars. Weeding is done two or three times. Katoully-Plowatt noted that wild grasses thrive in red soil while brush flourishes in black soil. One very bothersome weed is the prickly *mimosa invisa* (Pham describes *Mimosa invisa* Mart. ex Colla. as a plant that grows wild on uncultivated land[23]), which Katoully-Plowatt claims was brought into the area in 1923 by a French planter named Maillot to combat the spread of imperata grass. He also identified a very tall weed as *Eupatorium odoratum,* known to the French planters as "herbe de Laos" and believed to have been brought by aircraft flying from Laos during the French period.

When the rice plants are around one meter high, each family performs the *m'năm tuh phŭn mdiê* ritual, which Maurice and Proux report is to "call back the Rice Soul" so that the plants may thrive and bud.[24] The Rhadé believe that each year following the harvest, the Spirit of Čŭ Jŭ (Black Mountain) and the Spirit of H'mu Mountain (called La Mère et l'Enfant by the French) imprison the Rice Soul in a cave. Dressed in ceremonial garb, members of the family join the shaman in a swidden to offer a pig and five jars of alcohol. The shaman sprinkles a mixture of pig blood and alcohol on the four corners of the field while he entreats the two mountain spirits to release the Rice Soul, whom he invites to return to the plants so they can bud. He then offers a chicken to the ancestors, asking them for a full harvest. As rice ripens, fields are invaded by sparrows, turtledoves, titmice, crows, peacocks, parakeets, parrots, pheasants, and wild roosters. To cope, the farmers employ a range of traps, wooden noisemakers moved by the wind, and scarecrows, one of which resembles a black vulture and is suspended from a pole to continually swoop over the field.

Rhadé informants report that when the first crop is ready to harvest, the family brings a jar of alcohol and a chicken to the field, where they call upon the deities invoked at the sowing ritual to come and taste the new rice. Several days later, they celebrate *m'năm puôt* to initiate the harvest, placing offerings of a castrated pig, alcohol, tobacco, and bits of cotton on an altar in a field. The shaman and senior woman of the household squat facing east while he chants an invocation to the deities associated with rice farming to protect the new crop. All able-bodied members of the family are mustered to assist with the harvest. The most common threshing method is *puôt mdiê.* The harvester clutches several stalks, pulling kernels by hand into a back-basket set on the ground. Certain varieties, such as glutinous rice or *hlie* late rice, are threshed by the *wia mdie* method in which stalks are cut with a knife and beaten on a

---

23. Ibid., p. 796.
24. Maurice and Proux, "L'âme du riz," pp. 167–77.

mat to disengage the kernels. Katoully-Plowatt explained that the latter technique is "Lao-Vietnamese" and inappropriate for most upland rice because the grains tend to be fragile and fall to the ground when the stalk is cut. He noted that some Rhadé at Ban Don thresh by having buffalo trod on the cut stalks. Portage of the rice to the granary (one elephant can carry six large sacks) is accompanied by a ritual in which the shaman breaks an egg into a bowl and pours it over a basket of rice while chanting a prayer to agriculture deities and ancestors.

The unit of measure is the back-basket. In Buon Ea Kmat, for example, Y Dhuat Nie Kdam reported that a good yield was one hundred baskets. Working in Buon Kram, Michael Benge and his assistant, Y Puk Buon-Ya, measured the yield in Y Bham Nie's one-hectare swidden planted in traditional varieties and it was three and a half tons. Pierre-Bernard Lafont found in the brush zone of black, sandy soil near Ban Me Thuot that the first-year yield was around 1,500 kilos per hectare.[25] The second-year yield was 1,000 kilos and the third year 600. In the forested red-soil zone the comparable figures were 2,300, 1,500 to 1,700, and 800 to 1,000.

The end of the harvest is marked by the *kăm m'ngăt mdiê* ritual in the main room of the longhouse. If the harvest has been good, custom calls for a buffalo sacrifice to Yang Mdie, the Rice Spirit that inhabits the plant, and other deities associated with rice farming, and a pig for the ancestors. Four jars of alcohol are offered for the household women and one jar for guests. On 22 January 1966 this ritual took place in the main room of a Buon Kram longhouse. At dawn a pig (rather than the prescribed buffalo) had been slaughtered and dressed. Later, garbed in ceremonial clothes, male kin and guests gathered around the large open hearth and a rice bin near the entrance while women sat on mats at the rear of the room. *Pô ngă yang,* the shaman for this occasion, was an elderly villager named Y Bioh, who had learned the prayers and format from other shamans. He had fashioned a miniature tree (*ana tăng*) of leafy branches, which he explained symbolized an abundance of rice. He placed it in the rice bin along with two small bamboo figures, one an elephant with a tiny basket on its back, the other a buffalo. Near them he positioned a bowl of alcohol, the pig's head and tail, as well as three bowls of its blood and two pieces of its liver. A roasted chicken filled a bowl, and a dish next to it contained a mixture of coagulated blood, raw pork, and chopped chicken innards.

The ritual began when the drum and gongs sounded. Squatting in the bin, Y Bioh chanted a rhythmic litany of deities associated with rice

---

25. Pierre-Bernard Lafont, "L'agriculture sur brûlis chez les Proto-Indochinois des hauts plateaux du centre Viet-Nam," *Les Cahiers d'Outre-Mer* 20 (1967): 37–48.

farming. As his voice rose, he poured alcohol into the bowl of pig's blood and then tore bits of chicken breast and pig's head to add to the mixture. Inviting the Rice Spirit to partake of the offerings, he poured some of the mixture over the base of the tree. As he did so, the drum sounded steadily, and the gongs increased their cadence. Meanwhile, outside the longhouse a group of little boys and girls perched on a log and imitated the gong players using old tin cans, battered basins, and chunks of wood which they beat with sticks rhythmically if erratically. Nearby a cooking fire had been built, and men chopped up pig intestines to mix in the pot with shredded banana seeds.

In the longhouse, the "chief of rice" (the eldest married daughter) stepped forward to take a bowl of blood and alcohol proffered by the shaman. She drank some, and then her younger sister repeated the act. Y Bioh poured the remaining liquid over the dish containing the coagulated blood and meat. Going to the *tung mnăm* section of the room, the eldest daughter sat on a low stool at the first of four jars being offered to the Rice Spirit by the household women, and as gongs sounded she drank through the bamboo tube. Her sister drank from the second jar, and their mother sipped from the first jar. Other household women sat down to drink from the third jar. The eldest daughter returned to the first jar, where Y Bioh held the roasted chicken over her while she sang a chant to the Rice Spirit. This was repeated at the second jar, and when her chant ended, the shaman placed a brass bracelet on her right wrist. A younger girl of the family sat at the fourth jar and chanted while Y Bioh put a bracelet on her wrist. A fifth jar was for the guest, who sat and drank while the shaman held the blood-alcohol bowl over his head and chanted as the chief of rice placed a bracelet on his wrist, marking the end of the ritual.

Rhadé Bih have wet-rice paddies along the Krong Ana River south of Ban Me Thuot. Some are in low-lying floodplains inundated in December and January, permitting a May harvest. In addition, there are paddies irrigated by diverting water from nearby streams, using dikes to force gravitational flow through small channels. These fields are sown in July and August and harvested in January and February. To transplant the rice, men drain the seedbed of any standing water and hoe the earth, after which women rake the soil. Some farmers have buffalo tread on the soil to loosen it and break up lumps. To germinate seeds, women place them in a basket, which is immersed in water for one night; then they are wrapped in wet banana leaves and placed in another basket for two days. Sowing is marked by a simple ritual in which the senior female's husband squats by a basket of germinated seeds to offer a mixture of a white chicken's blood and alcohol to M'tao Kla, chief of agriculture. Moving into the field, women level the soil with their feet in preparation for men to broadcast seeds. Afterward, everyone returns to the longhouse to offer more chicken blood and alcohol to deities associated with farming. Soil in the larger field is turned over by men using hoes. After twenty-one days the seedlings are transplanted. Should a farmer lack either time or labor, he may broadcast the seeds in the larger field without transplanting. Men maintain dikes and channels, and women do the weeding. Everyone joins in harvesting, after which there is a ritual resembling that after the swidden harvest.

Rhadé women in the vicinity of Ban Me Thuot have for many years brought garden produce to the market for sale, although this was not a daily activity and crops were not grown with the explicit purpose of selling them. By 1930, French planters employed twelve hundred laborers, some four hundred of whom were Rhadé.[26] Some workers began to grow coffee trees near their longhouses, eventually starting small estates. The headman of Buon Pan Lam, who had worked on a plantation, related that he began to grow coffee trees on a small plot and it grew to an estate of 1.5 hectares. At Buon Kosier, Y Bram Eban, a teacher, began in 1945 to grow coffee, lime, guava, jack fruit, and banana trees on a sixty-by-thirty-meter plot. As the grove thrived and produce sold, he expanded it into a small estate.

Boys are taught at an early age how to hunt using a crossbow. Y Yok Ayun described how the "good hunter" (m'gap), almost invariably successful, performs the tuh hna (tuh is "sacrifice" and hna is "crossbow") ritual in the main room of the longhouse, offering a young rooster to the spirits, imploring luck in the hunt. According to Y Yok Ayun, many hunters use poison extracted from certain trees, and the deadliest is from the ana kam tree. Certain villages, notably those in the Mdhur area, produce the most effective poisons. Y Yok recalled that his father tested poisons he purchased on mice kept in a basket. For hunting, poison is mixed with tobacco juice and smeared on the shaft just below the arrowhead so it can enter the animal's bloodstream, bringing death in less than ten minutes. In addition to a wide range of small game, the hunter goes after older deer (never younger ones) and wild boar. If there is a tiger in the vicinity, he will stalk it for two or three days, but the Rhadé believe that when the tiger is aware of the "good hunter," he will flee because he fears poisoned arrows. The hunter dresses and cooks his game (including tigers) in the forest near the village, whose residents are invited to partake of the food and a jar of alcohol. The head and neck are taken back to the longhouse, where they are offered to the spirits in the bŏng kŏ ritual, after which they are boiled and shared with kin and neighbors. Wild elephants often raid gardens and swiddens, devouring

26. Hickey, *Free in the Forest*, p. 137.

manioc and maize, but Y Yok pointed out that the Rhadé neither kill nor eat them. Moreover, elephants always move in herds of two to five but sometimes numbering as many as fifty or a hundred, and they stalk the hunter.

Rushing water in streams carries fish into traps set along the edge and in temporary dams. Hand traps also are used, as are nets purchased in the markets. Sometime in the February to April period the whole village participates in the *tuh eâ* (*eâ* is "water") ritual. Men fashion a bamboo spirit house (*sang yang*) that is placed along the path leading from the village to a stream. Around 9:00 A.M. a procession of villagers go to the stream, where they offer the spirits a jar of alcohol and a chicken. Everyone then joins in fishing with hand traps and nets. Around 2:00 P.M. they all walk back to the spirit house to offer the same deities alcohol and chicken meat. They then return to the headman's house, where a similar offering is made.

Local Leadership

Leadership is reserved for those who are destined (*dhut*) by a spirit named Yang Rong to exercise authority (*knuih-kơhưm*). Y Bling Buon Krong Pang noted that an infant who cries a great deal is thought to be so favored, but it is customary to await further manifestations such as unusual intelligence and good luck in farming, hunting, or fishing. Y Yok explained that a leader is "someone everyone listens to and obeys," and "when he has a sacrifice, everyone attends." Y Bling observed that such a person "can go from village to village or through the forest at night without fearing enemies, tigers, or snakes." One with potency comes to possess a talisman (*hriêl*), such as a curiously shaped stone, symbolizing Yang Rong. He also must avoid being under female garments associated with sex organs so he cannot walk under a longhouse. Nor must he ever touch blood associated with childbirth. Usually "great potency" (*knuih prŏng*) is associated with the well-to-do (*mdrong*) because a leader must annually offer Yang Rong a buffalo and other animals along with many jars of alcohol and be the host at large feasts. A leader with very great potency (such as chiefs renowned in lore) may be identified with the title *mtao,* which appears to be a cognate of the Cham title *potao,* "king" or "lord." A lesser potency, *knuih diêt,* enables a person to assume lower-ranking positions such as village headman. There is the possibility of increasing one's potency by making yearly ritual offerings to Yang Rong. Violation of the taboos (*člŏm*), however, threatens loss of potency, but it can be rectified by making many offerings to Yang Rong.

Those not endowed with potency but who nonetheless undertake tasks that require it are inviting a condition called *rai* or *m'ang,* which can bring misfortune. Y Bling cited a 1955 incident when some ordinary Rhadé captured a white elephant, a rare and revered animal whose captors should have grand potency. The luckless captors had no end of trouble so they decided to present the elephant to Y Keo, the judge in the Ban Me Thuot indigenous court, a man with grand potency. Y Keo, however, had an unfavorable dream about the elephant so he declined the gift, but he proposed that they offer it to President Ngo Dinh Diem. With great publicity, the president accepted the elephant, which was transported to Saigon, where it was left free to roam the extensive landscaped grounds surrounding the Independence Palace. An ordinary person must be very careful in his relations with those who have grand potency. It would be dangerous, for example, to share a room with one so favored because when sleeping, his soul could consume that of the person without potency. Y Bling related that it was for this reason he avoided sharing a room with some of the "great chiefs," who accompanied him as fellow members of a highland delegation sent to Saigon in 1955 to participate in the celebration of President Diem's victory over the Hoa Hao, Caodaists, and Binh Xuyen.

According to Y Yok Ayun, authority of the village headman (*khôa buôn*) is symbolized by his possession of ritual accoutrements. Normally the role is retained within the same longhouse group, but circumstances determine who will assume it. In Yok's village of Buon Brieng, the headman had for a long time been his father-in-law, the husband of the senior female. When the headman died, no one wanted the eldest daughter's husband to succeed because he had no wealth, a sure sign that he had no potency. The second eldest daughter's husband became headman, and when he died the position was offered to Y Yok, who, because he had become a Christian, did not want it. The sisters then conferred and decided that the eldest sister would become household head and village chief, and so she officiated at the communal rituals.

According to Y Thih Eban, conflicts that cannot be resolved within and between kin groups are judged by the chief, who must be obeyed. Anyone who fails to obey is criticized as "a reed trying to be higher than the bamboo," or "a voice trying to be louder than the roar of a tiger." Offenses against the chief's authority call for a buffalo sacrifice, a costly punishment. A serious crime such as wanton destruction of the forest could in the past result in the guilty party being sold into slavery or banished from the village. Y Thih described ordeals to resolve interpersonal conflicts. In the ordeal by water (*nǔ eâ*), the two parties share an animal sacrifice, after which they are immersed in a stream, and the one who comes up first is the loser. In *mah braih,* a quantity of cooked rice is stuffed into the mouth of the accused, who, after chewing it, must eject every last grain or be judged guilty. The hand of the accused is covered with seven large leaves in the *tuh kmrak* ordeal, and then molten metal is poured over them. A burned hand indicates guilt.

With the advent of the French provincial administration early in the twentieth century, the *résident* began naming village chiefs, but it was done with consensus of villagers. In addition to his traditional duties, the headman took on new administrative functions such as collecting taxes, recruiting corvée labor for public works, and registering births, marriages, and deaths. In 1955 the Ngo Dinh Diem government imposed a Vietnamese administration on Darlac province.[27] The traditional village (*buôn*) became a hamlet in a larger unit based on the Vietnamese village (*xã*). The villages of Buon Ko Sier and Buon Pan Lam, for example, became hamlets in the village of Cu Kplong. The Rhadé headman now became a "hamlet chief," and the provincial administration named a village chief and vested him with formal responsibility for running community affairs with the assistance of a village council. To let the Rhadé law court languish and replace it with a Vietnamese tribunal, stipends for the judge and clerks were canceled, as were funds for the buildings.

The Vietnam War and Communist Rule

Communist infiltration was countered by the organization in October 1961 of the Village Defense Program by the U.S. Central Intelligence Agency, using Buon Enao village near Ban Me Thuot as the pilot project. Males were recruited, trained in village defense, and given arms. Many of the local Bajaraka leaders, who spoke English learned at the Protestant mission, assumed key roles. The Special Forces became involved, and by September 1962, Rhadé recruits included 1,500 Strike Force personnel and 10,600 village defense militia.

The appearance in 1964 of the FULRO movement launched a wave of ethnonationalism that swept through Rhadé Kpa villages. Its leader was Y Bham Enuol, a Protestant from Buon Ale-A who had been in the colonial agricultural service. Most of the militia in the Special Forces camps that rebelled in September 1964 were Rhadé, who also made up the greater part of the FULRO membership. As a result of the government's attempts at accommodation, instruction in the Rhadé language was restored in the school curriculum, Rhadé were named to important administrative positions, and the Rhadé law court was reinstated.

As the Vietnam War intensified in the mid-1960s, refugees from Rhadé subgroups began to make their way into the Kpa area, where the concentration of Vietnamese troops and American units at Ban Me Thuot

27. Information on the period from 1955 to the end of the Vietnam War is taken from Hickey, *Free in the Forest*, pp. 45–46, 73–131, 135, 199–200, 212–15, 267–69, 299.

provided security. Refugees built lean-tos until they could construct longhouses using metal roofing supplied by the American aid program. The shortage of males altered the division of labor. Women joined teams that built longhouses, and they took on more arduous tasks in swidden farming, as did older people. In November 1967 a group of older men and women harvesting a field near Buon Kmrang Prong lamented that because of the lack of manpower and disruption caused by artillery shells landing nearby, their crop gathering, which normally would take a week, would require twenty-five days. Cropping patterns changed. In September 1967, Katoully-Plowatt pointed out that the large influx of refugees created a shortage of land for swiddening, prompting readaptations. The twenty-year fallowing period was trimmed to less than ten. The usual three-year cultivation period was extended a year by using dung, straw, leaves, and other organic materials for compost. Y Dhuat Nie Kdam explained that although chemical fertilizer had been available in the 1950s, Rhadé farmers were afraid that it would "burn the soil." By 1965, some farmers near Ban Me Thuot began using it around fruit trees with impressive results. Some farmers began spreading it on the swiddens so they could be farmed for longer periods. Y Bham Nie described how in 1966 at the Ea Kmat Agriculture Research Center (which had been established in the late 1950s near Ban Me Thuot), he encountered a four-month rice. His eye also fell on a black-kernel "American rice," one of the "miracle" varieties that matured in three months. Y Bham and Michael Benge obtained seeds of both, and in the 1967 planting season the yield was four and a half tons per hectare, one ton more than he realized farming traditional rice.

There also were changes in paddy farming. At Buon Jat, some forty-five kilometers east of Ban Me Thuot, villagers had "since the time of the ancestors" farmed wet rice in a low-lying marshy area fed by the Ea Kwang stream using channels and bundings to control water. They grow *gur lao,* a wet rice said to have come from Laos, that matures in three and a half months. East of the village stretches the Chru Su swamp, and in 1968, Y Dhe Adrong, a Rhadé leader who had a coffee estate nearby, devised a plan to dig a canal from the Ea Kwang and arrange a system of dikes and channels. Each adult villager dug six square meters, and by the end of 1969 the canal was carrying water to the area, where new fields were cleared and ready for farming.

In Buon Ea Khit, forty kilometers southeast of Ban Me Thuot, on marshy land between two hills, Y Bok Buon Dap farms *gur lao* wet rice on gently terraced fields. He explained in 1970 (when he was seventy years of age) that the fields had "for many generations" been farmed by his wife's family, who are Rhadé Bih. On the nearby hills the family also cultivates swiddens. In 1967 Y Bok embarked on a plan to enlarge the

Photo 2. Local militiamen at Buon Jat paddy fields (1969).

terraced paddies by tapping the stream coursing through high ground behind the hills. With the help of kinsmen, he cut terraces on the slopes, dug a canal through the draw between the two hills, and constructed an earthen dam in the stream to divert water. Channels and breaches in bundings carried water to the fields. By 1969 the system was working. To cope with the manpower shortage, Y Bok raised money by selling rice and cattle to purchase a Kabota eight-horsepower tractor and a rototiller from a fellow villager and mechanic (who had built a hydroelectric generator and had once been arrested by French authorities for fabricating rifles without approval). Although during its first plowing the tractor got stuck in mud and had to be extricated by an elephant, it proved a success. From Lynn Cabbage, an American with the International Voluntary Service (IVS), Y Bok obtained some high-yield IR-8 rice seeds which he planted on a one-hectare plot, realizing a harvest of three hundred kerosene cans (each held twelve kilos, for a total of thirty-six hundred kilos). Y Bok found the rice "a bit hard but good to eat," and it made excellent rice alcohol. For cash to pay for machine maintenance and fuel, he sold one hundred cans of rice to Vietnamese from nearby Kim Chau village and rented the tractor and rototiller to other Rhadé

Photo 3. Y Bok Buon Dap and his paddy fields (1970).

farmers. In 1970 he began using chemical fertilizer, which "made the plants much greener."

With the wartime influx of Vietnamese civil servants, military personnel with dependents, and Vietnamese refugees from the Land Development Centers, the vastly increased demand for fresh produce prompted the appearance of a market on Route 14 in Buon Ale-A. Buyers were mostly Vietnamese while the vendors were Rhadé women who had expanded their cash cropping in gardens and swiddens. Y Ju Eban reported that he permitted his female neighbors to grow cash crops in his fallowing swiddens (each family staked out plots fertilized with straw ashes and manure). Five boys from the village began selling ice cream and fruit-flavored ices. Each day they sold the wares, keeping some money for new stock, allotting some for lunch and candy, and dividing the remaining cash to take home to their parents.

In 1966 a Buon Ki villager and his family planted a two-hectare banana grove and sold the crop to Vietnamese. Two additional hectares were planted in 1969, and two years later they had 520 thriving trees. They had planted an additional hectare with 120 grapefruit and lime trees, selling the fruit by the bag. In 1957, Y Ju Nie Kdam of Buon Kosier, who worked on the nearby Roussi plantation, shifted from wet rice to *robusta* coffee on a five-hectare holding. He planted banana trees and pineapples between the rows of seedlings to provide interim income. By 1966 he had 5,000 coffee trees and sold the berries to Chinese merchants. In 1965 Y Yong Nie Ktuol of Buon Drie Hling cleared a half-hectare plot for 300 coffee seedlings obtained from a nearby estate, and by 1970 his yield was 450 kilos. In 1968 he arranged on a nearby marshy depression a hectare of paddy fields in which he planted IR-5 and IR-8 high-yield varieties using chemical fertilizer. He realized 6.8 tons of rice, and by 1970 he had added an additional two hectares of paddies. At Buon Ea Khit, Y Ngung Knuol had a coffee estate of four hectares with 4,000 trees, and because of the wartime price rise his profits increased tenfold between 1965 and 1970. In 1969 he decided to open a rice mill, a risky venture because most Rhadé husked rice by hand. His niece quit school to run the mill, which attracted around thirty Rhadé women a day. They brought their rice in gunny sacks, which they put on a scale, and unlike any Vietnamese mill operator, the niece accepted the customer's weight figures without recording them. The customer was charged a set price per kilo, but if she did not take the bran, the milling was free. Most did not take the bran, which Y Ngung sold to the Vietnamese as pig food. As of 1970 there were 326 registered Rhadé coffee planters with estates totaling 531 hectares and a median holding of 1.0 hectare.

Before 1965 all of the shops near villages were run by Vietnamese, but after that year the Rhadé opened shops. In Buon Kosier near Ban Me Thuot, one proprietor, a former corporal in the Special Forces, had saved part of his pay and did not want to return to farming. Another was headman of remote Buon H'drah who escaped his Viet Cong captors and took refuge with kinfolk, who helped him start his shop. Other Rhadé shopkeepers included wounded veterans unable to farm and those who could not return to villages in insecure areas. In 1967 a few Rhadé Kpa began to engage in the transport business. Y Hue Buon Ya of Buon Kram purchased a three-wheel Lambretta carrier with cash saved while he was in military service. He made four trips daily between his village and Ban Me Thuot, interrupting service when he was needed to help with farming. He explained that he did not follow the usual pattern of buying cattle with available cash because security was crumbling, and should he and his family have to flee the village he might lose his cattle. With the Lambretta, however, he could pack everyone on board and go into Ban Me Thuot, and if he needed money he could sell the vehicle. (Ironically, he was interviewed in Buon Kram the day before the 1968 Tet Offensive began with a violent attack on Ban Me Thuot.)

In the late 1960s, the violence of the Vietnam War reached the hitherto secure zone around Ban Me Thuot. In January 1966, American fighter

Photo 4. Rhadé children playing with a homemade toy helicopter amid shell casings (1968).

jets accidentally bombed the Rhadé Adham village of Buon Ea Mur, destroying nine longhouses and badly damaging six others, with loss of lives and valuable gongs and jars. About the same time, a jet bombed Buon Kram, leaving the primary school and a longhouse in ruins. Early in the morning of 29 January 1968 the Communists launched their Tet Offensive with an attack on Ban Me Thuot. Communist forces massed in Rhadé villages to the south and north of the town, taking the people's rice and livestock for food. Many villagers died in the heavy fighting in Buon Ale-A, where Communist troops also slew five American Protestant missionaries. When fighting subsided, some four thousand Rhadé whose food had been stolen by the Communist troops sought relief in Ban Me Thuot.

On 10 March 1975, with the collaboration of a FULRO splinter group, North Vietnamese units attacked and captured Ban Me Thuot, precipitating the rout of South Vietnamese forces and the military conquest of South Vietnam. A large number of FULRO followers, now calling themselves Dega-FULRO, most of them Rhadé, went into the forests to organize resistance to Communist rule. When large Communist forces moved against them, the Dega-FULRO insurgents' only support came from the Khmer Rouge. According to Y Yok Ayun, in 1984 some 307 Dega-FULRO insurgents, discouraged by lack of outside support, elected to move across Cambodia to reach Thailand a year later. Two Rhadé in the group had since their youth participated in elephant hunts in Cambodia so they knew the trails. Foraging, fishing, and hunting sustained them, and in lean times they ate elephant meat, normally not in the Rhadé diet. Adjusting to the different environment, they ate leaves that ants were eating and in water containing a bullet cartridge they put leaves, which were thrown away if they turned dark. After a period in a Thailand refugee camp, 200 of these refugees, of whom 126 were Rhadé, were sent in November 1986 to North Carolina.

Since 1975 Hanoi has settled vast numbers of Vietnamese in the Rhadé country without regard for land claims. The *Wall Street Journal* reported on 22 July 1988 that more than four hundred thousand had moved into New Economic Zones in Dak Lak (former Darlac) province, where they were to grow coffee, pepper, and cashew nuts.[28] A 16 April 1989 article in the *Washington Post* noted that the Rhadé had been reduced to less than 30 percent of the population.[29] Coffee profits also lured a large number of "unofficial migrants," known locally as "coffee cowboys." According to the May 1989 *Far Eastern Economic Review,* an official complained that the Vietnamese squatters were "destroying our forests" and "forcing the minorities to move because they have no land."[30] The Communists also forced Rhadé families to move out of their longhouses into Vietnamese settlements. *Đại Đoàn Kết* (Great Unity) reported on 24 April 1985 that there was "a movement to redelineate villages" through "household separation."[31] In June 1985, *Tạp Chí Cộng Sản* (Communist Review) declared that the "campaign to discontinue the use of longhouses has become official policy."[32] On 31 July 1985, *Đại Đoàn Kết* reported that 4,405 families from 261 Rhadé villages had been moved onto state farms, where, under the surveillance of political agents and military personnel, they were intermixed with Vietnamese.[33] Rhadé refugees in the United States corroborate this, adding that the resettled villagers were not permitted to do swidden farming or observe traditional religious practices.

28. Barry Wain, "Vietnam Moving Millions to Its Highlands," *Wall Street Journal,* 22 July 1988.

29. Keith B. Richburg, "Vietnamese Pioneers Move Westward," *Washington Post,* 16 April 1989.

30. Murray Heibert, "Taking to the Hills," *Far Eastern Economic Review,* 25 May 1989, pp. 42–43.

31. Translated in JPRS—SEA, July 1987.

32. Translated in JPRS—SEA, 2 July 1985.

33. Translated in JPRS—SEA, 18 October 1985.

Chapter 2
Roglai and Chru

The Chru, who live in the beautiful Danhim Valley, and the Roglai, who live in the surrounding mountains, have through time sustained a curious kinship that is reflected in their strategies to preserve harmony among man, nature, and the cosmos. These strategies also reveal changes over time. According to oral history related by Touneh Han Tho, Chru ethnic identity evolved as a result of intermarriage between Cham who took refuge in the Danhim Valley when the Vietnamese threatened their last coastal enclaves and the indigenous Roglai (who call themselves Orang Glai, People of the Forest). The coastal Cham referred to the group in the Danhim Valley as Cham-ro or "Cham in refuge," and this eventually became Chru. In this context, the Roglai bear witness to a relatively aboriginal upland swidden-farming adaptation that predates a Cham presence in the area while the Chru attest to a Cham readaptation to the valley environment. As a mixed group, Chru society displays both Cham and Roglai components. The Chru retain an Indian-style script (known until recently by a small group of elderly men). The Chru also have a Cham-style water management system for the gently terraced wet-rice farming in the valley, but on the slopes they still practice swidden farming similar to that of the Roglai. Both the Roglai and Chru have matrilineal descent groups that show signs of disintegration. Chru use back-baskets (see Figure 22), rice-alcohol ferment, and plows made by the Roglai. Although the Chru observe certain Cham cults, they share with the Roglai a pantheon of cosmic forces and seek the services of Roglai shamans. For the Roglai, potency is demonstrated in unusual farming or hunting skills. For the Chru, potency is bestowed by Yang Nga Po'tao, which destines one to leadership, and it suggests Cham influence.

Pre-1960

According to French scholar E. M. Durand, in the mid-seventeenth century, during the reign of Po Nrop (1651–53), the last of the Cham rulers in the Panduranga dynasty, Cham leaders sought to establish redoubts among the highland people.[1] Bernard Bourotte expresses the view that the Cham were able to survive in Panduranga during the seventeenth and eighteenth centuries because of assistance from highland groups such as the Chru, Roglai, and Sre.[2] Touneh Han Tho related that historically Chru elite were of the Bahnaria clan, whose chief, selected by its members, was a vassal of the Cham ruler, who bestowed upon him the title *potao,* symbolized by a Cham saber. This leader was expected to send the Cham king annual tribute consisting of rabbits, horses, peacocks, parakeets, goats, and parrots. Every year the clan chief made a pilgrimage to the Po Nagar temple near Nhatrang to offer a horse, goat, and rabbit in honor of the deceased *potao Cham,* the Cham kings. The last great clan chief was Bahnaria Quang, who was recognized by the Cham, Vietnamese, and French from the late nineteenth century to 1930. According to Bahnaria clan history, Quang's maternal great-grandmother married a Cham general, who recruited Chru to fight the Vietnamese. In the villages of Diom and Tamiang there still are forges that were used to make weapons for the Cham army. Quang was guardian of the Cham general's ceremonial hat, robe, medals, and sabers. One saber, thought to have magical qualities, could not be removed from its sheath until a goat or chicken had been offered to the spirits. In his role as arbiter of disputes, Quang made the parties take an oath on the saber. Etienne Aymonier reported in 1885 that Roglai villages in the mountains west of Phan Rang were guardians of some ornaments, which legend had it were entrusted to them by Cham kings.[3] At two annual rituals the villagers made offerings of bananas and betel to deities associated with the ornaments in the belief that failure to do so would cause epidemics.

In his list of gifts sent by the Cham kings as tribute to the Chinese court between the fourth and eleventh centuries, M. Georges Maspéro mentions eaglewood, which was gathered by the Roglai.[4] When he visited

1. E. M. Durand, "Notes sur les Cham," *BEFEO* 5, nos. 3–4 (1905): 385. For further information on the Cham presence in the highlands, see Gerald Cannon Hickey, *Sons of the Mountains: Ethnohistory of the Vietnamese Central Highlands to 1954* (New Haven: Yale University Press, 1982), pp. 78–120.

2. Etienne Aymonier, "Légendes historiques des Chames," *Excursions et Reconnaissances* 14, no. 32 (1890): 193–206.

3. Etienne Aymonier, "Notes sur l'Annam," *Excursions et Reconnaissances* 10, no. 24 (1885): 310–11.

4. M. Georges Maspéro, *Le royaume de Champa* (Paris: G. Van Oest, 1928), pp. 92, 133; Hickey, *Sons of the Mountains,* pp. 33, 117, 160, 185–88. Eaglewood, also known as

Photo 5. Chru paddy fields and hillside swiddens (1966).

Cochinchina early in the seventeenth century, Cristoforo Borri noted that eaglewood came from the mountains of the Kemois (a designation for highlanders), and Etienne Aymonier describes how in the late nineteenth century the Roglai still traded eaglewood with the Cham.[5] Cham in the Phan Rang Valley had a dignitary called *po-gahlao* (lord of eaglewood), who every dry season organized the search for eaglewood. After making offerings to Po Klong Garai, Po Rome, Po Nagar, Po Klong Kashet, and Po Klong Garai Ghok—the "protectors of eaglewood"—the Cham proceeded to the villages of the Orang-Glai (Roglai) where the *po-va,* or village headmen, would assemble bands of men to assist the Cham in their search for the precious wood.

By the end of the eighteenth century the last Cham enclave at Panduranga fell under Vietnamese control. Chru and Roglai contact with the Vietnamese was largely through trade, which by the mid-nineteenth century came under control of corrupt tax agents who exploited the

aloeswood, is the heart of the *Aquileria agallocha,* a tree found in tropical Asia. When burned, the wood emits a fragrant odor, making it a highly valued offering in Cham, Vietnamese, and Chinese rituals.

5. Cristoforo Borri, *Cochinchina: Containing Many Admirable Rarities and Singularities of That Countrey* (London: Robert Ashley for Richard Clutterbuck, 1633); Etienne Aymonier, *Les Tchames et leurs religions* (Paris: Ernest Leroux, 1891), pp. 72–77.

highlanders. M. Brière reports that another form of exploitation was the annual offering of eaglewood, hardwoods, rhinoceros horns and pelts, resinous torches, rattan, thatching, special mats, and certain oils for the court of Hue. Provincial authorities collected these items, and in the late 1880s the Cham, Chru, and Roglai complained to Brière that they were never compensated for what they furnished.[6]

Probably the first European to visit the Danhim Valley area was physician-explorer Dr. Alexandre Yersin, who in June 1893 reached the Lang Bian peak (future site of Dalat) and then descended into the valley, stopping at the Chru village of Diom before continuing down to the coast.[7] In 1909 a French administrative post was created at Dran, and Bahnaria Ya Gut, a noted musician and kinsman of Bahnaria Quang, was named Tri Huyen (judge in the highlander court) to serve as intermediary between the administration and local populations and also to arbitrate conflicts among highlanders. His role required that he recruit Chru villagers for the detested corvée for road construction. Another Chru leader early in the century was Touneh Han Dang (father of Touneh Han Tho). Going into the upland Roglai country, he obtained valuable elephant tusks and wild honey, which he traded for salt, fish sauce, and metal pots in Phan Rang. Around 1907 Han Dang began launching economic innovations that he felt would improve the lives of Chru villagers. First, he arranged for some Cham women to go to the Danhim Valley and teach better weaving techniques to the Chru. Second, he sent his cousin, a woman named Ba Cam, to Phan Rang to learn the Cham methods for making clay pots. She returned to start a whole new pottery style. Less successful was his campaign to get Chru males, who customarily wore loincloths, to adopt trousers. In 1922, Han Dang became Tri Huyen, and he established the first primary school in the valley. He decided to replicate in the Danhim Valley the annual ritual held in Nhatrang to honor Cham kings. This led to construction in Diom of a temple honoring Yang Vamong as a reliquary for robes said to have belonged to Cham rulers. Each July there was a "people's offering" of three goats at the temple. Later Han Dang officiated at a ritual in which a horse bedecked with royal Cham robes was led into the temple while the shaman (*po juru*) intoned prayers. Han Tho reported that he saw the horse (thought to be possessed by Yang Vamong) sweat and neigh in agitation. Afterward it was fed boiled eggs, rice alcohol, and fodder while everyone drank and feasted.

According to Roglai informants, the French named local headmen for both the clustered longhouses of the Southern Roglai and the scattered

6. M. Brière, "Notice sur les Moi du Binh Thuan et du Khanh Hoa," *Excursions et Reconnaissances,* no. 32 (1890): 248–50.

7. Yersin's expedition is described in Hickey, *Sons of the Mountains,* pp. 245–59.

longhouses of the Northern Roglai. In 1905 the French began con-struction of a dirt road from Phan Rang to Dalat via the valley, and in 1912 the road was improved as Colonial Route 11. Colonial Route 20 between Saigon and Dalat opened in June 1933, and the following year a railroad running through Dran linked the coastal Saigon-Hanoi line with Dalat. During the Indochina War the Danhim Valley was relatively quiet, although some young Chru joined the French and others followed the Viet Minh. The Vietnamese ruler, Bao Dai, made scholarships available to young highlanders to attend the Lycée Yersin in Dalat, and among them were several Chru, including Touneh Han Tho.[8] With the 1955 establishment of the Republic of Vietnam, Vietnamese and Tai-speaking refugees from the north were settled in and around the Danhim Valley, introducing new rice-farming techniques.

Roglai

In 1967 the Roglai population was estimated at around 57,000, and the 1989 Vietnamese population census reports 71,696 Ra-glai (see Ap-pendix A). Roglai are dispersed in three groupings. Northern Roglai, sometimes called Radlai or Adlai, are in the mountains west of coastal Nhatrang. Southern Roglai are in the uplands west and southwest of the coastal city of Phan Rang, while to the northwest is a small grouping, called Cac Gia by the Vietnamese. The Roglai adaptation is based on swidden farming with rain-fed upland rice and maize the principal crops. Maxwell Cobbey writes that until 1960 the Northern Roglai lived in scattered longhouses with little contact among themselves or with out-siders.[9] Occasionally men of the family walked down to lowland Viet-namese markets, where they traded forest products for salt, knives, and cloth. Cobbey reports that the first written materials in the Roglai lan-guage were produced in the mid-1950s by a French Catholic priest. Subsequently, members of the SIL also wrote textbooks, but literacy among the Roglai was limited to a small group of men.[10]

Religion

Vurnell Cobbey points out that because the Northern Roglai (who num-ber twenty to twenty-five thousand) are dispersed in scattered long-

8. Ibid., pp. 312–17, 330–34, 416–18.

9. Maxwell Cobbey, "A First Case of Historiography Among the Roglai," in *Notes from Indochina on Ethnic Minority Cultures,* ed. Marilyn Gregerson and Dorothy Thomas (Dallas: SIL Museum of Anthropology, 1980), pp. 61–62.

10. Transcriptions of Roglai terms are based on the orthography used by Ernest Lee and Maxwell Cobbey.

houses throughout the mountainous area west of Nhatrang there are some variations in their pantheons, myths, and religious practices.[11] One category of supernatural beings are *yac,* the most powerful of which is *Yac Brom* (also called *Yac Catan*), who lives in the sky or at mountain summits and vents his wrath on anyone violating taboos. One woman told of six people who defied a taboo against sleeping in a certain cave. First *yac brom* warned them with lightning nearby, which they did not heed, then lightning struck the cave itself, killing all six. Another powerful spirit is *Yac Talac.* One informant said she had no idea where this spirit lived but that if a person suffers a great misfortune, such as falling into slavery, he can implore this spirit for help after promising to sacrifice a buffalo. A man from another area reported that *Yac Talac* resides near Cam Ranh Bay on a mountain that bears its name and that it prefers goats as sacrifices. *Yac Padai,* the Rice Spirit, is an important deity associated with rice farming. Also, when a member of the family falls ill, bananas, meat, and cooked rice in a miniature house made of leaves are offered to the rice spirit. If the ailment persists, the family summons the shaman (*vijou*), who communicates with the spirits to determine what propitiatory animal sacrifice is needed to restore health. According to Touneh Han Tho, some Roglai families also sacrifice rabbits and monkeys.

Yac dlai (or *yac choq*) are the mountain-forest spirits associated with upper elevations where one must avoid talking loudly, cutting trees, or tumbling large stones lest this spirit be disturbed. For this reason, it is taboo to clear a swidden near a summit. When burning a swidden on a slope, farmers are careful not to allow the fire to creep upward. When angered, this spirit can "catch peoples' souls," bringing grave illness. To propitiate, the male household head offers in the forest cooked rice and meat wrapped in leaves. Other deities associated with mountaintops are the wind spirits (*yac vaniaq*), which can steal a person's soul and smash houses.

Yac gahlou live in the eaglewood tree and can cause stomach pains and sore eyes that lead to blindness (the tree exudes a sap that burns eyes, causing blindness). Newborn children are particularly vulnerable to this spirit so they must be kept away from eaglewood trees. *Yac vinuq* are malevolent spirits that live at the bases of banyan trees, which should be avoided. One Roglai informant said that no one should ever try to fell a banyan tree, but another claimed that several men could chop down a banyan, forcing the spirits to go elsewhere. Large rock formations are the abode of *yac tac* (or *yac platou*), who possess metal bows enabling

11. Vurnell Cobbey, "Some Northern Roglai Beliefs About the Supernatural," *SA* 2, no. 1 (1972): 125–29.

them to shoot stone chips and wood splinters into the body of anyone who offends them. A villager related that a *yac tac* shot his body full of stone chips, causing him to ache all over. He summoned a shaman, who in a ritual drew out the chips, healing him. Evil spirits are associated with two types of snakes called *ula nac* and *ula garai,* which are found in caves. Equally dangerous are *yac ia,* water spirits lurking in rivers and waterfalls who capture souls, causing grave illness. There are no prescribed rituals to these deities, but when a mother bathes her child in a river, she first puts red pepper and yellow *cunhit* root in the water to make the spirit sneeze, causing it to depart. More benevolent are house spirits.

Cobbey translates *vungaq* as "the soul of a living person," but it also is used in the context of a special potency that some people possess. One who is exceptionally skillful at farming or hunting is said to be *samu vungaq,* "the same soul" with that activity. There are seven *vangaq* residing at the top of the head and on the shoulders. Malevolent spirits can steal one of these souls, bringing on sickness. The primary soul is *vungaq cachua,* which, following death, can be reincarnated in the body of an infant just before birth. Birthmarks and deformities are clues to a previous existence of the soul. If the child, for example, has a harelip, the soul previously inhabited a person so afflicted. In 1965 a young man named Macraq was killed by the Viet Cong outside Phuoc Luong village, and when the body was found, the liver had been removed. At the time, his sister was pregnant, and her baby bore a long scarlike streak on the right side of its abdomen, a sign that it was the reincarnation of Macraq. Lois Lee reports that club feet or stump feet point to leprosy in the previous existence, and withered limbs indicate a prior paralytic condition.[12]

Cobbey's informants were vague about what happens to the remaining six souls after death. One said that they simply "went into the air," while another held that they might inhabit an animal's body. Informants also spoke of *vunaq asu,* which Cobbey translates as "incarnate spirit," a condition of souls just before or immediately after death. She notes that "old people before they die may sometimes have *asu,*" and "if someone goes to the forest alone and sees something like a dog behind him, he knows it is an *asu,*" a sign that someone has just died. Ancestors' spirits, for whom there are no rituals, are called *asu amoq, asu acoi, yac amoq,* or *yac acoi.* Should anyone encounter trouble in the forest, he implores the ancestors for help. Ancestor spirits, however, can be malevolent, causing sickness and poor crops as revenge for their having been treated badly in life. Cobbey translates the word *atou* as "corpse" but specifies

---

12. Lois Lee, "Pregnancy and Childbirth Practices of the Northern Roglai," *SA* 2, no. 1 (1972): 49–50.

that it also can be used to designate a certain type of "ghost" manifest briefly after death. It can come in the night, causing a victim to suffer a sensation of coldness and stiffness leading to paralysis. Speaking the name of a deceased person can draw the wrath of the ghost unless the name is prefixed with the word *atou*. [13]

Settlements and Houses

The Northern Roglai traditionally live in scattered longhouses, each of which was occupied by an extended kin group related through the female line. The longhouse is built on piling "as high as a man," as one informant put it, to protect the inhabitants from tigers (an ever-present menace reflected in one villager's report that tigers killed all eight of his buffalo). The main support columns (*goq*) are of sturdy hewn logs. The "house spirit" (*yac sac* or *yac goq*) inhabits the central column, which is taboo to strike. At one end of the house is the veranda (*atuoh*) with an entrance (*bac atuoh*) used only by the family. The main entrance (*bac ina*) is in the center of the house and is gained by a log in which steps have been cut. According to Rim, a woman about twenty-seven years of age from west of Nhatrang, inside there is a large room divided by a bamboo pole tied to the floor. *Chhoq,* the section by the entrance, contains the principal hearth, abode of the "hearth spirit" (*yac havou patou licat*). Family meals are prepared on this hearth over which there is suspended from the roof beams a rattan shelf used for drying meat, rice, and maize. Vurnell Cobbey reports that should anyone steal something from the house, the family head will take ashes from the hearth to scatter outside while calling upon this deity to "eat" the soul of the thief. [14] According to Rim, the other section of this room (*khrah*) is the center of family activities and a storage area for alcohol jars, gongs, rice, maize, and clothes. When ritual celebrations are held, jars of alcohol are placed around the revered main column. This is where guests at celebrations sleep and tasks such as maize husking are done. Here also women weave textiles and men weave mats and baskets, some of which are traded with Chru. Family members sleep in the area adjacent to the main hearth. Between the family sleeping area and main hearth is a small space called *caq,* where menstruating women sleep to avoid having their blood contaminate others, particularly males, who would suffer grave misfortune in fields or forests. This space also is reserved for childbirth. Rice granaries, built on piling, are near the swiddens. Kitchen gardens are sewn with the first rains. Areca

13. Cobbey, "Some Northern Roglai Beliefs," pp. 128–29.
14. Ibid., p. 125.

palms produce nuts that are rolled in a betel leaf and garnished with lime to provide a slightly astringent, mildly narcotic quid.

Some Roglai have long lived in villages adjacent to the coastal plain where Vietnamese influence is relatively strong. One such village is Suoi Cat, west of Nhatrang, which in 1970 consisted of thirty households that had been there "several generations." The houses were built on the ground and had wattled mud walls and thatched roofs similar to those of local Vietnamese houses. Villagers practiced swidden farming on nearby hills and gathered firewood, which they sold to the Vietnamese.

Family

Roglai descent is reckoned through the female line. There also are traces of disintegrated matrilineal clans, whose names have fallen into disuse. Rim recalled that her mother's clan was Chamaliaq and her father's was Pipu. She also remembered Pinang (Areca Nut) as a clan name. (The eleventh-century Cham ruler Harivarman III was reported to have belonged through his mother's line to the Areca Nut clan.[15]) Touneh Han Tho reported that the Chru clan name Yolong was also found among the Roglai. There are indications that the traditional rule against marrying consanguineal kin has been changing with an emerging pattern of matrilateral cross-cousin marriages. The Roglai also have bride-price, which is not found in other highland groups in which descent is through the female line, perhaps reflecting Vietnamese influence.

As Appendix B2 indicates, in Ego's generation siblings are age-graded with *sa-ai* for older siblings and *adoï* for younger, and sex modifiers distinguish brothers from sisters. Sibling terms are extended to male cousins; female cousins are *awoï* and are age-graded with modifiers *ghong* (older) and *ben* (younger) relative to Ego. In addition, female cousins related through the female line are identified as *goq cumoï preh* ("female living in the same house") as opposed to those of the male line, who are *goq cumoï lingao* ("female outside the house"). Sibling terms are extended to a spouse's siblings, who are age-graded relative to the spouse and are identified as affines by the modifier *matou*. In the first ascending generation, parents' fathers are *ama*, a term also extended to the father's brothers. Mothers are *awoï*, also the term for the parents' sisters. *Miaq* identifies the mother's brothers. All of these siblings are age-graded relative to the parents using the same modifiers as those for Ego's female cousins. The parents' fathers are *acoï* while the mothers are *amoq*, both terms used for their siblings. Those on the father's side are

15. Hickey, *Sons of the Mountains*, pp. 70–71.

identified by adding *vanah ama* ("father's side") while the mother's kin are indicated by the modifier *jŏc* ("to beget" or "to create") because, as one informant noted, these kin were responsible for his "having been begotten." In the fourth ascending generation the term *canau* means "long time ago." Children are *anaq* with modifiers for sex and age priority added. Siblings' children are *camuŏn*. Direct-line kin to the seventh descending generation are recognized.

Rim reported that in the past it was strictly forbidden to marry consanguineal kin (identified as *gŏq apoq*). She related that her sister married their mother's mother's sister's daughter's son, despite disapproval from kinfolk, who saw it as a violation of the taboo. Rim observed that in recent decades the influence of Koho-speaking neighbors has become strong among the Northern Roglai, and one result has been a spreading pattern of cross-cousin marriages with the mother's brother's daughters. Also, exchange marriage (*sidua bu huaq*), in which a brother and sister marry a sister and brother, has become common. In plural marriages the first wife is *sidiuq phut* (*sidiuq* is "wife" and *phut* is "tree trunk"), and the second wife is *sidiuq la-o* (*la-o* is "last bud of a tree").

Young boys and girls play in the same groups, where most courtships begin. A young man should work hard and obey his parents ("eats the parents' chins"). The ideal girl is physically attractive, of good reputation, and hardworking. Most girls marry (*huaq bu*) when, as Rim put it, "their breasts begin to sprout" (she used the same term to describe the appearance of new teeth or a sprouting plant). To initiate formal courtship, the boy and girl meet, chat, and exchange areca nuts and betel leaves. Sexual relations must be carefully hidden or the couple will face punishment. The boy and his intermediary, an older male or female friend, arrange a visit to the girl's parents. The boy remains silent while he puts before them gifts such as a blouse and skirt. The parents then ask the girl if she agrees to wed, and when she answers "yes," everyone drinks from the alcohol jars. The head of a freshly killed chicken is put in boiling water and then is placed on a bowl of cooked rice. If the beak closes evenly, it presages a happy marriage, but if not, it bodes badly and the proceedings end.

Roglai weddings are festive occasions that last for days and may draw as many as one hundred guests from the surrounding area. The first phase takes place at the bride's house, where rice and fish are readied for the meals. Rim noted that weddings do not involve any animal sacrifices, but chickens, pigs, or, if the family is rich, a buffalo, are slaughtered to provide food. It is taboo to serve flesh of wild animals and impolite to serve vegetables ("one never serves vegetables to guests"). As his representative (*manuih ngaq januq*), a kinsman of the groom leads him and his family to the house to present the bride's mother's brother with a bride-price (*thoc sanraq*). Traditionally it consists of five spears if the girl is the eldest and three if she is not, a set of gongs, and perhaps some animals for the feasting. Rim noted that in villages near the coast, cash and cloth are substitutes for spears. She added that the bride's kin may quibble if they deem the gifts insufficient. The chicken-beak divination ritual is repeated. Then the bride's father offers rice alcohol (*keh topai*) to the ancestors (*asu acoï asu amoq*—"spirit of grandfather, spirit of grandmother"). Putting a drinking tube in an alcohol jar, he flicks a finger in a gesture called *chadac,* which is the ritual act of offering, once for the bride and once for the groom. The couple sits before a low table laden with food and bowls of alcohol. Male kinsmen bring rice, which they feed to each other. This act is repeated with pork and with sips of alcohol. Afterward they offer food and drink to their kin and other guests, a signal that the feasting can begin. The couple remains at the bride's house. At an unspecified time after the wedding, the couple gives a similar celebration (*damp*) to which the same guests are invited.

The longhouse group (*preh*) is the basic unit of Roglai society. The groom becomes part of the group, but he makes periodic visits to his parents' house. On the death of his parents, the eldest son must return home to see that family property remains intact and undivided. The newly married couple is given a sleeping area in the *khrah* section and may arrange a curtain for privacy. They share meals with the parents (the son-in-law must avoid joking with his parents-in-law) until they have a child, at which time they arrange their own cooking hearth. The eldest male is the household head, who in consultation with his wife makes decisions for the family. He has responsibility for teaching his sons how to perform male tasks such as farming, hunting, and fishing. Some Roglai specialize in making plows with metal blades that they sell to the Chru. When a small child does something wrong, the parents punish it, but chastising an older child is left to the mother's brother.

According to Lois Lee, Roglai knowledge of the female reproductive system is restricted to concepts of "a house of the child" (the womb) and blood. Women have no "seed," and when the "seed" of the man enters this house, it coagulates with the blood there, soon forming a lump that in weeks produces an infant that will grow inside the mother. Barrenness is thought to be caused by the husband having no "seed," the wife having no uterine blood, or a curse by a shaman who at the time of the marriage was angry with the couple. They can give the suspected shaman a pig or a valuable jar so he will lift his curse. When a couple has remained childless, the husband often takes a second wife in the hope of having children. Another recourse is adoption. Birth control is unknown, and abortion is not practiced. Lee estimates that about half the pregnancies are miscarried.[16]

A pregnant woman should avoid eating armadillo and anteater for fear that the child will roll up and come out back first. To consume turtle will result in the unborn child hiding its head and refusing to be born, and if a woman eats twin bananas, she will have twins. A baby will have webbed feet if its mother eats duck when pregnant. A pregnant woman bathing in the stream must not submerge her body lest the soul of the baby escape the womb and be carried away in the current. High places should be avoided because the fetus might be seized with fear and later be a nervous, excitable child.

Most Roglai prefer that the firstborn be a girl. Lee attributes this to the matrilineal descent system and the practice of having daughters remain in the parental house (a guarantee that family property will remain in the house and that someone will be there to care for the aging parents). Lee adds that it also is important to have boys so girls will have a brother to stand up for them if they have trouble with in-laws. Serious marital and family disputes are taken to the maternal uncle, and it is he who advises his sisters and their daughters about the disposition of family property.

Some midwives learn the skills from their mothers, while others assume the role because, as the Roglai say, "the spirit-gods use her and guide her in what to do." The most common need for the midwife during the second trimester of pregnancy is to alleviate by massage severe backaches brought on by carrying heavy back-basket loads. Massaging also is used to reposition the fetus. Delivery takes place in the special space (*caq*) in the house. Out of fear that spirits might peek during delivery, every wall opening and crack is covered. When labor begins, males must avoid the compartment, and the mother or older sister calls upon the ancestors to keep evil spirits at bay and watch over the delivery. If the midwife is present, she will implore the help of deceased midwives. A household member fixes a burning firebrand sprinkled with salt at the main entrance. Those who enter must hold their hands, feet, and anything they carry over the smoke to chase evil spirits.

The woman sits on a low stool while a kinswoman or midwife positions herself behind the knees against the back for the woman to lean on and push when pains begin. Delivery problems are usually attributed to a disgruntled shaman who does not want the couple to have children. To counteract this, the husband performs in the forest "the sacrifice to placate the shaman" (*pon luo vijou*), offering cooked rice and meat on *sula* leaves. As delivery proceeds, the midwife tugs gently on the emerg-

16. Lee, "Pregnancy and Childbirth Practices," pp. 26–52.

ing baby or massages the mother's abdomen. If labor has reached the expulsion stage and the baby does not emerge, the mother is given a bitter root (*jrau moq*) to chew, and because "the baby cannot stand the bitterness, it will come quickly."

After delivery, the cord is tied with a small piece of a type of vine also used to bind arrowheads, and it is cut with sharpened bamboo (use of scissors or a knife is taboo). The husband buries birth products along with the mat on which delivery took place. Mother-roasting is "staying by the fire" so that blood can drain, and then hot stones wrapped in cloth are placed on her abdomen in the belief that this helps the uterus contract properly. This is repeated "until the womb is ripe." For the first day or two the mother is given rice gruel, and when she can take other foods she still must refrain from eating chicken, turtle, fatty meat, okra, eggplant, and squash leaves (which cause the uterus to itch).

During the first days of life, the infant is highly vulnerable to evil spirits so only the mother can have contact with it. Anyone entering the long-house must perform the aforementioned firebrand ritual to prevent evil spirits from following. The father avoids swimming in the river lest the baby's soul follow him and be swept away in the current. Seven days after birth, the family observes the "sacrificial feast" (*djuq buai*), marking the end of this dangerous period. It begins with the father shooting an arrow into the air to frighten away malevolent spirits. A chicken is cooked, and the father takes a bit of the liver, calling on the ancestors and spirits of dead midwives to keep evil spirits away, allowing the child a long, happy life. The mother then chews some liver, passing it from her mouth to that of the baby. She also performs the chicken-beak divination ritual to determine the baby's destiny. At this time the family presents the mid-wife with a new skirt, kerchief, blouse and perhaps some cash. The child is allowed to breast-feed as long as it desires.

According to Northern Roglai informants, alliances are made through rituals that involve sharing something while promising lasting friendship and mutual aid. In some rituals, blood of both parties is mixed with alcohol and drunk by them. In others, the two simply smoke together. *Twaq yut* is an alliance binding two males as brothers or two females as sisters, and should one of them die, the other must care for the deceased's children. Another alliance binds two members of neighboring ethnic groups, each party becoming a "grandchild" of the other's group. One informant's father, for example, made such an alliance with a Tring (a mixed Rhadé-Jarai group), thereby permitting him to marry a Tring woman. In their alliance ritual, they drank each other's blood ("when two people mix blood they become one body") and shared a meal of pork and rice.

Livelihood

The primary crop is upland rain-fed rice (*padai*) farmed in swiddens (*apu*). Farmers look for black soil on which robust trees are growing, where they "can make rice fields." Such sites can be cultivated for three years and then are allowed to fallow for five years. Some Northern Roglai pointed out that because their longhouses are widely dispersed, there was much land to farm so they did not consider fallowing. Poor soils are reddish in color and have an abundance of small stones, but they nonetheless can be farmed for one year. Household groups share farming tasks, usually working two swiddens, one devoted to maize, the most important secondary crop. Because of the need for mutual aid, kinfolk farm in proximity, but it is taboo for nonkin to farm nearby because it would anger the Rice Spirit, inviting misfortune.

For Northern Roglai the planting season begins in late January, when rains have tapered off. They rise "when the cock crows the second time" (around 4:00 A.M.) and "when the birds play in the trees." At the time the rains begin, maize is planted, an exclusively female task. Using dibble sticks, women move in a group making holes in which they drop three or four kernels, tamping the earth with their feet ("so you can see footprints, and know where you've planted"). They do no weeding. "When the maize is as high as a chicken's back," rice is planted. *Du,* a variety with a round kernel, is the most popular ("you can eat *du* every day and never tire of it"). It matures in three months (the Roglai measure time by the phases of the moon) whereas other varieties take six months. Often in the same swidden they farm *duri,* a long-grain rice, and *wac.* Other varieties are *suac,* a reddish, long-grain rice; *tliq,* a glutinous rice good for making alcohol; and the fragrant *vo-anuoq* ("necklace bead"), which is the favorite food of the *ngiaq* ("tiny") bird.

For fear of offending the rice spirit, who will seize a person's soul and give it to malevolent spirits, it is taboo to take a bush scythe into the planted field. Small children are never taken into the fields for fear that one might pull up a rice stalk, causing the rice spirit to steal the soul of the child's mother. Before harvesting there is a ritual for the rice spirit in which offerings of bananas, meat, and cooked rice are placed in a small house fashioned out of leaves and set in the field. If there is a young boy in the family, the father also puts a necklace in the house. A tree is felled across the main path to indicate that for three days the field is taboo, and the boy stays in the longhouse. On the fourth day the father returns to the field, and shakes the necklace, invoking the boy's souls to come to the swidden. Returning to the longhouse, he puts the necklace on the boy. Everyone in the household helps gather crops. Holding the stalk, the harvester pulls the grains off with his hands (which makes them very sore), and rice is carried to the granary in back-baskets. A seven-day supply is taken to the house, where it is spread on flat, round baskets to dry and then be husked. Squash (*pluoi*) and pineapples (a Roglai riddle asks, "What is red-red at the edge of the field?" and the answer is "pineapples") are planted in swiddens where burned wood has left thick ashes (*uhuh*).

Hunting, a male activity, is done using spears and crossbows. Often the arrows are rubbed with poisons or drugs, one of which renders the animal unconscious for half an hour. Pet dogs usually accompany hunters, especially if the prey is wild boar. Fishing is another male activity. When men make periodic trips to the coastal towns to sell forest products, they purchase Vietnamese fish nets.

Chru

The Chru are a relatively small group, estimated at 15,000 in 1967; the 1989 Vietnamese population census reports 10,746 Chu-ru (see Appendix A). They live in the beautiful Danhim Valley nestled on the eastern side of the Annam Cordillera. There are nine small lakes in the valley, which, according to a legend told by Touneh Han Tho, came about as the result of violation of an incest taboo and a taboo against bringing mangoes and fish together. Long ago a woman gathered mangoes, which she tied to her belt. On the trail she encountered a man from her clan who had some fish affixed to his loincloth. The two lay on the grass and made love. Suddenly the sky darkened, and the earth shook and heaved. Everything was tossed about violently; villages were crushed, killing almost everyone. Where some objects landed, lakes were created and they still bear the name of the objects. A heavy wooden pestle (*rasung*) for husking rice landed where Danau (lake) Rasung is now located, and Danau Monu is where a chicken (*monu*) came to rest.

Religion

In the traditional Chru cosmology, described by Touneh Han Tho, the most powerful deity, known by two designations, Po Alak Longi (*longi* is "sky") and Po Yang Longi, has complete control over all other supernatural beings. *Yang siam* are good spirits and *yang rac* are evil ones, and both are associated with physical features. In addition, there is host of other deities, which, Han Tho pointed out, are similar to those of the Roglai. They include the mountain spirit (*yang chu*), the tree spirit (*yang kiou*), the forest spirit (*yang bonur*), and others associated with the physical surroundings. The Rice Spirit (Yang Coi) is an important deity.

Shamans are endowed with potency to perform certain rituals. The *gnau nga* or *iou yang* are called upon to officiate at village rituals during which they chant in a special language. *Po juru* (or *guru*) are male shamans who invoke spirits at certain rituals, notably those to cure ailments. According to Han Tho, most shamans learn prayers and ritual forms from the Roglai, and many Chru seek the services of Roglai shamans (he noted that one celebrated elderly shaman had to be carried down to the Danhim Valley). *Camo' lai* are sorcerers, usually males, who employ special poisons on their victims. Often of shamans' families, they usually are poor outcasts, who live in "low houses and treat their wives and children shabbily." According to Han Tho, before the French administration, sorcerers wielded power based on fear. Some were reputed to eat cadavers, and they could be slain only by using special crossbows. One sorcerer brought before Han Tho's father, Touneh Han Dang, at the tribal court was executed after it was proven that he had poisoned a fellow villager. Another sorcerer confessed to French officials and showed them in the forest his special poison-producing, flesh-eating plant that he fed live chickens. The French confiscated his poisons and jailed him. Han Tho related that during the 1960s, a sorcerer showed Father Darricau his special poison-producing plant, which resembled a miniature banana tree.

Settlements and Houses

Chru villages are oriented along the Danhim River, which flows from the northwest through the valley and merges to the south with the Dong Nai River. Settlements, composed of farmsteads oriented in no particular way, are close to paddy fields while swiddens are on the slopes of the valley. There are two traditional house types. According to Han Tho, in the past most Chru lived in "low houses" (*sang chru*), built on the ground (Figure 13). Less popular was the *sang glong* house built on piling, but after 1950 it was preferred as a symbol of highlander identity. Most Chru retained the low house, which became a *sang bep* (*bép* is Vietnamese for "cook") or "cookhouse."

To preserve harmony with nature and cosmic forces there are prescribed house-building rituals honoring Po Yang Longi, the wood spirit, forest spirit, and mountain spirit. For both types of houses, hardwood for main columns and beams is carefully selected and omens are heeded. Although Western saws have replaced axes for felling trees, logs are still hand-hewn. When the frame is finished, imperata cylindrica grasses are gathered for roof thatching. Outer walls of the low house are either of grass mixed with mud or woven bamboo wattle. The entrance is toward one side of the house, and the interior is divided into three main sections. At the far right is the granary where rice is stored in bins, the size reflecting the family's wealth (*p'vung* are large and *so* are small). To the

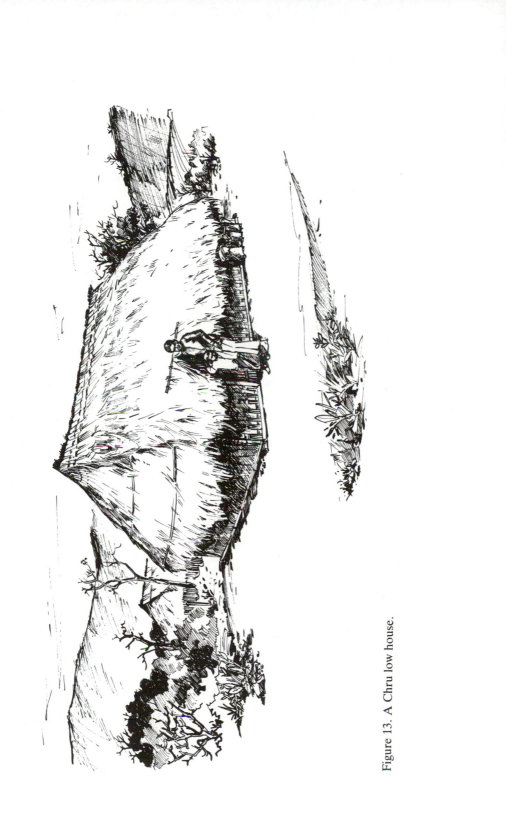

Figure 13. A Chru low house.

far left is a room that serves as the parents' sleeping quarters and kitchen with a large open hearth over which a rack contains food for the daily meal and red rice dried for making alcohol. Along one wall are jars of drinking water and back-baskets used for storing clothes. Large back-baskets (*jot*) are used to carry such items as rice and firewood while the smaller baskets (*jo*) are for storing clothes and carrying fish. The center section of the house has an open hearth and a low wooden platform where at family celebrations elderly women sit apart from the other guests and where food dishes are placed. The rear wall behind the platform is lined with alcohol jars, the most precious of which are called *stok,* large in size and dark in color. They are said to have been obtained long ago "in exchange for slaves." Gongs also are stored along the wall, and because it is taboo to set weapons on a house floor, they are hung along the wall. Affixed to a bamboo pole suspended from the beams are skulls of large animals, trophies attesting to the men's hunting skills. Above the platform is a sizable wood-bamboo storage deck hung from the roof by poles lashed to the beams with rattan cord. Heat and smoke from the hearth preserve containers of fish and meat (notably venison), buffalo hides (used for making animal tethers), maize, and husked rice. Houses on piling have the same floor plan but no platform. Floors are of wooden planks, and the hearths are arranged on earth bases with logs around the edge. Han Tho reported that his father, Touneh Han Dang, and his uncle Touprong Hiou built wooden houses on the ground in the Cham style with verandas graced with carved wood and Vietnamese furnishings.

Family

The Chru have matrilineal descent and exogamous matrilineal clans. The thirteen clans are Touneh, Touprong, Yolong Prong, Yolong Ade, Banaharia, Sahao, Charau-Ale (*ale* means "small bamboo"), Kabao-Volu (Fighting Buffalo), Mohi, Chru-Yang, Gonong-Sang (House Post), Yango, and Yanang-Roc. There is preference for cross-cousin marriage, particularly with the father's sister's daughters. Subclan groups claim land, which is managed by a senior female land guardian (*po-lan*). Historically the introduction of family-owned paddy fields diminished the importance of the land-guardian system, and since the 1950s it has weakened further, accompanied by an incipient disintegration of matrilocal residence and the rule for female ownership of family property.

As kin terminology transcribed by Touneh Han Tho (Appendix B3) indicates, there is age-grading in Ego's and the first ascending generations. Terminology in Ego's generation reflects preferential cross-cousin marriage as well as exchange marriage in which a brother and sister of

Photo 6. A Chru house on piling (1966).

one family marry a sister and brother of another family. In Ego's generation there are three basic terms for siblings—*saay, adây,* and *go*. The first two are for older and younger siblings respectively, and both can be used as modifiers for the age-neutral *go*. Sex modifiers are added to all three, and modifiers added to the first two terms identify the eldest and youngest siblings (the same modifiers identify the eldest and youngest children). The term *saay lokây,* older brother, is extended to the older male parallel cousins (father's brothers' sons and mother's sisters' sons) while *saay komây,* older sister, is used for older female cross-cousins (father's sisters' daughters and mother's brothers' daughters). By the same token, *adây lokây,* younger brother, and *adây komây,* younger sister, are extended to the younger male parallel cousins and younger female cross-cousins. Not age-graded, male cross-cousins are *prui* while female parallel cousins are *go komây,* which also is a term for sisters (and for female Ego, *go lokây,* a term for brother, is extended to male parallel cousins). Eugene Fuller reports that these terms are used similarly to designate affinal kin of this generation.[17]

17. Eugene E. Fuller, "Cross-Cousin Marriage and Chru Kinship Terminology," in *Notes from Indochina on Ethnic Minority Cultures,* ed. Marilyn Gregerson and Dorothy Thomas (Dallas: SIL Museum of Anthropology, 1980), pp. 113–18.

In ascending generations there is a bifurcation between kin related through the female and male lines. Parents' siblings are age-graded relative to the parents. There also is a common term, *tomahama* (which also means "original family property"), for father's sisters. Han Tho notes that the generic term for ancestors is *akây amo phŭn*. Fuller reports that the mother's maternal ancestor (*mò*) in the fifth ascending generation is identified with the modifier *tơnah rơya* ("of the land"). Similarly, the modifiers *kŏ kùt* ("at head of the tomb") and *akha rơlàng tơlàng kơbàu* ("root of the thatching grass and bones of the buffalo") identify maternal ancestors of the sixth and seventh generations respectively. Children are *ana* with sex modifiers to distinguish sons and daughters. This term also is used for the brothers' children and some affinal kin. Sisters' children and certain affinal kin are *komoan*.

According to Han Tho, the Chru prefer cross-cousin marriage, and in most instances it is with the father's sister's daughters. Marriage with parallel cousins is considered incestuous and is particularly grave when it involves members of the same clan. Violation offends the ancestors (*yang agap*) and invites misfortune to the guilty and bad crops for the clan. The guilty pair must perform a buffalo sacrifice to the ancestors, during which they cut their foreheads to mix their blood with that of the animal, thereby cleansing them, but they must separate. The levirate and sororate are practiced. Polygyny, sometimes sororal, is by and large restricted to the well-to-do.

Courtship is initiated by the girl's parents, although in most cases the couple has already developed a mutual affection (which they are forbidden to show publicly). A male or female intermediary, someone close to both families, makes the overtures, and because it usually is a cross-cousin situation, assent is immediate. After seven to fifteen days the girl and her parents visit the boy's house, where the hosts bid their guests to be seated and offer them tobacco. In the ensuing conversation the hosts ask in a very indirect way why they have come. Fuller reports that the guests will reply with words such as, "We are not able to see or smell and have come here because we are hungry and thirsty," an indirect way of requesting a betrothal. The girl's father then may add, "We have come to ask about hiring your young buffalo. Is that alright?" The boy's father will respond, "Oh, that buffalo is very inexperienced. How would he know how to work?" The girl's parents explain, "We were that way. If one is to speak he must practice. If he drags wood, he must tie it together, and if he wants to work he must learn." The girl's parents or the intermediary take a ring or necklace from the girl's hand to put on the boy, who feigns protest. Then the girl's parents ask that he take good care of the girl, reminding him that whether she is pretty or not, she can cook, for even "a black pot cooks rice done." A necklace is put on the boy while a jar of rice alcohol is brought out and at the urging of the girl's father, the boy's father drinks, after which everyone drinks. After half an hour the girl's parents ask for a bowl of alcohol, which they offer to their daughter. They put another necklace on the boy, and the girl rolls a cigarette for him. His parents give him a bowl of alcohol, a ring, and a necklace for the girl. As she sips from the bowl, he puts the necklace on her and the ring on her finger while everyone wishes them good luck and "as many children as the ants and termites."[18]

The next event is a feast at the girl's house, but his parents stay away in the belief that their presence might bring bad luck. Pigs, goats, and chickens are slaughtered, and many jars of alcohol are provided. The hosts present each guest with a ring and a necklace. The boy's mother's brother sings to him a chant advising him to treat his fiancée well and not misbehave. For one week, the boy remains in her house, and then they go to his house, but they cannot sleep together. A week later the wedding takes place at the bride's house. As the couple sits before an alcohol jar, her maternal grandfather invokes the ancestors and a host of other spirits while a rooster is placed on the rim of the jar. If he should fly away it is a bad sign and the wedding does not proceed. The grandfather places a chicken's head, feet, and wings on a plate, which he presents to the bride's father, who performs a divination ritual, dropping the parts to determine the couple's future by the way they lie. Afterward the couple is taken by her maternal grandfather to the bridal chamber arranged in a corner of the room.

The bridal couple remains in confinement for a week to avoid any inauspicious incidents (such as being hit by bird droppings). At the end, the girl's parents place a cooked egg and bowls of alcohol and water at the head of the bridal bed while chanting prayers to the spirits of the house and paddy fields. The couple then goes to the groom's house for two weeks "to care for his parents" and then returns to her house. Residence after marriage is strictly matrilocal for the eldest daughter, who is given her parents' bed while they move to a corner of the main room. Other daughters and their husbands reside in the house for a period, and then with help from all of the family they build their own residences nearby. When a daughter leaves the parental house she receives family goods such as jars and animals and also some family land, which she and her family then work themselves. Villagers noted that this is to avoid conflict later. When the youngest daughter has established her own household, the parents go to live with her. If a widower is elderly, he usually takes up residence with a sister or a sister's married daughter. Because he has contributed to his wife's family income he will receive some of their

18. Ibid., pp. 118–23.

animals. But even though he brings some goods to his kin's household, he may not be welcome. In May 1966, an elderly man encountered in a field near Diom was described by neighbors as a widower living in a lamentable situation with his sister's family. Diom villagers explained that the situation is better if it involves patrilateral cross-cousin marriage, citing the example of a widower who lived happily with his son and his wife, the widower's sister's daughter.

Villagers also noted that one way to avoid living with kin is to have several wives. Polygyny is common among the well-to-do. Touneh Han Tho's father, Han Dang, had two wives, one Cham, the other Vietnamese. Because he did not marry a Chru, Han Dang's children took his clan name. A kinsman, Touprong Hiou, had five wives and twenty-six children (all of whom he delivered himself). Both men deviated from traditional practices in establishing their own residences and owning their own paddy fields.

Women do what little weaving of textiles survives among the Chru. Touneh Han Tho described how men make rice alcohol using red rice dried over the kitchen hearth. The rice is boiled and spread on a mat, and some "ferment" is shredded over it. Made of powdered roots and bark, the small loaves of ferment are now purchased from the Roglai, and in recent years, commercial yeast purchased at the market has been used. The mixture is put in a basket, covered, and allowed to stand for three days, after which it is covered with rice husks in a jar that is sealed with banana leaves and a paste of water, cinders, and rice husks. After three months the alcohol, now "sweet and strong," is ready to be served at a celebration.

When someone falls ill, the family immediately summons the shaman (*po juru*). The family provides cooked rice, roasted chicken, and alcohol, which the shaman puts on a low table along with his wooden rattle to which feathers are attached. He also ties a string of small bells to a roof beam. Sitting at the table with the family gathered about, the shaman covers himself and chants a long prayer invoking Po Yang Longi, the Spirit of the Mountain, the Forest Spirit, Wood Spirit, and the malevolent *yang rac*. Periodically shaking the rattle and string of bells, he inquires which deity is causing the ailment and what it wants in propitiation. Han Tho recalled that when he was ill as a youth, the Roglai shaman "looked like he had just finished a long trip" when his prayers ended. He put a betel leaf in a silver bowl of water, placed it on Han Tho's upper arm, and then bit it. Tickling Han Tho on the chin, the shaman spit out a small stone. He then announced that Han Tho was "haunted by a spirit" that wanted a *manhum prong* (*manhum* is "drink" and *prong* is "large"), meaning a buffalo sacrifice.

With the exception of infants and very small children, who are consigned at death to the Tree Spirit and are buried at the base of a tree, all villagers of the same clan are interred in a common, carved-wood tomb. A coffin is fashioned out of a large log, and three days after death, the shaman officiates at the sacrifice of a chicken, pig, or buffalo, depending on the familly's means, as the coffin is placed in the tomb. Five days later the family conducts a ritual "to give food to the dead," after which they return home to join kin and neighbors in an animal sacrifice and feast. For several years the family saves money to have "the feast of the tomb" (*p'thi*). Young men cut wood to build a shelter twenty to thirty meters in length near the tomb, and they fell a solid tree that can be hewn into a sacrificial stake painted in red motifs and decorated with shaved-bamboo festoons. In the first ritual act, the deceased's sisters intone prayers to his spirit while family members remove from the tomb his bones, which are sorted out and then mixed in with other entombed bones. At dawn the following day, everyone gathers at the shelter decorated with flowers and fronds, where musicians squatting on a low bench play gongs and a drum. In the center is a row of alcohol jars behind which is a long bamboo rack for holding offerings and, on either side, fires burn in metal containers. Aged guests gather on a wooden bed next to which are arranged separate mats for men and women. The shaman chants while at the stake a buffalo is sacrificed, as are chickens and pigs. At noon, weeping and wailing family members carry parts of the animals, alcohol, and glutinous rice cakes to the pile of bones. After they return to the shelter, music sounds as male kin and then female kin dance eight times around the row of jars. Young men with gourds of alcohol stand at either end of the row to give swigs to the passing dancers. Parts of the buffalo and new garments are placed on the rack, and then everyone joins in drinking and feasting. Departing guests are given morsels of meat.

The following afternoon there is a "youth festival" for all young people who labored for the funeral. At sunset they have a feast, after which they place buffalo meat and rice on a bundle of thatching to circumambulate the sacrificial stake while the shaman invokes spirits of the dead. Several years later the family has the memorial *abong kok* ("eat the head") ritual, which involves animal sacrifices and feasting.

Economic Activities

So they could farm wet rice, Cham settlers who intermarried with the indigenous Roglai readapted to the new and alien Danhim Valley by arranging a sophisticated water management system based on the one they practiced on the coastal plain. They retained existing swidden farming. Their Chru descendants have maintained this paddy-swidden adaptation, making readaptations in recent years. Until recently they also preserved farming rituals geared to preserve the man-nature-cosmos harmony so that their crops will thrive.

According to Chru oral tradition related by Touneh Han Tho, in the distant past, segments of clans had claims to land in the Danhim Valley, and the guardian of each territory was the eldest female, who carried the title *po-lan*. She regulated use of land (farming), forests (tree felling and hunting), and water (fishing), suggesting that the system was similar to that of the Rhadé. Han Tho speculated that it was geared to a society with swidden farming, and when the Cham came to the valley and introduced wet-rice agriculture, individual families claimed ownership of paddy land, thereby lessening the importance of the land-guardian system. Clan claims to other lands, however, pertained until recent times, when the *po-lan* system eroded further, part of the broader disintegration of the matrilineal descent group and its functions. One reason, according to Han Tho, was squabbling among sisters. Those who married wanted more land than the eldest female was willing to give, and they questioned the authority of the clan land guardian. Another source of change was leaders such as Touneh Han Dang and Touprong Hiou, who eschewed some traditional rules associated with the matrilineal descent system. In the 1950s, they were joined by younger Chru who had left the village society for military service, higher education, or specialized training and were exposed to French and Vietnamese ways. They returned to the valley and accumulated land, houses, and furnishings, which they claimed as their own. Han Tho emphasized that the most severe blow to the *po-lan* system was the influx of Vietnamese in the mid-1950s. The government gave the settlers "unused land," some of which was claimed by the guardians though they had no titles. When this encroachment began to occur, Touneh Han Dang and other leaders urged the villagers to arrange sales of their uncultivated land in the valley and on the slopes to kin and fellow villagers. Although this helped preserve Chru lands, it further weakened the *po-lan* system. Only valley lakes remained under traditional control of the guardians.

In a traditional land transfer, the two parties invite all fellow villagers to the field, where the buyer has assembled jars of alcohol, a chicken, and either a goat or a pig. Payment is made before the gathering in buffalo, although in recent times it includes some cash. Animals are slaughtered, and both parties rub blood on a large stone, which they bury at the edge of the field to symbolize the sale. The buyer also distributes coins to the children to imprint the event on their minds.

Touprong Hiou, a leader in Labroye' village, explained in May 1966 that by and large, Chru farmers have clung to traditional rice-farming methods. Most have buffalo and implements, notably wooden harrows and plows of wood with a metal blade, which are made by the Roglai (who, ironically, do not use plows). Mutual aid arrangements provide needed labor. On the plane to undulating topography paddies are gently terraced. Water from the Danhim River and hillside springs is controlled by a system of dikes, canals, and field channels. Breaching of bundings allows flooding and draining of individual fields. Every Chru village has at least one "water chief" (*gnau ya*) (Han Tho's village, Diom, had two) responsible for mustering villagers in the dry season to clear canals and repair dikes. He also meets with other water chiefs to coordinate care of the valleywide system.

Just before the rains come, the villagers have a ritual to invoke the ancestors and a host of spirits, particularly Yang Wer, an evil being associated with banyan trees, which are taboo at all times. They carve figures of animals decorated with pig blood, the yellow of a certain root, and juice from betel leaves. At dawn, near a banyan tree, villagers gather around the shaman (*gnau nga*), who chants in a special language. Everyone then joins in a feast. In midafternoon the animal figures are carried in a large hammock along the trail about one kilometer, where they are dumped to let everyone know that the village is taboo for three days. In May everyone listens for the sound (like that made by a woodpecker) of a certain bird, the signal to make a ritual offering of boiled chicken and eggs in the house and to repair farm implements. After some ritual offerings to "good spirits," maize is planted in the swiddens. This done, the farmer plows and harrows his paddy fields, and after "allowing the soil to air" for three days, he plows again, but in a perpendicular direction. Touprong Hiou related that in 1938 he was the first Chru farmer to employ chemical fertilizer, and other farmers followed suit.

According to Touneh Han Tho, each household maintains a cult to the Rice Spirit (Yang Coi) symbolized by an egg-shaped rock (*dec sa-tay*), which is perfumed with sandalwood. It is kept in a special reliquary (*grii*), which should be something valuable such as a copper case, bronze pot, or antique porcelain plate. Han Tho related that in 1917 his father was digging out a rat tunnel in his field when he came upon two curious stones. He took them home and placed them inside two ancient bells he had purchased two years before in Hanoi, where he represented the highland people at a conference, thereby creating a *grii*. This reliquary is kept in the family rice bin, and a member is given responsibility for maintaining it and making periodic offerings of a chicken and a jar of alcohol. Han Tho pointed out that if a farmer is unsuccessful it is because the Rice Spirit no longer inhabits the *grii*, and anyone who buys the farm has no duty to retain the *grii*, which will be abandoned. For the rice-planting ritual, jars are set in the field amid bamboo poles decorated with flowers, and the family forms a procession to carry the reliquary to the site. Spirits are invoked while a buffalo (every three years) or a pig and chickens are sacrificed.

Bring is rice farmed in the July–September period, and between July and December *p'diy ana* is grown. Rice seeds are placed in a back-basket lined with leaves from a certain tree, and the basket is immersed in water for a day. As the seeds dry, they begin to germinate. Meanwhile, the field is drained of any standing water so it can "warm up" for the sowing. Women broadcast seeds, and for a month the family carefully guards the field against marauding birds. When sprouts appear, the field is flooded. About a month later, the water is drained so that small crabs that have invaded the fields in search of seedlings can be caught. The field is then flooded again, and for the remainder of the growing season women weed and maintain dikes with earth and mud. Han Tho related that in the late 1950s his kin began to adopt Vietnamese settlers' method of first planting rice in seedbeds, then transplanting the seedlings in the fields. He added that at this time everyone hunts burrowing paddy rats (a seasonal delicacy) that come down from higher elevations where they feed on fruit and tree roots. When the rice plants are thriving there is a ritual offering of chickens and pigs to thank the *yang* for the promising crop. The family invites the water chief to officiate at a preharvest ritual in which he squats by the field and intones the names of the deities, inviting them to accept the offerings of new rice, cooked chicken, and eggs. Starting at the edges of the field, the harvesters work inward, leaving the area around the *grii* until last. Cutting the stalks, workers spread them on open, hard ground so that buffalo can thresh by trodding on them. The rice is taken in back-baskets to a hut with a rice-straw roof, and as the wind blows, women standing on platforms winnow by pouring the rice onto mats. The rice is then taken to the house, and the *grii,* decorated with chicken feathers, is carried there for the final ritual at which the water chief, offering pigs, chickens, and jars of alcohol, invokes the Rice Spirit and "good *yang.*" Han Tho recalled that when he was young he would become vexed at long intonations because he was hungry and food was getting cold.

Here and there along the slopes of the Danhim Valley are swidden patches in the forest, where upland rain-fed rice (including a glutinous variety), maize, and vegetables are grown. In selecting a swidden site farmers inspect the predominant flora and the color and texture of soils. In addition, members of the family sleep at the site, and if they have unfavorable dreams, it is not cleared. In February at the field the family sacrifices a chicken, pouring blood on the soil in a divination ritual to determine the best day for planting. Prior to sowing maize, farmers set in the field a "tree of hope," a bough on which red, black, and white ears of maize are hung. A ritual to the Rice Spirit also is observed. Secondary crops are grown in the swiddens and in gardens near the houses. Swiddens are farmed for three years and allowed to fallow for at least ten years.

Forests around the Danhim Valley abound with small game, and more remote forests harbor big game. The Chru restrict themselves to the former, stalking deer and wild boar. In recent times traditional crossbows, spears, and traps have been replaced by firearms. A popular annual event is the hunt for delectable flying termites, which build mounds in the forest when heavy rains sweep the valley in August. The entire village joins in, using special trap-baskets which they place over the mounds. Smoke blown into the top of the basket forces the termites to exit their holes and cling to the sides of the basket, which is then placed inside a large bag of woven grass and shaken briskly, causing the termites' wings to fall off. The bag is carried back to the house, where the termites are fried and relished.

Families living near the valley lakes arrange small pools around the edge for fishing. Once a year the clan land guardians grant villagers in the vicinity permission to fish for large snails (the size of a hand and considered a great delicacy), catfish, and big-mouth bass. On the designated day, villagers gather at the water's edge clutching their hand traps that have a hole in the top to extricate the catch. At a signal from the *po-lan* everyone rushes into the water, plunging the traps in an atmosphere of merriment.

Leadership

According to Han Tho, certain individuals (mostly males) are endowed with potency by virtue of Yang Ngă Potao ("Spirit That Bestows Leadership") becoming part of their being at birth. This potency (*bongă ayua*) manifests itself in external charisma (*gonuh seri*) marking a man as having a "destiny to leadership" (*lot ngă potao*). Leadership also implies wealth, which is demonstrated by hosting lavish rituals and feasting. When in 1922 Touneh Han Dang was appointed Tri Huyen, he organized the *kaitra* ritual honoring Yang Ngă Potao, offering buffalo, goats, pigs, and many jars of alcohol with feasting and dancing for three days. Han Tho related that one often hears villagers refer to someone as "*hu bongă*," meaning he has manifest *bongă ayua* potency, but they are just as likely to chide a politically ambitious person, saying, "You can't be village chief because you don't have Yang Ngă Potao." Villagers look for signs of this favoritism in children. When a leader dies, his family puts charcoal marks under his ear, on the top of his chest, and on a thigh. Children born of his line are carefully examined at birth to see if there are any natural marks at these places, signs that the newborn has the soul of the ancestor and his potency. Han Tho's uncle's wife gave birth to twins (a rare event), prompting him to give a buffalo sacrifice to declare that they were "destined to leadership." Other signs of favoritism are strange rumblings in the night, a favorable dream by a kinsman, or a sudden rash of good luck. Outward manifestations (*gonuh seri*) in a child include a high forehead, bright eyes, clear intelligence, and robust health; such signs accord him special treatment. Han Tho was adjudged such a child, and he was addressed with the honorific term *on* ("sir") and was cautioned to eat sparingly, avoid certain foods, and not to urinate in strange places. As such a child grows older he takes on a majestic air and speaks with a voice that commands attention. His crops flourish, he invariably bags game, and he realizes good fish catches. As Han Tho put it, "He can cross the mountains without fear of tigers, snakes, sorcerers, and evil spirits (*yang rac*)." Han Tho reported that his father, Touneh Han Dang, could detect this charisma in photographs of leaders, including President Dwight Eisenhower, French president René Coty, and General de Lattre de Tassigny, as well as in the person of King Bao Dai.

At the risk of losing the spirit, the adult must avoid "unclean" things such as feces, rotten meat, old worn clothes, and garments associated with sex organs such as loincloths. The male must never be physically under a woman or anything associated with women. Han Tho's father, a leader who had this charisma, never walked under a house on piling, and he avoided clotheslines (and was aghast at a French physical culture exhibition in Dalat when a Frenchman hoisted a girl up on his shoulders). In Saigon Han Tho was going to dine at a Chinese restaurant located at the end of a narrow lane, but overhead were many clothes on lines so he had to go to another restaurant. One woman who had this charisma was the celebrated heroine Mo Co ("White-haired Lady"), who led resistance to French rule and collected money for Sam Bram, the nativistic figure of the late 1930s, for which she was imprisoned at Lao Bao, where she died.[19] After 1960 there appeared a new type of young Chru leader, who had been to school in Dalat or Saigon. Most of these leaders were kin, reflecting a pattern of intermarriage among elite Chru families. They also were part of the larger highland kin network (described in *Sons of the Mountains* and *Free in the Forest*). Imbued with the spirit of ethnonationalism, they favored retaining traditions (such as houses on piling) to preserve a highlander ethnic identity. But at the same time they eschewed the traditional matrilocal residence rule (for the eldest daughter). They also were among those who had acquired land, houses, and other property and therefore opposed restoration of indigenous Chru laws reflecting matrilineal-descent-group practices, notably female ownership of land and other family property.

19. Hickey, *Sons of the Mountains,* pp. 39, 266, 335, 343–58.

A radical change occurred in February 1962, when Touneh Han Dang became a Catholic, and practically all of the Chru followed his example. Touneh Han Tho pointed out that Christian families abandoned their previous religious cults, notably those related to farming. Cousin marriages and sorcery also faded.

The Vietnam War

Maxwell Cobbey reports that around 1960, Northern Roglai families began to migrate to the lowlands when Communist insurgency brought insecurity to their areas, marking the movement of Roglai refugees that would continue throughout the Vietnam War.[20] Louis Wiesner reports that in 1961 the Viet Cong occupied the Roglai village of Tan My on Route 1 between Phan Rang and Phan Thiet.[21] Some six thousand villagers had been relocated from the mountains, and between 1957 and 1959 more than six hundred had died from sickness, starvation, and heat. Those who tried to leave were imprisoned, so they followed the Viet Cong back into the mountains. In 1970 the refugee village of Suoi Hiep, west of Nhatrang, contained two thousand Roglai and some Chil and Tring. The Roglai explained that they had come from the Cau River uplands, "a one-night's walk" to the coast, where they thought it would be better to group their isolated farmsteads. One man noted that had they not done so they would have been likely targets for military aircraft (his remark drew laughter from the group). Readaptation to the dry coastal plain was arduous. The refugee village was a collection of army tents and badly constructed buildings (one collapsed during a storm, killing a young girl). The refugees were allowed to have swiddens in the hills, but they complained that they "did not know the soil," and rainfall was sparse. Poor yields forced them to sell firewood, but the hills were rapidly becoming denuded. Some had begun working as day laborers on nearby Vietnamese farms. They declared that they would like to return to the Cau River area, but because they had been under government control the Communists would treat them harshly. Lois Lee reports that in the refugee setting there emerged a new prenatal taboo which required the pregnant woman to avoid watching aircraft dive-bombing lest the newborn baby make a sound like an airplane engine and lose its breath.[22]

The Roglai who fled into the Danhim Valley fared better because they had had historical contact with the Chru, and the physical surroundings were not completely alien. The Chru allowed the Roglai to build houses

20. Cobbey, "A First Case," p. 61.
21. Louis Wiesner, *Victims and Survivors: Displaced Persons and Other War Victims in Viet-Nam, 1954–1975* (New York: Greenwood Press, 1988), p. 24.
22. Lee, "Pregnancy and Childbirth Practices," p. 31.

in or near their settlements, and there was ample land for the Roglai to farm swiddens. Some Roglai readapted, renting paddy fields from the Chru, who taught them how to grow wet rice.

In the early 1960s the Vietnamese government completed a hydro-electric dam on the Danhim River, bringing a prime example of modern technology and a new lake, which the Chru saw as a potential source of irrigation water. But the electric-relay towers became targets of Communist sapper squads that also severed the railroad running from Dalat to the coast and mounted ambushes on National Route 11. Chru villages, however, remained relatively unaffected by the war, and it was a time of considerable innovation. Through the provincial agricultural service the American Aid Program made available chemical fertilizers and tractors at low cost. Touprong Hiou introduced new cash crops, including garlic, avocados, artichokes, cauliflower, escarole, celery, potatoes, and plums. He was the first to hire Chru farm laborers, and he joined with Chinese businessmen to open the first private bank in the valley.

In 1975 the Communist regime nationalized all of the land, and Touneh Han Tho noted that it marked the death knell for the already weakened clan land guardian system. All of the Chru leaders were rounded up and sent to reeducation camps and prisons, where some died under harsh conditions. North Vietnamese troops also occupied every village, forbidding residents to visit kin without permission. When the harvest occurs, army trucks bring troops to carry away the yield. Letters Han Tho received from kin lament the jailings, severe food shortages, forced conscription of young men, and other hardships.

Chapter 3
Stieng

The southwestern reaches of the central highlands form between the mountains and the flat Mekong River delta a sweeping transitional terrace zone distinguished by its only (and unexpected) peak, Mount Bara, which rises some 733 meters (2,405 feet) near the market town of Song Be. In their scattered villages, composed of longhouses occupied by patrilineal kin groups, the Stieng observe prescriptions for preserving harmony with nature and a host of spirits (*yang bra* and *weeng,* a term that also connotes a "dream image" of the human soul). The Stieng were first mentioned in 1765 French accounts when Monsignor Pigues, apostolic vicar of Cochinchina, reported that there were "montagnards" between Cambodia, Laos, and Cochinchina who were amenable to conversion. He identified them as Stieng and "others, Proue, Queraie, Penong, etc." Five years later, Father Juget attempted to start a mission among the Stieng in the Prek Chlong area of eastern Cambodia, but he died in 1774 and his efforts were not continued. In 1861, Father H. Azémar founded a mission at Brolam, near present-day Bu Dop. When in 1866 Pu Kombo, a Buddhist monk, who claimed to be the son of the Khmer king, Ang Chang, mounted a revolt, it swept into the Stieng country, and rebels destroyed Brolam, forcing Father Azémar to flee. To launch a pacification program among the Stieng, the French in 1913 established a military post at Bu Dop. But the murder in 1914 of French explorer Henri Maitre north of the post and the death in 1915 of Truffot, a French officer, at Sre Chi inside the Cambodian border, spread unrest through the Stieng country, ending French efforts to bring it under control. Then in 1927, the possibility of developing rubber estates in the Bu Dop area prompted the formation of a mapping expedition led by Commandant Carrier into the thick forests of the Stieng country west of Mount Bara. The following year, Théophile Gerber became the administrator at Bu

Dop and began a systematic study of Stieng language and customs, which he later published. In 1929 it was decided to build the stretch of new Colonial Route 14 from Saigon to Ban Me Thuot through the Stieng territory. Construction proceeded, but on 29 October 1933 Morère, the administrative representative at Mount Bara, was assassinated, and in January 1934, a force of some three hundred Stieng attacked the French post at Bu Coh. By the early 1940s the section of Route 14 into the Stieng country was open to traffic from Saigon.[1]

The Stieng language is included in the South Bahnaric subgrouping of the Mon Khmer family within the Austroasiatic stock.[2] Lorraine Haupers notes that the Stieng language does "not exhibit the interesting vowel register phonemes of many other Mon-Khmer languages," but its "extensive use of semantic pairing, onomatopoeic forms, and internal rhyming make Stieng a colorful and fascinating language." Haupers also reports that the Stieng "divide themselves into two major groups: bulo 'the people above' (upstream) and budeh 'the people below' (downstream).[3] Stieng informants also identified local groups called Bulach and Budip. Because the Stieng extend into neighboring Cambodia, obtaining population figures for the entire group in recent years has been difficult. Gerber reported in 1951 that there was a total of 60,000 Stieng in Vietnam and Cambodia.[4] In 1967 those in South Vietnam were estimated to number some 30,000, and the 1989 Vietnamese population census reports 50,194 "Xtieng" (see Appendix A).

Between 1960 and 1974, Ralph and Lorraine Haupers of the SIL spent nine years conducting linguistic research among the Stieng. Five of the nine years were spent living on the edge of Bu Kroai village at the foot of Mount Bara some five kilometers from Song Be. My fieldwork on the Stieng in 1966 and 1967 was conducted with the help of the Hauperses and their Stieng assistant, Bi. Bu Kroai was the focus of research, and in the course of gathering general ethnographic data, a kin-network survey of eight households embracing seventy-one people was conducted. The survey supports Haupers's view that wealth is measured by ownership of cattle, water buffalo, alcohol jars (notably the prestigious *srung* jars),

1. Gerald Cannon Hickey, *Sons of the Mountains: Ethnohistory of the Vietnamese Central Highlands to 1954* (New Haven: Yale University Press, 1982), pp. 200, 216–17, 320, 326–28. Théophile Gerber's two publications on the Stieng are *Lexique Française-Stieng* (Saigon: Imprimerie du Théâtre, 1937) and "Coutumier Stieng," *BEFEO* 45 (1951): 227–68.
2. David Thomas and R. K. Headley, Jr., "More on Mon-Khmer Subgroupings," *Lingua* 25, no. 4 (1970): 398–418.
3. Lorraine Haupers, "Notes on Stieng Life," in *Notes from Indochina on Ethnic Minority Cultures,* ed. Marilyn Gregerson and Dorothy Thomas (Dallas: SIL Museum of Anthropology, 1980), p. 143.
4. Gerber, "Coutumier Stieng," p. 227.

gongs, and bondmen and by the men having plural wives.[5] The survey also suggests that within village society heads of wealthy patrilineal groups have the wherewithal to demonstrate potency not only in rituals and feasting but also in paying costly bride-prices for themselves and for less affluent kinsmen. The survey also reveals that the levirate allows plural wives without payment of bride-price. Survey data too bring out a functional link between bride-price and divorce, residence (flexibility of the patrilocal-residence rule), and debt bondage (which is also linked to costly buffalo sacrifices to cure illnesses).[6] Cases in the survey illustrate that the bondman lives as a member of the family (the "quasi-assimilation" into a more successful lineage observed by A. Thomas Kirsch[7]) and though he cannot be sold, he can be passed to another family as part of the bride-price. Marriage patterns in Bu Kroai reflect patrilineage exogamy, the rule against marrying the father's sister's daughter, and preference for marriage with consanguineal kinswomen of the mother's patrilineage, especially the mother's brother's daughter (matrilineal cross-cousin) because this had been prescribed by Tieng Lieng, common ancestor of the Stieng. The survey suggests that child marriages between cross-cousins tend to be more stable than other arrangements.

The elite status of some patrilineages combined with Stieng history raises the question of whether in the past there were "great patrilineages" (such as those that existed among the neighboring Maa) that enjoyed autocratic authority and organized armed revolts against the French. One way or another, the survey suggests that although Stieng society still retains some autocratic features (such as elite patrilineages, costly bride-price, and debt bondage) it has swung in the direction of becoming more democratic, with marriages between elites and nonelites and equal access to farmland by all villagers.

Between 24 June and 4 July 1967 a Walter Reed Army Institute of Research team headed by Captain Andrew Cottingham, M.D., conducted thick blood film examinations for malaria and filariasis in Bu Kroai (see Appendix C). Of the fifty-three villagers examined, the Plasmodium vivax parasite was found in seventeen (32.08 prevalence ratio), Plasmodium falciparum was diagnosed in one (1.89), a mixture of the two was found in one (1.89), and Microfilaria was detected in ten (18.87).

5. Haupers, "Notes," pp. 152–54.

6. Debt bondage is different from slavery, which existed in the past. A person found guilty of witchcraft was banished into slavery, and war captives became slaves. These distinctions are described in Gerber, "Coutumier Stieng," pp. 229–32.

7. A. Thomas Kirsch, *Feasting and Social Oscillation: Religion and Society in Upland Southeast Asia,* Department of Asian Studies, Cornell University, Southeast Asia Program Data Paper no. 92 (Ithaca, N.Y., 1973), p. 27.

Settlements and Longhouses

Stieng settlements usually have five to ten longhouses. The village of Bu Kroai has eight longhouses arranged in two uneven rows with entrances facing an open area in between. Elderly villagers recalled that at one time it had stood on a site not far away, enclosed by a log stockade. Each village has a guardian spirit (*me b'rǎ dum'rong*) for whom annual rituals are performed by a male with the title *me b'rǎ dum'rong blau*. But if there is another village nearby the residents share farming rights. An outsider must have permission of village leaders to farm in the territory but not to hunt, fish, or forage.

Houses in the Song Be area are constructed on the ground, but Ralph Haupers noted that Bu Kroai villagers said that in the 1950s they had been forced to do so by the Vietnamese government. They lamented that Stieng houses should be solidly constructed of hardwood and elevated on piling, and they were "not proud" of the present abodes. The main columns, *jarong mê* ("mother post"), at each end of the house and the central column, *jarong kloong,* support the longitudinal thick bamboo ridgepole (*noor booc*) that serves as the peak of the roof. At the four corners are posts, *jarong coon* ("child posts"), that support the two longitudinal purlins (*tòwòr*) running the length of the house and two latitudinal tie beams (*cang*) at each end. Roof rafters (*socaq*) are affixed to the *tòwòr* beams and the ridgepole. To support thatching, longitudinal bamboo poles are lashed to the rafters ("spirits of the rafters" are invoked at weddings that take place in the house). Panels of thatching (*ya*) are made by tying the ends of five or six bunches of dried imperata cylindrica grass with bamboo strips. Beginning at the bottom of the roof, the thatcher uses rattan cord to tie panels to the bamboo longitudinal poles, imbricating successive panels and bending the top ones (specifically designated *pu ja*) over the ridgepole. Exterior and interior walls are of split bamboo tied to thin bamboo (*pondaap*) to form panels (*ponir*) that are affixed to bamboo poles (*pendoong*). The number of entrances (*lpong*) depends on the length of the house.

Internal arrangements vary, but the common pattern is to have bamboo platforms about one foot high and open hearths, each of which consists of three large stones set in a hole in the ground. Near an entrance there is a large platform that serves as a place to receive visitors and a general work/storage (of family possessions) area. The Stieng draw a sharp distinction between the ordinary rice alcohol jars used in rituals and the old, highly valuable *srung* jars, which are part of bride-price. Bi explained that sets of gongs used in rituals also are prestigious items. There is a set of six flat gongs (*chêng*) of different sizes enabling them to be stored one inside the other, and each has a name. The largest, for example, is *boang* (the same term for a married woman without chil-

Photo 7. Interior of a Stieng longhouse in Bu Kroai village (1967). On platform from right: clay pots, water gourds, back-baskets, winnowing basket, and *srung* jar. On the floor are a mortar for husking rice and a back-basket.

dren). The fifth is *taal,* a term used to indicate children between the eldest and youngest, and the sixth is *coon,* the term for children. The last two terms are also used to indicate the two smallest of the set of five gongs with protrusions in the middle. Family farm tools are stored in this compartment, as are "singing kites." The rest of the house is given over to platforms, partially or entirely enclosed by bamboo partitions, where family members sleep, eat, and store personal effects.

Granaries built of wood, bamboo, and thatch on piling are located near the longhouses. The granary of Household 1 in Bu Kroai is innovative in having multiple functions. An area on the ground in the front section of the structure serves as a place for metalworking. To the rear, the upper part of the structure is for rice stored in large woven bins. The lower part is a coop for chickens and ducks and a storage area for dried grasses.

Bu Kroai Kinship

The Stieng trace descent through the male line. As Appendix B4 indicates, kin are recognized to the third ascending generation and the third descending generation. In Ego's generation *bi* is the common term for older siblings, and the modifier *rôh* identifies the older sister. Younger siblings (*oh*) are differentiated by sex modifiers *clau* (male) and *dở-ur* (female). *Ghêq* indicates very young siblings. Sibling terms are extended to male cousins, who are age-graded relative to Ego, and female cousins, not age-graded, are *rôh*. In the second ascending generation *mê,* the term for mother, is used for parents' sisters with the modifiers *rôh bươp* and *oh nur* to identify the father's and mother's sisters respectively. Father's brothers are *moon,* and mother's brothers are *côônh*. Informants note that *côônh* identify the father's collateral kin above the first ascending generation and the term *con côônh* indicates marriage with consanguineal kinswomen of the mother's patrilineage. Ego's and brothers' children are *coon* while sisters' children are *moom*.

In Bu Kroai, Bluq, head of Household 3, explained that *phung mbaang* refers to all consanguineal kin, and "close *mbaang*" are patrilineal, usually those within three ascending and three descending generations, while "distant *mbaang*" are others. Ralph Haupers noted that the term *mbaang* is stable, but the term *phung* is not, varying with dialect differences in the region. Bluq observed that everyone knows the name and village of kin of the second or third ascending generations. Weddings and funerals bring patrilineal kin together to strengthen their ties not only by contact but also through recitation of ancestors' names as ritual offerings are made (the only occasions when these names can be said).

Bu Kroai has eight households with a total of seventy-one residents (see Chart 1, which outlines kin ties). Patrilineage A includes Households 1, 2, 3, 4, and 5, all descended from Moi, while Patrilineage B is made up of households 7 and 8, all descended from Bie. Yueh, head of Household 8, observed that the respective ancestors were not related but were "pha gơna poh." Ralph Haupers explained that *pha* means "different" while *gơna* is "same,' and *poh* is "village." The "same" indicates same village, while "different" implies different kin groups in that village. Patrilineage C is not anchored in any household, but one member is a debt bondman (*dek*) in Household 7, and female members married men in Household 2, 6, and 7. Household 6 is a nuclear family linked by marriages to all three patrilineages.

Villagers in Patrilineage A trace common descent to an ancestor named Moi. His son, Mei, had three sons—Bom, Soruong, and Chhieng. All thirteen members of Household 1 are affiliated with Chhieng, who had two sons, Uq and Leq, as well as a daughter, Buoc (she and her husband, Yuot, remained in her paternal house). Uq married a distant kinswoman, Noi, now living in Household 1 with her two sons, Cling, head of Household 1, who married a girl from another village, and Nhooch, the younger brother. In addition to their families, the household includes Thuoc, the orphaned son of a sister, and a male patrilineal cousin, Mbong, son of Leq. Leq (a village patriarch who died in 1966) had paid bride-prices for

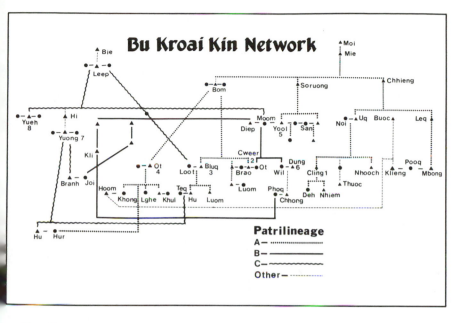

Chart 1

his sister's son, Klieng, and also for his brother's sons, Cling and Nhooch, who are now in debt to his son, Mbong. Cling's wife's brother and his family came to Household 1 as refugees and arranged a matrilateral cross-cousin marriage between their small daughter and Cling's small son, Nhiem, before moving to a refugee camp. Because the affianced children are young, they continue to live with their respective parents. Cling's daughter, Deh, and her husband were living temporarily in the house. Previously, two sons of Cling's father's sister, Buoc, had lived in the house. One of them, Hoom, married Khong, a daughter of Ot, head of Household 4 (she is of a nonwealthy branch of Patrilineage A). Not wealthy and unable to pay the goods and money he borrowed to pay the bride-price, Hoom became a bondman to his creditor in another village. At the time of the survey he and his wife were residing at Ot's house. The other son, Klieng, died, and normally, in conformity with the levirate, Hoom would have married Pooq, the widow. But because Leq had paid Klieng's bride-price, he declared that Pooq would marry his son, Mbong. Klieng's daughter, Brong, is a child bride and lives with her husband's family in another village. As a child, Mbong married two girls whose bride-prices were paid by his father. One girl, when she grew up, ran off with a young man from another village who joined the army (and failed to repay Mbong's bride-price). Mbong gave the other bride to Sol, his distant patrilineal kinsman who is a bondman in Bu Dru.

Leq attained his status as village patriarch by his demonstrated potency as a wealthy man who made impressive ritual sacrifices accompanied by large feasts. Potency also was manifest in his paying costly bride-prices for his son Mbong's two child marriages as well as for his older brother's sons, Cling and Nhooch, and for his sister's son, Klieng, not a member of the patrilineage. Payment of Klieng's bride-price enabled Leq to negate the levirate.

Cweer, head of Household 2 (seven members), and Bluq, head of Household 3 (nine members), are sons of Bom's first wife, and they represent a nonwealthy branch of Patrilineage A. Cweer's first wife, Ot, and her sister (married to Dung, head of Household 6) are daughters of Moom, a member of Patrilineage B, and her first husband, Diep, of Patrilineage C. Cweer related that Diep left Moom because "he didn't like her" so he forfeited the bride-price. Cweer pointed out that if the wife is guilty of adultery she must return the bride-price. Moom then married Yool, head of Household 5. After the death of his elder brother, who had married Brao, a distant kinswoman, Cweer adhered to the levirate and took the widow as his second wife. Her son and his wife live in the household.

In Household 3, Bluq, the head, is married to Loot, a woman from Patrilineage B (her mother was a daughter of Leep). Bluq's son, Hu, took as his second wife Tec, a kinswoman of his mother and daughter of Yuong, head of Household 7 in Patrilineage B.

The mother of Ot, head of Household 4 (ten members), was the second wife of Bom, making Ot a half-brother of Bluq and Cweer. It was noted above that Ot's daughter, Khong, married Hoom, a kinsman from Household 1, who is a bondman. Hur, another daughter of Ot, lives with her husband, Hu, son of Yuong, head of Household 7 in Patrilineage B. Yool, son of Soruong, is head of Household 5 (nine members), another nonwealthy branch of Patrilineage A. His first wife, Pheh, died, and when his brother, Yoot, died, Yool took his widow, San, as his third wife. His second wife, Moom, had been married to Diep, of Patrilineage C, and one of their daughters is first wife of Cweer in Household 2, while another is the wife of Dung (Household 6).

Dung (head of Household 6, five members) explained that he had paid his bride-price so he was free to live where he chose, and he elected to settle in Bu Kroai so his wife could be near her kin. His son Chhong (about seventeen years of age) is married to Phoq, an eleven-year-old kinswoman of Patrilineage C, daughter of Kli, a debt bondman in Household 7. Phoq assumes adult female responsibilities in Household 6. While I was interviewing there on a very hot afternoon, Phoq entered carrying a

Photo 8. Hu, son of Bluq, head of Household 3, in front of his longhouse (1967).

back-basket containing around twenty-five pounds of firewood. She set the basket down and splashed water from a can on her face and the upper part of her body. Later she returned with a baby (daughter of Sol and his deceased wife, the former child bride of Mbong of Household 1) in a sling, feeding it some thick chicken-rice soup.

Households 7 and 8 constitute Patrilineage B, whose members trace a common ancestor, Bie, through his son, Leep, who had two wives. By the first wife, Leep had Yueh, elderly head of Household 8 (two members) and Moom, wife of Yool (Household 5), as well as Hi, father of Yuong, head of Household 7 (sixteen members). Their half-sister's daughter, Loot, is the wife of Bluq (Household 3). Yuong is wealthy, a man of demonstrated potency who has cattle and buffalo for sacrifices and feasts, two wives, and a bondman. As was noted above, Yuong's son is married to a daughter of Ot (Household 4). Yuong's other daughter, Tec, wed Hu, son of Bluq (Household 3). Kli, the debt bondman (whose father's brother, Diep, was married to Moom), his wife, and daughter are treated as members of the household. Kli's other daughter, Phoq, is wife of kinsman Chhong, son of Dung (Household 6). One of Kli's father's brother's son's daughters, Joi, is married to Yuong's son, Branh, a distant kinsman. Kli (who married his mother's brother's daughter) related that

Photo 9. Phoq, child bride in Household 6 (1967).

he became a bondman when he fell ill and the shaman recommended a pig sacrifice. Kli borrowed a pig, but his creditor demanded a buffalo as payment. Yool (Household 5) provided the buffalo but wanted a *srung* jar in return, so Kli became his bondman. While his daughter, Phoq, was small, Kli arranged the marriage between her and Chhong, son of Dung (Household 6), who agreed to pay a bride-price of three *srung* jars, a buffalo, six pigs, and then regular rice-alcohol jars. The first *srung* was duly paid and given to Yool, freeing Kli from debt, but the remainder of the bride-price was not forthcoming. When Kli's half-brother wanted to marry a girl from another village, her family wanted two *srung* jars, a buffalo, three pigs, and fifteen ordinary alcohol jars. The family gathered all but the two *srung* jars so, in lieu of them, Kli went as their bondman. When a boy from that family married a girl from Household 7 they gave Kli in lieu of three *srung* jars, which were part of the bride-price. Dung (Household 6) still owed Kli the remainder of the bride-price, including two *srung* jars, but, unfortunately, Kli's wife fell ill, and he had to sacrifice a buffalo, which he borrowed from his son-in-law, Chhong, who demanded a *srung* jar in return. They were still working out the rest of the bride-price owed Kli, but meanwhile he remains a bondman in Household 7.

Marriage and Household

Although the Bu Kroai survey includes only three examples of matri-lateral cross-cousin marriage (Cling's son in Household 1, Bluq's son in Household 3, and Kli in Household 7), it appears to be more prevalent in village farther removed from town influence. On 29 June 1967 Ralph Haupers conducted a survey of a random sample of thirty-two male refugees from twelve outlying villages concerning their marriages. Twenty-five (78 percent) had married their mothers' brothers' daughters. One was engaged to his cross-cousin, but she lived in a village under Viet Cong control. In another case his elder brother had married the only cross-cousin available. One said that he had elected to marry a girl who was not related.

This survey and the Bu Kroai survey both contain examples of *con-côônh* marriages with matrilateral non-cross-cousin kinswomen. In the survey of refugees, two had married their mothers' mothers' brothers' sons' daughters. At Bu Kroai, in Household 1, Hoom's wife, Khong, is his mother's father's brother's son's daughter, and this relationship is replicated in Household 6 with Choong's wife, Phoq. Bu Kroai also has two examples of marriages with distantly related nonpatrilineal kinswomen on the male side. Bluq, head of Household 3, married Loot, who is his brother Cweer's wife's mother's half-cousin's daughter in Patri-lineage B. He explained that he did this because his mother's brother's daughter, whom he was expected to wed, died. He observed that marrying a matrilateral cross-cousin is desirable but not obligatory. If, for example, the girl is lazy and a poor homemaker, the boy does not have to wed her. In Household 7, Yuong's son by his second wife is married to a girl who is his father's father's sister's second husband's father's brother's son's daughter. Yuong's son, Branh, by the first wife, is married to Joi, who is his father's father's sister's first husband's brother's son's daughter.

In child marriages either all or part of the bride-price can be paid. The girl will remain with her parents until she is eight or nine years old, at which age she can assume a role in her husband's family's division of labor (exemplified by Phoq in Household 6). After a child bride reaches puberty, she and her husband can cohabit. A man in Bu Ghir (some fifteen kilometers northwest of Song Be) related that as a young man he was in the French army and upon returning to the village he married his very young cross-cousin who went to live at his house, where after puberty she began bearing his children. To satisfy a debt a couple may give a young daughter to their creditors, and when she reaches puberty one of the sons may take her as a wife, paying no bride-price. Should none of the sons want to marry her, she is sent back to her parents and the full debt must be paid.

According to Bi, for unarranged marriages, each side obtains the services of an intermediary, a male kinsman. On an appointed day the boy and his parents, bearing a spear and bush scythe with a curved handle (*wiêh ưưr,* highly valued because it requires skill to make and is used in rituals), visit the girl's house. If her parents accept the marriage bid they serve his parents a meal of buffalo or pork, and together they set the wedding date (which cannot be three days after the agreement or any combination of three). Then they discuss in bargaining fashion (the term for this, *toh laas,* also is the word for "trading") the bride-price, which is largely determined by the relative wealth of the boy's family and the girl's qualities (physical attractiveness, industriousness, and whether she is a virgin). In her description of marriage procedures, Haupers reports that the usual bride-price is one bondman, one *srung* jar, twenty regular jars, a buffalo, three or four pigs, five bush scythes, and five spears. She explains that "the value of a *srung* jar is measured in cubits (that is, the length of the forearm from the elbow to the tip of the middle finger)." A jar that measures one cubit is normally worth one bondman, and the most valuable jars are worth as many as five bondmen.[8]

Paying the bride-price is a great burden for most young men. The Bu Ghir headman said that bride-price items consist of "big" things such as a debt bondman, *srung* jars, and buffalo and "small" things such as spears, knives, and ordinary alcohol jars. For his first wife the headman had to pay a bondman, a *srung* jar, a buffalo, and ten rice-alcohol jars. He added that bargaining with the girl's parents is easier than dealing with her kinfolk, who "begin demanding things." Many in the male refugee group interviewed by Ralph Haupers explained that they worked for their future in-laws to help pay their bride-prices. They said that there are many instances when a boy who is taking a long time to pay the bride-price may be invited to live at the girl's house until he makes full payment, whereupon the couple will move to his parents' house. A Bu Ghir villager said he was living with his wife's family while he tried to pay the bride-price, which consisted of a bondman, a *srung* jar, four pigs (one large and three small), two spears, two bush scythes with curved handles, and ten regular jars. The Bu Kroai survey reveals variations in providing the bride-price. In Household 1 the rich uncle paid his nephews' bride-prices, which gave him the right to declare who would marry a deceased nephew's widow (and his decision negated the levirate). Chhong in Household 6 paid only part of the bride-price for his child bride, Phoq, daughter of Kli, a bondman, but the girl nonetheless went to live at his house. Kli in Household 7 illustrates that someone can help pay a kins-

---

8. Haupers, "Notes," pp. 153, 159–62, 171. Marriage procedures also are discussed in Gerber, "Coutumier Stieng," pp. 259–64.

man's bride-price by becoming a bondman and perhaps be passed on to another household as payment of bride-price. Observation of the levirate in Households 2 and 5 illustrates that this practice allows polygyny without bearing the cost of a bride-price.

If a boy is too poor to pay any bride-price, he may take up permanent residence at the girl's house. Bu Kroai informants explained that a young man has the right to borrow from his sister's husband a *srung* jar for a bride-price. Although such a jar may be worth two to four buffalo, he is only expected to pay back one buffalo. He also presents a pig, which the brother-in-law must offer in a ritual to which everyone is invited.

Haupers relates that all patrilineal kin gather for the first wedding celebration, "bringing the gifts to them" (*jên drap a bu*), held at the girl's house. The boy brings three pigs called "sacrificial pig, looking-for-a-wife pig, and spear-and-bush-scythe pig" respectively. The pigs are sacrificed by the boy's intermediary while he invokes the spirits. Nearby the couple stands facing each other with their right feet on a buffalo horn. Using the knife employed in the sacrificial slaughter, the intermediary mixes pig blood and a piece of the liver with rice alcohol and a mashed tuber called *gun,* associated with cosmic forces (it also is used for love potions and for rendering a dog hostile to outsiders). He smears the mixture on the bride's foot and then the groom's foot as he entreats the ancestors and spirits of the sky, graves, and house rafters to guard the new home and bring prosperity. He presents the knife to the groom, who must guard it. The groom drinks either two or four (three is taboo) buffalo horns of alcohol from a jar while the bride places a red bead necklace around his neck. As she drinks, he places the necklace around her neck. Feasting begins when the bride gives her husband a handful of rice and he reciprocates, a symbolic pledge to live and work together. Young men weave with astonishing speed many small bamboo baskets for guests to carry home some of the sacrificial meat. The couple remains temporarily at her house and then takes up permanent residence at his house.

The final marriage ritual, "our son brings his wife home" (*jên coon seq a sai*), marking payment of the bride-price and patrilocal residence, follows the harvest and is part of its celebration. It is important that the alcohol served be made from the new rice to ensure the success of the marriage (the Stieng emphasized that Vietnamese commercial alcohol cannot be used because the spirits are not accustomed to it). A delicious type of glutinous rice is cooked in bamboo tubes. Three pigs are sacrificed. One is the "sticky-rice pig," symbolizing the fact that the bride's kin can enter the groom's village. The second is the "stepping-on-the-sleeping-mat pig," to mark the founding of a new household in the groom's village, and the third is "entering-the-bed pig," a symbol of the couple's cohabitation.

According to Bi, because it is taboo for the bride to sleep on the same platform as her father-in-law, the newly married couple is given its own compartment and cooking hearth. By the same token, when visiting her parents, it is taboo for the boy to sleep on the same platform as his mother-in-law. Also, the two may not touch under any circumstances (Bi noted that this would be true even if she were drowning and he was the only one who could save her). They may, however, converse and joke. The only use of teknonymy is when a mother-in-law addresses or refers to her son-in-law.

Bu Kroai survey data reflect some characteristic Stieng living arrangements. All of the households have large platforms near the main entrance. Ot (Household 4) noted that at night he hung a wasps' nest outside the main entrance to prevent evil spirits from entering. In Household 1 Cling, the eldest male and therefore household head, and his wife and two young sons occupy a large compartment where they eat, sleep, and store personal belongings. Deh, the daughter, and her husband have another compartment, as does Cling's brother Nhooch and his family. The next two compartments are for the brothers' mother, Noi (when she died in 1968, hers was dismantled), and their cousin Mbong and his wife. Another is occupied by Cling's wife's brother, a refugee, and his family (later they moved to a refugee village). Dug into the earth in the corridor near the platforms are six hearths of stones. Members of the extended family share cooking hearths, but each nuclear family takes its meals in its own compartment. In cases of plural marriage each wife and her offspring occupy a compartment and have their own cooking hearth. In a nearby refugee settlement a man with three wives related that his house had four compartments, three of which were occupied by the wives, one of whom had a small son. Two married sons who had paid bride-prices lived in the other compartment with their families. Another son lived with his wife's family because his bride-price had not yet been paid. Each wife had her own cooking hearth, and the husband took meals with the wife with whom he had spent the previous night. He noted that he had to rotate continually to avoid jealousy among the wives.

In the past, farmers grew cotton, which women spun and dyed, but now thread is purchased in the market. Loincloths worn by men on ceremonial occasions have elegant motifs.[9] The section that hangs in

9. Mattiebelle Gittinger, research associate for Southeast Asian Textiles at the Textile Museum, Washington, D.C., did the following analysis of a Stieng loincloth: "This Stieng loincloth is created by three panels joined in a continuous strip to form a long narrow cloth. The center panel is black cotton worked in a warp-faced plain weave with simple marginal stripes in white, yellow, and black patterned in a float weave. The two end panels are red artificial fiber with white continuous and discontinuous supplementary weft patterns worked on a warp-faced plain weave ground. The supplementary wefts make geometric

Photo 10. Stieng woman weaving a loincloth (1967).

front usually has a red and white maze design called *mê* ("mother") and a smaller design of diamonds within diamonds called "melon-seed village." Other motifs are called "eclipse," "butterfly," and "parrot." To honor a taboo, the loincloth is woven so that the motifs in front are not aligned with those in the back. In the home or working in fields, women wear only small loincloths, which they cover with a black wraparound skirt (handwoven in remote areas) when going to market. When a woman reaches puberty she draws her long hair into a loose bun, and in the Song Be area she does not cut her hair until her spouse dies. Ear plugs (*pi blŭc*) of ivory or boar tusk, which girls receive at puberty, are common, as are metal necklaces and wrist and ankle bracelets. Women also make small pots for cooking rice and storing cooked rice. One elderly woman in Bu Kroai is particularly adept at it, and so she produces pots on order. She described how at the river's edge she digs gray clay from under the topsoil, allows it to dry, and reduces it to a fine powder, which she mixes with water to the right consistency. On a semicircular thick board with a depressed center she forms pots of varying sizes. While the clay is still wet

patterns organized in horizontal bands. White embroidery inserted beneath the supplementary weft creates diagonal lines in some fret patterns. Additional embroidery lightly embellishes some narrow lateral stripes. The fringe ends are cut and piped with white cotton. Total dimensions 339 × 21 cm (apportionment: 91, 264, 84 cm) The Textile Museum TD 389.4."

she uses a stick notched on the top four corners to incise designs on the exterior. Vegetables are cooked in small green bamboo tubes, while other foods are prepared in metal pots purchased in the market. In a deviation from the usual highland pattern, women do some of the fishing.

Most men still have long hair gathered in a bun held in place with a stylized metal comb made in the village. According to Haupers, boys learn basketry by weaving the simplest types first.[10] The most common back-basket (*sah*) is for carrying heavy loads of wood, rice, or gourds of water. A loosely woven basket (*waas*) is used exclusively for gourds of water while a quart-sized basket (*cupiêng*) with a lid and one shoulder strap is for carrying cooked rice to the field. A long, narrow basket (*sôôr*) with two straps and a pointed bottom serves either as a quiver or for bagged small game. The harvester has a gallon-sized tightly woven basket (*khiêu*) tied to the waist to hold grains and a more or less tear-drop-shaped flat basket (*dôông*) some four feet in diameter used for winnowing. When a bush scythe (*wiêh*) is no longer usable, the blade is fitted to a two-foot-long bamboo handle to make a hoe for weeding maize and tobacco. Every man fashions his own small knife (*pêh*) by inserting a blade in a small curved portion of bamboo shoot. The sheath is made of two pieces of wood tied with braided rattan cord, and the knife is always tucked into his loincloth on the right side. Once important in warfare and hunting, spears now are used only to kill buffalo in rituals. Crossbows (*sơna*), used to kill small game such as squirrels, porcupines, and groundhogs, are carved of hardwood. Poison extracted from bark of the *jar* tree is used on the bamboo arrows, and blood and fur of the first animal killed are put on the carved tip of the crossbow stock. Men also weave bamboo fish traps. One placed in the rushing water of a stream has a trip-spring that shuts the opening after the fish has entered. In a deviation from the general highland pattern, men help with foraging for food and a tree oil. Some men forge metals using bamboo bellows and plungers with rags. Smiths produce metal parts of farm tools, spearheads, metal combs, bracelets worn by men and women, and women's ankle bracelets. For pleasure, men fashion "singing kites" (*clêêng*) of bamboo and paper. A bow with a very thin reed is swung around to tune it in the Stieng six-note scale after which it is attached to the bottom of the kite. As the kite soars and dips, it "sings" incessantly. Haupers reports that male villagers make a woodwind instrument called *khôôm buôt* ("blow-joined") consisting of a gourd into which six varied lengths of bamboo are inserted and held with pitch (similar to Figure 10). The "gong horns" (*chênh kêy*) are a set of six buffalo horns hollowed out to give them when blown (only at night during the harvest season) notes equivalent to those of the set of six

10. Haupers, "Notes," pp. 147–48.

gongs. Every young boy makes a six-string banjo (*dênhdut*) entirely of bamboo and carves small wood tops (*pi blir*).

Bi explained that birthmarks or physical deformations are signs of *coon phaan* ("child of deceased"). A man in Bu Kroai, for example, has a short fourth toe on each foot, and because his grandfather had the same toe formation, the man is *coon phaan*, that is, identified with his grandfather's soul. If a small child dies, its arm is marked with charcoal, and should another child of the family be born with a similar birthmark, it is *coon phaan*.

Personal objects that play a role in childbirth take on new significance, and it is taboo to part with them. They include the small homemade knives, which fathers use to cut umbilical cords, and ivory ear plugs, which a woman rubs on her newborn daughter's body. It also is customary for a man to rub his pipe on the body of a newborn son while imploring the spirits' protection. A villager encountered in 1967 described how he had done this, first spitting on the side of his seasoned Rhadé pipe. Another villager related that when his wife was in labor he stuck his spear (about five feet long) in the ground so she could clutch it while giving birth. Now he must protect the spear, using it only for sacrificing animals in rituals.

The Stieng traditionally have one name, which does not have particular meaning. A child can be named after an ancestor even though names of deceased kin are avoided. Sometimes a parent dreams of a name, which is then given to the baby. There is a mild taboo against telling one's name to anyone. A third party is asked to provide that information. Often nicknames are bestowed on the basis of some physical trait. One boy in Bu Kroai has a chronic skin ailment, earning him the name "sick skin." During the 1950s the government required surnames for identification cards, so all Stieng were given the name, Điểu.

Infants are rarely left alone. Mothers nurse them, and older siblings care for and play with them. Late in the day, fathers carry their infants in a sling while they socialize with their friends. Relations between children and fathers appear to be easy. While I was chatting with Bluq (Household 3), his little daughter came running into the longhouse with some wildflowers, and, sidling up to him, she put one of them in his ear, saying, "Father has a flower in his ear." This evoked great peals of laughter from Bluq and the women and children present. One discussion with a father and his small children turned into a lesson (for Ralph Haupers and me as well) concerning the names of the fingers. The thumb is *mê ti* ("mother of the hand"), and the index finger is *lniep boh* ("finger that licks salt"). The middle finger is *dong clung* ("middle finger"), the fourth finger is *sar* (a term also used for a fallowing swidden), and the fifth finger is *teet* (also the name of a species of small parrot). An example of small boys learning male tasks took place in the longhouse of Yool (Household 5), who was sharpening his bush scythe using a worn stone and a bowl of water and sand. When he had finished, his grandson Doong, a boy of about ten, copied the same method to sharpen his small personal knife. When a child reaches puberty a common practice is to break the four front teeth (by peers for a boy and by an older brother for a girl) lacquering what is left. A rock or heavy stick is struck against a knife held in front of the teeth, breaking most of them unevenly. Several young Bu Kroai Stieng declared that "since we know the Vietnamese" it is no longer done. Some of the Haupers's assistants who had broken teeth purchased "gold" false teeth in Song Be shops.

Haupers reports that the Stieng divide people into "good people" (*joh*) and witches (*chaac*), who inflict sickness and death.[11] With the exception of death in battle, all violent deaths (*chhêt briêng*) are thought to be the work of witches. If a person is killed by a tiger, for example, everyone knows that it was raised by a witch who fed it rice. An auto accident results from a witch making the driver temporarily lose his sight. When a person falls ill, a witch is eating his liver or brain.

Between 23 June and 5 July 1967, Captain Andrew Cottingham, a member of the Walter Reed Army Institute of Research, treated villagers from Bu Kroai and the surrounding area, including Stieng from refugee settlements, recording the diseases he observed. Among the normal childhood illnesses he found were mumps and chicken pox. There also were viral fevers and diarrheal diseases as well as tuberculosis and plague. Fungus infections included tinea capitis, tinea corpus, tinea cruris, tinea pedis, tinea imbricata, tinea versicolor, otomycosis, and candidiasis. Malaria (plasmodium vivax and plasmodium falciparum) and filariasis (wuchereria bancrofti and brugria malayi) had already been noted. Cottingham found yaws and the venereal diseases, syphilis and lymphogramuloma venerum. Eye diseases included viral conjunctivitis, trachoma, abscess of the upper lid with orbital cellulitis, probably secondary to staphylococci infection (hordeolum), and interstitial keratitis secondary to congenital syphilis. Some Stieng showed symptoms of intestinal parasites, nutritional diseases (kwashiorkor, marasmus, nutritional edema, and vitamin deficiencies), leprosy, and warts (Molluscum contagiosum and Verruca vulgares).[12]

Haupers notes that one means of avoiding sickness is to wear an amulet consisting of small pieces of the sacred *gun* tuber fashioned into a

11. Ibid., pp. 150–52, 168.
12. Andrew Cottingham, "Diseases Observed in the Village of Bu Kroai, RVN, 23 June–5 July 1967," mimeograph, Walter Reed Army Institute of Research (Saigon, 1967), pp. 1–2.

Photo 11. Captain Andrew Cottingham, M.D., Ralph Haupers, and a Special Forces medic treating Stieng villagers (1967).

necklace.[13] When sickness does strike, the household head can kill a chicken and smear its blood on a spirit pole, which he then places outside the village gate. He chants a plea to the *bon brah,* which includes ancestors, and spirits of the forest, mountains, rivers, rock, and trees, asking that they take pity on him because a member of his family is sick and he promises a sacrificial offering if that person is healed. An alternative is to obtain the services of a male shaman (*chơndrông*) to perform the *prông* ritual. He first rubs the victim's body with homegrown cotton wet with his saliva, then holds the cotton behind a lit candle to determine what animal the spirits want as a sacrifice. After the animal is killed and roasted, a morsel from each part of its body along with rice and alcohol are placed on a tray and deposited outside the village gate. It is essential that each village family receives meat of the sacrificed animal.

Another course is to summon a "spirit woman" (*mê brah*), who orders the sacrifice of a chicken and dog before she performs the *mhom* ritual. On 22 June 1967 a "spirit woman," a married woman with children, was

13. Haupers, "Notes," pp. 168–70.

Photo 12. Stieng "spirit woman" shaman (1967).

encountered in the Son Trung II refugee camp near Mount Bara. About fifty-five years of age, she related (as she chewed a quid of areca and betel) that as a young girl she began to have headaches and one night awoke to find in her hand a "magic stone" (*tmau tlaar*), which she knew was a symbol of her "wedding with a husband spirit." She would hence-forth address the stone as if it were her husband. (When Ralph Haupers asked if she feared losing the stone, she replied, "How can you lose your husband?") This stone gave her the power to heal ailments "caused by the spirits," such as fevers, internal pains (but not diarrhea), and swell-ings. It is an individual gift that may be bestowed on a woman, but it cannot be passed on. Several men listening to her story volunteered the information that there were not many of these shamans, and she was the only one in the vicinity. She explained that the first step of her ritual healing is to determine which spirit is causing the ailment. She explained that it might be an evil spirit or perhaps that patient's own spirit. Or the sickness might be the work of a witch. Rubbing the stone on the affected part of the body, she goes into a trance to communicate with her patron spirit. She noted that in most cases the ailment is the result of the patient having offended a spirit by, for example, violating a "sacred place." She added that villagers all know the "spirits' places." The offended spirit lets it be known what propitiation it expects, usually a chicken, goat, pig, or even a buffalo. The sacrificial offering should take place where the offense occurred, but if that is inconvenient, it can take place anywhere. If a chicken is sacrificed, she receives half of it. For a large sacrifice such as a buffalo she is paid cash. When villagers gather with minor ailments, she heals by simply rubbing the stone on the affected part while invoking her patron spirit but does not make a sacrifice. The shaman explained that the stone is kept in hiding, brought out only for healing rituals. After her death the stone loses its significance and is thrown away.

Gerber observes that a long illness during which a patient of little means must sacrifice buffalo (or more than one) can result in falling into debt.[14] As the case of Kli in Household 7 indicates, this can lead to debt bondage. In writing about illness and death, Haupers observes that the consequences of a sickness can be even more dire. Occasionally a person who falls ill dreams that a fellow villager, a witch, is eating his liver. As a warning, the victim's family gives every household a notched piece of bamboo (*khaac*) to put by the hearth. A kinsman of the victim goes into the forest to drop molten lead on a round section of bamboo while calling the name of the accused. If the lead forms the shape of a buffalo horn, the accusation is made public and a trial by ordeal is needed. Seven layers of leaves are packed on the accused's hand, and a razor-sharp bush scythe is held next to the hand to keep it from moving. Molten lead is poured on the leaves, and if it drips to the ground to form the shape of a buffalo, the accused is guilty. If, however, the burns on the hand are only minor, he is innocent. In an alternate trial based on the belief that a witch cannot hold breath under water, the accused is submerged in a stream for a brief period. The guilty can be saved only if the shaman heals the sickness. In the past, the witch could be sold into slavery, have his fingers chopped off, or be tortured to death by afflicting on his body deep cuts into which chili peppers are rubbed. Haupers notes that in 1968 there were some villagers who had witnessed such trials even though they were forbidden by the government.[15]

Haupers relates that all of the deceased's kin gather at his sleeping platform to call out in a wail their exact relationship with him. This continues day and night while men fell a hardwood tree to fashion a coffin; one group carves the top half while another hews the bottom. Out of fear that food brought from the village might bring something of the illness associated with the death, each man prepares his own meals. The family sacrifices a buffalo or a pig, and the body is placed in the coffin (if death was caused by an accident, only close kin are willing to touch the corpse). As the coffin is sealed, mourners perform the *seen cǒmôôch*

14. Gerber, "Coutumier Stieng," pp. 229–30.
15. Haupers, "Notes," pp. 170–74.

ritual, each placing a morsel of meat, some rice, and a bit of tobacco on the coffin. At the grave some of the deceased's personal belongings (including his bush scythe and crossbow) are buried with the coffin. A woman's back-basket is burned and a man's favorite alcohol jar is smashed. A thatched shelter is built over the grave on which are piled the remaining possessions, notably those that are worn and shabby because in the next life everything is opposite so the deceased will have all new things (this also discourages stealing from the tomb). As mourners make their way back to the village they stop to bathe and wash their clothes (*ôm bôôc*) in the stream. At the longhouse the closest kinsman lights a fire in which the sleeping platform of the deceased is set and kept burning six days for a woman and seven for a man. A widow cuts her hair and smears ashes on her face; a widower and children cut the locks on their forehead. Next day, the closest kinsman places a finger-sized tube of rice and fish on the grave. On the sixth or seventh day, kin gather while a sealed bamboo tube is thrown on the fire to explode, after which a gourd of water is added to break and extinguish the fire, ending the funeral observances. The dead person is referred to only as "the deceased" (*cmôôch*). Bi explained that *ta moh phaan* ("naming the deceased") is the taboo against uttering the name of the dead. Should a close relative say the name, the departed spirit might mistakenly think that it is being invoked, which occurs only at weddings or funerals. Also, to say the name of a deceased person in front of his kin will make them sad. When such a reference is unavoidable, a relative of the deceased will utter a kin term, adding a modifier to indicate that he is dead. A nonkinsman can use a word that rhymes with the name of the deceased, a practice known either as *khoï phaan* ("avoid the spirit of the dead") or *chôôl kheet* ("to talk around").

Economic Activities

When searching for new swidden sites, farmers examine vegetation and soil, avoiding rocky places. A grasslike weed (*la siêt*) indicates fertility. Swiddens are named for the numerous streams and rivers that course through the Stieng country. Before clearing the site for a new swidden, the farmer performs the first part of the Pe Lnoong observance called finding the field. He clears a space about five square feet in the center of which he places a bamboo pole with the top split into four strips cut so that three touch the ground while one remains upright. On the upright strip he fixes *la siêt* weeds and invokes the spirits, notably *weeng ba,* spirit of unhusked rice. In her detailed description of farming rituals, Haupers reports that part of the prayer entreats: "I am trusting here. I want to

Photo 13. A Stieng woman working in a rice swidden (1967).

plant. Even if I should plant the hardwood tree, have it bear fruit. If I should plant a pestle used for husking rice, let it sprout." Out of fear that wild animals will invade the field if it is planted, the farmer avoids any contact with visitors for several days. He and his family await omens such as unfavorable dreams indicating whether the site is auspicious. If none occurs he returns to the field for the second part of the observance called the testing, in which he clears a ten-foot-square area while listening for signs, notably the cries of certain birds or the sound of a falling tree ("the sound of your coffin being made"). If none is forthcoming, the rest of the field is cleared for farming. The pattern is to farm field A and the following year to farm field A again but to clear and farm field B. For the third season, B and C are farmed, but if field A is adjudged to show signs of exhaustion it is left to fallow for fifteen to twenty years. Bi described how men do heavy work such as felling trees and the abundant bamboo that abounds in this area. Swiddens tend to be larger in the bamboo areas because it is easier to cut than felling trees. Wood is left to dry and is then gathered into piles, which are set ablaze. The soil is hoed, and as soon as the rains begin maize is planted (it matures in three months). Later, when the rains come daily, upland rain-fed rice (there are ten varieties) is planted in alternate rows. Men use dibble sticks to make holes ("women do not know how to do these things"). Women drop seeds from bamboo tubes, tamping down the soil with their feet.[16]

Haupers reports that just before rice buds appear the family observes the "Sprinkling of Rice" (Broh Ba) ceremony, which begins in the village with the sacrifice of a pig and a chicken. Chicken liver is impaled on a bamboo "spirit pole" (*cõnhjoh*) and blood from both animals is smeared on the pole's decorations. Meat from the sacrificial animal and rice from the top of the pot are taken to the original ritual clearing, where, next to the Rice Spirit House, a model of the granary, they are offered to the spirits. The meat and rice, along with betel, areca nuts, lime, and tobacco, are set in the Rice Spirit House. Taking a bamboo tube in which he has mixed some of the sacred *gun* tuber (grown by the field hut) with water, the farmer sprinkles it on four sides of the field and on the path while he calls upon the Rice Spirit to bring an abundant harvest. Putting the empty bamboo tube in the Rice Spirit House, he takes some of the meat and the spirit pole to the stream, where he invites the Water Spirit to partake of the offerings. At harvest, rice around the Rice Spirit House (the last gathered) is put in an old back-basket for storage in the granary as the "spirit's own rice." The Harvest Ceremony (Pu Ba Khiêu [*khiêu* is the basket tied to the waist at harvest]) is held immediately after the harvest at the smaller clearing, and no rice in the granary can be eaten until it is observed. The Rice-Spirit basket is removed, and a chicken and a pig are sacrificed. After smearing sacrificial blood on a newly made spirit pole, the farmer sticks it in the basket along with the pig's head and the chicken. Glutinous rice is steamed in a finger-thin bamboo tube, which is then cut every inch or so to make it flexible enough to wind around the top of the pole. Numerous food dishes and bowls of rice alcohol and water and a dish containing betel, areca, and lime are placed in the basket. The household head invokes the spirits, calling attention to the offerings while he asks them to bring prosperity, good fortune, and health. The celebration ends with feasting and drinking.

Haupers reports that to scare predatory birds and animals the farmer arranges bamboo clackers (*pooh*) attached to a system of rattan cord that can be jiggled from the field hut. In Bu Kroai the women thresh rice in large, flat, circular baskets using their feet, and winnowing is done by flipping a heart-shaped basket in the wind to separate rice from chaff. Haupers also points out that farmers in the Song Be area grow sesame in their swiddens for sale to Chinese merchants.

Where there is level land with a source of water some Stieng have arranged paddy fields. Mbing of Household 1 has a paddy field some two kilometers from Bu Kroai, but the government established a strategic

16. Ibid., pp. 155–56, 166–68.

hamlet there so he has not been able to farm it. His younger brother also has a wet-rice field near the Be River. Another kinsman who farms paddy (and has a small pepper and coffee estate) is Soon, a Stieng teacher and leader in Bu Dop, who has a primary school education and studied in Hue. When a field is cleared for wet-rice farming, the bamboo-pole ritual done for a new swidden is conducted to determine the auspiciousness of the site. Then there is the *tel lnôông* ritual breaking of a few chunks of earth. Mbing noted that because they did not own a plow, he and his brother used a buffalo to break the earth. Soon reported that at Bu Dop they germinate the seeds by soaking them in water and then leave them in the air. Seeds are broadcast in a seedbed, and when the fields are flooded, seedlings are transplanted.

Behind longhouses are gardens where the usual highland secondary crops are grown, in addition to peanuts, mint, and a long squash (*plai dien*), whose vine and leaves are a favorite year-round food. Foraging is done throughout the year, and though it is predominantly the occupation of women, girls, and boys, adult males sometimes participate. In lean times most edible plants are gathered, but when harvests have been abundant the less preferential wild foods are bypassed. Favorite dry-season foods are cashew fruit and nuts, which are soaked in water, boiled, and then roasted. Other favorites are the tops of rattan plants and kapok flowers. A variety of swamp vegetables and algae on river rocks are gathered. Rainy-season wild foods include bamboo shoots, mushrooms, squash, and manioc roots. Men also cut the bark of a certain type of hardwood tree and light a fire to extract the oil, which is sold to Vietnamese merchants (who sell it to boatmen).

Domestic animals include ducks (a variety that does not require much water), and the well-to-do have buffalo. Using crossbows or spears, men hunt throughout the year (Figure 14). Barking deer and mouse deer about one foot in height are favorite prey in the Mount Bara area. Other small game are wild boars, porcupines, squirrels, and civet cats. Snakes, including pythons, are hunted. In the more remote areas hunters stalk elephants, tigers, leopards, gaurs, and honey bears. The Stieng are skilled at producing drugs and poisons from roots, leaves, and bark. Informants contend that one of their deadliest poisons, which they smear at the base of the arrowhead, will kill a sizable tiger within minutes. Other preparations stun animals, which are then captured or killed.

Both men and women fish. Groups of women use woven bamboo scoops in shallow streams. Men place bamboo traps containing bait on streambeds. In periodic group fishing efforts men dam a stream, and all available villagers gather downstream from a point where men squeeze a milky substance from the root of a particular tree (*gle*) into the water. It kills small fish and stuns larger ones. Laughing and rushing about, men,

Figure 14. A Stieng firing a crossbow.

women, and children with baskets hurriedly gather up the catch, which is shared by all.

The Vietnam War

By the early 1960s, Vietnamese leaving the Land Development Centers (established in the late 1950s) when Communist insurgency threatened them began encroaching on traditional Stieng village territories, thereby precipitating disputes. At the same time, along the Cambodian border, Viet Cong insurgents (including Stieng who had gone north in 1954) went into Stieng villages to recruit, demand food, and engage in propaganda. A favorite technique was to sing propagandist songs, one of which urged the villagers to make bamboo stakes to place in paths and to dig traps (as the Stieng had done to harass the French in the 1930s). One song, translated from Vietnamese by Neil Jamieson, went:

> Comrade Stieng, strive to strike the invaders
> As we catch spies, we smash, we strike!
> We diligently make stakes, make traps,
> Dig trenches, dig ditches
> Everyone, from old men to young children.[17]

17. Gerald Cannon Hickey, *Free in the Forest: Ethnohistory of the Vietnamese Central*

In November 1963, the U.S. Special Forces opened a camp at Bu Dop amid rubber plantations northwest of Song Be, where the French had established a military post in 1913.[18] Its militia consisted entirely of Stieng men recruited from villages in the area. The government ordered ten Stieng villages near Bu Dop to relocate into a large "strategic hamlet," which necessitated changes not to the villagers' liking. Some recalled in 1967 that in the new settlement they missed their traditional Stieng longhouses and being near kin and friends. Many cleared new fields, but most went back to their old fields. Because they could not go back and forth to the fields every day and the government would not permit them to stay in the fields at night, a good deal of the crops were lost to predators. They did note that one advantage in making the move was that the Viet Cong could not come to take their rice and chickens. In February 1966, the headman of Bu Ghir, fifteen kilometers to the north of Bu Kroai, led a group of men, women, and boys to Song Be in a quest for rice. He explained that he had taken refuge in Bu Ghir in 1965 after the Viet Cong had captured him and other villagers. During the two months they were held, they were given a cup of rice every day and often were kept in stocks at night. Finally, dislike of the Viet Cong prompted him and over a thousand others to move to Bu Ghir, leaving behind everything, including buffalo. A refugee encountered in Bu Kroai in May 1967 declared that he was from a village a half-day's walk from Bu Kroai, but after the Viet Cong burned it four times he and his family fled.

In June 1967, Stieng in one section of the Son Trung II refugee village near Song Be related that they were forced to relocate in 1965. They were told they could take their rice with them, and it was duly placed on American chinook helicopters, but when the villagers arrived they found that it had been given to other refugees. Although they were promised assistance, they received no housing, food, or clothing from the government. Some cleared swiddens but had no rice seed. Vietnamese refugees from Land Development Centers, however, were given good houses, food, and clothing, and their villages became showplaces for visitors. Son Trung II village was finally built in February 1967, and when a Japanese relief agency brought clothing, representatives of the press were there, making a great fuss as if the Stieng had just arrived. Because of a land shortage caused by the influx of refugees, farmers resorted to clearing fallowing fields, but harvests were meager. In desperation, some women returned to farm near their old villages, where they had to attend the

Highlands, 1954–1976 (New Haven: Yale University Press, 1982); material on the Stieng in the Vietnam War in this work can be found on pp. 120, 167, 234, 249–50, 270–71.

18. Francis J. Kelly, *U.S. Army Special Forces, 1961–1971* (Washington, D.C.: U.S. Department of the Army, 1973), pp. 71, 187.

Communists' indoctrination sessions (if men returned they would be pressed into service by the Communists), but they lived in constant fear of being shelled by government forces.

By March 1967, Vietnamese refugees moving into the Song Be area had taken so much of the swidden areas in the territory of Bu Kroai that the villagers were forced to farm on the slopes of Mount Bara. Yool (head of Household 5) complained that their traditional farm implements were breaking because of the rocky condition of the slopes. In the Song Be area refugees began to experience chronic food shortages and lower living standards. To cope, some Stieng began to vend tobacco, rice, dried fish, and alcohol in their villages, an activity once done exclusively by Vietnamese. At the same time, cash became more commonly used by villagers, not only for purchases but also for borrowing and paying debts.

As the more remote areas became insecure and inaccessible, good wood for artifacts and ivory and boar tusks for women's ear plugs became scarce. Men in the refugee camps were producing imitation versions of their traditional crossbows, which they carried to Ralph Haupers, who in turn had them sent to be sold in the large military exchange in Saigon. Haupers thereby provided a reasonably steady cash income badly needed by the refugees. By this time it was common for them to spend almost every night in bunkers near every longhouse. During the Bu Kroai survey, for example, as Bu Kroai villagers lined up to be tested for malaria and filariasis, a firefight broke out near the village, sending the entire sample to the bunkers.

On the lighter side, Haupers describes how as the sights and sounds of war came closer to the Song Be area, children began to make toys imitating the real things they saw all around. Taking the center blade of a banana leaf, they cut a series of slits which they could bend. Running the forefinger along the slits produced a "tat-a-tat-tat" sound reminiscent of the M-16 automatic rifles. After seeing paratroopers practicing jumps nearby, village boys skillfully made their own parachutes with bits of cloth and string.[19]

When in July 1967 Ralph Haupers received the first primers in the Stieng language, a large group gathered in a Bu Kroai longhouse. Haupers explained what the primer was, noting that he had devised an orthography using Vietnamese-type diacritical marks for vowel shadings. Because Soon, a leader from Bu Ghir, read Vietnamese, he was able to read the Stieng in the primer. As he did, a hush fell on the group, and then there was a collective sigh of wonder at the realization that their language was in print. One elderly woman remarked, "Now we have a written language like the Vietnamese!" Another leader was Huynh, a

19. Haupers, "Notes," pp. 152–54, 156.

Stieng pastor living in An Loc, who spoke Vietnamese and some English. For two years he had studied theology at an institute in Nhatrang and had represented the Stieng at meetings in Saigon. As a result, he had become acquainted with leaders from other highland groups such as Nay Luett, and unlike other Stieng, he was aware of the FULRO movement.

The year 1967 brought new violence to the highlands in the form of nocturnal attacks on villages by the North Vietnamese army forces. One of the worst bloodbaths of the Vietnam War took place on 5 December at Dak Son, a Stieng refugee camp near Song Be. According to Ralph Haupers, the Communists had been sending warning notes to the camp, ordering the villagers to join them in the forest on the Cambodian side of the border with the threat of "punishment" if they did not adhere. Undoubtedly the Stieng were to be used to carry arms and supplies through the area. Few villagers obeyed, so the North Vietnamese assaulted the camp. The Stieng men rallied to the defense with spears, crossbows, and a few rifles while the women and children hurried to the bunkers. The Stieng were no match for the Communists with their Russian weapons. Once inside, the Communists attacked the bunkers with grenades and flamethrowers. Over two hundred of the Stieng were murdered. Haupers visited the village the following day to find charred bodies of adults, children, and tiny infants in the scorched earth of the bunkers. Their metal wrist and ankle decorations were melted into grotesque shapes. Survivors, most of them wounded and burned, picked through the ruins and ashes in the hope of finding some of their missing family members still alive.

On 6 April 1972, North Vietnamese army units captured Loc Ninh and threatened An Loc, both on the western fringes of the Stieng country. Many Stieng refugees were caught in the fighting, and large numbers of them sought refuge in An Loc. The town was surrounded by Communist forces, who subjected it to constant shelling, attacking it several times with Russian tanks. Huynh, the Stieng pastor, described how he and his kinfolk huddled in bunkers during the two-month siege, going out only to try to get some of the food being air-dropped from American aircraft. The stench of decaying corpses lay heavy over the town, which daily was being reduced to rubble. Huynh said sadly that many of his relatives died in the stricken town. Early in June word spread through the town that Route 13 was open. Around ten thousand desperate Vietnamese and Stieng, caked with red dirt, emerged from their bunkers and, making their way through rubble and burned vehicles, moved in a mass down the road. There were among them elderly people, women with small children and babies, and boys and girls whose parents had been killed carrying younger siblings. Ignoring the fighting and attempts by the Communist troops to stop them, they pushed on to Phu Cuong, where

Photo 14. Stieng and Vietnamese fleeing besieged An Loc (1972). (Photograph courtesy of AP/Wide World Photos.)

there were refugee centers. On 5 June 1972 a large group of Stieng refugees appeared in central Saigon, clutching their bush scythes as they made their way to the Ministry for Ethnic Minorities' Development to seek food and shelter. They had walked from the vicinity of An Loc, avoiding embattled Route 13, and were the first highland refugees to enter the capital. Haupers reports that in 1973, some ten thousand Stieng were resettled in Lam Dong province east of their traditional territory.[20] On 6 January 1975, after a week-long siege, Song Be fell to the Communist forces, the first provincial capital to fall in the final campaign of the Vietnam War.

20. Ibid., p. 143.

Chapter 4
Katu

The Katu live in one of the harshest and least hospitable physical environments of the central highlands. In his 1938 article on the Katu, J. Le Pichon describes the relief of their country as being "very broken, a confusion of mountains." It is a place where rivers (often rendered unnavigable by boulders and rocks in their beds) rush through tortuous valleys cut by innumerable streams with rapids and waterfalls. The mountains are covered with thick, somber forests in which open patches reveal the sites of swidden farming. At lower elevations there is a profusion of tropical growth where liana vines interlace with branches to form impenetrable barriers to passage. Here and there, hardy bamboo dominates, its dead stalks cover the ground, cracking underfoot, while overhead foliage finely filters sunlight. Le Pichon observes that "Katu paths, slippery and filled with leeches, push ahead, plunging and replunging into rivers, scaling the steep mountain slopes (the Katu do not ask 'where are you going?', but rather, 'where are you going up to?'). At dawn the cries of monkeys mix with songs of peacocks and chatter of blackbirds. Then in the torpor of noon all is quiet. But as darkness descends one can hear crickets, night birds, the belling of deer, and rustling of thousands of insects, a signal that the hunting hour of the tiger, lord of the forest, is at hand."[1]

In this environment the Katu are very close to nature and reliant on cosmic forces for survival. Fertility for the Katu is a constant concern, and potency is demonstrated not only in wealth, rituals, and feasting, but also in conducting raids to obtain human blood to offer the spirits. Any adult male can conduct such raids, an egalitarian feature added to other

1. J. Le Pichon, "Les chasseurs de sang," *Bulletin des Amis du Vieux Hué* 25, no. 4 (1938): 362.

characteristics of the "democratic" society described by Kirsch.[2] There are no village boundaries, and the household rather than the patrilineage is the most important social, religious, and economic unit. Beyond the household, kindreds diffuse patrilineal ties by extending nonpatrilineal social relationships even to neighboring ethnic groups. Males participate equally in functions at the men's house, and bride-prices are adjusted to family means. But at the same time, successful raids for human blood combine with wealth to lend certain individuals a potency identified by their stylized way of speaking.

There is much to suggest that existence has been relatively precarious for the Katu. They must avoid the deep, steamy valleys with their tropical growth and build their villages on higher slopes, but farming there is arduous and all too often unrewarding. All of the Katu informants noted that their main swiddens are a long walk from the village. Also, lack of sufficient arable soil often forces relocation of villages every decade. Seasonal food shortages are not uncommon, and Katu legend tells of a time in the golden past when they were "well and fat" and not "skinny" as now. Game must be shared with fellow villagers, and at ritual animal sacrifices all of the community partakes in the feasting. Frequent food exchanges are prescribed not only for close kin but also for members of the far-flung kindred networks. In addition to the constant struggle to sustain, the Katu face almost daily physical peril in surroundings fraught with danger, even death. Le Pichon sees that danger as the basis for the Katu obsession with a "good death," that is, one caused by old age or sickness leading to a blissful afterlife. The opposite is a "bad death" resulting from attacks by wild animals, accidents, or other "unnatural causes," which condemn the deceased to an existence as an errant malevolent spirit (and force relocation of his village). "It is impossible," he writes, "to understand Katu life without grasping the important role that death plays. Death is the great spirit that prowls the forest. It lurks most often at the bottom of the precipices, leaving there from time to time on the wings of the wind to roam the villages. Death is an unreal thing that assumes unexpected forms. It is a tiger lying silently in wait as night falls for the Katu coming from the fields, or it may be a cobra rising to hiss in the sultry noon. It is in a mad torrent whose waters sweep away the unwary. Yes, death stalks everywhere." Despite all of these perils, Le Pichon found the Katu to be "vain and boastful, but hospitable and generous."[3]

There are indications that the Katu ethnic label and identity as an

2. A. Thomas Kirsch, *Feasting and Social Oscillation: Religion and Society in Upland Southeast Asia,* Department of Asian Studies, Cornell University, Southeast Asia Program Data Paper no. 92 (Ithaca, N.Y., 1973), pp. 24–25.

3. Le Pichon, "Les chasseurs," pp. 379, 385.

ethnic group are of relatively recent origin. Historically the Vietnamese knew the upland population of Quang Nam province simply as *mọi* ("slave" or "savage"), the generic designation for highland people. Vietnamese in coastal settlements greatly feared the upland people because of their frequent raids on villages, less to pillage than to kill and obtain human blood for their ritual sacrifices. During the reigns of Minh Mang (1820–41) and Thieu Tri (1841–47) the "blood raids" were so numerous that the royal court was prompted to organize ceremonial presentations of buffalo and other gifts to tribal chiefs in the vain hope of ending the raids. Many Vietnamese also thought of the highland people as being less than human. French visitors to Annam in the late nineteenth and early twentieth centuries were told of "savages with tails" living in upland Quang Nam. In 1928, Dr. Gaide, a French military physician posted in Annam, reported that articles in the 1896 issues of the *Revue Scientifique* and the *Bulletin de la Société de Géographie* in Paris claimed that Vietnamese had captured a *mọi* with a tail-like appendage at the base of his spine. During his stay in the 1920s, Dr. Gaide was often told by Vietnamese mandarins, doctors, and civil servants that they had heard stories about men in the Quang Nam mountains who had tails resembling those of monkeys.[4]

During the pre-French colonial period the only Vietnamese who had contact with the upland people of Quang Nam were the traders (*các lái* or *lái buôn*), woodcutters, and those in search of precious oils.[5] During the reign of Gia Long (1800–1820), traders based themselves at Ben Hien on the Con River and at Ben Giang on the Cai River, where they traded salt, blankets, iron spearheads, pottery, and jewelry for fruit, betel leaves, and medicinal plants brought to the market by highland people. Traders also served as intermediaries between upland chiefs and coastal Vietnamese mandarins, levying a tax on goods exchanged and remitting part of it to the mandarins. Despite their familiarity with the highlanders, it was not unusual for traders to fall victim to blood raids.

The first Frenchman to penetrate the Quang Nam highlands was Captain Debay of the Infanterie de la Marine, who in 1901 was commissioned by Governor General Doumer to conduct a survey of the region in search of a site for a hill station and sanitarium to serve the French living in central Vietnam. In his report, Debay described the highlanders as "industrious" but given to raiding. To launch an effort at bringing the region under colonial control and to put an end to blood raids, the French

---

4. Dr. Gaide, "Les hommes à queue," *Bulletin des Amis du Vieux Hué* 15, no. 1 (1928): 107–19.

5. Le Pichon, "Les chasseurs," pp. 359–67, 397; Gerald Cannon Hickey, *Sons of the Mountains: Ethnohistory of the Vietnamese Central Highlands to 1954* (New Haven: Yale University Press, 1982), pp. 11–12, 278, 329–30.

in 1904 established a Garde Indigène post at An Diem on the Con River east of the Ben Hien trading post. In 1913, Sogny, commandant of the post, conducted a survey, reporting a population of about ten thousand in 250 villages. He concluded that the population was "one race" with its own dialect, and he gave it the name "Ka-tu." Subsequently the label Katu appeared in French sources and on ethnolinguistic maps.

By 1935, plans for construction of Colonial Route 14 linking Kontum and Tourane (Danang) called for construction through the Katu country. Their bellicose reputation raised concerns about the safety of the workers so it was decided to open another Garde Indigène post at Ben Giang, where Route 14 would pass through the valley at the confluence of the Cai and Giang rivers. At the beginning of 1937, the Katu launched a series of blood raids on Vietnamese villages near An Diem, prompting the French to close that post and open a new one at Ben Hien farther west in the troubled zone. The commander of the new post was Le Pichon, and he set out to visit the Katu villages as far west as the Laotian border to gather information and to gain cooperation of the Vietnamese traders who still visited these villages. Le Pichon found that in each village the residents identified themselves as the "people" of that village. Knowing that "katu" in their language meant "savage," he inquired, "Do you know the katu?" and was not surprised when they invariably responded that the "katu" lived farther up in the mountains. Receiving this answer all the way to the Laotian border, Le Pichon observed with amusement that "I could not but conclude that there were no savages in the entire region." He did find to his satisfaction that the Katu (he continued to use this label) comprised one large ethnic group with a population of around twenty-five thousand. In noting some variations among them, he found in the vicinity of A-Ro a pocket of Lao-influenced villagers better fed and more sedentary than other Katu. In contrast, Le Pichon also learned of another band of Katu who at some time in the past had retreated (probably, he surmised, because of intervillage conflicts and blood raids) to the inaccessible higher elevations, where, like "true savage beasts," they dressed themselves in animal skins, lived in rude shelters, and survived by hunting, fishing, and foraging.

In a 1972 interview, Kithem, a Katu leader in Saigon for an Ethnic Minorities Council meeting, described his experiences with the Vietnamese and French. He had been born around 1915 in Pi Karong village. He recalled how periodically a French administrator from Kontum would arrive on horseback with an escort of Bahnar, Jeh, and Sedang militiamen. The French needed a Katu chief who could speak Vietnamese to deal with the inhabitants of some twenty Katu villages, so they selected Kithem's mother's father. After he died, Kithem's father's brother assumed the role, and he was succeeded by the mother's brother. When

Kithem was a young man the French pressed him and other Katu into service with the Garde Indigène, but en route to Faifoo (Hoi An) for training, "many ran away." After serving nine years, he returned to his village, where he functioned as an interpreter for the French. On the death of his maternal uncle, Kithem was named chief of the area from Ben Hien west to the Laotian border and north to Thua Thien province. One primary responsibility was to muster corvée labor (fifteen days a year), mostly for construction of Route 14 through the Katu country. He also arbitrated conflicts that could not be resolved at family and village levels. "Not to stab the Vietnamese, not to stab the Katu," was the expression he used to explain his role in heading off trouble between Katu and Vietnamese, notably in marketplace dealings in which the Katu exchanged chickens, rice, ducks, honey, betel leaves, and areca nuts for salt, metal, axes, woven mats, cloth, and alcohol jars. When in 1945 the Japanese came to the Katu country, they too used the villagers as laborers. The Japanese also had Katu guide them into the mountains, where they conducted some unspecified research. After the Japanese left, the Viet Minh arrived and "talked against the French," but when the French returned, the Viet Minh fled into the bush. "Later," Kithem added reflectively, "the Viet Minh became the Viet Cong."

In August 1957 I made a field trip into Katu country with Reverend Gordon Smith, an American missionary, and Philip Hodgeson of the British Embassy. Having already visited the area, Reverend Smith knew that blood raids normally do not take place in August, a time when villagers experienced food shortages. So he arranged with the priest in charge of the Catholic Relief Services in Danang to obtain rice, which would be accompanied by a Vietnamese nurse in a larger boat. At Hoi An we boarded sampans which hardy Vietnamese women rowed against the current to move upstream in the Thu Bon River. Three days later we reached Thanh My on the Cai River, the last Vietnamese settlement where Katu gathered to trade. From among them we secured bearers to carry our gear and food, and Reverend Smith also retained the services of a Vietnamese wood vendor who spoke Katu. The brush on either side of the winding path was an impenetrable tangle of jungle growth, which here and there gave way to patches of tall elephant grass. After the sun rose, the heat became stifling. On the path we met a file of Katu women with open-weave back-baskets (*jong*), followed by men in loincloths. Farther along we encountered a young couple. She had a back-basket, while he had a man's pack (*talek*) with compartments for a knife, a pipe, some tobacco, and a quiver of arrows for the crossbow he held.

Walking the better part of the day, we approached the village of A-To, surrounded by a high stockade. The gate was closed, and along the path were freshly made bamboo symbols, raising the question of whether they were taboo signs. The wood vendor went to the gate, where a young man informed him that the village was indeed taboo (*diang*). The vendor then talked to the headman, who relented, saying that we could enter the village and go directly to the men's house for a very short time marked by passage of the sun. The village was strangely still, doors were closed, and we could see eyes peering at us through cracks in the bamboo walls. In the semidarkness of the men's house with its smell of smoke and walls covered with heads of buffalo that had been sacrificed, the headman sat on a mat. Around him was a group of long-haired young men garbed in very brief loincloths and clutching long hardwood spears with sharp blades that are used in blood raids. Talking through the wood vendor, the chief expressed dissatisfaction at having "Frenchmen" in the village, saying that the "Viet Minh" would not like it. He noted that there were Viet Minh in the forest, adding that his brother, who had "gone north," was now with them. When the headman mentioned a food shortage, Reverend Smith said that if his men went to Thanh My they could get some rice from the boat. The chief, however, shook his head. "The Viet Minh would be angry if we took food from the French."

Leaving A-To, we walked to the neighboring village of O-Mo, which had a small men's house but no stockade. Its longhouses (somewhat ramshackle compared with those in A-To) were arranged around a sacrificial stake. Smoking his long pipe, the headman welcomed us and explained that survivors of epidemics that had ravaged two villages had banded together to found O-Mo. They were now plagued with more sickness and a shortage of food. We slept in the main room of the chief's house (and the first night were attacked by an army of black ants lured by our supply of food). When the relief boat arrived at Thanh My, men from the village carried bags of rice to each longhouse. The nurse from the mission was kept busy tending the sick. In talking with the Katu at Thanh My and O-Mo, Reverend Smith and I found (as did Le Pichon) that people identified themselves by the village from which they came. The "katu" were those people living farther up in the remote mountains. Nancy Costello of the SIL, who conducted research on the Katu language, identifies two subgroups—High Katu and Low Katu—that vary not only linguistically but socially as well. The former are located at higher elevations while the latter are found in the lower area adjacent to the coastal plain.[6] In their classification of highland languages, Thomas and Headley have a Katuic branch that includes Bru, Pacoh, Katu, Kantu (High Katu), and Phuang.[7] In 1967 the Katu were estimated to

6. Nancy Costello, "Socially Approved Homicide Among the Katu," *SA* 2, no. 1 (1972): 77–78, 87.

7. David Thomas and R. K. Headley, Jr., "More on Mon-Khmer Subgroupings," *Lingua* 25, no. 4 (1970): 398–418.

Photo 15. Katu women of O-Mo village (1957).

number around 40,000, and the 1989 Vietnamese population census reports 36,967 "Co-tu" (see Appendix A).

Religion

According to Costello, the Katu believe that there is one supreme deity, master of all other deities, whose name cannot be spoken, so he is referred to variously as Manuih Pleng ("Sky Being"), Malai, or Patar.[8] Although they say that they "do not know much about him" and "cannot talk about him," the Katu reveal that by and large he is favorable toward human beings even though he once used his power over the elements to inflict a catastrophic flood. He created the world, visiting it to determine where banana and other trees would grow. He influences the Katu search for "good ground" on which to locate villages, and he controls sickness and death. Before every meal the Katu scatter a bit of uncooked rice on the ground while imploring this deity for health, good crops, and a "full belly."

The Sky Being's son, Bulô Bule, lives somewhere between earth and sky, and he had a wife and children who perished in the great flood. It is

8. Nancy Costello, "The Katu Tribal People of Quang Nam, South Vietnam," mimeograph, n.d., pp. 1–5.

imperative to honor him with ritual offerings because he acts as intermediary between the Sky Being and humans, "sending rain" and bestow-
ing good upon those he favors while those out of favor suffer hunger and
sickness. Evil spirits fear Bulô Bule, who has power to give them human
souls, but he also can retrieve souls they have captured. Katu legend also
tells of the Sky Being's two daughters, Maaih and her younger sister,
Achal, both of whom had long hair. On earth, two brothers, Tau and his
younger brother Ong, became discontent with mortal girls so they went
to the sky and sought the two sisters in marriage. After they wed, the four
went to earth, where the girls worked in the rice fields like mortals, but
they kept a rope enabling them to return to the sky and visit their
parents. On earth the girls became unkempt and ate feces so Tau abandoned his wife to wed a Katu girl. In the heat of anger the two sisters
killed him, but when they saw his rotting corpse, Maaih raised him to life.
The two couples then fled back to the sky, where they have remained.

Another deity, I Yaang, "came from the sky" garbed in a green loincloth and mantle, carrying a spear, crossbow, and dagger, all colored
green. He carries messages from the Sky Being, and it is he who outlined all the taboos the Katu must observe. A particularly fearsome deity
is Sayiing Krung, described as having an enormous stomach and gro-
tesquely matted body hair. Among other things, he tries to steal the
bodies of the newly dead, so corpses must be carefully guarded while
awaiting burial.

Abuĭ are spirits associated with all aspects of nature (including rice
and maize crops) and with houses as well. When in a benevolent mood
they bestow abundant crops and heal the sick, but when malevolent they
force people to do harm, destroy crops, cause ailments, and inflict "bad
deaths." Chills result from the *abuĭ* dunking the victim's soul in cold
water, and roasting a soul over a fire leads to profuse sweating. An *abuĭ*
can enter someone's stomach, causing abdominal pains, and it can drive
out the person's soul, bringing on madness. Swelling, headache, and
giddiness are signs that a spirit has forced water into the body, struck the
head, or shoved the victim. Aching extremities indicate that an *abuĭ* has
bound the hands and feet. The Katu avoid places in the forest believed to
be the abode of *abuĭ,* and for the same reason, certain trees cannot be
felled. One should stay away from grave sites lest an *abuĭ* living in the
earth bite the intruder. A dream about a stranger is a sign that an angry
abuĭ is present.

Costello reports that certain individuals and some animals have the
inherent power to inflict minor ailments such as sores and temporary
nausea simply by having physical contact with someone. To counteract
this power, the victim must take some hair from the person or animal
with whom he had contact and place it on his own head. High Katu

informants say that the Low Katu have this power, and it is one reason they avoid lower elevations. Low Katu, however, claim that the High Katu can impose hexes (*pagun*). A hex, for example, can be put on one of the low, carved-wood stools found in Katu houses, and anyone who sits on it will die. Another hex causes the victim to become antisocial and suffer excessive weeping and loss of appetite. The Low Katu also contend that at night High Katu sneak up on their villages to blow air at passersby, killing them.

If villagers hear a female (usually one with children) talking to herself in a strange manner, she is said to be conversing with spirits. If in her speech she uses many rhyming words, she is adjudged to be an *abô,* a shaman who derives her gift of healing from spirits, notably the powerful Sappong Pleng. There is one for about every five villages, and although the role of shaman is not a desirable one, a woman must nonetheless follow her calling. She cannot consume the flesh of chickens or pigs because they eat feces. If someone sneezes near her, it puts her in danger of death. Should she fall ill, one of her children or a younger sibling must rub her body with bird blood, and during her sickness it is taboo to sacrifice buffalo in the village. While attending a funeral the shaman cannot drink from alcohol jars because those who touched the corpse washed their hands in the same stream from which water added to the jar was drawn.

Responding to a call from a family struck by illness, the shaman goes to the longhouse, where all of the fires have been extinguished. Left alone with the patient, she holds a bowl of rice to her head and then to her mouth while she chants the names of spirits (such as spirits of treetops, animal traps, and snake markings). The shaman may, for example, determine that a pig spirit has been trying to "eat the soul" of the patient, so she will recommend a pig sacrifice. After the pig has been killed, the shaman takes a tuft of its hair, scorches it, and places it on the patient, chanting, "return soul, return and stay in a good person." If a buffalo sacrifice is in order, all villagers participate, dressed in their best clothes. For the women this means an ankle-length skirt (everyday skirts reach just below the knees) of Lao textile enhanced with silver thread. Men wear multicolored loincloths with mantles draped about the shoulders. The buffalo is tied to a decorated stake, and while drums and gongs play, the shaman dances. It is imperative that the patient dance, even if he is so weak he must be propped up by kinsmen. As all of the villagers join in the dance, the movement and sounds agitate the buffalo, which is speared by the closest kinsman. The patient is carried on the back of a relative who assists him in making a ritual thrust of the spear into the animal. Dipping a large leaf in the blood, the shaman smears some on the sacrificial stake, on herself, and then on members of the patient's family.

The patient's brother rubs (the prescribed movement is from left to right) blood on the patient's forehead and chest. The Katu say that with these actions "the spirits eat the blood." While the family prepares a large feast, the buffalo is dressed out, and parts are presented to the guests. For six days following the sacrifice the patient's longhouse is taboo. In another healing ritual the shaman rubs the body of the ailing person with sand while asking the water spirit to stroke and heal the body. She also may pat the body with *achong* leaves, which are used in preparing a medicine, or mix a potion obtained from the spirits, enabling a client to see his dead kin.

Chicken-foot divination is used when sickness strikes, during marriage rituals, and in deciding whether to organize a blood raid. The foot contains four claws. The outer one, resembling a thumb, represents the person whose destiny is involved. The second claw is Bulô Bule, son of the Sky Being, while the third is the Sky Being, and the fourth is the *abúi*. When the foot is severed, if the Bulô Bule and *abúi* claws come together it indicates the deities' disfavor. If all remain apart it is a favorable sign.

Costello notes that there are individuals who have power (*gun*) to protect others from malevolent spirits, and for doing so they charge a fee. Such an individual can protect a child by rubbing certain leaves on its head or by giving it a necklace of delicate shells containing *koq,* small worms that spirits fear. Tatooing around the nose, mouth, and wrists certain motifs such as a snake's head affords protection against evil spirits (who fear serpents). Katu tatoo motifs described by Le Pichon include two sunbursts at the lips, a series of dots over the eyebrows and extending to the ears, and a "dancing lady" (*pâdil yayah*) on the forehead. Louis Bezacier, however, questions Le Pichon's interpretation of this motif as representing a dancing lady, suggesting instead that it might be a symbolic depiction of the soul.[9]

Human Blood Sacrifices

There are two types of human blood sacrifices among the Katu. One involves the slaughter of a victim, whose blood is ritually offered to the spirits. The other entails the offering of blood from a live victim, who afterward is slain. Both include blood hunts carried out by raiding parties, and in some cases the head of the victim is removed and taken back to the raiders' village, where it is kept in a special hut. Motivation for blood raids is mixed. Le Pichon, Costello, and Katu informants all agree

9. Le Pichon, "Les chasseurs," pp. 365–66; Louis Bezacier, "Interpretation du tatouage frontal des Moi 'Ka-Tu,' " *IIEH* 25, no. 2 (1942): 117–25.

that appeasing the spirits with human blood is a primary goal. Then, too, the raids offer an opportunity to display personal bravery and potency. Costello notes that "a person who has killed is considered clever and powerful," and she adds that "a village which has suffered loss of life at the hands of outsiders, while claiming the raiding party did wrong to kill, will also say that the killers were nonetheless brave." When a man who has claimed many victims dies, his kin organize a raid for blood to offer his soul. Le Pichon quotes the lyrics of a popular Katu song that goes, "My husband is strongest of all, his spear has killed more men than there are hairs on my head." Costello notes that a victim village will more than likely organize a revenge blood raid, and Le Pichon echoes this, citing the Katu saying, "blood calls for blood."[10]

Le Pichon notes in his description of a blood raid that the need to appease the spirits is prompted by such events as a bad death in the village, death of a shaman, or a poor harvest. Adult males gather in the men's house to decide whether a blood raid is called for. After they drink from the jars while invoking the ancestors, the eldest man performs a chicken-foot divination to determine the will of the spirits. Outside, children circumambulate the sacrificial stake, beating drums and crying aloud to the souls of the dead. If the spirits favor a raid, the men select a victim. Should they identify a particular individual, a second chicken-foot divination is held, but this time it is performed by a man empowered to communicate with spirits. He may, for example, recommend that the raiding party walk in the direction of the rising sun for two days, and on the third morning they will find the blood they seek.[11]

After talking, drinking, and singing all night, the blood-hunt party leaves at dawn. Wearing blue mantles over their shoulders, they clutch spears with sharpened blades and crossbows with arrows smeared with a poison Le Pichon describes as a kind of "curare derived from the strych-onose tree." Full of swagger, they march all day, avoiding the beaten path, slashing their way through the brush to cross the mountain. Le Pichon notes that the Katu never attack directly, preferring to lay an ambush at nightfall by hiding in foliage near a trail used by their intended victims. Whoever comes along the path is felled by a poisoned arrow, and the raiders quickly emerge to spear the victim. Blood must flow profusely to satisfy the spirits so each member of the party spears the fallen victim. "Happy is he whose spear is rusted with human blood," Le Pichon observes.[12] Go, the headman of Bo Lo village, described to Le Pichon how he soaked his hands in human blood and smeared it on his face.

10. Costello, "Socially Approved Homicide," pp. 77–78; Le Pichon, "Les chasseurs," pp. 391–92.
11. Le Pichon, "Les chasseurs," pp. 391–94.
12. Ibid., pp. 392–94.

Leaving the body on the path, the party returns to its village, where for several nights as gongs and drums play, everyone feasts and drinks while the men boast of their exploits and chant descriptions of their deeds to the ancestors. Should the victim be from a village known for its fierce warriors, fear of vengeance will more than likely cut short celebrations as preparations are made for a possible revenge blood raid. Men dig traps and fix stakes of sharpened bamboo along the paths. Bamboo tubes of poisoned water are set in the huts by the swiddens to lure the unwary thirsty attackers. Lookouts are positioned in trees. If the villagers feel that they cannot withstand an attack, they bury gongs and jars before fleeing into the forest.

In October 1969, Kmeet related that two specific spirits associated with human blood sacrifices are the Dog-Stone Spirit and the Black Cobra Spirit. A person walking in the woods who hears a dog barking should look for a white stone that bears the likeness of a dog. Such stones, manifestations of the Dog-Stone Spirit, are believed to have fallen from the sky. The finder has the option of leaving the stone in place or taking it home after declaring that he will follow the spirit. If one should encounter a black cobra he should club it to death and bury its head. If a plant grows on that spot, the person must decide whether to follow the Black Cobra Spirit manifest in the plant. Anyone who elects to follow either spirit will be rewarded with success in farming, hunting, and fishing. But the time will come when the spirit will let it be known that it craves the human blood of a speared victim. Barking of a dog at night brings the message of the Dog-Stone Spirit, and the Black Cobra Spirit relays its will through the "snake plant." If the follower does not provide human blood, the consequences can be grave. "The dog will bite," said Kmeet, explaining that the bond with the spirit is irrevocable and is passed on to succeeding generations through the male line. He cited as an example two brothers who as followers of the Dog-Stone Spirit enjoyed great success in blood hunts and in stalking elephants (rare in Katu country). After the brothers died, their four sons eschewed any relationship with the spirit and threw the Dog Stone away. Not long after, all four died.

Costello points out that the soul of a blood-hunt victim remains with the killer and is "like a brother," adding its voice to those of the Dog-Stone Spirit and Black Cobra Spirit in demanding blood to drink.[13] When this happens, the follower behaves like a madman and must be restrained. He is given chicken blood to drink, and when the madness has passed, he tries to persuade other men to accompany him on a blood hunt. Victims are always sought in distant villages because it is taboo to

13. Costello, "Socially Approved Homicide," pp. 78–81.

take blood in a village where one has kin, and a man cannot take a wife from a victim's village. In addition, should two individuals discover that there have been blood raids between their villages they cannot eat or drink together.

Kmeet explained that a blood-hunt party consists of from ten to twenty men (it must be an even number). For one day before their departure the village is taboo. Equipped with male backpacks, crossbows, and spears, they walk from two to twenty days, during which time they are forbidden to bathe. If the blood of a dead victim is to be sacrificed, the killing must take place where the victim is encountered. One strategy is to lay a nocturnal ambush (as in Le Pichon's description). Another is to seek a victim in a sleeping village. Four of the men remain in the forest with the packs, while the rest approach the village stockade, where they utter a magic formula "taught by the spirits" to induce deep sleep in the residents and watchdogs. Raiders then split into two groups and whistle softly to signal that they are in place at the enclosure. Stealthily they enter the village. The village chief is a particularly desirable victim because he is a figure of prestige and killing him would demonstrate great potency. Furthermore, his death would render it unlikely that the village will seek revenge. As the killing takes place, the packs left in the forest begin to tremble and shake, a sign that the victim's soul wishes to remain with the raiding party. Inside the village the raiders dip their spears in the victim's blood. If the chief has been the target, his head is severed and carried away by the raiders.

Back in their own village the raiders stick the blood-encrusted spears in front of their longhouses. The chief's head is put in a special hut. The blood hunters then retreat into the men's house (which becomes taboo), where they remain incommunicado for one month, during which they cannot bathe. There they perform for the victim's soul a ritual in which a bowl of rice, a chicken, a red flower, and a red blanket (red is associated with souls) are placed on a mat as offerings. When the raiders emerge from the men's house, the village is declared taboo for six days of celebrating with lots of feasting with rice alcohol. As gongs and drums play, men dance around the bloody spears while chanting to the spirits, "You wanted this blood, so we bring it to you. Don't kill us, give us good health, abundant crops, and enough to eat." Afterward, women join in the dance (Figure 15).

Kmeet related that the hut in which the chief's head has been deposited is sacrosanct. Should the village be threatened, the elders will open the hut to implore the help of the souls associated with the heads. Very often when blood hunters set out on a raid they take a head so its soul can persuade victims to submit to the spears. Villages involved in blood raids

Figure 15. A Katu woman dancing at a ritual.

can end them by holding the *teeng tabah,* a large feast during which the headmen drink blood of a buffalo together. This establishes peaceful relations, but intermarriage is still not possible.

According to Kmeet, the blood of live victims sometimes is used for sacrifices. The victim is taken prisoner, and because it is difficult to carry an adult back to the raiders' village, children are the preferred targets. The Katu claim that during a raid the child comes to his captors willingly because he is guided by the spirits. The child is placed in a large back-basket (*prôm*) with a top, which is carried back to the village. There a bowl of rice, a chicken egg, a red blanket, and a red flower are placed on a mat as offerings. The child is told to squeeze the blade of a sharp dagger. Should he refuse, one of the men holds his hand over that of the child to force the act. As blood flows, the men chant to the spirits, "You wanted this blood, so we are bringing it to you. Give us health, good crops, and enough to eat." Then the child is speared and his head is severed and put in the special hut.

In a 1964 conversation Gordon Smith related that subsequent to our 1957 trip, he and his wife, Laura, organized another sojourn that would take them farther west into the High Katu country. They stocked their motorboat with food (including rice for the villagers) and medicines, and with two Vietnamese assistants they went up the winding rivers to a remote place accessible to High Katu villages. The Smiths and one assistant walked up the slippery, tortuous path for hours, finally reaching a village encircled with a stockade. Once in the village it became readily apparent that the headman had decided that Reverend Smith would be a prestigious victim for a blood sacrifice. The situation looked bleak, but Smith pleaded with the headman, saying that if he were killed, his wife would be left alone. This moved the chief to change his mind, but he ordered them to leave the village immediately. The stress of the situation, however, caused Laura to have a crippling attack of sciatica, rendering her almost immobile. Gordon and his assistant carried her into the shade of a tree outside the stockade. The Smiths remained there while the assistant returned to the boat to obtain help. Night fell, and from time to time, the Katu, looking very angry, appeared at the village gate but did not approach. The Smiths knew well that if anything went amiss in the village they would be blamed and suffer the wrath of the Katu. They prayed together, and with morning light the Vietnamese assistants arrived with a litter to carry Laura down to the boat.

Settlements and Longhouses

Low Katu settlements have between ten and twenty longhouses (in 1957, A-To had twenty). Vien (a High Katu of about sixteen who had been wounded during a skirmish between Special Forces and Communist troops west of A-Ro) described villages as having five or six longhouses. Le Pichon reports in his 1938 article that "important" Katu villages had as many as fifty longhouses.[14] Vien noted that a large settlement poses

14. Le Pichon, "Les chasseurs," pp. 370–71, 393. Le Pichon data in this section are from this source.

problems because of the practice of sharing all game and fish with fellow villages. Blood raids and intervillage warfare require that there be a stockade with only one entrance, which can be closed in the event of an impending attack or when the village is taboo. Paths through the forest leading to the village are purposely labyrinthine to confound outsiders. Anyone using a path should be aware of any taboo signs, indicated by fresh notches in a nearby tree telling the number of taboo days or a stick in the path with similar notches. One informant claimed that he once touched a taboo sign and immediately fell ill. Anyone violating a taboo must pay the village a pig of "three hands height" and two jars of alcohol. To dispel evil spirits, carved figures with varying motifs, some of them fearsome, are placed along paths. Le Pichon relates that when the French *résident* of Faifoo was making his first tour of the Put Valley he inquired why the villagers did not go to Ben Giang to trade. They responded that "there is a malefice near Ok-Ba-Lua that prevents our passage." Soon after, the commander of Poste 6 investigated and found by the forest path a weathered sacrificial stake decorated with two saber blades and a niche containing a human skull.

Longhouses and the men's house are always oriented around an open space in the center of which is a sacrificial stake (*sinur*). Vien described High Katu villages as usually shaped like a tilted "ell" with the top to the north and a row of dwellings oriented in a line from north to southwest. The "corner" of the "ell" is due west, and a second row of houses is oriented along a line to the southeast. Due east of the "corner" is the stake where sacrificial animals are tied, and east of the stake is the men's house. Vien emphasized that at dawn the sun must ascend behind the men's house.

Artistic endeavor is focused on the sacrificial stake, which in many respects is the centerpiece of the village. Le Pichon says the stakes are commonly carved with "sacred animals," such as toucans, fish, snakes, iguanas, and turtles, along with depictions of crosses, stars, and the sun. Some stakes have elaborate stylized wings at the top. Decorative coloring is provided by using burned wood for black, lime for white, and areca nuts for red. Informants note that motifs include trees and buffalo, and a red color also is derived from red flowers. For village sacrifices the stake is decorated with festoons fashioned by shaving bamboo in thin layers.

According to Le Pichon, Ben Hien area houses are built on piling with a central column (*tonal*) five to eight meters in height. At the ends of the roof's peak are carved symbols depicting silhouettes of men, stylized animals, and phalli. Inside beams are decorated with hunting or fishing scenes and geometric figures. In the Katu village of O-Mo (visited in

1957) house interiors consisted of one large room with open hearths for preparing meals. Farm tools, weapons, and fish nets were stored on the rafters. Costello reports that the *jadoh* is a small round basket for keeping money and tobacco, and *katroh* is a loosely woven oblong-shaped basket that is hung on the wall to store dishes.[15] Cornmeal is kept in the *ja-duar,* a basket wide at the bottom tapering to a two-inch top. Similar in form is the *daru,* used to store cornmeal, fish, crabs, and meat.

According to Costello, before building a house the Katu performs a divination ritual to determine if the site is auspicious. Drawing a line on the ground, he places two small live creatures found near watercourses (such as frogs) on either side of the line. The one above the line is called *machau abuï,* identified with the *abuï* spirits, while that below is *machau manuih,* associated with humans. If the former crosses the line first, it is seen as a sign from the spirits that the site must be abandoned, but if the latter crosses first, construction can begin.[16]

Every Katu village has a men's house (*guol*) distinguished by its unusually high roof. Great care is expended on the construction and decorative art so that the building will be imposing. Here, in the presence of ancestors who died good deaths, men gather to make decisions affecting the whole community, to prepare for war, and to plan blood raids. Young men and often older men sleep in the men's house. Le Pichon reports that the men's house at A-Ro slept up to one hundred men, and its central column attained several dozen meters in height. Hunting and fishing scenes were painted on the interior walls, which also contained the heads of sacrificial buffalo and game such as deer, foxes, and toucans, along with pheasant plumes symbolizing their "souls," which remain in the men's house. There are at least two open hearths and as many as ten (the number must always be even). Sometimes there are masks depicting grimacing faces (*kabei*), which the headman of Bo Lo village said were war masks.

The men's house at A-To in 1957, although not elaborate (it had heads and plumes on the smoke-blackened walls), was sturdily constructed. Vien described the men's house in his High Katu village as having a high roof decorated with wood carvings. The large interior has two hearths, and a slightly raised rear section is the sleeping area. The central column is fashioned from a thick hardwood trunk, and drums used in celebrations are lashed to the crossbeam. Heads of sacrificial buffalo adorn the walls. He described how the men gather to conduct rituals, drink from the jars, and chat informally. Women bring food and water to the main entrance but cannot enter.

15. Nancy Costello, "Corn Processing in Katu Culture," mimeograph, n.d., pp. 8–9.
16. Costello, "Katu Tribal People," p. 7.

Family

The Katu have exogamous patrilineages in which the basic social-economic unit is the longhouse group (*kabuh*), which consists of from two to ten nuclear families and is headed by the eldest male. There also are kindreds that regulate cross-cousin marriage, permitting marriage with the mother's brother's daughter but forbidding it with the father's sister's daughter. The kindred also prescribes mutual hospitality and gift exchanges.

As Appendix B5 indicates, in Ego's generation siblings are age-graded and these terms are extended to the father's brothers' sons, mother's siblings' sons, and mother's sisters' daughters. The term *mamooq* identifies the father's brothers' daughters, who, until they marry, occupy the same longhouse as Ego. Members of the patrilineage that gives wives to Ego's patrilineage are *shuya,* while members of the patrilineage that takes wives from Ego's group are *cha chaau.* In describing the rule that Ego can marry his matrilateral cross-cousin but not his patrilateral cross-cousin, Vien said, "If a boy calls his cousin *shuya* and she calls him *cha chaau* they can marry, but if she calls him *shuya* and he calls her *cha chaau* they cannot marry." *Cha chaau* is used for the father's sisters' children, and it is taboo for Ego to use their given names. In ascending generations no distinction is made between patrilineal and nonpatrilineal kin. There are explicit terms for the brothers' children while sisters' children are called by the kindred term *cha chaau* because they are members of patrilineages that took wives from Ego's patrilineage. It is taboo for Ego to use any of their given names until they have reached the age of puberty.

Children are brought up with the idea that they will marry cross-cousins, and courtship begins after puberty. In the rare instance when a boy refuses to marry his mother's brother's daughter, he must nonetheless pay the bride-price. Le Pichon points out that the ideal young male is "strong and handsome . . . one who has followed his kinsmen in war and whose spear is renowned in the region."[17] Katu informants report that the usual pattern is for the boy to visit the girl's longhouse, where they are accorded privacy in a curtained-off corner. He plays an instrument that resembles a Jew's harp, and they chat. They are not supposed to have sexual relations, but often they meet in an unused hut by a swidden to make love. If discovered, they must give the men's house a pig or a buffalo to sacrifice for the ancestors. Should the girl become pregnant, the couple must leave the village for six days, then offer a pig or a buffalo and a jar of alcohol to the ancestors, whereupon they are considered married without any further ceremony.

According to Katu informants, the boy normally informs his father

17. Le Pichon, "Les chasseurs," p. 376.

that he intends to marry, and the father obtains the services of an elderly male friend to serve as intermediary. At the next full moon the intermediary visits the girl's house to partake of a large meal and discuss the bride-price, which prescriptively includes some jars of rice alcohol, cloth, animals, and cooking pots. A poor family may offer pigs with a minimum of the prescribed gifts, but a well-to-do family will present twenty jars, two or three buffalo, a great deal of cloth, many pots, and also some spears and daggers. After the bride-price has been agreed upon, a roasted chicken is given to the intermediary, who deftly cuts off its right foot for a divination ritual. The large claw is *krun,* and if it closes between the other two, called *pâdrui* ("man") and *pâdil* ("woman"), the marriage should take place, but if all three close together it is an unfavorable sign.

The groom decorates the village sacrificial stake to which a buffalo is tied on the day of the wedding when the groom and his family present the bride-price to the girl's parents. Either the bride's father or her elder brother then spears the buffalo, which is immediately dressed out. The bride's parents give the boy's parents some buffalo meat and cloth, which constitutes the final act of the marriage ritual. A wealthy man may take a second wife, who may be the first wife's younger sister. When a man dies, his younger brother has the option of marrying the widow, but when a woman dies her younger sister is obligated to wed the widower.

Residence is patrilocal, but a Low Katu informant said that in his area it was temporarily ambilocal, and the newly married couple eventually settled in his longhouse. They are given a curtained-off sleeping area and a cooking hearth as they assume their place in the division of labor. When a pregnant woman is ready to deliver, she goes into the forest, and while kinswomen keep watch, she cuts the cord with a bamboo knife, which is buried with the placenta. Returning to the house with the infant, the mother rests in a curtained-off area next to a blazing hearth, not bathing for three days and nursing the infant at night. An elderly kinswoman chews rice, which is fed to the baby. Le Pichon reports that as birth approaches, the husband and his kinsmen gather in the men's house. When news of the birth arrives, they kill a pig (provided by the husband) for a celebration. Costello writes that if the mother and child die within seven days of birth, both deaths are considered "bad." For a given period no food can be cooked or consumed in the house, and residents of the village are not welcomed in neighboring villages.[18]

According to informants, a child is not given a name for at least six months, and it cannot be named after any relative. It also is taboo for patrilineal kin to use words that rhyme with names of any members of the patrilineage. To observe this custom, they alter the phonemes of perti-

18. Ibid., p. 375; Costello, "Socially Approved Homicide," p. 82.

nent words in the same way. One result is that each patrilineal group is known for its peculiar pronunciation of ordinary words. A child is nursed until the next child is born so it is not uncommon for breast-feeding to continue until the age of three or four. Le Pichon notes that a small child is fed a boiled mash of rice, manioc, maize, and herbs. It is carried in its mother's arms or in a sling on her back and sleeps in a bamboo crib placed near an open hearth. A lullaby from Pa San village goes:

The buffalo are back in the village
Drink and sleep.
Don't cry because night falls.
Drink and sleep.
May good spirits bring pleasant dreams.
Drink and sleep.
Slumber 'til the cock crows![19]

Kmeet and Vien described how boys go to the men's house, where elderly males teach them traditional songs and legends as well as male skills such as carving crossbows, making animal traps, weaving baskets, and designing motifs. At an early age they begin learning hunting and fishing skills, and after puberty they sleep in the men's house. Young girls take on the usual highland household chores. Vien said that among the High Katu, "late in the day the women weave cloth while the men fish in a nearby river."

A major responsibility for the eldest male as household head is to resolve conflicts, and in conflict between outsiders and a family member, the head "will speak for him." Kmeet related that if a man has a married sister in the village, from time to time he must cook fish and bring it to her longhouse, where the two share a meal. Should she live in another village, he must visit her annually, bringing rice and fish in a *ndal* back-basket. When a married sister returns to her parental longhouse, the adult members of her patrilineage (*cha chaau*) must give her food to take back to her family (*shuya*). If a sister's husband is successful in hunting or in trapping rats, he must invite his brother-in-law, a *shuya* kinsman, to partake of the meal at which the rats are served. *Pling* is the prescribed presentation of fish, frogs, pork, chicken, and wild game such as rats and birds to *cha chaau* kin, notably sisters' husbands, and also to *shuya* kin, particularly the wife's brothers.

Costello reports that "while the Katu threaten death for adultery, the elders apparently never carry it out." Both the man and woman are considered guilty, and they must give the cuckolded husband some cloth.

19. Le Pichon, "Les chasseurs," p. 377.

It is not uncommon for the husband to try to kill his wife's lover, but in most instances his fellow villagers prevent any violence. If the lover is from another village, the husband and a band of kin and friends go there to demand compensation in the form of a pig, cock, or buffalo. According to Le Pichon, the fine for an adulterer who is not a kinsman is two buffalo—one for the offended husband and one for the village. An adulterer who is a kinsman pays a lighter fine of one pig for a meal to which the whole village is invited. Divorce is permitted, and if the wife's lover wants to marry her he must pay her husband a bride-price. Children remain in the custody of the father.[20]

Costello reports that according to legend, the Sky Being long ago distinguished "good deaths" from "bad deaths."[21] When someone dies a good death (from old age, or sickness), the closest kin wash the corpse, carefully avoiding contact with the forehead and knees in the belief that to touch them would cause the family to forget the deceased and not dream of him. The corpse is then dressed in ceremonial clothes and wrapped in cloth. The longhouse is lit with candles, and it is important that the body be guarded to prevent evil spirits from snatching it. One popular story tells how family members were keeping watch, and as the night wore on, all but one man who was ill fell asleep. In the early morning hours he was startled when in the doorway appeared the figure of Sayiin Krung, the evil spirit identifiable by his large stomach and matted body hair. Knowing that this spirit coveted the corpse, the man grabbed a piece of flaming wood from the hearth and hurled it at the intruder, who fled into the darkness.

Unless death occurs during the second and third lunar months, when rice is being planted and it is taboo to attend funerals, kin and friends gather for the first burial. Each sister of the deceased male is expected to contribute a buffalo (a pig if the deceased is a child). Costello notes that "she does this so that her brothers will love her and later give their daughters as wives for her sons in the Katu custom of cross-cousin marriages."[22] To slow, rhythmic gong-and-drum music, the assemblage dances around a buffalo tied to a stake while family members shout praise for the deceased, citing such merits as his wealth and hunting skills. When the buffalo is ceremonially speared, everyone implores the deceased to claim the animal's spirit. The buffalo head is placed on the roof of the longhouse, after which the family and guests drink from the alcohol jars and partake of a feast. Fearing sickness, guests do not take

20. Costello, "Socially Approved Homicide," p. 84; Le Pichon, "Les chasseurs," p. 377.

21. Nancy Costello, "Death and Burial in Katu Culture," in *Notes from Indochina on Ethnic Minority Cultures,* ed. Marilyn Gregerson and Dorothy Thomas (Dallas: SIL Museum of Anthropology, 1980), pp. 102–5.

22. Ibid., p. 103.

any leftover food, and they carefully wash their hands before departing. On the second day the body is placed in a coffin. One male dry-season activity is to fashion from a hardwood log an elaborately carved coffin, which is stored in a cave (and for one month afterward it is taboo to build a new house). The deceased's clothing, baskets, and rice-alcohol jars are placed by the coffin. The spirits frown on burial as dark approaches, but because the spirits see everything as opposite to what it is in the human world, the Katu know that they can bury the coffin in the late afternoon, which the spirits will think is early morning. The grave is shallow, and a bowl of rice is placed upon it to provide food for the soul, which remains with the corpse until the second burial.

Because the second burial entails a buffalo sacrifice to which the whole village is invited, it may not take place for several years, and it is not unusual to have one second burial observance for two or three deceased kin. The coffin is exhumed and carried to the common village tomb (*ping*), a solidly built structure with a wooden roof over an excavation about four meters deep in which coffins are stacked. The coffin is placed outside the tomb for three days of celebrations. While gongs and drums play, everyone dances as the buffalo is speared, after which all drink from the alcohol jars and partake of food. If the deceased had claimed many blood-hunt victims, his kinsmen will organize a raid on another village to obtain human blood, which is offered along with the buffalo blood. When celebrating ends, the assemblage gathers at the entrance of the tomb, where a pig is slaughtered and its blood rubbed on a stone that is cast into the tomb while the men ask the spirits to receive this soul and make it happy. The buffalo's head, some jars of alcohol, and bowls of rice are placed in the tomb. Sometime after the second burial the soul goes to *maraaih,* a place inside the earth where existence resembles life in a Katu village.

Writing about death practices, Le Pichon reports that ancestors who have died good deaths keep watch over their descendants. "It is they who put the peacock eggs on the path to signal their presence, it is they who knock down the large tree on the trail or who make the tiny gold bird cry in the reeds with rhythms that haunt the passerby." These signs tell the Katu that "he must return quickly to his village to utter the incantations that will appease them." In one incantation he implores, "Benevolent spirits of the forest, you will struggle against the evil forces, you will protect your family and those of your clan if they know how to honor you, if you find in your former hearth or around your tombs ritual offerings—good newly harvested rice, the best jar of alcohol, and blood of a hardy cock that had marked with his songs the hour of your awakening." Le Pichon adds, however, that should these spirits become irritated, dire manifestations such as an epidemic or spoiled harvests call for offerings of blood, either of a human or a buffalo, to restore calm.[23]

The ancestors figure in village celebrations marking such events as the clearing of new swiddens, sowing crops, harvesting, or building a new men's house. Le Pichon describes a celebration that took place in A-Pat village on 9–10 November 1937. The sacrificial stake in front of the men's house was festooned with sprays of shaved bamboo, and an altar of the ancestors was covered with blankets and loincloths. When night fell, two fires were lit, a buffalo was tied to the stake, and bowls of rice and alcohol along with a chicken were placed on the altar. Striking long drums in cadence, six men circled the buffalo. Behind them came two dancing men tapping gongs, one in a slow rhythm and the other in a staccato fashion, bending and twisting his body as if "he were animated by an interior demon." The musicians were soon joined by six women wearing blue mantles, moving in a circle with their hips swaying in slow rhythm and their hands stretched skyward. With shrill cries they invoked the ancestors. Music and dancing continued well into the night.

Early in the morning the dancing resumed, this time done by eight men clutching bush scythes. Jumping close to the buffalo, on a signal from one of them, all formed a circle. Around nine o'clock the aged chief of A-Pat, holding a copper pan in which charcoal burned, began to dance around the buffalo. Suddenly he lunged at the animal, stabbing its snout with a dagger. Collecting some of the flowing blood in a bowl, he placed it on the ancestors' altar. The dance rhythm increased as young men, slightly bent, jumped from one foot to the other. One played a blowpipe while the others marked cadence by striking an iron ring suspended nearby with their bush scythes. The headman came forward and plunged his spear three times into the buffalo's heart as the dance accelerated, lasting until the buffalo lay still. The tip of its tail was cut off, and each of the villagers took turns trying to throw it into a basket tied to the top of the sacrificial stake. To succeed was a sign of good fortune, and those who did so were given larger portions of buffalo meat. At eleven o'clock buffalo meat was boiled and placed on the ancestors' altar. Village elders then led everyone in feasting and drinking from the jars, flicking a bit of alcohol from their index fingers as offerings to the spirits. At sundown the buffalo head and feet were affixed to the sacrificial stake.

Those who die in blood raids remain with their killers, but souls of those who die bad deaths as a result of accidents, attacks by wild animals, childbirth, and suicide go to *bayo,* abode of evil spirits. Kmeet related

---

23. Le Pichon, "Les chasseurs," pp. 385–87, 396–400. The following two paragraphs are based on this source.

that in his village two sisters married to the same man quarreled incessantly. After one violent conflict, one of the sisters hanged herself in the longhouse, bringing bad luck to her family and the whole village. The clothes of one who died a bad death are burned, and when the corpse is being wrapped, the family avoids touching it. There is no funeral ritual, no incantations, and no mourning. The corpse is hurriedly buried deeply in a dark corner of the forest well removed from trails and fields. Le Pichon reports that in the event of a "very bad death," such as being devoured by a tiger, all domestic animals in the village, including dogs, must be slaughtered and left to rot. Everyone must move into the forest for six months. A new village site is selected, and carved-wood figures, some with huge faces, are placed along the trails, at the entrances to longhouses, and around the men's house to frighten away evil spirits. The sacrificial stake is left in the old village. Le Pichon notes that in less than one year he witnessed two relocations of Mey Ra village, once when a new men's house had just been completed.

According to Costello, the Katu believe in resurrection of the dead. Legend relates that a long time ago, all who previously had died rose again and, "shedding their old bodies like a snake sheds its skin," they acquired fat new bodies, heralding a golden age. While Costello was conducting her research in the 1960s, Katu refugees repeated resurrection stories that had been circulating in the villages. One told how the soul of a deceased man became troubled when his son-in-law failed to have a second burial for him. The soul goaded the young man, who promised to hold the ritual, but he did not have the means to buy a buffalo and became very frightened. Evil spirits appeared to him asking what he wanted, and he said he wanted to see his father-in-law. When he found himself at the place of the dead, he explained to his father-in-law that he did not have the means to purchase a buffalo. The older man showed him a buffalo, saying, "Here, take this animal you had sacrificed when I died." He added that the buffalo should be taken to the center of the village to be sacrificed in the morning or it would turn into charcoal. The son-in-law returned with the buffalo to his village, where he duly held the buffalo sacrifice, and all went well.[24]

Subsistence Activities

According to Vien, for swiddening, the High Katu farmer looks for black soil and large trees (indicators of fertile soil), avoiding red soil. Most households have two swiddens. A small one is near the settlement, "where the grandparents can help farm," while the main swidden is worked by younger adults some distance away. Before clearing a new

24. Costello, "Death and Burial," pp. 102–5.

swidden, the farmer performs a divination ritual similar to the ritual to determine the auspiciousness of a new house site. Clearing takes place in the late January to early February dry spell, and if thunder is heard at any time during farming, fields are taboo for the remainder of the day. Dried wood is set ablaze, initiating *pajarom,* a two-day period during which fields are taboo. When a certain type of tree sheds its leaves it is a sign that red and white maize should be planted (High Katu have one crop while Low Katu have two). As men play gongs, women dance, and everyone drinks from the jars, a pig, a chicken, and a dog are offered to the spirits. Afterward, men make holes with dibble sticks, and women follow to dispense kernels from a round rattan basket (*achui*) tied about their waists. As plants grow, women weed using knives with straight or curved blades.

When leaves of a certain tree turn red it is time to plant rice. First, there is a ritual offering to the spirits that resembles that held for maize planting. Men move across the swidden making holes between the rows of maize plants, and women follow to sow. While planting takes place, the village observes the *baluich* taboo for two days. With the rice crop sown, secondary crops are planted in the field and along the edges. Cotton (*araang*) is planted in a separate swidden, and while this is being done it is forbidden to visit anyone. *Pai araang* is the taboo against using any new cotton while the crop is being gathered. Tobacco, grown in a small patch, is dried and either rolled into crude cigars or shredded and smoked in long pipes by men and women.

Costello reports that among the Low Katu, red maize is harvested two months and ten days after planting; the white is ready in three months. It is forbidden to eat any ripe maize in the fields during harvest, but some unripe ears are boiled or roasted in hot ashes for consumption. Mature ears are cut and placed in the large, loosely woven *jong* back-basket. Stalks are cut down and left between the rows of rice plants, but roots are dug up and allowed to rot. Some unripe maize is placed over a hearth for one month to dry, then dusted with ashes to ward off insects while it is stored for three months to provide seed maize for the next season. Ripe maize is placed on a large, flat, circular basket (*apoq*) to dry for three days. The kernels are removed from the cob, dried further, and then stored. To provide snacks, maize is roasted in the hot ashes or kernels are popped on a flat pan over the fire. Kernels also are crammed into a bamboo tube to heat on the fire. During lean periods when there is no rice, maize is either steamed using two pots or simply boiled. Low Katu also use maize as pig feed. Women shell it using a mortar and pestle, after which it is winnowed in a flat, pear-shaped basket (*aring kiar*). The crushed kernels are sifted through a basket so that the final product is a fine cornmeal, which is stored in a *daru* basket. Meal is boiled with leaves, papaya skins, and other edible garbage to provide pig food. Costello relates that the Low Katu were astonished to see pigs eat ears of uncooked maize given to them by Westerners, and many quickly adopted this feeding method.[25]

Katu informants say that weeding is done when rice plants are around one foot high, and the crop matures in five months. Women do most of the harvesting, pulling the grains from the stalk to fill the small, square, tightly woven *arê* baskets tied to their waists. When the baskets are full, they pour the contents into the similar but larger *ndal* basket that stands on four short legs. *Chu duach* is the interdiction against eating any new rice during the harvest. Women carry rice to the granary (built on piling near the swidden) in square back-baskets to spread it on large circular baskets to dry. Women and girls husk daily using a mortar and pestle. Rice is boiled and served in a special basket (*apơq mók*) about twelve inches in diameter with four legs. People sit on the floor and help themselves using their hands. Informants report that fields are farmed up to three years. The dried maize and rice stalks are burned, after which farmers use hoes and their hands to level the soil. A portion of rice is used to make alcohol. According to Le Pichon, the Katu in the Ben Hien area also ferment maize and manioc. In the vicinity of Poste 6 the villagers produce a palm alcohol (*bavak*) that he found to be "tart" but agreeable.[26]

An important source of food is hunting, using crossbows, spears, and traps. Accompanied by dogs, hunters, each wearing the male backpack, go in groups to stalk small game, deer, and wild boar. Le Pichon reports that in the Ataouat range the Katu are adept at imitating calls of wild chickens and game birds such as toucans and peacocks as well as the cries of wild goats and roe deer. Hiding in a thicket or in a tree, they lure their prey, shooting them with arrows that often are poisoned. Meat from the hunt is shared by all villagers. Most of it is eaten as soon as possible, but some is salted and stuffed into bamboo tubes, which later are placed on the edge of a hearth to cook. Considerable bravado is associated with hunting, and trophies are proudly displayed on the walls of the men's house. Le Pichon recorded the following hunter-song lyrics from Bo Lo village:

In the men's house of my village there are
one hundred deer's heads,
There are a hundred fox tails, a hundred peacock plumes
that I hung up with my own hands,

---

25. Costello, "Corn Processing," pp. 1–2, 4–6.
26. Le Pichon, "Les chasseurs," pp. 367, 378–79, 383–84.

For I am the most adept hunter in the village.
At my voice the birds come,
the stupid toucan, the light magpie,
I know where sleeps the pheasant
whose tail is more beautiful than that of the peacock.

Katu villages are invariably accessible to one or more watercourses in which men fish, using traps and nets. One commonly used bamboo trap is cone-shaped with the wide end set in an earthen dam so that the fish are carried into it by the current. Cotton thread produced by the women is fashioned into fishing nets, and some Low Katu buy nets from the Vietnamese. Nets either are cast or tied to the end of a long bamboo pole that is quickly dipped into the water.

Le Pichon reports that in the 1930s trading was the affair of each household group, which dealt with itinerant Vietnamese merchants who from time to time visited the area. Periodically the village headman organized communal exchanges with Vietnamese traders, arranging a meeting at Ben Hien (figured on the basis of days of walking and phases of the moon, recorded on folds of a bamboo strip). On the appointed day the Vietnamese trader disembarked from a sampan containing cotton cloth, glassware, salt, rice-alcohol jars, necklaces, and spearheads. Soon there appeared a long file of men armed with crossbows, spears, and bush scythes and women with back-baskets filled with maize, betel, glutinous rice, fruit, and roots of certain trees. Occasionally small parties made their way to coastal towns such as Danang.

In August 1957, after we had returned to Gordon Smith's Danang compound from our trip into the Katu country, we learned that two Katu in the central market were being taunted by Vietnamese because they were wearing loincloths and had long hair. We went there to find a man in his twenties and a boy of about fifteen, who explained that they had come to Danang to trade areca nuts and betel leaves for salt. The older one had been to Danang once before, but it was the first time the boy had been out of Katu country. Their ride in a vehicle was a frightening experience, and they were mystified by the traffic policeman in uniform waving his arms. At the compound the Katu were astonished at running water in the kitchen, the stove, and glass in the window (which they refused to touch). They clearly felt at home, however, with the compound pets, particularly the gibbon. Some months later a group of Katu en route to the central market stopped at the compound to sell Gordon Smith a small elephant tusk exquisitely carved in a praying mantis motif. In the past most High Katu obtained lowland goods through exchange with the Low Katu. Vien reported that his High Katu village traded with a Lao-speaking upland group called Katu Da Riiu, who farmed paddy fields, exchanging forest

Photo 16. Katu trading party on the trail (1957).

products for rice-alcohol jars and skirts with borders elegantly woven with gold and silver thread.

Village Leadership

The headman (*taka*) is selected by the inhabitants of the village from among older men versed in traditional ways. It is preferable that he be a man of prestige, wealthy and credited with successful blood raids, all reflecting potency. Le Pichon observes that Katu headmen and well-to-do villagers assume a stylized way of expressing themselves, prefixing commonly used words with "a" so that the word *ca* ("dog"), for example, became *a-ca*.[27] Kayi, a Low Katu from the vicinity of An Diem, said that the headman must be able to "speak out" and make decisions. If in the course of his tenure the chief's decisions are frequently questioned or if the village should experience misfortunes such as crop failure or an inordinate number of deaths, the household heads gather in the men's house to select someone to replace the headman, who steps down gracefully because it is the will of the ancestors. Vien reported that in his High Katu village and in neighboring villages there was no headman. Rather, adult members of the households form a collective leadership. When

27. Ibid., p. 378.

asked about decisions (such as relocating the village), he always responded, "Everyone knows what to do."

Most internal problems are resolved by household heads acting with their members. Should this fail, the problem is brought before the village leaders. When there is conflict between two villagers, the accuser usually demands compensation, and if the accused refuses, there may be a death threat. The accused will then ask village leaders to intervene. In their discussions of leaders' roles in preserving moral order, Le Pichon and Costello agree that theft is one of the most serious breaches with which they must contend. According to Le Pichon, although a Katu rarely steals from his own village, it is not uncommon to steal from a neighboring one, which can lead to endless intervillage warfare. Although the Sky Being condones a revenge raid on the thief's village and helps the avenging party slaughter its victims, any blood spilled cannot be offered to the spirits. A village that does not seek revenge is an easy target for aggressors and is dishonored so its inhabitants must avoid others and refrain from eating buffalo meat. The headman and elders are responsible for organizing a revenge raid, reconnoitering ways of gaining entrance to the target village. Usually the raiding party consists of from eight to ten men, although occasionally one man, considered extremely brave, conducts the raid alone. In preparation, the young men arrange special "war coiffures," intertwining their long hair with bamboo sticks, cones of bone, and wild boar tusks. These conflicts can go on for years, resulting in a village being wiped out. In one case a village lost one member and exacted a toll of seventy in a revenge raid. Costello reports that theft, although rare, is considered more grievous than murder, a value reflected in a villager's statement that "if we kill a man on the trail or in a village, we never steal from him." The Katu saying, "Ask and you will live, steal and you will die," also reflects the gravity of theft. For the first act of thievery, particularly if the item stolen is not of great value, village leaders impose a heavy material fine. A person guilty of chronic stealing, however, is stabbed to death or buried alive. In one case village leaders ordered the stepson of the thief to have him killed by a man from a neighboring village. The stepson duly led the thief to a place on a wooded trail where the executioner waited, and as the stepson fled, he was stabbed.[28]

Costello observes that murder is relatively rare because of the Katu habit of expressing anger audibly so that the whole community knows that two parties are in conflict, prompting the leaders to intervene. Murderers are either speared to death or buried alive, after which the

---

28. Le Pichon, "Les chasseurs," pp. 377, 387–89; Costello, "Socially Approved Homicide," pp. 79, 81–86.

leaders must sacrifice a buffalo to cleanse the village ground, dispelling evil which might lead to more murders. Informants point out that sorcery and witchcraft resulting in death are forms of murder. In most instances, however, it is difficult to identify the offender because villagers, fearing the malevolent powers involved, are reluctant to accuse anyone. Also, the accused usually denies the charge, and if the leaders are not convinced by the evidence, the accused has the right to slay the accuser.

According to Costello, insanity is the result of having angered the Sky Being. If the insane person is only a minor nuisance he usually is kept tied to a pole. If, however, he becomes a threat to the community, custom calls for leaders to see that he is buried alive by members of his family. He is placed with his knees against his chest in a hole so small he cannot move. The hole is then filled with dirt to a level that allows enough air for the victim to survive five to ten days during which time a member of the family checks to see if he is still alive.

In telling of the death of his friend Go, headman of Bo Lo village, Le Pichon provides some insights concerning aspects of Katu culture already discussed. Go was "young and lithe with laughing eyes" and proudly wore on his forehead the "dancing lady" tatoo. In a playful mood he would run ahead of the Garde Indigène column to hide in a tree, imitate the calls of different animals, and then suddenly leap from his perch to startle everyone. He was very knowledgeable about Katu customs, and he had the reputation of being the most adept singer in the region. Something of a boaster, he liked to tell about the numerous enemies he had slain. One day Le Pichon confided in Go his dream of having all Katu united under the French administration. Not long after, Go disappeared. His fellow villagers said that he gone on a blood raid. Twenty days later, however, Le Pichon was surprised to see the arrival in Ben Hien of a group of fifteen village chiefs and men from the remote Ataouat sector. Two months after that, Go, leading some twelve headmen, arrived to take the oath. Le Pichon greeted him enthusiastically and gave him gifts of glassware. Go seemed very happy, but soon he appeared at the Frenchman's door declaring that he was sick because the Katu of Ataouat had cast a spell on him. Le Pichon gave him some alcohol and quinine, and Go departed. A few days later, a Vietnamese trader carried the unconscious Go to Le Pichon's house, where he died. The Frenchmen had his body taken to An Diem, suggesting to the Katu that they accorded him the burial of a great chief. Go's family, however, responded that he had died a bad death so they would have nothing to do with the corpse. Le Pichon therefore arranged for Go to be buried with full Garde Indigène honor guard and a rifle salute. Several months later, one of Go's brothers came to see Le Pichon, relating that Go had appeared to him in a dream saying that the brother should kill Dinh-Mai, the Vietnamese trader who had poisoned him. The Frenchman proposed that instead they sacrifice a buffalo for Go. The ritual was duly held, but nonetheless the village of Bo Lo was abandoned and its inhabitants went to live in the forest for the prescribed period before relocating.[29]

The Vietnam War

Remarks concerning Viet Minh activities made by the headman of A-To village in 1957 substantiated reports that Katu were among the southern highlanders who went north with the Communists in 1954 to be re-grouped as insurgents in South Vietnam during the early 1960s.[30] In May 1962, Communist activities in the Katu country prompted the opening of a Vietnamese-American Special Forces camp at Nam Dong in the Ta Rau Valley. A month later another post was established at An Diem on the site of the former French fort.[31] Although in other areas of the central highlands the Special Forces succeeded in recruiting militiamen from among the local ethnic groups, here they attracted very few Katu, so they brought in Vietnamese recruits from Danang. In May 1964 I visited the Special Forces camp at An Diem. Close by there was a small settlement of Katu refugees—women, children, and elderly people, most of them kin, all of whom had been crowded into a longhouse. The American Special Forces team hired the men as laborers and gave them thatching and wood to build houses, which they oriented around a flagpole that served as a sacrificial stake. They had a grove of banana and papaya trees, vegetable gardens, and not far away were small swiddens.

Not long after I visited the camp at Nam Dong, where there was a small settlement of Katu refugees who lived in shacks and were farming small swiddens in the nearby forest. Early on the morning of 6 July 1964, a reinforced battalion of seven hundred Viet Cong newly arrived from North Vietnam mounted an attack that left two Americans, one Austra-lian, and a large number of Vietnamese militiamen, civilians, and Viet Cong dead. In the fighting, the post was completely destroyed, and my field notes from the 1957 trip into the Katu country and those from recent visits to highland villages were burned. The American team leader, Captain Roger Donlon, was the first American in Vietnam to receive the Congressional Medal of Honor.

Early in 1965 there were reports of Katu in large numbers moving westward into a Communist-controlled area. One apparent reason was

29. Le Pichon, "Les chasseurs," pp. 387–99.
30. Hickey, *Sons of the Mountains*, pp. 13–16.
31. Francis J. Kelly, *U.S. Special Forces, 1961–1971* (Washington, D.C.: U.S. Depart-ment of the Army, 1973), pp. 68, 182–83.

Photo 17. Katu refugee children frolicking in a monsoon rain at An Diem (1964).

revealed in May during an interview with the Vietnamese province chief of Quang Nam. He expressed strong anti-Katu sentiment, declaring that he had ordered all of the upland interior to be a "free-strike zone" for the South Vietnamese airforce. He added ominously, "That will take care of our Katu problem." Katu leader Kithem recalled that in 1964 the area from An Diem west to Ben Giang was subjected to heavy bombing. He lost several houses as well as his precious jars. Katu refugees who had remained near the An Diem camp after it closed in July 1964 told Nancy Costello that local Vietnamese ransacked their village, taking the wood and thatching and forcing them back to the longhouse they had previously occupied. One day an aircraft flew low, broadcasting a message on a loudspeaker, but it was in Vietnamese and they could not understand it. Fearing military violence, they put their jars in an abandoned brick building at An Diem and went into the forest. Soon after, jets swooped in, dropping bombs on the longhouse and the An Diem buildings, leveling the one containing their jars. Kithem and the refugees also described how the whole area was sprayed by low-flying aircraft. Soon after, their rice and yam crops died, leaving them to subsist on leaves and roots gathered in unaffected woods.

In July 1965 Vien had provided Nancy Costello and me with ethnographic data. During an interview, he described terraced paddy fields, which seemed unusual because everyone who had visited the Katu country had found only swidden farming. When asked if his people had always farmed that way, he smiled and turned away. Later, in a discussion about the men's house, he astonished us by taking a pen and writing a sentence: "Where is my older brother and older sister?" He used the same diacritical marks as the Vietnamese to indicate vowel differences. He beamed and noted that I had written similar terms for "older brother" and "older sister" the day before (using Costello's orthography). It turned out that he knew a complete alphabet, which Costello judged to be well done. When asked where he had learned to write, he smiled and looked away. It would appear that these innovations had been introduced among the Katu by the Communists, the only outsiders who had been in the High Katu area for many years.

By 1969 Thuong Duc was the only U.S. Special Forces camp remaining in the Katu country. The militia included only three Katu soldiers, and nearby was a settlement of 120 Katu refugees. According to Touneh Han Tho, in September a report from Thuong Duc revealed that a young Katu male who had been picked up by a U.S. Marine patrol claimed to be part of a group of 900 to 1,000 Katu who had moved from a Communist-controlled area near the Laotian border to a valley west of the camp. Under the thick forest canopy they had constructed lean-tos similar to those built by the swiddens and were farming small garden plots of manioc, pineapples, and bananas. They also hunted, fished, and foraged. According to the report, they had become discouraged with the Communists' unfulfilled promises so they wanted to rally to the government side. But, fearing attacks by either side, they were afraid to make their presence known. Not long after, some Katu began to filter into the vicinity of the camp. In August 1970, however, the Communists began daily shelling of Thuong Duc, culminating in a ground assault in October that left heavy casualties on both sides. In July 1971, Touneh Han Tho and Minister Nay Luett visited Thuong Duc, where some 1,888 Katu refugees had gathered. They had constructed a settlement and had crops of yams, bananas, and beans and were receiving relief rice from the government. Nay Luett proposed that some of them be sent back into the mountain forests to encourage other Katu to come to Thuong Duc. They did so, and by September there were an estimated 2,500 at the camp site. In addition there were around 100 children whom American and South Vietnamese troops found in abandoned villages. Nay Luett adopted two of them; the rest were sent to the orphanage operated by Reverend Gordon Smith at Danang. In 1972 the Ministry for Ethnic Minorities' Development moved 1,000 Katu from Thuong Duc southward to Buon Blech in Darlac province. On 9 March 1975, North Vietnamese forces captured Thuan Man district town and began moving in the direction of Buon Blech. The Katu and Bru joined the Buon Blech garrison retreating to the town of Cheo Reo. On 15 March, Ban Me Thuot fell to the Communists, prompting the evacuation of Kontum and Pleiku, with masses of Vietnamese military personnel and civilians pouring down Route 7 into Cheo Reo. As the Communists shelled the town and attacked refugees, Cheo Reo became the scene of confusion and death. The fate of Katu who had gone there is not known.

A 1986 article by Anh Trang in the *Vietnam Courier* reports that in 1976, a group of "formerly nomadic" Katu came to Nam Dong (Ta Rau) Valley, and at Huong Huu they were organized into four production collectives totaling 1,454 people, 482 of whom were of "working age." The author notes that the settlement, with its rows of thatched-roof houses set in gardens with fish ponds, could easily be mistaken for those of the Vietnamese. The Katu deputy head of the cooperative (who had adopted the Vietnamese name Nguyen Minh Liet) related that "for generations our only farming tools were bush-knives and dibbles. It was the farmers coming from the plains to establish new economic zones who taught us how to grow rice, preparing the soil, sowing, transplanting seedlings, tending the plants, and harvesting." Anh Trang noted that the three longhouses that made up the Katu village of U Rang were now spread among forty-four small houses. Gone are "worship of spirits" and the practice wherein a "man would 'inherit' the widows of his brothers" (the levirate). Gone too are "infant marriages" (probably a reference to cross-cousin marriages) and "costly weddings" (a reference to bride-price).[32]

32. Anh Trang, "Nomads Settle Down to Sedentary Farming," *Vietnam Courier,* no. 6 (1986): 20–21.

Chapter 5
Bru and Pacoh

Inland from the coastal plain city of Quang Tri the mountains are covered with emerald forests well watered by the southwest and northeast monsoons, which sometimes bring misty drizzle or chilly torrents that lash foliage, sweep the shuttered villages, and swell the fast-running rivers. Then the rains give way to bright, clear sunshine and everything seems renewed. This is the country in which, until 1960, the Bru and Pacoh had achieved relative harmony among man, nature, and cosmic forces. The Bru (sometimes spelled Brou, B'ru, or Baru) have no subgroups. Pacoh means "Mountain People" (*pa* is "people," while *cŏh* is "mountain"). A subgroup located closer to the plain is called Pahi ("Lowland People"). The Vietnamese have long grouped both Bru and Pacoh under the name Van Kieu. The 1989 Vietnamese population census reports 40,132 Bru-Van Kieu while in 1967 the Bru population was estimated at 40,000 and the Pacoh numbered some 15,000 (see Appendix A). The Bru have well-defined patrilineages while the Pacoh have patrilineal clans. Both have kindreds that have numerous social and economic functions and regulate marriage with the mother's brother's daughter (matrilateral cross-cousin).

Historically the Pacoh have been more isolated than the Bru largely because a trade and invasion road (that later became Route 9) from Quang Tri to the Mekong River town of Savannakhet in Laos passed through the Bru country via the Ai Lao pass. In 1282, for example, after conquering some Cham territory, the Mongol armies of General Sogatu moved westward through the pass into the Khmer kingdom. The Ai Lao pass also figured in Vietnamese expansion into Lao principalities during the reigns of Vo Vuong (1738–65) and Gia Long (1802–20). Minh Mang (1820–41) ordered construction at the Ai Lao pass of a prison for Christian exiles. For around two hundred years before the arrival of the

French, the Vietnamese maintained the section between Quang Tri and Lao Bao, and in 1904 French engineers began mapping improvements for the entire road. Félix Polin related that in 1921, his father, Eugène, established an estate to grow *robusta* and *arabica* coffee near the present town of Khe Sanh, where on a nearby rise the French built a fort. Initially Polin hired Bru as laborers, but they proved "unreliable" so they were replaced by Vietnamese from the coast. With the upsurge in Vietnamese nationalism during the 1930s, the French administration constructed a political prison in the pass at Lao Bao, and one renowned inmate was Ho Chi Minh. In May 1964 the ruins of the prison were still standing amid wild growth near the settlement of Lao Bao, whose inhabitants were Lao. The Geneva Agreements of July 1954 made the seventeenth parallel a demilitarized zone between the two Vietnams, putting the Bru and Pacoh on the front line in the struggle that would become the Vietnam War.[1]

Bru

In Bru society the patrilineage is the most important social and economic unit. Its head serves as steward of religious prescriptions for preserving harmony with the patrilineage patron spirit (or spirits) and the ancestors, both protectors of the kin group, who bring good fortune, health, and abundant crops. The head's potency is symbolized by divination blocks he uses in rituals to learn the will of cosmic forces. Heads of wealthy and strong patrilineages also demonstrate potency by hosting lavish rituals during which buffalo are offered, followed by feasting. Such patrilineages function as local elites into which smaller, weaker patrilineages sometimes ask to be assimilated.

Religion

The Bru relationship to cosmic forces is captured in John Miller's observation that "the entire course of a Bru individual's life is integrated with the world of supernatural beings, spirits, which control his destiny from beginning to end and even beyond. A Bru is therefore careful not to offend a spirit intentionally, and if he should offend one, he makes every attempt to appease it, generally by offering a stipulated sacrifice."[2] The

---

1. Gerald Cannon Hickey, *Sons of the Mountains: Ethnohistory of the Vietnamese Central Highlands to 1954* (New Haven: Yale University Press, 1982), pp. 85, 159–60, 167, 179, 193, 210, 359, 430; "Note sur la province de Quang-Tri," *Revue Indo-Chinoise* 5, no. 69 (1907): 1587–94.

2. John Miller, "Bru Kinship," *SA* 2, no. 1 (1972): 65–66. Transcriptions of Bru terms are based on the orthography of John Miller and Caroline Miller.

Bru have an extensive pantheon of spirits (*yiang*) intrinsic to all aspects of the physical environment. According to informants, Yiang Sursei is the supreme deity, who is considered "good," although the Bru tend to be vague about his other characteristics. There are no particular ritual sacrifices prescribed for him. Another powerful being is Yiang Cutêq, Spirit of the Earth, associated with soil fertility and good crops. Very much feared is Yiang Phi Mana, the Death Spirit. At the moment of death, however, it is Yiang Ca Mui who carries off the soul while the wail of Yiang Comuiq can be heard. Whenever an inordinate number of people fall ill or if someone should see a tiger emerging from the forest, villagers know they must offer a sacrificial chicken, pig, or buffalo (depending on the gravity of the situation) to the spirit, Lampẽ. In May 1964 at Lang Kat a family performed such a ritual, sacrificing a chicken and burning sandalwood gathered in the forest.

Mondo, one of Miller's assistants, explained that because illness is a manifestation of a spirit's discontent, divination must be performed to determine which spirit is responsible and what it wants by way of propitiation. The most common divination is *satêh,* a ritual that can be performed by anyone. Three kernels of uncooked rice are placed on the edge of a bowl while the name of a spirit is uttered, and should the kernels remain in place, that spirit is the cause. Most spirits want chickens or pigs, but Yiang Abon, Spirit of the Rice Field, must have a white buffalo, a very costly sacrificial animal.

There is at least one male shaman (*mo*) in every village, and the role most often is passed down within a family. It is by means of *liam* ("to learn what the shaman does") that a boy apprentices, doing such things as repeating a special prayer (*yao*) in a divination ritual (*mul*). In the course of a session, a shaman may employ one or more divination techniques. He might, for example, do the *satêh* ritual, adding his own invocations. Or he may select a special shaman's ritual in which he holds a raw egg in one hand and a lit candle in the other, putting the egg close to his mouth to implore a spirit in a special language. Then, blowing out the candle, he breaks the egg in a rice bowl and pours it over a broad leaf. Only the shaman can interpret signs in the egg telling whether that spirit is responsible and what it demands as propitiation. Mondo noted that the one sign everyone knows is a sizable spot on the egg yoke, the symbol of *sưo,* a pile of dirt from digging a grave and a portent of death. If the ailment persists following the sacrifice, the shaman will perform the *siang* divination, in which a knife is stuck in a large bowl of uncooked rice while the shaman addresses the spirit identified in the previous ritual. If the knife remains upright that identification was correct, but now propitiation will require a larger and more costly animal.

Some divination involves both shaman and kin of the ailing person.

Mondo described how when his mother fell ill he was obliged to perform a divination ritual that normally would have been his father's responsibility. Fashioning a cup out of a large leaf, he filled it with uncooked rice, and taking it outside the house he implored the spirits, saying, "If you want some food, let me know and don't fool me." Carrying a bowl of rice and a candle, he went to the shaman, and sitting on the floor with his legs crossed (a gesture of respect), he indirectly asked the shaman to determine which spirit was causing the sickness. The shaman agreed and on a bamboo tray with legs he placed the bowl of rice and lit a candle. Chanting, he poured the rice on the tray and filled the bowl with water. Then he performed the *satêh* ritual, learning from the responsible spirit that it wanted a chicken sacrificed. To verify this message, the shaman performed a second ritual in which three rice kernels were placed on water in a bowl, and when they remained afloat it substantiated the findings of the previous divination. The chicken sacrifice was duly held, and Mondo's mother recovered.

In May 1964 a divination ritual was observed in the Bru village of Lang Troai on the east bank of the Sepong River (which in this area marks the border between Vietnam and Laos). The patient was an elderly man who suffered from fever and severe coughing. One of five village shamans had determined that the responsible spirit wanted a chicken, which was duly offered, but the ailment persisted. The shaman then recommended a pig, another offering that met with no results. A second ritual revealed that the spirit demanded a buffalo, and when the village was visited, preparations for the sacrifice had begun. The patient was in a bed by an open hearth where a bright fire burned. Along one wall were seven small rattan family altars honoring seven different spirits. Affixed to the opposite wall on bamboo sticks were cone-shaped woven rattan symbols in which rice bowls containing dried bits of previously sacrificed animals were set. The newly made symbol (still empty) for this sacrifice was attached to the wall. In a nearby corner were two low carved-wood tables containing a lit candle, a basket of cooked chickens, a cooked egg, a gourd of rice alcohol, and three bowls containing glutinous rice, water, and a mixture of leaves and bananas. On the floor next to the tables were a large platter of uncooked glutinous rice and small jars of alcohol. In front of the house a buffalo was tethered to a stake.

In midmorning kin and friends gathered in the room. The offerings on the small tables had been moved to the floor in front of the new conical symbol. Next to them one of the sons had placed a pair of carved-wood divination blocks, rounded on one side and flat on the other. Men began playing gongs, drums, and a tambourinelike instrument, while the wife and two sons carried the platter of glutinous rice and basket of chicken out of the house to hold them close to the buffalo's mouth. Returning to the house, they set these dishes amid other offerings while the sons chanted and lit candles. As the rhythm of the music increased, the sons sprinkled glutinous rice over the offerings and the conical symbol. The elder brother then took the divination blocks and dropped them until one flat side and one round side came up, a sign that the spirit accepted the offerings. The sons snuffed out the candles and covered the offerings with a large purple and gold Laotian cloth.

Early in the afternoon the buffalo was slaughtered without ceremony and dressed out immediately. Portions of seven parts were placed on the seven altars in the house. The cloth was removed from the offerings, and baskets of buffalo meat were set among them. A rice bowl filled with bits of the offerings and morsels of buffalo meat was put in the conical symbol. As the music began to play, the sons sat on the floor, and while one poured glutinous rice on the mat before the offerings, the other chanted as he dropped the divination blocks until they signaled the spirit's acceptance. The Laotian cloth was again spread over the offerings to end the ritual. The family and guests then sat on the mat, where in a convivial atmosphere they drank alcohol from small cups and partook of the many food dishes.

Broken bones, sprained joints, eye problems, toothaches, swelling of the foot from stepping on a certain type of worm, and a wide range of wounds (including gunshot wounds) are each associated with a particular spirit. Healing rituals invoking this spirit involve blowing air on the affected area, and this can be done only by a *mo blong* ("shaman who blows air") using special formulas. In most cases this information is passed down in a family, but any adult who learns one or more of the formulas can practice. It is possible to pay a shaman to impart such knowledge, but informants note that this is costly because for each ritual he receives a fee, such as rice alcohol, a chicken, or some silver French colonial coins, making the practice lucrative. One informant reported that he had learned an incantation in a ritual language combining Bru and Lao (one passage went "stop the blood, wound become closed—a scab"). He also was to tell the patient to avoid a certain type of fish. When this healing technique was tried, however, it did not work, and the informant felt that the shaman from whom he had learned it cannily left out some important parts.

Mondo described a type of sorcery called *pân cuai* (*pân* means "to shoot" as in shooting a gun), which is done through the intervention of Yiang Chiat. In the *chat* ritual the sorcerer, using a *can chai,* a stone tube "as smooth as a rice kernel," shoots a projectile (*can triên*) of metal or wood into the victim, causing illness. The sorcerer knows a ritual for removing the projectile, but if this is not done the victim will die. In the past it was necessary to apprentice (which involves being given a stone tube) in upland Laos among the Carai (or Crai), a "backcountry Lao" group who live near Lao Bao and speak a dialect of Lao mixed with words borrowed from neighboring upland groups. Mondo's mother's brother was such an apprentice, and though he no longer practices the shooting, he continues to perform the removal ritual for a fee. This type of sorcery is evoked for the most part in interpersonal conflicts. Mondo cited as a hypothetical example the desire for vengeance by an old man who feels that he has been insulted by a young man from a neighboring village. The old man consults a sorcerer, giving him the young man's name (this is important) and paying him a fee to have *pân cuai* performed. The shaman first prepares the projectile by wrapping a splinter of metal or wood with thread. Then in the *chat* ritual he inserts the projectile in his stone tube, which in turn is put into a bamboo container. Shaking the container, he invokes Yiang Chiat in an incantation mixing Bru and Lao asking that the projectile be shot into the body of the victim (who is named). Unseen by human eyes, the projectile penetrates the victim's body, causing localized pain where it enters and then a general malaise. Mondo noted that one aspect of the vengeance is that the victim's family will fruitlessly do the usual sacrifices, depleting their livestock, leaving them destitute.

The projectile can be removed only by another sorcerer equal or superior in power to the one who shot the victim. First, this sorcerer examines the victim, after which he stands back and, with hands clasped in a gesture of respect, declares whether or not the ailment is caused by *pân cuai*. The victim then asks the sorcerer to "force" (*êp*) the projectile out of his body. Placing four nuts around the inside of a rice bowl and lighting a candle, the sorcerer informs Yiang Ca Mui (the spirit who takes the soul) that he wants to cure the victim (who is named). Holding the candle, he pours alcohol into a bowl, and after sipping a bit of it, he sprinkles the remainder over the sick man's body. Then, taking the leaves of the *apuac* tree (which Bru identify in Vietnamese as *cây bi,* the *bi* tree[3]), the sorcerer rubs (*ramoon*) them over the painful area of the body while he calls upon the projectile to concentrate where it entered, the only place from which it can be removed. In a second ritual several days later, the sorcerer dips *apuac* leaves in rice alcohol and then rubs them on the victim's body as he calls on the projectile to concentrate. When he squeezes the leaves in a bowl of alcohol, there are likely to be some bits of substance which everyone thinks is from the projectile although only

---

3. In Phạm Hòang Hộ, *Cây-cỏ Miền Nam Việt-Nam* (Flora of South Vietnam) (Saigon: Bộ Văn-Hóa Giáo-Dục và Thanh-Niên [Ministry of Culture, Education, and Youth], 1970), p. 427, the *bi-điển đồng-chu* tree, whose botanical designation is *Bridelia monoica* (Lour.) is described as being native to the area of Hue and Quang Tri so it is very likely the tree they call *apuac*.

the sorcerer can see it emerge. This ends the ritual, and the family treats the sorcerer to some alcoholic drinks (Mondo said laughingly that a sorcerer who likes to drink is apt to return several times to take advantage of the family's hospitality). After the patient recovers, his family visits the sorcerer to make a ritual presentation (*tuoh cliêi*) of rice, a chicken, a container of alcohol, and silver French coins.

Settlements and Houses

Each Bru village has a defined territory, the use of which is supervised by the headman. Settlements have from ten to twenty houses, and married sons usually live near their parents so kin clusters are common. Enclosed kitchen gardens are located near the house and along the banks of nearby watercourses. Bru houses vary in size and some construction materials, but roof thatching is invariably of imperata cylindrica grass. All houses are on piling most commonly six feet in height for dwellings on level ground. An ordinary house has six hewn tree trunks as basic columns, and attached to these with rattan cord are small logs to support the floor (Figure 16). Larger houses of the well-to-do have hardwood frames and roofs rounded at the ends to accommodate storage lofts. Many roofs have carved decorations, the most common of which are buffalo horns (Figure 17). Many houses have two entrances, one exclusively for the family.

Ordinary houses usually have one room (Figure 18), where mats are spread by the open hearth for sleeping. When the eldest son marries, an addition may be built to accommodate him and his family. Larger houses have two rooms, one of which is used by the women to receive their female guests, while the other is where males gather and family celebrations are held. Meals are prepared on hearths, over which are bamboo platforms where salt in banana leaves, beans, tobacco, and maize are kept dry. Water gourds, baskets, ropes, a broom, and bundles of sticks are suspended from the ceiling. Personal belongings, baskets of unhusked rice, and tools are stored along the wall. Spears are kept on the roof beams.

Family

Kin terms (see Appendix B6) reflect the fact that the Bru have exogamous patrilineages (*sâu*), membership in which is traced through the male line upward to the fifth ascending generation and down to the fourth descending generation. *Ai* is older brother, *dī* is older sister. *Clúng* and *ndī* may be added to identify the eldest and second eldest siblings. *A-ễm* is younger sibling differentiated by sex modifiers *mamsẽn* for broth-

Figure 16. Bru house construction details.

Figure 17. Bru house buffalo-horn roof motifs.

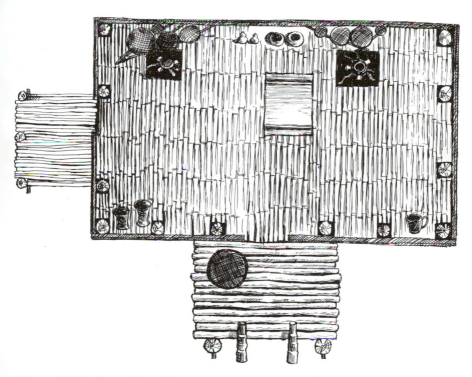

Figure 18. Bru house floor plan.

Photo 18. A Bru village near Khe Sanh (1964).

ers and *semieng* for females with the modifier *ralŏh* identifying the youngest sibling (it also is used for the father's youngest sibling and Ego's last-born child). Male Ego may address or refer to any female siblings by the term *amuaq,* and a female Ego may use the term *amiang* for male siblings. Sibling terms are extended to cousins, who are age-graded relative to Ego. In addition, *semai* is a generic expression for male cousins and *semaui* for female cousins. Both terms can be used with other appropriate kin terms to specify a relationship. The son of the father's younger brother, for example, can be referred to as *semai con anhi* or "male cousin, child of father's younger brother." Age-grading is extended to Ego's affinal kin.

In the first ascending generation, father is *m'poaq* and mother is *m'piq,* but west of Khe Sanh these terms are *m'pua* and *m'pi* respectively. With the exception of mother's brothers (*cūq*) the parents' siblings are age-graded relative to the parents. *Bac* is the term for father's older siblings and mother's older sister. When addressing the father's older sister, the modifier *ayoah* is added. Parents' younger sisters are *avia.* Only collateral kin of the patrilineage are recognized using father's siblings' terms, and they are age-graded relative to the father. *Cūq,* mother's brother, is the only kin term not used bilaterally, and this appears to be related to the Bru preference for matrilateral cross-cousin marriage as well as to the unique role the maternal uncle plays in his sister's daughters' marriages and in distribution of inheritance in his sister's family. The parents' siblings' terms are extended to affinal kin of this generation. Emphasis is placed on male-line kin of the second ascending generation with terms for the father's father's siblings. Addition of the modifier *õng* identifies the paternal grandparents while the modifier *muq* is used for the mother's parents. Only kin of the direct male line are recognized in the third, fourth, and fifth ascending generations. In the first descending generation the same modifiers as are used in Ego's generation identify the first, second, and last-born children (*con*). *Con* also is the vocative term, but the affectionate *ai* for sons and *amoq* for daughters is more commonly used. Siblings' children are *ramon*. Collateral kin in the second descending generation are recognized, but only direct male-line kin are identified in the third and fourth descending generations.

Elders of the exogamous patrilineage (*sâu*) keep careful track of membership. In one informant's village there were thirty-two families divided among four patrilineages, and membership in them extended to neighboring villages. Some Bru patrilineages even claim membership among the Pacoh. Although in principle the *sâu* is a consanguineal group, should members of a very small patrilineage fear that their group might die out, they can affiliate themselves with a larger *sâu*. This entails the assent of the larger group's members and a sacrifice of two buffalo. Mondo said he and his brother were the only surviving members of their *sâu* in the village, but they did not have two buffalo. When they approached the head of a very large, wealthy patrilineage, he asked them, "Why do you want to join our *sâu*? Will you do bad things? Will you steal from us?" The brothers responded that they wanted only to be good members. It was agreed they could join without a buffalo sacrifice. They and the *sâu* members cut their fingers, letting the blood drip into rice alcohol which everyone drank.

Within the *sâu* there is a small, patrilineally linked residential group, the *tóng*, which consists of a father, who is chief, and his married sons. This unit functions in many respects as the social and economic building block of the patrilineage. When the sons have children, the group expands to include three generations, but with the death of the father it disintegrates and each son becomes head of a new *tóng*. One informant was member of a *sâu* composed of six *tóng*, but within a year it dwindled to five.

The patrilineage is a more enduring group, whose solidarity is generated by the role of the group head and common veneration of a *sâu* patron spirit (or spirits) and the ancestors. Harmony with these cosmic forces will bring abundant harvests, health, and good fortune. Each patrilineage venerates a special spirit (or spirits) that at some time in the past was selected by its members from the Bru pantheon. One informant, for example, reported that his *sâu* spirits were those who bestowed upon people the ability to be good singers and storytellers. The group head bears the title Cuai Yong Asaiu, "He Who Possesses the Blocks," a reference to the carved-wood blocks he uses in rituals honoring the patrilineage deities. Each patrilineage is known by the name of its head. Mondo, for example, is a member of *sâu chua Agni* or "patrilineage of Agni's grandfather." The head usually is an older man of good reputation, and it is important that he want the position. Should he for whatever reason (such as there being too much criticism of his performance) want to quit, he is free to do so.

Mutual aid is an important principle within the *sâu*. There often are needy, elderly, or handicapped members, and sometimes a family is left destitute. The head sees to their material welfare by soliciting contributions from *tổng* leaders. A widow is free to marry out of the patrilineage, and in doing so she cuts all ties with it. If she has been a good and faithful wife, however, she may approach the *sâu* head to ask her husband's kin for some mobile family goods. She also may seek the good offices of the head to get her children released from their father's patrilineage so they can join her new husband's patrilineage. If a family needs additional labor in building a house, the head will provide it, and he can be asked to help gather goods for a bride-price.

Miller observes that the *sâu* head derives certain legal prerogatives from the fact that if a member does not adhere to the Bru moral code, the spirit will become angry and wreak misfortune on the whole group.[4] He arbitrates conflicts within the group. Any grievance against a member by an outsider is a grievance against the entire kin group, which must be resolved on a group-to-group basis with their heads as mediators. If a woman is caught in adultery with an outsider, for example, it is considered less an offense against her husband or the group than against the *sâu* spirit. The head will therefore deal appropriately with the woman and demand heavy retribution from the outsider's patrilineage to placate the spirit.

Souls of the dead enjoy bliss only if prescribed offerings are made to them and to the *sâu* spirit in a ritual which the head must organize. After death, the burial, which must have the approval of the village headman, is relatively simple. The body is placed in a coffin roughly hewn from a large hardwood log (the bumps on the log are called "feet and breasts"). A few personal possessions and perhaps some money are packed around the corpse, and burial takes place without ceremony. In the isolation of the forest, the *sâu* head maintains a spirit house (*dống soc*), a miniature

4. Miller, "Bru Kinship," p. 65.

of a Bru abode. He is the only one allowed to touch the house, and when a member of the patrilineage dies he places a small bamboo stick inside (for "bad deaths" such as those resulting from childbirth or an attack by a tiger, there is a special spirit house with a rounded roof). The head organizes annual offerings of chickens, a pig, eggs, and jars of alcohol, and to obtain these he visits the lineage households to solicit contributions. This can be a bothersome task, and it is one of the reasons the role of head is not sought after. The Millers related that unbeknownst to them, one of their Christian converts continued to give chickens for this ritual. The man finally admitted that even though he knew it was wrong, he did it out of fear that if he did not, the *sâu* head might resign and nominate him as successor.

Gathering at the spirit house, members of the patrilineage present their offerings, after which the head intones a prayer to the *sâu* spirit, saying, "We are bringing offerings of pigs, chickens, eggs, and alcohol, so you must protect us because if anything happens to us there won't be anyone to make offerings and feed you." Mondo explained that this was to induce a response (*xui giuc*) from the spirit in the block-divination ritual that follows. Holding a block in each hand, the head drops them, and if one flat side and one round side come up (the blocks are dropped until they do), it is a sign that the spirit has "eaten the offerings." The animals are then slaughtered, dressed, and cooked while everyone drinks from the jars.

When a large number of sticks have accumulated in the spirit house, the head announces that the spirit has manifested its desire to have a final ritual for the deceased. Prescriptively twelve buffalo should be the main offering, but smaller patrilineages offer half that number. This occasion provides an opportunity for the patrilineage to demonstrate its wealth, which also reflects the potency of its head. On the appointed day, all patrilineage members gather at the spirit house, where the head invites the *sâu* spirit and the ancestors to partake of the offerings. The animals are slaughtered, after which the head removes the sticks from the spirit house, placing them in a miniature coffin fashioned from a log. He sets fire to the spirit house, and as it burns he addresses the spirit and the ancestors, saying that all of the offerings have now been made so they should be at peace. The coffin is buried in an isolated place that must be avoided. A new spirit house is built to begin a new cycle. Subsequent misfortune may be taken to mean that the spirit and ancestors are not content with the offerings. The head must then seek more contributions and make another offering and be very firm in pointing out that it is the *final* ritual.

Marriages create a constantly changing network of kindred ties, expressed in the terms *khoi* and *cuya,* that Ego shares with male members of his patrilineage. For Ego, all of those in patrilineages whose members have taken wives from his patrilineage are *khoi*. Members of the patri-lineage from which Ego's male kin have taken wives are *cuya*. In other words, for Ego, the *sâu* that takes wives is *khoi,* and the one that gives wives is *cuya.* The kindred regulates marriage with the rule that "the *khoi* can take from the *cuya,* but the *cuya* cannot take from the *khoi.*" This in effect means that Ego can marry his mother's brother's daughter but cannot marry his father's sister's daughter. Kindreds duplicate many of the social-economic expectations found in the patrilineage such as hospi-tality and mutual aid in house building and in accumulating goods for a bride-price.

According to informants, the Bru in times past adhered to the prefer-ence for matrilateral cross-cousin marriage, but in recent years young people have been exercising more free choice in the selection of mates. Mondo reported that his mother urged him and his brothers to marry her brothers' daughters because "it is closer, and the family will give help when it is needed." One brother did marry his maternal uncle's daughter, but another wed a girl who was not related. Mondo felt that if he married a cousin he could not "tell her off" when the occasion called for it. Parental approval is necessary before a marriage can take place. In Bru villages it is common for children of around eight years to sleep away from their own houses in an informal arrangement in which boys tend to group in one house and girls in another. After puberty, the boys go to visit the house where the girls sleep to talk and play musical instruments. The ideal girl is one from a good, reasonably well-off family with no history of oddities. Physical beauty is desirable, but it is ranked be-low qualities associated with being a good housekeeper such as "good-hearted," truthful, faithful, and industrious. Physical handicaps, if they do not render the girl an invalid, are not an impediment to marriage. The Bru say that a handicap does not reflect the curse of spirits nor does it indicate "bad innards" (bad character). The Millers cited the case of a girl who was a deaf-mute, but she had such a good reputation as a house-keeper that villagers agreed she would have no problem finding a hus-band.

A boy and girl attracted to each other arrange secret meetings through friends, secluding themselves in places such as provisory shelters built near swiddens. They are apt to begin having intercourse, and should the girl become pregnant, marriage arrangements must be made imme-diately. Normally when a courtship reaches the point that parents see it leading to marriage, they confer with their children. The couple spends a night together, and the following morning the boy gives the girl a token gift as they declare their intention to wed. The boy's parents enlist an older reputable family member of either sex to act as intermediary (*mo so͞u*). The village headman, who will serve as "leader of the wedding" (*thâu kei*) is duly informed. In the "send for" ritual, the boy, accompanied by the intermediary and friends, goes to the girl's house with gifts (metal pots, knives, necklaces, beads, bracelets, tobacco, and recently some cash). They wait outside until one of her parents asks what they want, and, bringing forward the gifts, the boy responds that they have come for the girl. The group is invited to enter the house and given food, drink, and places to sleep in the main room. In the morning the girl's parents take from among the gifts a string of beads, tobacco, and a cooking pot, which they give the boy. He descends the entrance ladder and then ascends it to place these things inside the main entrance. The girl's parents then invite him to enter, giving him glutinous rice wrapped in a banana leaf, regular rice, onions, and bananas. The boy and girl leave and go to his house, where his parents sacrifice a pig and a chicken to introduce the girl to their *sâu* spirit. Afterward there is a gathering at the girl's house to eat and drink. Among the alcohol jars there is one with eight bamboo drinking tubes, and it is forbidden for members of the couple's patrilineages to drink from it (this jar is also used in a later ritual). They must also refrain from eating rice cakes, and until the first wedding ritual they should avoid one another's houses.

In preparation for the first wedding ritual (*rabeing*), the intermediary approaches the village headman and the girl's parents to work out the bride-price, which usually does not involve any bargaining. The minimum is a large sow, a suckling pig, a hen, a rooster, and a set of gongs. Additional items such as beads, bracelets, metal pots, pans, and trays will be given, depending on the boy's family's means. Male members of both patrilineages gather at the girl's farmstead to eat and drink while discussing wedding arrangements, but because it is taboo for those of the boy's group to enter her house, a special shelter is built. About one week before the wedding, the girl goes to visit her mother's brother, who is responsible for making arrangements for the ritual and feasting. The girl informs her uncle that she plans to wed and asks his assistance. He responds by soliciting contributions of cooked food, chickens, pigs, and fish from males of the patrilineage.

On the day of the celebration the groom's party gathers in the temporary shelter near the bride's house, where they are greeted by the "intermediary for the bride's side" (*mo so͞u cuya*), to whom they present the bride-price. These gifts are carried into the house and given to the "wedding leader" (village headman), who in turn passes them to the bride's parents. They look the gifts over and put them in baskets, a gesture of acceptance that lifts the taboos for both patrilineages so the groom's party is now free to enter the house. As five chickens and a suckling pig are sacrificed, the bride's "wedding guardian" (her father or one of her brothers) informs the *sâu* spirit that she is married and has left the patrilineage. The groom's family then presents cloth and food to the bride's parents. With the bride's maternal uncle playing host, everyone joins in drinking and eating, and the bride performs menial tasks to demonstrate that she is a conscientious housekeeper. Bru informants also noted that this is the last time she will play a role as a member of her paternal household.

When this celebration ends, members of both patrilineages are forbidden to enter the lofts in one another's houses. This taboo is eliminated when the final wedding celebration (*coul*) is held at the wife's paternal house to mark the *khoi-cuya* linking of the two patrilineages. For this event the wife's former patrilineage (*cuya*) contributes mats, husked rice, and jars of rice and maize alcohol while the husband's group (*khoi*) presents a buffalo, pigs, and chickens. Because of its cost, this ritual may be put off for a long time. One informant noted that he and his wife had four children, and they still had not observed it. When both sides agree on a date for the ritual, it is recorded on a long cord of knots. The married couple assumes a position at one side of a sacrificial buffalo while the wife's father stands at the other side. He passes the husband a woman's skirt and blouse, and the husband hands him a knife and gong. The wife then holds a bag containing salt, a knife, and fresh fish over the buffalo's head. Reaching into the bag, she removes the knife, handing it to her father, who slits the animal's throat. After the buffalo is dressed out, meat is roasted and seasoned with the salt from the wife's bag. The jar of alcohol with eight drinking tubes that had been prepared at the time of the engagement is brought out. The couple's parents are first to drink, followed by the two intermediaries and the village headman. While other guests drink, the bride's father performs a divination ritual with his patrilineage's blocks (obtained from the head) to determine if the *sâu* spirit has accepted the offerings.

Residence is temporarily patrilocal with the couple sharing his parents' cooking hearth. Eventually the couple builds a house nearby, and with the consent of his father they may farm their own swidden. At Huc Van village in 1964 a very well-to-do villager had a large, elaborate dwelling, and next to it his married eldest son had just completed his new house, a simple, one-room structure. After marriage, until a child is born and teknonymy pertains, the groom often is referred to as "husband of so and so," or he might be known by the name of his wife's village added to the term *khoi*. If she, for example, were from Huc Van, he would be called "*khoi* Huc Van." The Bru division of labor reflects the general highland pattern with some exceptions. Men join the women in planting seeds and in foraging. While men weave back-baskets, women weave the shoulder straps. In addition, men fashion bracelets of metal and bead necklaces.

Both men and women prepare a tasty quid of areca nut wrapped in betel leaves and garnished with a dash of lime. In the past, filing teeth at a puberty ritual was common, but by 1964 it was fading. In Lang Troai, for example, only a few villagers, most of them females, had filed teeth. A great many Bru still blacken their teeth with lacquer. Among young men, tatooing two or three rows of dots on the forehead before marriage is very popular.

Miller reports that although all of the land within a village's recognized territory is under supervision of the headman, household heads do obtain "rights" to swiddens being farmed or fallowing.[5] On the death of the father, this usufruct is part of the inheritance, which also includes household furnishings, farm implements, and domestic animals. The eldest married son, assisted by his mother's brother, sees to the distribution of the property. Because females marry out of the family (and take personal possessions with them), sons tend to inherit the bulk. Married daughters nonetheless often receive some token goods. Obligations and debts of the deceased fall to his heirs, who must be informed of them before the father's death. Should a couple divorce, such things as duration of the marriage and which party is responsible for the breakup determine whether the wife must return part of the bride-price.

Economic Activities

In selecting the site for a new swidden, the Bru look for black or brown soil and places with abundant growth, notably large trees. Most families farm two or three hectares. The task of clearing a swidden begins in January, when the rains are tapering off. Should farmers decide that because of late rains "the soil is not ripe," the head of the patrilineage organizes a ritual sacrifice to ask Yiang Cuteq, Spirit of the Earth, for good growing conditions. Both men and women make holes with dibble sticks to plant upland rain-fed rice and glutinous rice (good for making alcohol).

In late October or early November, everyone, including children, joins in gathering the crop. Yield is measured in back-baskets, which informants claim hold around twenty kilos of unhusked rice. They say that most families realize between twenty-five and thirty baskets per swidden. One informant noted that a field of two hectares with very fertile soil can yield as many as seventy baskets. Depending on adjudged soil fertility, swiddens are farmed between one and three years. "We do not like to cut young forest," farmers observed in explaining that they allow substantial regrowth before farming again. Secondary crops are planted in and

5. Ibid., pp. 63–65.

around swiddens and in gardens along watercourses and next to the houses. South of Khe Sanh at lower elevations there are orange and lime trees, and villagers close to the French estates have adopted coffee cultivation. Well-to-do villagers have elephants, which are used as draft animals.

Both men and women forage for seeds, roots, and wild fruits and vegetables. For hunting, shotguns have come into use, although men carve crossbows, and the village of Huc Van gained a reputation for producing superior crossbows. Men also fashion hardwood spears and in 1964 a Vietnamese smith in Khe Sanh made most of the blades. Groups of adept hunters venture into the mountain forests to stalk tigers and elephants with spears and crossbows, the arrows of which are smeared with poison just below the arrowhead. The poison, extracted from a local tree, is said to kill quickly. In the past women made skirts from the bark of this tree, detoxifying by immersing it in water.

Normally the Bru do not grow cash crops, nor do they engage in commerce. There are times, however, when poor crops and other circumstances (such as wartime disruptions) force villagers to exchange vegetables, bamboo, firewood, and sometimes livestock for rice and salt with Vietnamese in the Khe Sanh market. Also, from time to time villagers sell or barter among themselves domestic animals (except dogs) and tigers. This is done indirectly using code words. One informant cited as an example the situation in which a woman in his village let it be known that she was willing to part with one of her pigs. A man approached her, asking, "Will you blow air at me," which she knew was a way of asking if she would invite him into the house to discuss the transaction. Inside the house he said, "I would like to have your rat." Both knew that "rat" meant a pig, so they worked out a price. Similarly, a buffalo is a "clawing ant," a goat is a "fox," and an elephant is a "large log." Bru inexperience with marketplace behavior was illustrated at the 1966 SIL workshop in Kontum, when research assistants from various ethnic groups shared quarters and took turns marketing for their meals. The Bru assistant was quickly relieved of this duty when on his first visit to the market he paid what the Vietnamese vendors asked without bargaining.

Village Leaders

Although the French and Vietnamese superimposed administrative systems on the Bru, duties and responsibilities of the headman (*ariaih*) persisted, and the role is hereditary so his sons decide who among them is best suited to succeed. If there are no sons, adult members of his patrilineage select his successor. According to Miller, the headman, with his superior knowledge of customs and laws, "must be consulted on virtually all transactions taking place within the village," and "if one does not abide by the decision of the chief, one is obliged to leave the village."[6] In addition to his roles in marriages and funerals, he regulates use of village territory, protecting a family's "rights" to swiddens, approving new swiddens, and even deciding whether large trees can be felled. He arbitrates disputes unresolved by the parties themselves or by their kin groups. The headman represents the village in any dealings with the local government agencies, for example, recruiting labor for village or government projects.

Pacoh

Historically the upland Pacoh have been relatively isolated although the Pahi at lower elevations had some contact with the Vietnamese. In a 1965 discussion, Richard Watson pointed out that the Pahi language displays some dialect differences that can be attributed to Vietnamese influence.[7] The Pacoh, like the Bru, have patrilineal descent, but they have clans, each of which has its name, a common ancestor, and legends. Some clans also have food taboos. The Pacoh have kindreds similar to those of the Bru, which regulate marriage. In addition to having wisdom manifested in wealth, Pacoh leaders demonstrate potency by their eloquent performances in "speaking contests" and "debates." Also, the role of female "*aboh* chief" has potency derived from a female-fecundity link with soil-rice fertility. Pacoh legend describes how they are descended from a man and his wife who survived the great flood. They had two sons and two daughters who mated, thereby setting the pattern for marriage with the mother's brother's daughter (matrilateral cross-cousin marriage).

Settlements

The Pacoh avoid building settlements high in the mountains because "they are too steep even for tigers." They also avoid places believed to be the abode of spirits (*yang*), such as forest ponds surrounded by wild fruit trees and caves with "clean" interiors. According to one Pahi myth, some caves are inhabited by female spirits who have one large breast in the middle of the body. One such spirit captured a Frenchman and held him in her cave for three years, during which time they had a child. One day she inadvertently left the cave entrance unguarded when she foraged for food, and the prisoner escaped. Male spirits in the mountains are mon-

6. Ibid., pp. 64–65.
7. The transcriptions of Pacoh words are based on Richard Watson's orthography.

strous, and they can imitate a human cry for help. The unwary person who responds is grabbed and frightened to death by the spirit's fiendish laughter.

Each Pacoh village has a well-defined territory (*cruang*) encompassing a large area, sometimes the better part of a river valley. It is administered by village elders and is for the exclusive use of residents. Each settlement is composed of longhouses, the length of which depends on the size of the resident extended patrilineal family. Cubuat, one of Richard Watson's assistants, described his natal village of Arum, located on the Laos side of a river marking the border, as having 600 residents divided among six longhouses with a total of 113 hearths. The smallest longhouse in the village had 1 hearth and 20 residents while the largest had 180 people and 42 hearths. In the hardwood-frame longhouses a large room (*mong*) with three or four hearths serves as a work area, reception room, place for family rituals, and dormitory for older boys. Extended in either direction are compartments occupied by males and their families. Each compartment has a hearth and its own entrance reached by a wooden ladder. Cubuat described the arrangement of kitchen gardens along the river, where residents also bathed, fished, and fetched water. They hunted in the nearby forests.

Family

Kin terms in Appendix B7 reflect patrilineal affiliation, age-grading, and preference for matrilateral cross-cousin marriage. Ego's siblings are age-graded, and younger brothers and sisters are distinguished by sex modifiers. The mother's brothers' daughters are identified by the term *lu lep,* and they are addressed by the familiar term *alep.* Sibling terms are extended to other collateral kin, who are age-graded relative to Ego. There is a common term for the father and his brothers, but the latter are age-graded relative to the father with the use of modifiers. His sisters are similarly age-graded. The mother's siblings are not age-graded. Patrilineal and nonpatrilineal kin in the second and third ascending generations are distinguished by the modifiers *choanh* and *preng* respectively. An alternate modifier, *yaq,* the term for "clan," can be used to identify the father's mother and father's father's mother. Only direct male-line kin are recognized in the fourth ascending generation. In the first descending generation, children are *acay* with sex modifiers used to distinguish sons from daughters. Siblings' children are *amon.* Only male-line kin in the second and third descending generations are recognized.

The names of patrilineal clans (*tong* or *yaq*) are Can Xŏiq, Prung, Kê, Xmpong, Pataq, Avceat, Ahár, Nguan, Tancoal, Tarlúc, Tayur, Hôi, Tuvên, and Aiq, all taken from designations for animals or plants. The

Kê and Tuvên have taboos against eating dog, and the Aiq must not consume cat. Legend has it that in the distant past the Prung and Kê were the only clans. There "were not enough people" so members of both clans took their belongings and went to a faraway place. There they offered pigs and chickens to inform the spirits that they were no longer members of their respective clans. After a period, they returned to their villages and intermarried with Kê and Prung clan members, thereby creating the additional clans.

One clan not named after a plant or animal bears the designation for the Pacoh word for the pestle used in husking rice. Clan legend relates that members were descended from a family of "lazy people," who, rather than carve a pestle as did other families, stole one from a neighboring longhouse. Suspecting them of the theft, their fellow villagers trimmed a bush near a much-used path in the shape of pestle and hid nearby. The father of the family came along the path and, thinking the bush was a pestle, he grabbed it but found it rooted to the ground. At that moment, the villagers emerged and declared that from that day his family would be known as "pestle."

Intercourse between members of the same clan is irreparable incest, an affront to the ancestors, and Pacoh law calls for the guilty couple to leave the village and not be allowed to enter other villages. Marriage is further regulated by the kindred, which resembles that of the Bru. For male Ego, all of those in clans whose members have taken wives from his clan are *khoy* while those in the clan from which Ego's male kin have taken wives are *kuya*. The *khoy* can take wives from the *kuya*, but the *kuya* cannot take wives from the *khoy*, which means that Ego can marry his mother's brother's daughter but not his father's sister's daughter. Pacoh informants report that in the past the rule was strictly adhered to because young men and girls were brought up with the idea that such marriage was ideal. Cubuat observed that marrying the father's sister's daughter is like marrying a sister, but to marry the maternal uncle's daughter is "to marry as one's father did." He added that he knew that his mother's kin would treat him well. If such a cousin is not available, a young man searches for a wife among his *kuya* kin. Cubuat and Avu (another assistant to Richard Watson) said that *khoy* are expected to visit *kuya* kin from time to time, bringing animals (but no fowl), pots, pans, knives, and clothing. The *kuya* make frequent visits to the *khoy* "because they are visiting the daughter who has been given in marriage," bringing fowl, cooked rice, and cloth. Such *khoy-kuya* mutual visits also allow marriageable cousins and their parents to become better acquainted. Cubuat's wife is a Phuang (the ethnic status of the Phoang, also called Phuang and Phuong, has yet to be determined) located south of the Pacoh, and they have the same kindred system with *khoy-kuya* linkages. Cubuat's marriage links him with Phuang kindreds, which, because of intergroup marriages, extend to the Katu farther south. Cubuat noted that should he travel into the territories of the Phuang or Katu, he would seek someone with whom he could converse to trace clan names similar to his in an attempt to locate himself in a *khoy-kuya* network so he "would know how to behave."

Cubuat describes in a text how some boys and girls meet during the maize harvest.[8] Boys take flutes and other instruments to the fields where girls are helping gather the crop. The boys tease the girls, who roast ears of corn for them to eat. When the adults return to the village, the young people remain into the night. There are sanctions against having intercourse, but should a girl become pregnant, out of fear that they "will meet a tiger when they go out of the village" the couple must confess to their parents who will have them sacrifice pigs to the ancestors to avoid misfortune for the village.

Cubuat observed that the high cost of getting married renders it difficult for a boy from a poor family to find a wife. He relates in a text that to initiate a courtship, the boy brings to the girl's house some cloth, perhaps cash, and something he knows she likes. This initiates a taboo against his giving her any cooked rice, chicken, or fish. The first day of the wedding is "the day when her parents give their child to another hearth, so they must kill a pig" and provide rice, chickens, rice alcohol, and sugarcane alcohol (fermented in bamboo tubes) for a feast called *aleq-uroq* ("dropping the banana-leaf stem through the top of the ladder") at their longhouse. The girl's father asks the boy's parents to bring a bride-price of "two or three large pigs and some old silver" (probably a reference to silver French colonial coins). The wedding is marked by three days of feasting at the groom's house. Following this, there is another celebration called "chop the child's head," held at the bride's house for her departure. The groom's family provides a buffalo sacrifice, some silver, gongs, necklaces, bracelets, earrings, and pots of various types. With this celebration the taboo against the boy giving the girl certain cooked foods is lifted.[9]

The couple remains at the groom's house. *Aboh* is the term for the residence group that normally consists of parents and their married sons' families, who share the same cooking hearth, farm together, and observe rituals for patrilineal clan ancestors at which the eldest male, head of this group, officiates. The eldest female, however, is the "*aboh* chief," who

8. Cubuat, "Customs of Pacoh Young People," trans. Richard Watson, mimeograph, 1964, pp. 1–2.

9. Cubuat, "We Pacoh Take Each Other's Children to Be Our Wives," trans. Richard Watson, mimeograph, 1964, pp. 1–2.

has a mystical tie with the Rice Spirit, associated with the family's seed rice. She officiates at the rice harvest ritual, and she alone can cook rice. At meals everyone must go to the hearth, where she serves portions of steaming rice. Women of the household are subservient to the *aboh* chief, who supervises preparation of all food (game bagged by the men is dressed out and cooked by her).

A newborn child is not named for several months (a practice that appears to be related to high infant mortality). Children are given names that begin with the same letter. When a child reaches prepuberty its peers bestow another name of three words. The first word indicates sex—"cu" or "a" for males and "cón" for females. The second word is a noun that rhymes with the given name, and the third is a verb associated with the second word. If, for example, the second word is "bamboo," the third might be "split," or if the second is "rock," the third could be "throw." At this time the given name becomes taboo.

Cubuat relates in a text that when illness strikes, the victim often is aware of having offended a spirit and awaits a dream that may reveal how to make amends. In most cases, illness prompts the family to summon a shaman. The male shaman (*mo ramón*) and female shaman (*curu*) contact spirits who sing (*cha châp* and *panôh*) messages through them. The family awaits nightfall to summon the female shaman. Sitting on the floor in torchlight, she adds some joss to a bowl containing hot embers, and as the smoke rises she intones a prayer to Yang Coh, asking which spirit has been wronged and what it seeks in propitiation so that the victim "will be released." Sometimes the shaman admits that the victim is close to death and cannot be saved by sacrificial offerings. More often, the shaman sings (in a strange language) a spirit message asking for a sacrifice, beginning with a chicken, and if the ailment persists, a pig, then a buffalo. Cubuat relates that when he was younger he became gravely ill, and the shaman performed her ritual and told his parents that they should sacrifice a buffalo for a spirit called *crúm*. They did so, and Cubuat recovered. Cubuat noted that some individuals have the special power (*cun*) to stop bleeding. When, however, such a person is extracting juice from the *tuvaq* tree, he may unwittingly bring his power to bear and the juice will stop flowing.[10]

The Pacoh distinguish between the spirits of "those who die a natural death" (*yang cumuiq*) and "those who die a bad death" (*yang pireng*). Burial customs for the former vary according to wealth. The very poor light candles, wrap the corpse in a mat, and bury it in a deep grave after

10. Cubuat, "Sickness for Us Pacoh," trans. Richard Watson, mimeograph, 1964, pp. 1–2.

which they sacrifice a chicken for the departed spirit. The well-to-do place the corpse in a hewn hardwood coffin with a hole in the bottom to allow body fluids to drain. Personal belongings and gifts are packed in the coffin, which is then sealed. The coffin is left aboveground, surrounded by a brightly decorated wooden enclosure. After a buffalo is sacrificed, mourners drink from jars and feast. Three years later, the bones are removed, washed, and placed in a new, smaller coffin in which gifts are placed. Mourners dance around the coffin, stopping periodically to eat and drink.

Once every four years the entire village observes the feast of the tombs (*gariaw ping*). Cubuat describes in a text how three months prior, word spreads that (using his natal village as an example) "Arum village is going to celebrate the feast of the tombs," which stirs up excitement because everyone wants "to go play, sing, eat, drink, and entertain." Villagers prepare rice alcohol and sugarcane alcohol, hunt game and birds, and trade with the Vietnamese and neighboring Ta-oi for chickens, pigs, rice, skirts, and shirts. They inform *khoy* and *kuya* kin so they can bring chickens and rice. Villagers without kin seek entertainers from other villages. Twenty days before the feast, the *khoy-kuya* kin and helpers from the vicinity are invited to Arum to prepare cakes and other food while the villagers build a lavishly decorated enclosure around a covered shelter in which a coffin sits on an earth mound. Lots of food and alcohol are available, and preparations are carried out in a very merry atmosphere. On the eve of the feast, *khoy* kin, helpers, and entertainers flood in to put on special garb such as loincloths and shirts, arrange their hair, and make up their faces. On the first morning of the feast, while musicians at the edge of the settlement play gongs, drums, flutes, and horns, villagers exhume and wash bones, putting them in the coffin. In the late afternoon *khoy* kin are invited to the houses of their in-laws, but when the elders declare that "if any debts remain unsettled, even though the tomb is completed, no one can enter," the village is taboo to everyone else. After debts are resolved, the taboo is lifted. Music soars as villagers and guests break into the "buffalo dance." *Khoy* kin are served rice, cakes, bananas, rice alcohol, and sugarcane alcohol, after which everyone else joins in feasting and drinking from the jars. Four buffalo (one explicitly for those who prepared the feast) and some cattle are sacrificed. The celebration continues for three days with music, dancing to honor the dead, songfests, speaking contests, feasting on many dishes, and drinking from the innumerable jars. When the guests leave to return to their villages, they are given glutinous rice, pork, chicken, and beef. *Kuya* kin are presented with mats, bowls, dishes, pots, pans, and silver French coins while *khoy* kin receive skirts, shirts, and rice. Cubuat ends his description lamenting that with the gaiety ended, a quiet loneliness descends on the village.[11]

The rainbow is a manifestation of spirits (*yang pireng*) of those who have been murdered, committed suicide, or died accidentally or in childbirth. The rainbow's bright colors ominously reflect the violence of these deaths and serve as warnings to live carefully so as to avoid a similar fate. Corpses are buried in isolated forest graves without ritual, and they are ignored in the feast of the tombs. A rainbow is a sign that an unhappy spirit is reaching from the tomb to slake its thirst in a nearby watercourse, and villagers say they have seen rainbows extending from *yang pireng* graves to streams. Condemned to wander aimlessly, these spirits allow the rainbow to be seen only when they wish it, but certain individuals endowed with *cun pireng* are empowered to see rainbows and allow others to see them.[12]

Farming

The four seasons of the Pacoh year are marked by crops, not weather. Permission to clear a new swidden within the village territory must be obtained from the elders. In April and May, before the rains begin, maize is planted in part of the swidden, after which rice is sown. Each household group venerates its own Rice Spirit, associated not only with the eldest female but with their seed rice as well. Seed rice can be given, bartered, or sold to outsiders for consumption but not for planting. Men enclose the swidden with a fence and build shelters for those who will guard against predatory animals and birds. They grow vegetables in a separate plot.

Maize is the first field crop harvested, and it is a joyous occasion, a time of plenty. Squirrels and birds abound amid the ripe maize, making the fields a good nocturnal hunting ground. Cubuat relates that "one sees the corn already yellow, delicious, ready to roast. From the heart one is happy, very joyful. They eat corn hash dipped in meat sauces." Women gather ears and shell them using a mortar and pestle. Part of it is kept in the longhouse bin for the family, and part is given to *khoy* kin. Cubuat observes that "at the end of the corn season one finds the mountain people very fat, physically fit, not skinny."[13]

When rice has ripened in late October, the *aboh* chief, who has a

11. Richard L. Watson, "Reduplication in Pacoh" (M.A. thesis, Hartford Seminary Foundation, 1966), pp. 119–28.

12. Cubuat, "*Yang pireng,* the Rainbow," trans. Richard Watson, mimeograph, 1964, p. 1.

13. Cubuat, "Corn Season," trans. Richard Watson, mimeograph, 1964, p. 1.

special relationship with the *aboh* Rice Spirit, must refrain from washing her hair. She also must avoid being near rushing water, which is associated with rice stored in the granary being washed away. On a sunny day seed rice is harvested, and then the remaining rice is gathered. Women strip the plants by hand, allowing kernels to fall into an open apron worn for this task. When all village rice has been harvested, granaries are closed, and everyone joins in a feast with meat preserved in bamboo tubes, fresh fish, sugarcane alcohol, and rice alcohol. Afterward, at each granary there is a ritual in which the *aboh* chief, carrying a bamboo container of water and roasted meat, ascends the ladder and enters, pulling the ladder in behind her. Inside she feigns sleep and then washes her hair with the water. She offers meat to the Rice Spirit and eats some of it herself, marking the end of the rice harvest celebration.

Village Elders

Leadership is vested in a group of male elders (*xaxai*), also known as "root of the village" (*areiah*), who are selected by resident adults. An elder is well-to-do from successful farming, and he must be one who is eloquent, a mark of maturity and wisdom. Watson reports that such eloquence is demonstrated in two kinds of formal dialogue. "What the Pacoh call *kârloy* 'speaking contests,' and *târqa* 'debate' are important to any festive gathering of village elders." These contests go on without break for three or four days, eliminating contestants until one man is left as champion. The elders regulate use of village territory, organize village celebrations, arbitrate conflicts that cannot be resolved at the family level, and punish those who violate Pacoh laws. Failure to respect the elders' authority can result in punishments, the most severe of which are expulsion from the village and death by clubbing.[14] Cubuat reports that "if someone accuses another of small theft, the two may be tested by tying their index fingers together and putting them gradually into a fire. Whichever party pulls back is guilty. If neither pulls back so that both are burned, the accuser must pay the accused for having accused him falsely."[15] A more serious offense invites participation by the village elders, and if the party found guilty refuses to pay for his crime the elders will order his family to do so. Should they refuse, the elders will confiscate all of their belongings. If the guilty party has no family, his possessions will be taken or he may be clubbed to death.

According to Cubuat, in cases of theft involving anything "the value of ten buffalos," each family head questions every member. If the culprit

14. Watson, "Reduplication," p. 117.
15. Cubuat, "Pacoh Justice," trans. Richard Watson, mimeograph, 1964, p. 1.

remains unknown, the entire village is summoned to stand judgment in the presence of the elders. There are four trials, and before they begin some joss is burned under a canopy of beautiful cloth to invite the spirits' intervention. In the first trial, villagers gather in a circle around a chicken, which is beheaded. The person on whom the fluttering chicken lands is guilty. If he does not confess and agree to pay a fine, he must undergo the second trial. The accuser (who suffered the theft) and the accused each plunges a live grasshopper under water, and the loser's surfaces first. If both come to the surface, the next trial takes place. Two candles are set just below their tops in water, and each party lights one. The guilty party's candle goes out first. If both continue to burn to the bottom despite the water, the last trial is held. The two parties are tied together, and their heads are submerged in a stream into which an arrow is shot. The one who is hit is the loser. Cubuat adds that during these trials the guilty one almost invariably confesses, and if he agrees to pay even part of the accuser's loss, the village will help him.[16]

The Vietnam War

When in the early 1960s Communist insurgency brought conflict, the Bru and Pacoh found themselves a people in between. Some Pacoh went eastward to lower-elevation Pahi villages where fellow clansmen and *khoy-kuya* kin would aid them.[17] Others moved westward into Laos, and some made their way south to the Achau Valley. At the same time, Bru were leaving their villages near the Demilitarized Zone and the Laotian border because the presence of Communist insurgents invited attacks by government forces. Some went into Laos, but most went into other villages, preferring those where they had kin with patrilineal or kindred ties. Others grouped in refugee villages near Khe Sanh, where there were government troops. In December 1962, a U.S. Special Forces detachment moved into the old French fort above Khe Sanh and recruited local Bru for the militia. Khe Sanh itself in May 1964 was a small town of some twelve hundred Vietnamese who lived in houses with tile roofs and wattled walls (the style of coastal central Vietnam) set in gardens of vegetables, fruit trees, and flowers. The center consisted of a few shops around a small covered market that was quietly bustling in the early morning. A stream ran through the town, and it was crossed by a stone bridge reminiscent of those in rural France. Surrounded by misty green

16. Cubuat, "Four Trials," trans. Richard Watson, mimeograph, 1964, p. 1.

17. For information on these groups in the Vietnam War see Gerald Cannon Hickey, *Free in the Forest: Ethnohistory of the Vietnamese Central Highlands, 1954–1976* (New Haven: Yale University Press, 1982), pp. 96–97, 125, 172, 185–86, 231–34, 252–53, 262, 277.

mountains, Khe Sanh seemed cut off from the outside world, giving the place a curiously timeless aura.

The influx of refugees, however, was a graphic reminder of the insurgency at hand. Huc Van, five kilometers from Khe Sanh, had by May 1964 grown from twenty-five houses to one hundred. Lang Troai on the Laotian border had grown from twenty houses to sixty-three. Leaders in the refugee village of Huong Loc near the Laotian border with 380 families lamented that they were on the horns of a dilemma. If they farmed close to the settlement, there was insufficient land and the Communists harassed them for being pro-government; if they farmed farther out where land was plentiful the government suspected them of supporting the Viet Cong. Most chose to farm close by, but their yields were small. The government gave each family a three-month supply of rice gratis, after which they had to pay for it, but few had the means. Villagers also complained that the soil was not as rich as in their former territory. In their small gardens they grew beans, yams, pineapples, and green leafy vegetables. When they first arrived in 1962, they planted papaya trees, but none had as yet borne fruit. Many resorted to foraging in bamboo stands for a wild grain that they husked and boiled. A village leader noted that out of desperation some refugees were moving into remote areas under Communist control where they could farm proper swiddens.

Not far away, in the refugee village of Lang Van Chuoi, the residents complained that because of small swiddens and meager garden yields, there was a serious shortage of food. Relief rice requested from the district chief had not come, forcing them to eat unpalatable relief bulgar wheat. One villager pointed out that although children attended one of two district primary schools opened in 1959, "they studied with empty stomachs." Some young men joined the army to get cash to send their families. Other refugees sold bamboo, thatching, baskets, and domestic animals in the Khe Sanh market for cash to purchase food. A few were able to find work in the Polin coffee estate. In March 1964, while driving his familiar yellow Citroen on Route 9, Eugène Polin and M. Llinares, a fellow coffee planter, were ambushed by the Viet Cong. Polin was killed, but Llinares escaped.

In April 1965, Félix Polin observed that an influx of refugees not only created a shortage of land for swiddening but raised the danger that much of the ground cover such as trees, brush, and fallen leaves would be removed, leaving the laterite soils exposed to sun and rain, possibly causing leaching. He explained that local soils lack sulphate and potassium, necessitating use of chemical fertilizers. He also described how some of the Bru refugees moved on to the bottom land near a stream that runs through his plantation. They arranged paddy fields, using buffalo to farm, and they had gardens with tobacco, yams, and manioc. Claiming that the area was insecure, the Vietnamese district chief ordered them to abandon their village and move closer to Khe Sanh.

In May 1965, the chief of Huong Hoa district (a Vietnamese army captain) reported that since 1962, some 4,000 Bru had moved into the Khe Sanh area from more remote villages. They had recently been joined by 120 Bru and around 500 Ta-oi from Laos. At the same time, there had been a movement of Bru into Laos and into zones controlled by the Communists. The refugees at Khe Sanh were being assisted by Father Poncet of the Missions Etrangères de Paris (who was killed in 1968) as well as by Félix Polin, the Millers (who lived in Khe Sanh), and U.S. Special Forces personnel. Father Poncet had a small chapel in Khe Sanh, and two Vietnamese nuns of a nursing order made visits to Bru villages to treat the sick.

In 1966 the Special Forces moved to a new camp on an airstrip on high ground above Khe Sanh. During May 1967 there were significant movements of North Vietnamese troops across the border from Laos into the Bru country with heavy concentrations in the hills dominating the Special Forces camp. Two battalions of U.S. Marines were dispatched to the airstrip, and they clashed with the Communists, capturing Hill 881 North overlooking infiltration routes. The marines then took over the base at the airstrip from the Special Forces, who moved farther west to a new camp at Lang Vei. In mid-January 1968 the North Vietnamese 304th Division crossed the Laotian border to join the 325C Division operating near Khe Sanh, while the 320th Division appeared to be getting into position along the Demilitarized Zone to attack Route 9 east of the town in the vicinity of Camp Carroll, where U.S. Army 175mm guns provided support from the marines. In June 1990, Daniel Kelley, a former marine corporal who had served at Khe Sanh and worked with Bru refugees, related that when North Vietnamese units surrounded the village of Ta Cong, near the Special Forces Forward Operating Base, they had with them Bru cadre who entered the settlement and told the residents not to evacuate. Near Khe Sanh, two battalions of the 26th Marine Regiment held a position, and on 16 January a third marine battalion was flown into the area as part of Operation Niagara II.

In his description of the Khe Sanh battle, Reverend Ray Stubbe, a chaplain, reports that the marines estimated that there were over ten thousand Bru clustered in villages within six kilometers of the base.[18] John Miller related that by 19 January, Bru in eight villages west of Khe Sanh had moved into villages near the base, but the old people

18. Ray William Stubbe, "Khe Sanh," unpublished manuscript (Milwaukee, 1989), pp. 384–85, 527, 680–82.

remained behind. When clashes between the marines and the Communists made it apparent that a major battle was in the offing, the Americans on 22 January ordered all the Vietnamese population of Khe Sanh to evacuate to the base, where they would be airlifted to Quang Tri. John Miller (who had sent his wife and children to Danang) described how his Vietnamese neighbors quickly packed their belongings and boarded up their houses. Busy packing his linguistic materials, Miller was the last one to leave Khe Sanh. Soon after, North Vietnamese troops began to infiltrate the abandoned buildings. The marines call in air strikes and artillery, completely destroying Khe Sanh. Stubbe reports that the Bru south of the base sent word that they wanted to be evacuated. The marines, fearing the Communists would use them as shields in attacking American positions, wanted all of the Bru to go, but an order from General Hoang Xuan Lam, the Vietnamese corps commander, forbade it. The marines' only recourse was to send ten thousand pounds of rice to the Bru settlements. As the sounds of violence grew louder and news of the Khe Sanh evacuation spread, fear gripped the Bru. Miller reported that some three thousand of them began to make their way on foot down the Bao Long Valley. After days of walking, they arrived at Cam Lo on the coastal plain, but many died during the trek.

On 21 January the marine positions on Hill 861 came under heavy attack. The marine battalion and a reinforced company occupying hills 558, 881 South, and 950 faced two North Vietnamese divisions numbering between fifteen and twenty thousand men plus an additional division within striking distance. With massive bombing, exchanges of artillery, and ground assaults, the battle was joined, marking the beginning of the Khe Sanh siege that lasted seventy-seven days. On 6 February 1968, a Communist regiment using artillery, flamethrowers, and nine Soviet PT-76 tanks assaulted the Lang Vei Special Forces camp. During an American air strike, some bombs were mistakenly dropped on Bru soldiers in the camp, killing many of them. For the next eleven weeks the marine base underwent heavy daily shelling (on 23 February, for example, some 1,307 rounds landed). Nonetheless, cargo planes continued to resupply the garrison, although some were hit by shells and exploded. One victim was Félix Polin, who was arriving on a C-130 that crash-landed.

Miller related that as the siege intensified, North Vietnamese troops occupied the Bru villages of Lang Khanh I, Lang Khanh II, and Lang Bu, forcing the residents to remain in order to deter any American bombing. Finally, one night, in desperation, 2,000 Bru left the villages and walked ten days to reach Cam Lo, already swollen with refugees. Stubbe reports that on 7 March half-starved Bru refugees began arriving at the marine base, offering their silver bracelets, fashioned from French coins, as payment for food. They were flown to the coast, and by 19 March, 1,247 Bru had been evacuated. Bru arriving at Cam Lo by foot on 22 March reported that North Vietnamese troops had been foraging for food in Bru villages that had been abandoned. There were still Bru in some villages, and they were caught in horrendous B-52 bombing (between 22 January and 31 March there were 2,602 sorties delivering 75,631 tons of bombs). Lang Bu and other villages south of Khe Sanh soon were demolished. According to Stubbe, Bru had gathered in villages west of Co Roc Mountain located southwest of Khe Sanh in Laos across the Sepong River from Lang Troai. When B-52s destroyed these villages, some Bru fled up the mountain, only to be killed. In a discussion with Bru leader Anha at Cua on 3 November 1969, he related that people from Lao Bao were refused entry to the marine base. As they made their way down the road to the coast, they were strafed by American planes. By May 1968 the Bru country had become a no-man's land with not one village left standing.[19]

Thousands of Bru at Cam Lo found themselves in the alien coastal plain, where the soil in the dry season is dry and hard, rendering it impossible for them to readapt by farming and gardening. The refugees lived in tents, which provided no respite from unrelenting daytime heat. There was only one well, and the water rapidly became contaminated. Relief rice was the only food provided, and women went into the hills (a free-fire zone) to forage for firewood. Daniel Kelley reported that he and James Perry, a U.S. Army medic, tried with limited resources to cope. They treated the Bru, who were suffering from dehydration, malnourishment, and severe diarrhea. Kelley organized the digging of latrines. Perry chlorinated the well to improve the water quality, but initially the chemical made the Bru ill. Refugees were dying daily, and their corpses were buried without coffins in shallow graves with no spirit houses or ritual offerings to *sâu* patron spirits. Judging that the reason for their plight was disharmony among themselves, nature, and cosmic forces, the Bru obtained a chicken to make a ritual offering to Yiang Cutẽq, Spirit of the Earth. Some eight hundred Bru who reached Cam Lo later reported that they had been forced by the North Vietnamese to go into Laos, but they refused to stay when they discovered that there was no housing and little rice.

By late June 1968 the siege of Khe Sanh had ended, although the heavy shelling and B-52 raids continued in the Bru country. Some five thousand Bru moved on military trucks from Cam Lo to Cua Valley, a wide expanse of grass and trees between low hills, but most of the land was already being farmed by Vietnamese. Nonetheless, the Bru attempted to

19. Ibid., p. 682.

readapt, immediately building shelters (there were insufficient materials to build traditional houses). On a piece of land they arranged one large paddy field, which they farmed communally, sharing the yields. Kelley, who with Perry continued to work with the refugees, reported that in addition to the ailments encountered at Cam Lo, Bru coming down from the mountains had terrible fungus infections caused by long stays in underground shelters. Kelley also related that the marines gave the refugees seven buffalo and some pigs. On one occasion a shaman (who chanted prayers in a strange tongue) organized a buffalo sacrifice, and there were several pig sacrifices. Shamans also performed healing and divination rituals. The refugees could now make their rice alcohol, which they drank on these ritual occasions.

When the refugee villages were visited in November 1969, the situation was grim. Paddy production was insufficient to feed everyone. Noting that the soils were very different from those in the uplands, a villager observed, "We plant a lot, but many things, even bananas, don't grow." He added that it was difficult to farm swiddens back in the hills because of the constant danger of being shot, and wild pigs and other marauding animals damaged crops. Their small gardens contained taro, yams, manioc, lemon grass, mint, and chili peppers. Some Bru had been producing charcoal, but gathering wood in the increasingly insecure hills was perilous. It required two days to produce one bag, and the nearest market was an arduous nine-kilometer walk. Citing all of the deaths in the harsh conditions, an elderly man lamented, "We will all die here."

Fathers R. P. Aimé Mauvais and Neyroud organized a center to provide assistance to the refugees and a school for between 120 and 170 children with two Vietnamese nuns providing instruction in the Bru language (using primers supplied by the Millers). Seven Bru boys and two girls were sent to Catholic schools in Danang and Hue. Father Mauvais reported that by the end of 1971, some six thousand Bru lived in Cua. The priest observed that the lack of food led to an increase in theft, a departure from the normal Bru pattern. Thieves made off with bananas and other produce as well as chickens, pigs, and even rice from the supply the Catholic nuns kept to feed children at their center. Some one thousand Bru had either gone back to Cam Lo, where Father Conan and two nuns had a center for twelve hundred Bru, or to the three camps that had sprung up amid the weathered-stone tombs of mandarins in the vicinity of Hue. There the Bru were joined by Pacoh refugees. With only some gardens, the refugees were completely dependent upon aid from private relief agencies.[20]

When on 6 January 1972, Nay Luett, minister for ethnic minorities'

---

20. R. P. Aimé Mauvais, "Lettre aux bien chers parents, amis et bienfaiteurs," Dong-Ha, South Vietnam, 1 January 1972.

Photo 19. Bru refugees and their huts amid Mandarin tombs outside of Hue (1972).

development, visited the camp, the Bru and Pacoh gathered in a cold, dismal rain to hear him announce that he had plans to resettle them farther south in Darlac province, the heart of the Rhadé country. The plan had been conceived in August 1971, when the worsening situation in the northern provinces of South Vietnam raised the possibility that the region would be adjudged undefendable and therefore expendable, becoming a free-strike zone for the B-52s. The resettlement plan was opposed by Anha, the Bru leader, who feared that his refugee funds would be reduced if they were resettled, and so it was stalled in the prime minister's office. Meanwhile, small groups of Bru were filtering down from Cam Lo and Cua. Camp leaders reported that the previous week some four hundred had arrived, and during the week of Nay Luett's visit there were two hundred newcomers.

On 31 March 1972, the Communists launched a large offensive that began with heavy shelling of bases and towns along the Demilitarized Zone. As the Bru at Cam Lo and Cua joined other refugees fleeing southward, North Vietnamese units, using Russian tanks, captured the former American bases at Cam Lo and Gio Linh. In Saigon, Nay Luett immediately formulated a new plan to move the Bru and Pacoh rapidly.

He dispatched Binh, a young Bru working at the ministry, to Hue while Luett and his staff flew to Darlac and selected a resettlement site at Buon Jat. Luett and Touneh Han Tho then went to Hue to find around two thousand refugees, with more arriving daily. Most of the Bru and Pacoh at Cam Lo and Cua Valley had been caught in the Communist sweep, and many (including Anha's wives and children) had been killed. Anha himself was with the Hue group, and he performed a divination ritual using a chicken, eggs, and rice to determine the spirits' will. The signs were unfavorable so he told the refugees to stay. Luett and Binh, however, pointed out that the situation north of Hue was fast deteriorating and advised them to leave. The Bru conferred among themselves and elected to move south, so they began to board Air America cargo planes.

At Buon Jat, local Rhadé militiamen built houses for the refugees (at first the Bru complained that the houses were not right because they resembled Rhadé longhouses). Rhadé from surrounding villages received the first arrivals, offering food and drink. Eventually, twenty-three hundred Bru and a small number of Pacoh were settled in Buon Jat. Shortly after most of the Bru had been airlifted from Hue the defenses north of the city collapsed, sending South Vietnamese troops and civilians flooding southward. After the population of Dong Ha had fled, David Elliott was in the abandoned city and reported seeing some Bru wandering around the silent streets. When fighting subsided months later, only an estimated four thousand Bru could be accounted for in Quang Tri province. By early 1973, the Bru at Buon Jat were well settled. Some had realized excellent profits, selling their crops of vegetables (maize, potatoes, yams, and white beans) to a Rhadé entrepreneur, who transported the produce to Nhatrang.

In 1973, some two thousand Bru were moved from Hue to Buon Blech in northern Darlac. On 8 March 1975, North Vietnamese captured the nearby town of Thuan Man, sending the Bru and Katu refugees, who also had been moved there, fleeing to the town of Cheo Reo, where they were caught in the disastrous events precipitating the fall of South Vietnam. Pierre K'briuh, who was for a brief period at the Ministry for Ethnic Minorities' Development after the Communist victory (and who subsequently was jailed and later escaped Vietnam by boat), reported that the authorities ordered the Bru at Buon Jat to return to Khe Sanh. The government did not offer any support, so the refugees were left to make the return trip on their own. In August 1991 the Millers related that they had heard from Bru in Laos (where they were organizing linguistic research) that some of the group in Darlac (now Dak Lak) had moved back north, but the Khe Sanh area was now filled with Vietnamese settlers who had taken all of the land. Bru who had lived there were moving into more remote regions, some making their way into Laos.

Chapter 6
Sedang

The Sedang live in high country where the green, forested mountains are stunning in the brightness of the dry season and brooding in the mist that accompanies the rains. Matching these moods, rivers running through the valleys change from placid to angry, rushing torrents of brown water flecked with the green of captive vegetation. The mountains build up to the cordillera's highest peak (2,598 meters, 8,573 feet), known officially as Ngoc Linh and called Ngo Eang—"Shining (or Brilliant) Mountain" by the Sedang. Legend has it that at the upper reaches wild sugarcane abounds and on the peak there rests a splendid gold pirogue. French investigator Georges Devereux reports that the Sedang call themselves Ha(rh)ndea(ngh).[1] Kenneth Smith of the SIL, who conducted considerable research on the Sedang language, writes that their own designation is Roteang ("Sedang Highlanders"). He places Sedang in the North Bahnaric branch of the Mon Khmer family. Smith identifies seventeen Sedang ethnodialects, which he notes lends credence to the "slightly exaggerated Sedang truism" that "every village speaks differently." In 1967 it was estimated that the Sedang numbered around 40,000, the 1989 Vietnamese population census reports 96,766 Xo-dang, and Vietnamese sources list "local groups" including the To-drah, Ca-rong, and Halang (see Appendix A). The Halang are generally recognized as a separate ethnic group. Ca-rong is a cognate of Kayong, and in Chapter 8 it is noted that the Halang are sometimes called Kayong. Thomas and Headley identify Todrah and Kayong as separate North Bahnaric languages.[2]

1. Georges Devereux "Functioning Units in Ha(rh)ndea(ng) Society," *Primitive Man* 10 (1937): 1.
2. Kenneth D. Smith, "More on Sedang Ethnodialects," *Mon Khmer Studies IV,* Language Series no. 2, Center for Vietnamese Studies and Summer Institute of Linguistics (Saigon, 1973), pp. 43–51; Smith, "Sedang Dialects," *BSEI* 42, no. 3 (1967): 196–255;

Stewards responsible for maintaining the man-nature-cosmos harmony are validated in Sedang society by their demonstrated potency.
Devereux reports that village membership is based on use of water from
a common spring (for which the village usually is named) and common
veneration of longhouse hearth spirits. He says that the household head's
wife lives in the half of the house associated with the "husked-rice soul"
and the "hearth soul" (which Leon Wit from Dak Brao identifies as
mohua phe and *mohua bao* respectively). This gives her a special link
with the rice spirit so that only she can cook the family rice and perform a
rice-planting ritual. Devereux notes that humans have "*mahua paon,*" a
type of "soul" he likens to "mana." Wit says that *mohua* associated with
individuals is potency, a gift of the spirits (he noted that the older
generation uses the term *mohua* while younger people use *seă*), manifested in wealth (rich harvests, cattle, buffalo, valuable jars, and gongs),
good luck, and wisdom. One risks losing *mohua* by engaging in asocial
behavior such as stealing or speaking badly of people or having contact
with women's skirts. An individual with a great deal of *mohua* is adjudged to be *kro,* a figure of unusual prestige who plays a leadership role.
Wit noted that Sedang sometimes use the term *poa potao* for a man of
power such as a headman (and the word *yang* for "spirit"), both terms
introduced in Catholic texts based on Bahnar-language texts. The word
apia has long been used in legends to describe an unusually beautiful
woman. It would appear to be a cognate of *bia,* the Cham word for
"queen," associated with the Kon Klor Cham vestige near Kontum.[3]

Pre-1960

The first mention of the Sedang in any historical accounts is in the journal
kept by Father Pierre Dourisboure, one of the small band of French
priests who founded the Kontum Mission.[4] Father Dourisboure arrived
in the highlands in 1851. He describes the Bahnar as being relatively
gentle and the Sedang as warlike. One problem was the periodic raids by
Sedang on Bahnar villages, where they pillaged, murdered, and carried
off residents, some of whom were later sold to Lao traders. Nonetheless,
the priest elected to work among the Sedang, settling in Kon Trang
village, a trading center where Lao merchants exchanged buffalo with

---

David Thomas and R. K. Headley, Jr., "More on Mon-Khmer Subgroupings," *Lingua* 25,
no. 4 (1970): 398–418. Transcriptions in this chapter are based on orthographies of Kenneth
Smith and Leon Wit.

3. Devereux, "Functioning Units," pp. 3–4.

4. Pierre Dourisboure, *Les sauvages Bah-Nars (Cochinchine Orientale) souvenirs d'un
missionaire* (Paris: Pierre Téqui, 1922), pp. 68–69, 92–93, 131–32, 172–73, 190–91, 213–14,
217–19.

Sedang and Rengao for slaves and gold panned in the Poko River and its tributaries. Father Dourisboure reported that Sedang spent several months each year working iron mined locally to fashion sabers, knives, and spears, which they traded with the Rengao and western Bahnar for cloth and with the Bahnar Alakong to the east for salt. French explorer Henri Maitre reported that the Sedang told him that in the distant past they learned ironworking from Lao who lived in the vicinity.[5]

Father Dourisboure devised an orthography for the Sedang language and wrote a catechism. One of his first catechumens was a youth named Pat from Kon Xokou. His village had been at war with neighboring Kon Hongol, whose men conducted a raid, capturing Pat and his family. Barely old enough to walk, Pat was well cared for so that later he would command a good price from Lao slave traders. When at ten years of age he was taken to Kon Trang to be sold, Father Dourisboure bought him, restored his freedom, and later Pat elected to become a Christian (by 1855 there were twenty Sedang converts). Kon Trang had lost a good portion of its population warring with the more powerful Dak Rode, but it rallied and captured four Dak Rode men, who were kept in the men's house. The priest succeeded in gaining their release, thereby restoring peace between the two villages.

Dourisboure mentions in his account sorcerers who used invisible bows and arrows to shoot a victim, causing sickness and death. He notes that the female shaman (*pojao*) had the responsibility of identifying any person practicing sorcery (who would be sold to Lao traders). Most of those accused were women of low status such as a widow without family or an orphan but never a woman of a wealthy family. The priest describes how the shaman performed a divination ritual with three eggs (which had been incubated so that they would crack more easily). Setting the eggs down, she chanted while gesturing. Then, taking one egg, she placed it between her index and middle fingers of the right hand and extended her arm. An assistant asked where the sorcerer resided and began slowly to name neighboring villages. With each name the shaman pressed the egg, and its breaking revealed the village where the sorcerer lived. The second egg identified the house, and the third, the guilty party.

The Sedang received brief mention in historical annals of the late nineteenth century through their unexpected role in the bizarre events surrounding the founding of the Sedang kingdom by a French adventurer named Charles David, who called himself the Baron de Mayréna (and was known simply as Mayréna). Sent on an official mission to the highlands in April 1888, he gained the cooperation of Father Jean-Baptiste Guerlach of the Kontum Mission. The priest helped Mayréna obtain a

5. Henri Maitre, *Les jungles Moi* (Paris: Larose, 1912), p. 476.

series of treaties with Bahnar, Rengao, and Sedang chiefs. Suddenly, on 3 June 1888, Mayréna promulgated the "constitution of the Sedang kingdom," in which he was named king. Other than having their name used, the Sedang have no particular role. Claiming his kingdom had gold and other riches, Mayréna offered to turn over authority to the colonial government but noted that if the French refused, he would deal with the Prussians. When French officials ignored him, Mayréna went to Hong Kong, where efforts to gain English and German support for his kingdom failed. Mayréna proceeded to Paris and then to Brussels, where a wealthy industrialist lent financial support for his return to Indochina to reestablish his rule. But British authorities blocked him in Singapore so he went to the nearby island of Tioman, where on 11 November 1890 he died mysteriously. Meanwhile, the French colonial government moved to abolish the Sedang kingdom, and in 1898 all religious, civil, military, and judicial powers over the central highlands were placed in the hands of Father Jules Vialleton, superior of the Kontum Mission.[6]

The Mayréna affair revealed that the Bahnar, Rengao, and Sedang had chiefs who exercised authority over groups of villages. At the end of the century, a Sedang chief named Thang Mau (apparently a Vietnamese designation) mounted raids on Vietnamese settlements close to Kontum (Vietnamese captives were sold to the Halang and Jarai). This act prompted the Garde Indigène to launch a military operation during which Thang Mau was killed, but it signaled a period of unrest. On 29 May 1901, a force of Sedang attacked a French military post on the Psi River, fatally wounding Robert, the commander. On 24 November 1901, some 450 Sedang assaulted Dak Drei, where Father J. E. Kemlin lived. The village defenses held, and a Sedang captive revealed the names of the chiefs who had been involved. The French then moved against them, restoring peace to the Sedang country. By the end of the 1920s construction of the Kontum-Tourane (Danang) section of Colonial Route 14 through Dak Sut had begun, requiring corvée labor of Sedang villagers.[7] Tran Van Than reports that the Sedang and neighboring groups forced into corvée labor were treated harshly and were victims of many accidents.[8] Time spent on road construction prevented them from farming their usual swiddens, resulting in serious food shortages. In his 1937

6. Gerald Cannon Hickey, *Kingdom in the Morning Mist: Mayréna in the Highlands of Vietnam* (Philadelphia: University of Pennsylvania Press, 1988).

7. Gerald Cannon Hickey, *Sons of the Mountains: Ethnohistory of the Vietnamese Central Highlands to 1954* (New Haven: Yale University Press, 1982), pp. 257–58, 279–80, 303, 319.

8. Trần Văn Thân, "Tìm hiểu phong trào chống thực dân pháp của người Sêđăng ở vùng đông bắc Kontum," (Understanding the Sedang anti-French colonial movement in northeastern Kontum), *Nghiên Cứu Lịch Sử* (Historical research) 150 (1973): 21, 25–26.

article Devereux writes that the Sedang village of Tea-Ha opposed the French and once dispatched a group of five men to kill those in a neighboring village who wanted to submit to the French. When in 1933 the French moved against Tea-Hat, "the whole region came to the defense of the besieged, and retreated only when it was observed that the justly famous fortifications of that village had fallen."[9] Paul Guilleminet describes how in 1937, when influence of the Python God movement reached Kontum province, the Sedang, Jeh, and Monom, armed with crossbows and spears, mounted attacks on Garde Indigène posts.[10] According to Tran, the French retaliated by destroying thirty villages, killing over two hundred Sedang.

While visiting the Sedang village of Dak Cho, some seven kilometers from Dak To, in March 1957, Father Paul Renaud, a French missionary, related that during World War II three downed American flyers came into the village, and he hid them in his house. One day soon after, he saw Japanese soldiers entering the village gate so he quickly warned the Americans. They fled into the forest, and later the priest learned that one had been captured and beheaded but the other two made good their escape.

Tran writes that between 1945 and 1948 the Viet Minh played upon the highlanders' discontent with the French to recruit in the villages.[11] By 1950 there were four guerrilla zones in districts north of Kontum embracing some two hundred villages. Fathers Renaud, Leger, Brice, and Beysselance still lived in Dak Cho, Kon Trang, Kon Horing, and Dak Mot respectively, but their mission work was severely restricted. Whereas in 1939 there were 25,212 Catholics in Kontum province, by 1949 this figure had only risen to 25,255.[12] On 1 February 1954 the Viet Minh seized the initiative, capturing Dak To. The following day the Viet Minh attacked French positions around Kontum town, which was evacuated five days later, leaving the entire province in Viet Minh hands. With the end of the Indochina War in 1954, Sedang were among the highlanders who were sent north to the Southern Ethnic Minorities School near Hanoi. Eventually they were sent south as insurgents.[13]

When Dak To was visited in 1956 and 1957, the Saigon government controlled all of the province with the exception of the zone north of Dak

---

9. Devereux, "Functioning Units," p. 2.

10. Paul Guilleminet, "Recherches sur les croyances des tribus du haut-pays d'Annam, les Bahnar du Kontum et leurs voisins les magiciens," *IIEH* 4 (1941): 32.

11. Tràn, "Tim hiểu," pp. 27–29.

12. Société des Missions-Etrangères, *Compte rendu des travaux de 1950* (Paris: Séminaire des Missions-Etrangères, 1951), pp. 88–89; Hickey, *Sons of the Mountains*, p. 418.

13. Gerald Cannon Hickey, *Free in the Forest: Ethnohistory of the Vietnamese Central Highlands, 1954–1976* (New Haven: Yale University Press, 1982), pp. 14–16.

Sut. At Dak Cho, Father Renaud told of Sedang fears of an influx of Vietnamese, who at that time were in Dak To—shopkeepers and soldiers, who sometimes entered villages to steal chickens and pigs.

Settlement Pattern

Villages have between ten and twenty houses, although some centers such as Kon Trang and Kon Horing are larger. All of the houses face east so that light from the rising sun hits the main entrance. In 1957, Kon Horing villagers explained that they still retained stockades with a gate (*cheǎng* or *chěa*) as symbols, but in previous times they were essential because of intervillage warfare. Villages normally remain in place, but Father Dourisboure noted that incidents such as houses catching fire, the capture of a villager by enemies, a particularly tragic death, or an inordinate number of deaths in a short period would lead the shaman to declare the site inauspicious.[14] The shaman then performed a ritual to implore spirits' guidance in determining a new, propitious site. In 1854, Kon Trang was moved three kilometers to a new location, and villagers slept in the forest until their new houses were completed.

Every Sedang village has a territory (*cheam beng*) marked by geographic features. Tua, a native of Dak Tea Pen, pointed out that when one spoke of "Dak To" or "Kon Horing," it was not a reference to the village itself but rather to its territory. Outsiders must have permission of the village elders (*kra*) to farm, hunt, fish, or forage. Residents are free to use the territory, but clearing a new swidden requires approval of the elders, who know the status of fields being farmed or fallowing.

Sedang longhouses are rectangular and built on piling with a hewn hardwood frame and a roof thatched with imperata grass. Most houses measure from ten to twenty meters in length, but some are as long as eighty meters. The main entrance, in the center, is reached by a large veranda used as a general work area. Immediately inside is a large work/reception room also used for family rituals. Corridors on either side lead to family compartments.

The central structure of the settlement is the men's house (*kuat* or *kuiet*), in many respects the heart of the village. In 1967, villagers of Dak Lung observed that "the land [village territory] belongs to the men's house." Its structure is of sturdy hardwood logs to provide relatively high piling and support the soaring roof decorated with woven bamboo motifs. The interior is undivided, and there are at least two open hearths to provide warmth. Along the walls are jars of alcohol, and one wall is covered with dried heads of animals sacrificed in previous rituals. Ac-

14. Dourisboure, *Les sauvages*, pp. 182–83.

Photo 20. Sedang longhouse at Kon Horing (1956).

cording to Father Christian Simonnet, tradition called for a young slave to be crushed beneath the main piling as an offering to the spirits in recompense for guarding the structure against fires and typhoons.[15] In the past it was the village defense center, where young men slept with weapons handy in case of a nocturnal attack, and it still serves as a dormitory for young men and boys. Adult males gather here for rituals and for making decisions affecting the whole community.

Kinship

The Sedang have bilateral descent, and it is forbidden to marry anyone identified as "close kin." Proximity and character of kin ties are expressed in terms that can stand alone or be used as modifiers. *On veáng* refers to members of the nuclear family, and *róping* identifies those of the extended household group. *Siam* ("source") is used for certain very close consanguineal kin, and *môjiang* ("to produce, bear a child, cause to become") is a modifier to indicate direct line. *Môi mo* designates close consanguineal kin such as parents' siblings and parents' siblings' children. *Tobó* ("left over") refers to certain relationships by virtue of remarriage.

15. Pierre Dourisboure and Christian Simonnet, *Vietnam: Mission on the Grand Plateaus* (Maryknoll, N.Y.: Maryknoll Publications, 1967), p. 242.

Sáng is the second wife, as opposed to *kodrai hodrói,* the first wife. *Tosêa* indicates distant affinal kin.[16]

As Appendix B8 shows, there is age-grading in Ego's generation and in first ascending and descending generations. Kin numeratives are used for older siblings so if the eldest is a sister, she is *na reng ta.* Younger siblings are *o* with sex modifiers *konóu* (male) and *kodrai* (female) added along with the same kin numeratives, so the eldest younger brother would be *o konóu ki reng ta.* *Tobó* is added to identify half-siblings (for example, *ngoh tobó* is a half–older brother). Also, because sibling terms are extended to cousins (who are age-graded relative to Ego) and to some affinal kin, siblings are specified by the modifier *siam.* In this generation the term *tosêa* might be used to refer to kinsmen related through a younger sibling of the grandfather. In the first ascending generation the modifier *siam* can be used to specify parents (because parent terms are extended to collateral and affinal kin). The terms *tăm* (father's younger brother) and *sáng* or *să* (mother's younger sister) are used for the step-father and stepmother respectively.

In the second ascending generation the terms *pôa* (father's father and mother's father) and *ja* (father's mother and mother's mother) are extended to any recognized kin so modifiers specify father's father (*pôa pa pa*), father's mother (*ja pa pa*), mother's father (*pôa pa nôu*), and mother's mother (*ja pa nou*). Also *môjiang* can be added to identify each parent's parents. *Môjiang pa* is "grandparents who gave birth to father," while *môjiang nôu* is "grandparents who gave birth to mother." *Tosea* as a modifier would indicate a kinsman related through his marriage with a sister of one of the grandparents. In the first descending generation the modifier *môjiang* is used to identify "one's own child," as opposed to *kuě tobó,* a stepchild. The same kin numeratives used for siblings are used for children.

Normally everyone in Sedang village society marries. Paul Guilleminet reports that in 1932 at Dak Kon Kan, Inspector Maulini of the Garde Indochinoise came upon a male villager dressed in female garb and playing the role of a woman.[17] When Guilleminet inquired about "men-women," he was told that they were rare among the Sedang, Bahnar, and Jarai. Not all dressed as females, but they lived as women although they never married or had intercourse. Such males when small are informed in a dream that they belong to the female sex. Guilleminet added that they are never subject to ridicule.

It is forbidden to marry anyone identified as "close kin," but one can

16. Kenneth Smith, "Homonyms in Sedang Kinship Terminology," mimeograph (Saigon: Summer Institute of Linguistics, 1969), pp. 18–19.

17. Paul Guilleminet, "La tribu Bahnar du Kontum," *BEFEO* 45 (1951–52): 524.

marry relatives who are *xa,* that is, related through the parents' parents' parents' collateral lines. According to Tua, young people select their own mates, but the choice is subject to the approval of parents and village elders. Kenneth Smith reports that in Sedang terms, when young people reach puberty it is time "to have company, to befriend someone" (*xrôk* or *sŏk*) with the implication of mating.[18] This prompts the young man "to get a wife" (*xo kodrai*). Tua related that when a boy is attracted to a girl he communicates his affection in conversation. In more recent times he might send her a note entrusted to a small boy (who cannot be a kinsman). If receptive, she invites him to visit her house "when the older people are out." The next meeting is at the boy's house. By this time the parents are aware of the courtship, assenting to it by remaining silent. A third meeting is arranged at the girl's house and a fourth at the boy's. According to Smith, when the couple "agrees to marry" (*torau dêi pó*), they are too "ashamed" (*komêi*) or "embarrassed" (*ôh ta xiap*) to inform village elders. Tua notes that this is done by obtaining the services of older kin, two men and two women, as intermediaries. The elders almost invariably give their consent as long as it is known that the couple has not had intercourse. Devereux reports that "secret pre-marital or extramarital intercourse may result in the burning of the village by the spirits."[19] If it is known that they had intercourse, the couple must, according to Smith, "offer the elders rice" (*dŏu vai kra phái*), which means that they "kill a pig" (*kodê chu*) and "drain the blood" (*xo mohêam*), which is mixed with unhusked rice on a flat circular basket that the couple places on the veranda of an elder's house.[20] Should the elders declare that the couple must "make up to the village" (*bro polê*), the offering is placed either on the platform of the men's house or at the village gate.

The elders and the couple "announce with beads" (*prêi hodró 'báng pri*) the engagement (*torak*), and the couple exchanges beads and the elders give them beads. During the engagement period (which may be two months or two years) the couple avoids intimate relations with anyone, and for kin and friends they give two or three feasts of chicken, pig, or buffalo (depending on their means) with jars of rice alcohol. At the end of this period, elders present the couple with rice, a symbol that they may live as a family. On the wedding day (*hai pokŏang*) they are *chiang,* that is "made into a family, brought together." According to Tua, the wedding takes place at either house. With no guests present, the couple sits side by side facing the two female go-betweens while the two

---

18. Kenneth Smith, "Engagement and Marriage," mimeograph (Saigon: Summer Institute of Linguistics, 1966), pp. 1–3.

19. Devereux, "Functioning Units," p. 4.

20. Smith, "Engagement," pp. 5–6.

males sit to their right, and the parents sit to the right of the couple. The bride presents glasses of alcohol to the female intermediaries, then to the males, the groom's parents, and finally the bride's parents. Taking a full glass of alcohol, the bride drinks half, passing it to the groom, who drinks the remainder, thereby sealing the marriage. Smith writes that the following day the couple is relieved from any tasks "because they want to know how to live together." They "go have fun" (*lám hêi*), "go to the water" (*lám a têa*), "go look for fish" (*lám táng ká*), "go bathe" (*lám huam*). After this day the couple is free to sleep together. They spend the first year at the bride's parents' house, where they are given their own compartment. Smith notes that the terms *ko-ói* ("pregnant") (Wit uses the term *de-ói*) or *aí kuán* ("to have a child") identify pregnancy after marriage while *xiu* indicates pregnancy before marriage and in animals. The term *hlo ma,* meaning "to see the eye," describes delivery. The Sedang have the levirate and sororate, neither of which is obligatory. Guileminet reports a 1939 case of polyandry—a woman in Kon Tobreng who was permitted to have five husbands, three of whom lived with her.[21]

The newly married couple assumes a place in the division of labor found throughout the highlands. Sedang women weave, and Devereux makes a passing reference to weaving a textile of "china grass" cultivated in kitchen gardens.[22] Guilleminet reports that in the past, when Bahnar and Sedang men went off on a war expedition to attack another village, all of the household and village responsibilities fell on the women.[23] They also participated in village defense, producing pointed bamboo stakes to stick in the ground outside the enclosure (these were also used by the Viet Cong and were called "ponji stakes" by Americans). Then, if the village was assaulted, women assumed positions on the enclosure to hurl rocks at the attackers.

At family rituals, men play gongs and drums and both men and women play the bamboo organ (*klŏ put chao*). Georges de Gironcourt describes ten boys and girls in Dak Lung playing a bamboo organ consisting of ten bamboo tubes set on long poles, each player cupping his or her hands to compress air into a tube.[24] Guilleminet describes a bamboo organ consisting of seven open-ended bamboo tubes whose interiors have been carefully polished.[25] The tubes vary in diameter and length so as to produce seven notes—*do, re, fa, so, la* (the pitch note), *do, re,* and are

21. Guilleminet, "La tribu," p. 547.

22. Devereux, "Functioning Units," p. 6.

23. Guilleminet, "La tribu," p. 545.

24. Georges de Gironcourt, "Recherches de géographie musicale en Indochine," *BSEI* 7, no. 4 (1942): 53–55.

25. Guilleminet, "La tribu," pp. 549–50.

set zigzag on two large bamboo poles. Three women on one side and three on the other play the organ by cupping their hand to compress air into the tubes. Four of the women are responsible for playing two tubes while the other two play three tubes (the end tubes produce low *do* and high *re*). Nancy Cohen reports that two Jeh songs, the *huai* and *ding-ding,* were borrowed from the Sedang.[26] The former is sung to lament lack of success in hunting or foraging, or someone might sing it in memory of a dead mother. The Sedang *ting-tin* is a love song, but it often is sung by children at play.

Within the household, authority rests with the eldest male, who, in Tua's words, "most teach the others." He organizes family rituals and feasts and makes decisions about such projects as clearing a new swidden, relocating the house, or making house repairs. The household head's wife has a special position because of her relationship with the "rice spirit," which gives her ritual roles in rice planting and harvesting. According to Devereux, the "spirit of husked rice" lives in the stones of the hearth used by the household head and his family, and she is the only one who can prepare and serve rice to members of the household group.[27] The household head also arbitrates family disputes. Devereux points out that intrahousehold disputes sometimes threaten the family unit, but breaking up of households rarely occurs. He describes the case in which a villager named Ngya, who felt that the wife of his household head was serving him unduly small portions of rice, stole one of her chickens. Accusing him of the theft, the wife explained that Ngya was lazy and did not contribute his fair share of work in the fields so he did not deserve more rice. Ngya threatened to move his family out of the house, but all of the kin group had already contributed money to purchase a buffalo for the planting ritual and they elected to remain together.

Shamans described by Father Dourisboure still function in Sedang villages. Leon Wit said that his mother-in-law and his male cousin are shamans. When illness strikes a family they summon the shaman to perform rituals to identify the spirit that is causing the sickness and find out what it wants as propitiation. The shaman also has healing techniques for certain problems such as sucking the nipple of a childless woman to make her fertile.

Shamans can communicate with spirits and with ghosts (*kia*), the character of which depends on the mode of death. According to Wit, those who die of natural causes such as old age are simply *kia. Kia*

26. Nancy Cohen, "Jeh Music," in *Notes from Indochina on Ethnic Minorities,* ed. Marilyn Gregerson and Dorothy Thomas (Dallas: SIL Museum of Anthropology, 1980), p. 86.

27. Devereux, "Functioning Units," pp. 4–5.

modrieŭ or *m'jiu* are ghosts of those who have died "bad deaths" from suicide, murder, an accident ("a tree falls on him"), or in childbirth. This ghost manifests itself in a strange light, and Wit said he had seen such a light while in the forest. His cousin, a shaman, informed him that it was a manifestation of his deceased mother, who had died in childbirth, became a *kia m'jiu,* and wanted to talk to him. *Kia modroh* are ghosts of those who die in epidemics, a different kind of "bad death." *Kia o'nga* is the ghost of an infant, and traditionally its body was hung on a tree where the villagers could hear its cries. Shamans are the only ones aware of the dire presence of evil ghosts called *kia m'droh, kia h'mat,* and *kia toro.* Wit cited an instance when his shaman cousin was with a group of men entering the gate of a village. Suddenly he began to perspire and warned his companions that there was a *kia modroh* in the village so they should walk straight through without entering any longhouses. Those who did not heed the warning fell ill within days. Wit also reported that male sorcerers *(deq)* can by invoking *kia h'mat* smash a victim's bones, leading to death. Wit's father, Bok Plum, a well-known leader, told of how when he was sleeping in another village he became aware that an evil curse by a sorcerer was trying to penetrate the walls of the longhouse. He was protected, however, because his *mohua* was more powerful than that of the sorcerer and he had had tattoos done by a Lao practitioner to ward off such curses. When Wit was young, his father took him to a Lao who tattooed three dots (representing his *mohua*—someone with great potency would have five dots) on his neck, arm, and leg. Another talisman is a snake or eel that has died. Wit related that the Sedang greatly fear Halang witches (whose power is transmitted through the female line), who they call *kia pi poa,* manifest in disembodied heads that float through night air seeking victims whose liver they eat, causing death. Wit once worked in Dak To with a Halang whose wife was a witch.

Wit related that when death occurs, the family wraps the corpse in a blanket and packs personal belongings around it for burial as soon as possible for fear that the deceased might return to the house. One of Wit's kinsmen, a boy of thirteen, died and "returned to life." Later, when Wit asked him what happened, he said that he had died and an "old man told him to return to his family." After burial, the attendees wash their hands and return to the house for a pig or buffalo sacrifice while the shaman calls upon the deceased not to return to the house. Younger kin stay with the family for a week to console them with songs and merriment. For those who die "bad deaths," there is no ritual in the village, and everyone but close kin is afraid to touch the corpse. Wit's mother died in childbirth in Kontum so her body could not be returned to the village.

Economic Activities

Preparation of swiddens for planting begins during the dry season in February. Hmou pointed out that in the Kon Horing area farmers cut bamboo and several kinds of pithy trees, but large hardwood trees are left standing. Wood is left to dry for at least a month before it is set ablaze (men place themselves around the edge of the clearing to control the fire). According to Hmou, most Sedang prefer to plant maize first. Using a "digging hoe" men and women plant either in rows along the swidden edge or randomly within the swidden. The common varieties are the long-ear *alai tei* (*tei* means "ordinary") and *alai nuan*, a sweet maize (both varieties are good for making alcohol). *Alai konoi* has kernels "the size of a thumb" and is excellent for popping in a lidded pot over a fire.

Hmou noted that it is well to wait until the maize seedlings have appeared before planting rice to avoid stepping on them. Before planting, the household head's wife invokes the rice spirit while a buffalo or pig (depending on family means) is sacrificed, after which there is a feast to which the whole village is invited. Devereux also describes this ritual, noting that one objective is to lure "rice souls" from other villages so as to increase the yield.[28] Kenneth Smith collected a list of Sedang upland rain-fed rice (*báu*) varieties. Four have white kernels with husks that vary in color. *Báu kôang* has a yellow husk while *báu khêi* has a red husk as does *báu tíng* (*tíng* means "tail," a reference to a small tail-like protrusion at the end of the kernel). *Báu práng* has a black husk. *Báu lóang ngo* is characterized by a short stalk two to three feet high. *Báu plôang* and *báu tosông* are glutinous types. Hmou said that in Kon Horing *báu khêi* and *báu tosông* are the most popular kinds of rice, and he added that villagers also have two favorites, *báu dé* and *báu khé* ("moon"), both easy to grow.

When the seedlings begin to sprout, men and women weed, and this task is repeated when the plants are about two feet high. If the swidden will be farmed again, there is a third weeding. To protect crops from predatory birds and animals, the Sedang have devised noisemakers (*tang kŏa*) ingeniously worked by the force of water gushing from hillside springs. De Gironcourt describes one such noisemaker, an elaborate chime made up of a great many bamboo pipes of varying diameters and lengths, which are struck by wooden hammers attached to a system of very thin bamboo poles, rattan cords, and bamboo scoops at the source.[29] The seesaw motion of the scoops as they fill and empty jiggles the whole system, producing a medley of xylophonic sounds. Another noisemaker has a similar arrangement, but the sounds are produced by flint pen-

28. Ibid., p. 4.
29. De Gironcourt, "Recherches," pp. 56–67.

dulums alternately striking a large suspended chunk of shale or limestone.

Before the harvest, the household head's wife offers an animal sacrifice for the rice spirit similar to the planting observance. Should crops fail for two or three years, she is replaced by another woman of the household. At a swidden near a village outside Dak To, in October 1970 a woman and her daughter (who carried a sling in which an infant slept) were harvesting rice. The woman placed a medium-sized basket (*chea*) with no straps on the ground. She grabbed a stalk with one hand and pulled loose the kernels with the other, putting them in the basket. When it was full she emptied it into a large back-basket (*monou* or *chang*), which she carried back to the village to sun the kernels by spreading them out. To winnow, she put kernels on a circular basket, which she flipped up and down, allowing the wind to blow away the chaff. At Dak Lung in 1967 farmers reported that they gathered between twenty and thirty backbaskets (we estimated that each held around thirty-three kilos of unhusked rice).

Normally, swiddens are farmed for two or three years, after which they are left to fallow for varying periods based on adjudged soil fertility and dominant flora. Relatively fertile soils are not cleared for about eight years whereas infertile soils fallow for ten years. In 1965, Dak Kang villagers explained that it was possible to farm a particularly fertile field for one year and allow bamboo to grow for a year before clearing again. Dak Lung farmers said in 1967 that they used swiddens for three years, and bamboo that grew afterward matured in five years.

According to Hmou, encouraged by the Saigon government, in the mid-1950s Vietnamese began settling in the Kon Horing area. The village had long been a market center, and the Vietnamese moved onto unclaimed land, where they arranged gardens and small paddy fields in terraces on slopes and limited bottomland, using water from hillside springs. After the neighboring Sedang saw the abundant harvests, they began to borrow Vietnamese techniques. By 1960 some Kon Horing Sedang had arranged wet-rice fields on slope terraces and on bottomland using a water management system in which channels and bundings guided water from springs into the upper terraces and then into the lower ones. In January, farmers using hoes break the earth in seedbeds and then release water into them. Both men and women broadcast seeds of two common types of wet rice, *báu klang* and *báu kơpôu* ("buffalo dung paddy rice"), and *báu ua,* a glutinous rice. Men and women hoe the larger fields, which, when seedlings are high enough, are flooded. Women do most of the transplanting. No fertilizer is used, and everyone assists with harvesting. Farmers with cattle or buffalo cut the stalks and have draft animals trod on them to disengage the grains. Those without draft animals pull the grains from the stalks in the traditional manner. The advent of wet-rice farming in Kon Horing also introduced for the first time the practice of family-owned fields. Paddy fields were regarded as the property of the farmers who arranged them rather than land under the authority of village elders. Paddies also were alienable, the selling price set in terms of valuable rice-alcohol jars and cattle.

In swiddens farmers grow secondary crops and kitchen gardens. Sugarcane is grown in separate patches near swiddens, and cotton is cultivated in a field close to the village. In a sparsely forested area close to Kon Horing, villagers grow pineapples in large fields; most of these are sold to Vietnamese in Kontum and Tan Canh. Some Kon Horing residents also have coffee trees, selling the berries to Vietnamese.

Ironworking described in earlier French accounts has continued, and every village has its specialists in the craft. They use double-piston bellows consisting of bamboo tubes and plungers fashioned from rags tied to the ends of sticks to force air into the fire. Devereux and Guilleminet report that on an embankment of the Akoi River, Sedang had ironworking furnaces on top of which were animal-skin bellows worked by hand.[30] Iron ore was extracted nearby and mixed with charcoal to produce iron. Guilleminet recalls that in 1928, French *résident* Jerusalemy launched a project to instruct Sedang villagers how to produce round woven-reed boxes and miniature back-baskets to sell in lowland handicraft shops. Devereux mentions that in the 1930s some Sedang villages produced pottery.

Village Leadership

Authority is in the hands of the headman (*kán polê*) and elders (*kra*). In the 1930s, Devereux found that the headman's role essentially was "to voice the collective feeling" and serve as "war-leader and the sacrificial priest."[31] Now the headman is selected by a consensus of adult villagers and must be one who "knows all of the ways" and is not argumentative or given to using bad language. It is important that village leaders have *mohua* potency (some use the Bahnar word *ai* to describe this potency), a gift of the spirits, manifest in wealth, good luck, and wisdom. Wit pointed out that one with *mohua* "always wins." When one with this potency dies, his soul joins other spirits in the sky, but the soul of one without it goes to the forest. At Dak Cho in March 1957 villagers pointed out that some village chiefs still had slaves from remote villages or other ethnic groups. They served as domestics and were treated as members of

30. Devereux, "Functioning Units," p. 2; Guilleminet, "La tribu," p. 524.
31. Devereux, "Functioning Units," pp. 3–4, 7.

the family. The headman can make decisions affecting the community without consulting the elders, although he is aware of their sentiments. The headman and elders cooperate in matters such as working out a division of labor for village projects, the clearing of swiddens in village territory, and preserving moral order. Anyone guilty of wrongdoing in the village is fined a pig or buffalo, which is sacrificed and then served at a feast. There are strong taboos against eating the flesh of animals paid as a fine by a kinsman. Devereux cites the case of woman named A-Ngye who was caught having premarital intercourse with a man during one of her uncle Ngue's celebrations.[32] The usual fine would have been a pig, but the elders allowed her instead to give Ngue a skirt, which he could trade for a pig. Devereux also points out that a chronic troublemaker (one who "breaks taboos, steals, causes quarrels, commits incest, etc.") who refuses to pay fines or atone can be expelled from the village to live in the forest in the belief that "he abandons his *mahua plao* and therefore his human status." But this does not mean that these individuals will languish and die. Devereux observes that "such persons are ostracized with admiration, and are credited with exceptional *mahua paon* [soul mana], which expresses itself in the fact that they usually become rich and return to the village, paying past fines, and humiliating everyone through their wealth." He makes the interesting point that somehow (perhaps because of their unusual potency) "they have no difficulty getting rich, since they do not have to brew alcohol with most of their crop, sacrifice beasts, etc., and are not preyed upon by jealous shamans always anxious to order sacrifices when anyone is too successful in animal husbandry."

32. Ibid., pp. 5–7.

Chapter 7
Jeh

Ngoc Linh, the highest peak of the Annam Cordillera, arises to the east of the Jeh country. For the Jeh (sometimes spelled Die in French works) it is the mysterious Peng Oi Mountain, and legend has it that in the distant past a young man made his way to the summit. There he found a huge rock formation shaped like a cooking pot, and he was startled to see large goats living in caves. The young man collected some stones that he brought back to his village, but they caused a strange malady from which he never recovered. No Jeh has since been tempted to repeat that experience, so they are content to observe Peng Oi from afar.

A Jeh legend explaining how the mountains came to be made of rice tells how in the distant past a woman and her granddaughter were working in a field when the woman instructed the girl to return to their longhouse and prepare rice. "How much rice should I put in the pot?" the girl asked. "Just one grain," the woman responded. When she was well along the path, the girl turned back to the field to ask again how much rice she should put in the pot. "Just one grain," the older woman repeated. When she had gone halfway to the village, the girl again returned and asked the same question. Vexed, the grandmother said, "You have asked three times, now go home and put *one* grain in the pot." At the longhouse the girl did not follow instructions, instead pouring the whole basket of rice into the pot. As it cooked, the rice bubbled, flowed over the pot onto the floor, and out of the house. It began to swell as it spread, becoming one mountain, then another, and still another until they were everywhere. And that is how the Jeh country became so mountainous.

The Jeh are one of the smaller highland groups, numbering in 1967 around 10,000, and the 1989 Vietnamese population census reports 26,924 "Gie-Trieng" (see Appendix A). Their language belongs to the North Bahnaric subgrouping within the Bahnaric branch of the Mon

Khmer family.[1] The relative isolation of the Jeh, which accounts for the scarce mention of them in French annals, diminished somewhat with the construction of Colonial Route 14 through Dak Pek during the early 1930s. Around 1932 the French administration established a political prison at Dak Pek for some four hundred Vietnamese who had been active in lowland nationalist movements. The inmates included Le Van Hien, who became minister of labor in the Viet Minh government and served as North Vietnamese ambassador to Laos; Ha The Hanh, one-time Viet Minh minister of information; and Nguyen Duy Trinh, who became minister of foreign affairs for the Socialist Republic of Vietnam after having held the same position in North Vietnam. The prisoners were used as laborers on road construction, and they once caused the death of a disliked French supervisor by felling a tree on him.[2] The Jeh did have considerable contact with the neighboring Halang and Sedang. Contact with Lao traders resulted in Jeh panning for gold in nearby streams and in ironworking (which has a special mystical tie with sha-manism). During the Indochina War the Viet Minh were active in the Jeh area and introduced some farming innovations.

In Jeh society, advancing age brings a certain potency (*kakayh*), a gift of the spirits, to men and women. This enables an older woman to become household head (she already may be the household's Mistress of Rice Planting and Harvesting, with a mystical link to the rice spirit) and join village elders in the communal house. But the primary stewards of religious prescriptions for preserving harmony among man, nature, and the cosmos and maximizing fertility must demonstrate "wisdom," which is equated with wealth (success in farming and the wherewithal to have many pig and buffalo sacrifices with attendant feasting). As "Grand-mother of Aning," an elderly lady from Dak Pek, put it, "Wisdom and poverty do not live in the same person." In Kirsch's framework the Jeh would be classified as having a "democratic" social system with bilateral descent, no entrenched elites, a system of household and village leader-ship open to both sexes, and a communal house accessible to all.[3]

In many respects the communal house (*mrao*) is the heart of village society. It is the meeting place for village leaders and site of village ritual celebrations usually marked by a buffalo sacrifice, which takes place in

1. David Thomas and R. K. Headley, Jr., "More on Mon-Khmer Subgroupings," *Lingua* 25, no. 4 (1970): 398–418. Transcriptions of Jeh in this chapter are based on the orthogra-phy devised by Dwight Gradin and Pat Cohen.

2. Gerald Cannon Hickey, *Sons of the Mountains: Ethnohistory of the Vietnamese Central Highlands to 1954* (New Haven: Yale University Press, 1982), p. 329.

3. A. Thomas Kirsch, *Feasting and Social Oscillation: Religion and Society in Upland Southeast Asia,* Department of Asian Studies, Cornell University, Southeast Asia Program Data Paper no. 92 (Ithaca, N.Y., 1973), pp. 32–34.

Photo 21. Grandmother of Aning (1966).

front of the building (where gongs and the deerskin drum used in these celebrations are kept). It is the dormitory for male and female children, so most courtships begin here, and the communal house is where older men instruct boys in basket weaving. Visitors stay there, an arrangement that Grandmother of Aning pointed out protects them from violating village taboos for which they would suffer the spirits' wrath.

Jeh express rhythms of life in music, both vocal and instrumental. Nancy Cohen describes four distinct types of vocal music (it is strictly taboo to sing while eating for fear of angering the spirits). There are the inevitable lullabies (*nhen*) and laments (*akah*), both of which are sung only by women.[4] The third type includes nine kinds of "happy"

4. Nancy Cohen, "Jeh Music," in *Notes from Indochina on Ethnic Minorities,* ed. Marilyn Gregerson and Dorothy Thomas (Dallas: SIL Museum of Anthropology, 1980), pp. 85–97.

(*kŏdoh*) songs, six of which (*huaĭ, ding-ding, ton, tŏret, tŏ'ngi,* and *kŏdoh kŏsăng*) are sung solely for entertainment while two (*si'ang* and *ayaă*) also are for ceremonial occasions. The remaining happy song, *bia-bia,* is sung only by the household woman designated as Mistress of Rice Planting and Harvesting when she invokes the rice spirit. Only children and young people sing the *huaĭ* and *ding-ding,* and the *kŏdoh kosăng* ("*kŏdoh* of long ago") are for older people. *Ayaă* are men's songs. The fourth category includes what Cohen calls "foreign tunes" and what the Jeh call *hat* (taken from the Vietnamese *hát* or "song"), Vietnamese and Western songs. Cohen notes that frequently the *akah* and all of the happy songs with the exception of the *tŏret, si'ang,* and *bia-bia* use metaphorical language to convey indirect messages. The Jeh have eleven musical instruments, none of which may be played outdoors. Men play panpipes, flutes, lutes, gongs, drums, and horns, and women play the bamboo organs. Everyone makes music on the Jew's harp.

Religion

According to Suai (from Peng Sal Peng near Dak Pek) and Brol (from Dak Bi near Dak Wak), both assistants to SIL linguists Dwight Gradin and Pat Cohen, one group of deities are spirits (*iang*). Some are associated with features of the physical environment, such as the malevolent water spirit (*kanam nhing dak*), while others, such as the rice spirit, are intrinsic to crops. The legend of Thao Thon describes beautiful celestial male and female beings called "sky people" who on occasion fly to earth. One of them, a female named Lu La, flew to earth and while swimming was captured by Thao Thon, who took her as his wife. She had a magic blouse that enabled her to fly, but Thao Thon kept it hidden in the rafters. Thao Thon decided to visit the lowlands in Laos, and he warned his mother not to let Lu La find the blouse. While he was away, sky people flew down to look for Lu La, who sat weaving a blanket. When she and her mother-in-law saw the sky people, Lu La said, "I still know how to fly like that. If you get me the blouse, I'll teach you to fly too. I'll just fly to the peak of the roof, and when you say the magic words 'pa hah,' I'll return." The older woman got the blouse, which Lu La put on with the intention of joining the sky people. As she reached the peak of the roof, however, her mother-in-law said, "pa hah," and Lu La descended, unable to escape.

An important deity, Ya Nguh, "ancestress of the Jeh," called "grandmother," is responsible for all human conception. She lives in a village on the moon with her two sons, Ntol (who created the earth, sun, and the "skin of the sky") and Jat, both of whom, unlike their mother, are spirits (*iang*). When in 1966 Dwight Gradin told Jeh villagers that American astronauts had landed on the moon, they asked if the Americans had encountered Ya Nguh. After Gradin replied, "no," the Jeh pondered and replied that the astronauts had more than likely landed in a place removed from Ya Nguh's village. Ya Nguh possessed a chicken that ate a water spirit and thereafter produced gold droppings. The Lao captured and killed the chicken. Jat heard the chicken's dying squeals and descended to the earth, where the Lao seized him and drove a nail through his kneecap.

Suai explained that every human, animal, and plant has a spirit called *rok,* and every human in addition has a *phol* (Pat Cohen noted that this term means "soul" or "blessing") that lives in the head. If a person has a bad dream, it is a sign that his *rok* has gone to the woods or the rice field, and though he might live for a year without it, he will become debilitated, perhaps unable to work. When someone does not feel well he will lament, "Oh, I have no *rok.*" Following a bad dream most Jeh consult a male shaman (*m'jao*) and provide him with a pig to offer the spirits, asking them to find out where the *rok* has gone and to have them make it return. Should the shaman determine the specific rice field where the errant *rok* has gone, it becomes taboo for the victim to eat any rice harvested there.

Suai, Brol, and Grandmother of Aning agreed that serious illness is caused by the absence of the *phol,* which may have been seized by the evil spirit, K'nam. "He doesn't have a *phol,*" the villagers say when a person takes to the sickbed, and a shaman who has power to see the *phol* is immediately summoned. A pig is sacrificed as the shaman entreats the spirits of the mountains, trees, and other physical features to bring back the missing *phol.* If the evil K'nam "bites the *phol,*" the victim dies. When this happens, the *rok* leaves the body and goes either to the woods or to a rice field. The next day the *phol* departs. Normally it goes straight to the sky to join the *phol* of the ancestors, but there are exceptions in the event of "unnatural death" or a rich person's death.

Settlement Pattern

The Jeh settlement consists of a cluster of longhouses, each set in a farmstead with gardens and groves, in the center of which is the communal house. Most villages number around two hundred people, although in the vicinity of Dak Pek some hold approximately five hundred. Yun, from Dak Trap, and Cho, a man from Plei Bong (near the Laotian border), explained that each village has its own territory (*sal ja*), the limits of which are known to the elders, who regulate use of everything within it. Everyone knows and respects residents' swiddens, including those fallowing, and everyone must respect the custom of not clearing zones where forests are dominated by large trees. Outsiders can hunt or fish within the territory, but they must obtain the elders' permission to farm, cut wood, or dam a stream.

In some villages longhouses are built on piling about one meter high while in other villages they are constructed on the ground. Grandmother of Aning observed that "some live on the ground and some in the sky," reflecting the Jeh concept that whatever is not on the ground is "in the sky." She added that in her natal Dak Pek the houses are on the ground, but beds in the main room are arranged on low platforms. Longhouse piling and structural framework are fashioned from logs (*sa*), hewn from dried dead trees or felled trees. The main entrance must face east to catch the warmth of the rising sun. At this entrance there is a log veranda called the "path" (*truang*), where women weave. The interior is divided into two sections: "the bed place" (*dang yong*) and "the cooking place" (*dang che*), where women prepare meals on open hearths and males never enter. The former is where the family sleeps (beds are placed by open hearths), but it also serves as a dining room (household members eat together), work area, reception room for visitors, and place for family rituals. A focal point for these celebrations is the central support column to which rice-alcohol jars are staked and around which the food dishes are arranged. Personal effects are kept in baskets; weapons and farm tools are stored on the rafters.

The communal house is built on piling four to eight feet in height, and the style varies. At Dak Pek, for example, it resembles an ordinary longhouse without a central column, whereas at Dak Wak it has a soaring roof in the style of Sedang men's houses. The interior is free of partitions, and the number of open hearths depends on the size of the village.

Family

The Jeh have bilateral descent with kin recognized to the third ascending generation and down to the fourth descending generation. As Appendix B9 indicates, in Ego's generation older siblings are *mĕe* and younger are *oh,* with sex modifiers *loulou* and *dridri* to distinguish brothers from sisters respectively. Sibling terms are extended to cousins, who are age-graded relative to Ego. In the first ascending generation, father is *băa* and mother is *uŭ*. Parents' older siblings are *mih* while their younger brothers are *nhu* and younger sisters are *ma*. Only the father's father's father (*boŏ ka baă,* which means "father's grandfather") is recognized in the third ascending generation. Ego's children are *kon* with sex modifiers to identify sons and daughters and modifiers to indicate eldest (*paseem*), youngest (*sut*), and those in between (*nay*). These modifiers also can be used for children's children.

Marriage between consanguineal kin is forbidden. Most marriages are between young people of the same village, so the communal house, which serves as dormitory for all village children, plays an important part in their courtship. During the day they live in their family longhouses, but when night falls they converge on the communal house to sleep under the watchful eye of an elderly woman or widower. Boys have sleeping mats at the rear of the large room, while girls sleep to the right of the main entrance. Before retiring for the night they gather by the fire to sing two "happy" songs, the *huaĭ* and *ding-ding* (both borrowed from the Sedang).[5] The boys like to sing "foreign" tunes such as patriotic songs learned in school.

When a young man becomes attracted to a girl, he is likely to sing one of the *huaĭ* songs to her. The lyrics of one recorded by Nancy Cohen go, "I want to buy a bracelet, but I do not have any money" (a reference to the bracelets exchanged in the wedding ceremony). According to Yun, romances most often begin when a boy is around eighteen and the girl is sixteen. If she is interested, the boy can go in the night to her mat, where they make love. Dwight Gradin notes that there are strong taboos against premarital pregnancy, and should it happen, the couple must leave the village to live in the forest for one planting cycle.[6] Yun related that before the French administration Jeh custom demanded that to shorten this exile, the banished couple would have to provide the finger of a victim, so the boy would either ambush a person and cut off his finger or dig into an isolated grave to remove a finger of the cadaver. The couple would take it back to the village, where it would be on public display, exonerating them. Yun said that now the couple goes to a distant place such as the Halang country, where the boy symbolically thrusts a spear in the air while declaring that he has snared a victim.

Yun observed that the couple's parents will inevitably become aware of the love affair, prompting one of the mothers to raise the subject of marriage. When the parents meet to discuss the situation, the mother who initiated it proffers gifts of green vegetables, sugarcane, and fresh fish. If they agree to the marriage, they select a disinterested elderly male or female to act as intermediary. Gradin describes how friends of the couple, the parents, and the intermediary plan the first ceremony of the marriage proceedings. On an appointed evening friends "kidnap" the surprised couple, taking them to the house of one of their parents for the *bla* ceremony in which the couple's hands are forced into a jar of rice alcohol while phrases of goodwill, long life, and prosperity are chanted by those present. Then a bowl of alcohol is given to the boy and girl to sip, after which they exchange bowls of alcohol and simultaneously drink the

5. Ibid., pp. 86, 92.
6. Dwight Gradin, "Rites of Passage Among the Jeh," *SA* 2, no. 1 (1972): 55–57.

contents. If one of them balks, friends wipe alcohol across his or her face, chiding, "If you have no desire to be married, why have you been sleeping beside one another?" The couple place hands momentarily on a live chicken. While more phrases are chanted, the chicken is killed, plucked, and cooked on the hearth. Yun said that if the legs stiffen and the beak is taut, it is a good sign for the marriage. If the lower jaw is awry, however, it is a bad sign and the ritual must be repeated. The boy and girl are given a handful of cooked rice mixed with bits of chicken thigh, liver, and gizzard, which they exchange and eat. Everyone then feasts and drinks from the jars. Cohen explains that the *ton, tŏret, to'ngi,* and *ko'doh ko'sǎng* happy songs are sung on such occasions, and in one the intermediary leads off, singing, "We're going to catch a chicken, an orphan chicken, and roast it and eat it." The girl's mother responds, "I don't have an orphan chicken," to which the intermediary sings, "Oh yes you do." Then the two mothers have a comedy exchange, listing skills their children lack although everyone knows that all young Jeh boys and girls learn such skills. The bride's mother sings, "My child doesn't know how to pound rice, carry wood or water, or look for wild vegetables." In a chorus the groom's family sing, "That's okay." The boy's mother responds, "My son doesn't know how to weave baskets," to which the bride's family sing, "That's okay."[7]

According to Gradin, the couple returns to the communal house, now free to have intercourse.[8] The *bla* ceremony is repeated at the other parents' house within the next month. Three or four months later there is the *taya* ceremony held once for each family (by the northern Jeh but not by the southern Jeh). Its goal is to implore the spirits to bring the couple good health, and its format resembles the *bla* ritual, although a pig rather than a chicken is sacrificed. At both rituals each family receives half of the pig, which they share with fellow villagers. Gradin speculates that the purpose of this ritual is to integrate the new nuclear family into the kin groups and village so that when the new couple eats meat and drinks alcohol provided by others or when others eat meat and alcohol given by them, "no one will contact sickness of any kind." In three or four months the *talu* observance is held at both families' longhouses just for family members. Its function is to join the two sets of grandparents, who will now have common descendants. There is no animal sacrifice, and when the couple drinks from the jar, family members tap on the mouth of it while intoning phrases of good fortune and long life. Everyone then drinks and feasts on chicken. For several weeks women of the girl's family gather firewood and stack it near the boy's house for the *long* ("wood") ceremony held by his family. The couple sprinkles rice alcohol

7. Cohen, "Jeh Music," pp. 88–89.
8. Gradin, "Rites of Passage," pp. 56–57.

on the wood and then taps on it with their fingers while invoking the wood to break any *kayh* ("to have an evil power radiating out from") that it may possess. Gradin explains that this derives from the belief that relatively large amounts of such things as wood, rice, and maize begin to emanate *kayh*. For this reason, he notes, Jeh seldom plant more rice than is necessary for the family's use, and surpluses are rare. After this ritual both families sit down to a large feast with pork dishes accompanied by jars of alcohol. Several days later, the boy's family gives the girl's family grass mats and bamboo baskets woven by the men, and the girl's family reciprocates with blankets, shirts, and loincloths woven by the women.

Until now the couple has continued to sleep in the communal house. Gradin observes that this is because most young Jeh are reluctant to settle down like adults with a bed in a longhouse, which entails appeasement of the ancestors' spirits. None of the marriage rituals contains any invocation or propitiation to the ancestors because the bridal couple does not have any ancestral spirits "following them" until they have a bed of their own. The final ritual is *choo yong* ("go to the home bed"), which has some elements of the *bla* ritual in that the same group of friends catches the couple unexpectedly and brings them to the longhouse of one set of parents. There they force the couple to hold a pig or chicken, which is slain while phrases are chanted. Blood and alcohol are sprinkled on a bed arranged for the couple. Everyone joins in a large feast of pork and chicken with rice alcohol. According to Yun, in the vicinity of Dak Pek the girl presents the boy with a rice-alcohol jar (or jars if her family is wealthy), and he reciprocates with animals, which for the ordinary Jeh means as many as fifty rats that his kinsmen trap, while for the well-to-do it is pigs and chickens (it is taboo to give wild chickens or barking deer). A few days later the bride's family invites the groom's family to join them in drinking alcohol, and his family arrives with many meat dishes for the feasting.

Normally the couple will remain in the house for three or four farming cycles and then move to the other parents' house. When the wife becomes pregnant, the couple must begin making offerings to the ancestors, placing fish tails on a split bamboo pole lying horizontally across two forked stakes. If the couple experiences good fortune, such as the birth of a healthy baby, it is taken to be a sign that the ancestors of the household look upon them with favor, so they will remain in residence there. Polygyny is practiced, and Brol noted that though the usual arrangement is to have two wives, he knows some men in villages near the Laotian border who have seven wives. Remarriage within the year following a wife's death is taboo because of the belief that the new spouse will also die. For remarriage no gifts are exchanged. Divorce is very rare, and Brol pointed out that the Jeh do not have the levirate or sororate.

The couple is given a place to sleep by an open hearth, and takes on labor in the household. Suai, Brol, and Grandmother of Aning explained that authority in the household rests with the head (*dradră*), an older, married member who has the potency of age (*kakayh*). He also should manifest the spirits' favoritism in having wealth (owning four or five pigs and two or three rice-alcohol jars) enabling many sacrifices, notably those for the ancestors. He must be generous, not given to berating (*hŏl*) others, and able to arbitrate family disputes with calm deliberation. He is supposed to be above reproach, and should he violate any customs, he must be replaced by another member of the family. In most households the head is a senior male, but there are instances when the position is shared by several males or held by a younger man or an older woman. In every household an elderly woman is designated as "rice mistress," a title reflecting her special relationship with the rice spirit and the rice crop. She performs rituals at planting and harvesting, and she is the first to cook the new rice. Before her death she must designate her replacement. Should there be several meager harvests, she must relinquish her role to another woman.

Cho explained that the Jeh rise before dawn and mark the day with six periods. First is the time "when you cannot see yet," which is followed by sunrise, midmorning, noon, midafternoon, and sunset. The Jeh have the same sexual division of labor as other highland groups, but men also work iron and pan for gold. In 1970 in the wooded garden by the Cohens' Kontum house, several of their Jeh assistants' small daughters were playing roles of women gathering wood in the manner of their mothers. Using a sharp knife, one girl busied herself cutting twigs and placing them in a tin can to which string straps had been attached in back-basket fashion. Another girl, also wielding a sharp knife, chopped branches, arranging them in stacks. Talking little, the two girls went about their tasks with great seriousness. When the tin can was filled with twigs, the girl slipped it onto her back. Two more girls appeared with their dolls in slings on their backs. They all chatted brightly and then in single file left the garden.

Cohen writes that the happy songs are interwoven with daily life, and women, for example, sing them when cooking rice or foraging.[9] The minor-key *ton,* borrowed from the Halang, has a narrow range with frequent ornamentation noticeable on the lower notes. The singer can whistle a phrase of the tune in midsong. A parent exhorting a child may sing the *ton* tune using such lyrics as, "Do your work well; do it quickly; don't take a long time doing it. Whatever you do, do well. Talk nicely to one another; do not talk to one another in a bad manner." A tune can

9. Cohen, "Jeh Music," pp. 86–89.

also express a person's emotional state. Cohen recorded a *to'ret* sung in a minor key by an older woman, "revealing that she feels inferior to others and that she is afraid when someone even speaks to her. She feels lazy and not as steadfast in working as when she was young." To recall times past, the elderly like to sing the minor-key *ko'doh ko'săng,* the most complex of the happy songs. One sung by a grandmother to a young man told of days long gone, describing such things as a river meandering past a village that now stands deserted.

Among the happy songs, the *si'ang* and *ayaă* tunes can be sung only at ritual celebrations in the longhouse and communal house or at informal gatherings when everyone drinks from the jars. At a dinner a guest might sing a major-key *si'ang* tune with lyrics praising the host's hospitality, calling attention to the tasty buffalo meat and good jars of alcohol. Cohen points out that the *ayaă,* sung only by men in a minor key, are unique among happy songs in that they are "lined." The host may, for example, start by saying, "I have no buffalo meat to serve you, no rice to give you, no alcohol for you to drink," after which he will sing the words to the *ayaă* tune with a strong beat. Then male guests will join him in a reprise while he snaps his fingers at certain places to indicate changes of interval and phrasing and also to keep the group singing in unison. One of the guests may take a turn, saying, "I go to look for gold, then I get cash and go buy a water buffalo," then singing the words to the *ayaă* tune, and the men again join the song. A variety of sentiments can be expressed in *ayaă* songs. Among those recorded by Cohen, one intones in a line, "Oh father, oh father, you died when I was a little child, you died when I was a little child." Lightheartedness is reflected in another line of a song saying, "When I was still a child bringing the pan to pan gold, slop, slop; I am the child bringing the pan to pan gold, slop, slop." A different feeling is present in a later line relating, "Day after day I carry a pack on my back, going off by myself; I carry a pack on my back, going off by myself." A final line reflects the view of the not rich that "there is someone rich and able to acquire possessions; we follow him but we're not able to acquire possessions; we follow him but we're not able to acquire possessions."

Cohen observes that musical instruments, like vocal music, are associated with specific social and ceremonial occasions. The large panpipe (*khen*) is played only by men at night when they are drinking from the jars, and it usually accompanies happy songs. In times past, gongs were played only by men during buffalo sacrifices, but more recently gong music accompanies drinking from the jars. Cohen notes that the large gong (*gong*) requires two men using a sling attached to a shoulder pole to carry it, and it is struck by a wooden hammer covered on one end with cloth or rubber. "When played, its sound echoes from mountain to mountain and can be heard up to a distance of four kilometers." The small gongs (*chiang*) are always in sets of four. One, beat with a wooden hammer, sounds the basic rhythm while the other three, struck by fists, play together. The large drum (*sigāl*) is made from a hollowed-out log with cowhide or deerskin stretched across both ends as drumheads. Cohen reports that its sound can be heard at an even greater distance than the large gong. The big horn (*dut-dut*) is fashioned from a water buffalo horn. In former times, when the Jeh sought victory over enemies, they performed a special ritual in the forest to implore the spirits on their behalf, after which men would blow this horn and beat a small model of the large drum. A small horn (*koliă*) is made from the horn of a white rhinoceros hornbill bird, and at a buffalo sacrifice it is blown by a man to introduce the *si'ang* tune invoking the spirits. Other instruments played only by men are the small panpipe (*ding hŏl*), bamboo flute (*chul*), and lute (*tēng nēng*), which consists of a hollow gourd resonator, a bamboo neck, and eight wire strings held in place by wooden pegs.[10]

The bamboo organ (*ding but*), similar to that of the Sedang and played only by women, is made up of twelve bamboo tubes of varying length (from one to two meters), laid crosswise on a wooden frame. Each tube has a different tone, determined by its length, and the sound is made by the player cupping her hands to force compressed air into the end of the tube. Four to six women (forming two or three sets of partners) sit on opposite sides of the instrument, each woman responsible for three or four tubes. Each set of partners takes assigned turns to sound each tube to play the melody, and a strict rhythm is maintained throughout the performance. Both men and women play the Jew's harp (*nhing gui*), which is made either of bamboo or brass. One end is placed between the teeth while the fingers of one hand flick the free end to make rhythm and to vibrate the tongue.

According to Gradin, when a Jeh woman approaches the time to deliver her child, her husband constructs a provisory shelter near the longhouse, and should the house have only one entrance, another must be cut out of a wall.[11] The child must be born outside the village in an isolated part of the forest, and several women assist with the delivery. After birth, the mother, father, and infant stay for ten days in the shelter because it is taboo for them to enter the house. Jeh believe that people can be "allergic" (*kane*) to one another so on the eleventh day, mother and child go into the house to observe *wieyh*, a ritual to dispel any potential allergy, thereby fortifying the whole family against diseases. Gradin adds that this ritual also is intended to integrate the infant into the

10. Ibid., pp. 92–96.
11. Gradin, "Rites of Passage," pp. 57–61.

kin group. The mother arranges a jar of alcohol in the main room, and all household children gather around the newborn, touching its hands. At the same time, the mother and other kinswomen chant, "Don't be cry-babies, and don't break out in scabies and other diseases." Afterward, the children dip their fingers in rice alcohol, wiping some of it on the chin or cheeks of the baby. Then the mother dabs some of the alcohol on the children's lips. Should anyone sneeze during the ritual, everyone must wait five minutes and begin all over again. A few days later, other household mothers repeat this ritual.

The second ritual, *pak pat* ("pierce the ear"), to name the newborn, takes place five days later. While kinfolk drink from the jars, a pig is killed, and an ear of the newborn is pierced and rubbed with blood, after which either the father or grandfather bestows a name, and parents and grandparents are referred to teknonymously. Gradin points out that Jeh pigs are a gray-black color, and during the mid-1960s, "pink pigs" were brought into the area (they were part of the U.S. aid commercial import program). In preparation for this ritual, a villager purchased a pink pig, but his wife refused to use it in the belief that it would cause the child to have pink skin blotches.

According to Gradin, an adult can arrange to have his coffin made at any time, and he is expected to provide the carvers with rice and meat for the six days of labor. A solid hardwood tree is felled, and a portion of the trunk is hewn with bush scythes into a coffin, which is kept under the communal house. The owner rewards the carvers with jars of alcohol and a meal featuring pork dishes. That evening, in a ritual held annually until the owner's death, he holds a live chicken over the coffin, allowing it to scratch the top with its feet. After killing the chicken, he mixes its blood with alcohol and sprinkles the mixture over the coffin while he utters invocations for a long life.

Gradin notes that although procedures associated with death vary from village to village, there appear to be two common rituals. When a person is approaching death, all of the villagers gather at his longhouse to keep vigil, drinking alcohol while musical instruments play. Then, when death is imminent, his kin grasp his hand, a gesture of farewell, which villagers repeat. Kin put uncooked rice in the mouth of the corpse, dress it, and lay it on a bed in the main room. In some villages salt is spread over the body. While the body lies in the house, villagers gather to eat and drink while to the music of drums and gongs some mourners dance around the corpse. The funeral usually takes place the following day, but the well-to-do delay it because they observe a series of animal sacrifices with many jars of alcohol. Also, the *phol* of a wealthy person must remain longer than others (not considered a desirable state) to guard the inheritance, which takes longer to distribute among his heirs. The surviving spouse oversees the division of goods and counsels the children (the youngest child receives the largest share) not to quarrel over them. Inheritable possessions include rice fields, domestic animals, gold nuggets, bush scythes, knives, loincloths from Laos, clothes, and blankets. Communal family goods include the longhouse, cooking pots, very old jars (*sem*), gongs, baskets, mats, crossbows, fish traps, rat traps, and guns.

For burial the body is carried to a place just outside the village gate for the *yah kanam* ritual that is performed by the shaman to determine the cause of death. Three small bamboo shavings are placed on top of one another on the corpse's chest, after which a blanket is spread over it. The shaman asks, "Did he die because of a supernatural power in the house?" Then the blanket is carefully raised, and if one or two shavings have slipped off, it is a sign that the supernatural power in the house "bit" the deceased, causing death. Brol and Grandmother of Aning identify this "supernatural force" as the evil spirit K'nam. They also pointed out that if the ritual is not held, other members of the family will soon die. If after several tries the shavings remain in place, it is an indication that the ancestors have summoned the deceased to join them. The body is then placed on a mat in the coffin, and the lid is sealed with mud. Four to six men carry the coffin to the burial ground while other mourners remain behind to sacrifice a pig and chickens to lure the ancestors' spirits to the grave site, where an enclosure and temporary shelter have been constructed. After all mourners arrive, the coffin is placed in the shallow grave with the top above the ground. A torch is set at the foot of the grave to keep the feet of the corpse warm. Material goods such as rusty knives and cracked alcohol jars (not necessarily the deceased's) are left within the enclosure. Then the mourners bathe in the nearest watercourse, an ablution to prevent spirits from following them back to the village. Everyone returns to the *yah kanam* ritual site for a feast with rice alcohol.

Anytime during the ten days following death, the spirit of the deceased can return to the hearth in the main room of the longhouse. On the first, fourth, and tenth days of this period none of the deceased's kin can go to the fields or into the forest for fear that the spirit will follow them to the house. On the tenth day the family gathers to sacrifice a chicken as one of them chants to the deceased, "Here, we give you a chicken; don't haunt us, don't return to the house anymore, just stay at the grave." After two or three months there is the final funeral ritual for which a pig is slaughtered. On a woven mat one foot square, thorny leaves are arranged in a circle, and bits of pig liver along with tufts of cotton and tobacco are placed on the leaves. A small bamboo tube of rice alcohol mixed with water with a straw inserted is set in the middle of the circle. A procession of kin and friends led by a child carrying the mat makes its way to the site of the *yah kanam* ritual, where the child places the mat on the ground. It is believed that when the spirit of the deceased comes to drink the alcohol and eat the liver it will prick its fingers on the thorns, jolting it into the realization that it is dead and should remain in the grave. The coffin is left in place, and after five years it can be used for another deceased member of the family. On this occasion, the lid is opened, and bones of a male are stacked at the head while bones of a female are grouped at the foot to make way for the new corpse.

Grandmother of Aning and Brol report that the *phol* of one who dies in an "unnatural way," that is, by murder, suicide, or being mauled by a tiger (tigers only get "bad people"), remains in the vicinity of the village, becoming *phol kanam Drieng,* dreaded wandering souls in league with the evil spirit Drieng. Wandering souls lead others to die unnatural deaths, so the Jeh fear rainbows, manifestations of Drieng catching rain to feed his wandering souls. Several months after an unnatural death, the villagers gather at the edge of the settlement to perform a special ritual during which members of the deceased's family place raw pig liver and rice alcohol on a broad leaf to propitiate Drieng. Suai related that two men from his village of Peng Sal Peng, militiamen of the Special Forces, were killed in combat, an unnatural death. The American advisers arranged to have their bodies returned to the village, and the elders elected to make an exception and allow normal funeral observances.

Economic Activities

According to Brol, in selecting swidden sites the farmers prefer black soil because red soil is not good for farming upland rain-fed rice. Patches of rotting leaves packed on the earth are signs of fertile soil, as are bamboo and large old trees, but they cannot be disturbed because these are "spirit trees" that harbor strong, malevolent earth spirits. When clearing a swidden in the vicinity of such trees, men beat gongs imploring the sky spirit to protect them from the earth spirits. After a site for a new swidden has been chosen, farmers "cut the stick" (*ko quy*), cutting branches of a certain tree, which they stick in the earth to mark the spot. In discussing the size of swiddens, Brol used the expression "one bed one field," meaning that a man and his wife will normally need one field to produce enough for themselves. He added that a couple may farm two fields "if they are strong enough." He also explained that in an extended family of parents, two unmarried children, and one son and his wife, the parents and two unmarried children would work three swiddens while the son and his wife would farm two. The household would therefore cultivate five swiddens, usually dispersed.

Describing songs associated with economic activities, Cohen reports that while clearing a swidden, men and women working sing happy (*ko̕doh*) songs.[12] According to Brol, should one of the workers have a bad dream, it is a sign that earth spirits are in the soil, and the site is abandoned. Wood from small trees is taken to the house as kindling, and remaining wood is left to dry for at least a month. In a new swidden the men hoe soil around the edge to form a low mound (*but*) about eight inches high. Brol said that "when distant thunder can heard to the southwest," the burning, which lasts twenty days, begins. First there is the "big burning" (*chou gik*) when wood is set ablaze and fire is spread by the wind. When the fire has subsided, partially burned wood is gathered into piles for the "second burning" (*grem gik*). After the fires die, men go fishing. Yun related that with the first rains, the household woman designated as Mistress of Rice Planting and Rice Harvesting for seven days refrains from bathing and eating onions, chicken, and fruit. On the eighth day a pig is sacrificed, and the woman goes to one of the swiddens to make ten symbolic holes in the soil with a dibble stick. Then, while pouring a secret herbal brew in the holes, she invokes, according to Cohen, the rice spirit *bia-bia* happy song, which has words asking the rice spirit for abundance of food and rice alcohol, happiness, smooth relations among family members, and no serious illnesses. She repeats the song as she ritually smears pig blood on prescribed places in the longhouse kitchen.

Upland rain-fed rice is sown in rows in between which cucumber, squash, and maize are planted. Brol pointed out that planting in neat rows is not traditional for the Jeh; it is a cropping pattern introduced by the Viet Minh during the Indochina War. Another Viet Minh innovation is the planting of maize on the low mound surrounding the swidden. He added that the Viet Minh also built sizable earthen mounds on which they cultivated secondary crops. When the rice plants are around six inches high, cucumbers begin to sprout. Brol noted that "the rice grows tall while the cucumber crawls along the ground." When rice reaches the height of one foot, men and women employ two kinds of short hoes (Figure 19) to dig out weeds and sickles to cut grass. Later, when the rice stands around twenty inches (and cucumbers can be gathered), grass is cut again. Squash is ready to harvest in three months, as is maize, which young people roast over fires in the field. Cohen writes that on this occasion they like to sing *si'ang* and *ayaă* songs.

The rice harvest takes place during October and November. First, a pig is sacrificed, and the Mistress of Rice Planting and Rice Harvesting performs a ritual for the rice spirit similar to that which preceded the rice planting. Singing the *bia-bia* tune with the same lyrics, she enters the swidden to cut the first sheaf of rice, which she then winnows and carries back to the granary. Continuing her song, she smears sacrificial blood in

12. Cohen, "Jeh Music," pp. 85–87, 90–91.

Figure 19. Jeh hoes.

the kitchen. She is the first one to cook new rice and serve it to the family. Jeh men never gather rice. Cohen notes that often, a woman with an infant in a sling while harvesting will sing a *nhen* lullaby (it is taboo to sing any other song when doing this task). The harvesting technique was observed in 1967 at a swidden farmed by Jeh refugees outside of Dak To. The two girls harvesting had small baskets attached to their waists with cords. With deft movements, they pulled the kernels from the stalks and put them in baskets, allowing very few to fall to the ground. When the baskets were full, they poured the kernels into a larger basket, which a boy periodically emptied onto a flat, circular basket with a relatively open weave. Grabbing it on both sides, a woman lifted and jiggled the basket, sifting the kernels onto a woven mat. She then poured the contents onto a large, closed-weave circular winnowing basket which another woman rhythmically jerked up and down, allowing wind to blow away any remaining chaff. The kernels were finally poured into a basket to be taken to the granary in the village.

According to Cho, swiddens are farmed only one year with the exception of those located in the vicinity of very old trees which can be farmed up to four years. *Puh* is the term for a fallowing swidden that has grasses growing in it, a sign that it has not been farmed for one or two years. From time to time a *puh* field will be farmed longer, but only when the soil has been adjudged very fertile. *Sal pok* is the field with bamboo stands that require four or five years to grow. A field on which trees have matured is an "old field" (*sal kra*) that has been fallowing for at least seven years.

The longhouse is set in a farmstead (*tang chal*) that functions as a general work area and place for sunning rice, roots, bark, and coconut husks (kindling) in large circular baskets. Close by is the kitchen garden (*tang*) filled with secondary crops. Yun pointed out that previously the Jeh did not grow bamboo shoots, but now it is common. In addition, there are special gardens for chili peppers (*tang wet*) and maize (*tang bli*), a pineapple patch (*tang priat kok*), and a banana grove (*tang priat*).

Cho reports that older women weave a special cloth from the stringy bark of a certain tree. It is cut into strips, soaked in a bamboo tube of spring water, and then the strips are twisted and woven into skirts that can be sold to other villagers but not to outsiders. All young girls are taken by their female kin into the forest to learn how to forage for wild vegetables and fruit. Cohen reports that foraging is a time to sing the *ton* and *huaĭ* happy tunes. A girl seeing wild fruit she cannot reach might sing, "I'm hungry and want to eat you, but I'm not able to reach you. Who will climb and pick for me?" While foraging with her friends, a girl, upon seeing a man farther along the path, may sing so her companions can hear, "What man is that?" Or the *ton* may be sung in the forest when a storm is approaching, using words such as "Don't let me get wet and cold." The *huaĭ* can be sung to lament lack of success in finding wild food. It also is sung by men who fail to bag any game.[13]

Iron portions of tools and weapons are produced by village iron-workers, who, like those among the Sedang, employ a bamboo double-piston bellows, and the products of those who are considered particularly skillful are sought after. Cho noted that any man aspiring to be a shaman must be an adept ironworker. (Cho himself was once a shaman, but he abandoned the role and claims to have forgotten the prayer chants.) He related that when modern warfare first came to the Jeh country during the Indochina War, ironworkers discovered that metal from shell fragments and shell casings could be worked into excellent blades for knives, bush scythes, sabers, and spears. Fishing, another male activity, is done using nets and traps inserted in dams so that the current will carry fish into them. Men also pan in nearby watercourses for gold that until the Vietnam War was traded with Lao itinerant merchants for highly valued gongs, rice-alcohol jars, and loincloths woven in Lao villages. Paul Guilleminet mentions very briefly in a 1951–52 article that the Jeh made jars, but they were of mediocre quality.[14]

Village Leadership

According to Suai, authority is in the hands of the council made up of household heads (*dradră*), who in his village of Peng Sal Peng number twenty. For the most part they are the eldest men in the household, who manifest potency by their wealth, but women and younger men sometimes assume this role. Suai noted in 1967 that with men absent in the war, women composed half of the council in some Dak Pek–area villages. Council members select the headman, who must have the special potency (*kakayh*) associated with age as well as a special potency that

13. Ibid., pp. 86–87.
14. Paul Guilleminet, "La tribu Bahnar du Kontu," *BEFEO* 45 (1951–52): 524.

identifies him as *yau* ("big"), a man of wealth ("one with gold from the river"), which is equated with wisdom. Cho pointed out that the headman is the "one who teaches, shows the way." He is addressed by villagers as *boŏ* ("grandfather"). The leaders organize the most important annual village "big feast," called *piyang,* honoring Iang Boŏ Ya, the ancestors. It begins with the shaman performing a divination ritual in which he places rice kernels in the palm of his hand, which he then jiggles. Should all of the kernels fall to the ground, it is a sign that the village must sacrifice a buffalo (and if this is not done, everyone will die). If at least one kernel remains, the sacrificial animal will be a pig. The headman makes the offering to Iang Boŏ Ya. Suai noted that he must do this, but in some village rituals, in his absence, his wife, who is called *ya* ("grandmother"), may perform the ritual, providing she is the wealthiest woman in the village.

The headman meets in the communal house with the council to make decisions affecting the whole community. Normally, conflicts within the household are settled by the head, but from time to time unresolved conflicts are brought before the leaders. Suai told of one instance in Peng Sal Peng when a villager accused his neighbor of stealing rice from his field. Both parties met with the headman and the council at the communal house, where they drank from the jars and settled the problem through discussion. In more serious breaches of Jeh custom the leaders issue judgments (*duyh*) and impose atonement fines, which in the past were pigs or jars. Suai related that in 1965 two village men named Apui and Akao were serving together in the army. Akao borrowed money from Apui, who later demanded payment, angering Akao. While on patrol, Akao shot and killed Apui. The village leaders decreed that Akao would have to pay Apui's widow the sum of thirty thousand piasters (which amounted to Akao's army pay for three years). In another case, a man shot at a deer in the forest, accidentally killing a woman. The leaders ordered him to pay the victim's family a fine of four thousand piasters. Sometimes the leaders cannot resolve internal village problems. Brol told that in Dak Bi, where he was born, conflict among families resulted in a division into three groups of households. The group to which Brol's family belonged left Dak Bi and founded a new village, which they named Dak Wak Hlat.

Trial by ordeal is another way of resolving serious conflicts. In one water ordeal based on fear of a malevolent water spirit (*kanam nhing dak*), the two parties are escorted by village leaders to a nearby river, where they are plunged into the water. Knowing that the water spirit can smell them and will enter the nose of the wrongdoer, killing him, the culpable one will invariably surface first.

Chapter 8
Halang

Northwest of Kontum town the frontiers of Laos, Cambodia, and Vietnam converge, but on maps the delineated borders are only approximations. This imprecision reflects the fact that the country is remote, ruggedly mountainous, and heavily forested, rendering it extremely difficult to carry out ground surveys to fix national boundaries. It is little wonder that the Halang who live in that country have until relatively recent times been an almost unknown group. Halang point out that they have only one designation for themselves, and there are no subgroupings. Outsiders sometimes refer to them as "Kayong." In neighboring Laos, where some Halang are located, they are called "Doan" or "Halang Doan." The Vietnamese classify the Halang as a subgroup of the Sedang, and the only available population figure is ten thousand in 1967 (see Appendix A). Thomas and Headley report that the Halang speak a language of the North Bahnaric subgrouping of the Mon Khmer family. James Cooper reports that the Halang have rhymes which "are not oral poetry in the usual sense, but are idiomatic formulas used by different speakers in different contexts." Most of the rhymes are found in legends and in invocations to spirits chanted during ritual sacrifices. Cooper adds that similar rhymes are found among the Mon Khmer–speaking Bahnar, Rengao, Sedang, Jeh, and Chrau as well as among the Austronesian-speaking Jarai.[1]

Halang live in scattered villages that range in population from 150 to 600. The basic social-economic unit in village society is the longhouse

1. David Thomas and R. K. Headley, Jr., "More on Mon-Khmer Subgroupings," *Lingua* 25, no. 4 (1970): 398–418; James Cooper, "An Ethnography of Halang Rhymes," *Mon-Khmer Studies IV,* Language Series no. 2, Center for Vietnamese Studies and Summer Institute of Linguistics (Saigon, 1973), pp. 33–34. Transcriptions of Halang in this chapter are based upon the orthography devised by James Cooper.

bilaterally linked extended family group. Primary stewards of religious prescriptions to maintain harmony among man, nature, and the cosmos are village leaders, men with *mahuol,* a potency bestowed by the spirits (*ya?*) and demonstrated in lavish rituals and feasting. Dinh, Cooper's assistant from Dak Rode, explained that those without this potency are prone to bad luck. He cited the case of a man he knew who joined the Special Forces program and was killed, prompting villagers to say that "he had no *mahuol.*" The Halang display a mixed attitude toward wealth. On one hand, as a sign of potency, it is respected and, given the custom of sharing meat from sacrificial animals in a rich man's large feast, the nonwealthy stand to benefit. But on the other hand, possession of material goods invites chiding by the nonwealthy. Luoi, Cooper's assistant from Plei Khok Hnar, pointed out that one way this is done is by goading the rich man into giving elaborate celebrations. In 1970 Luoi cited as an example his brother-in-law, who, soon after he became a policeman with a good salary, was subject to jokes by fellow villagers about his newfound affluence, forcing him to give a series of lavish buffalo sacrifices with feasts that taxed his income sorely. Chiding is also intended to goad the well-to-do into declaring disdain for material possessions. One time in the past, when Luoi was wealthy, he was drinking from the jar with a friend, who began to ridicule his collection of jars and gongs. Finally, Luoi had to smash one valuable old jar to demonstrate how little he cared for material wealth.

This attitude toward the well-to-do and other characteristics suggest that the Halang have what Kirsch calls a democratic upland society.[2] Slavery, previously an indicator of wealth, has disappeared. Kin networks extend through villages, linking rich and poor alike, marriage is not restricted to any particular group, there are no bride-prices, and all males have access to the men's house. A poor person can form an alliance with a rich man, and consensus of all adults is the rule for making decisions affecting the village community.

Henri Maitre reports in his 1912 work that during the early nineteenth century, when the kingdom of Vientiane was expanding eastward, the Lao formed the "ephemeral province" of Muong Satha on the Boloven plateau, and its territory included "all of the Halang country." He also mentions that in 1893, French official Prosper Odend'hal found that the Halang villages of Dak Rode, Plei Jar, and Plei Khok used the Lao *peng* as a unit of measure for gold panned in local streams. Villagers' legend attributed this to a Lao chief named Pha Sai, who ruled the Halang.

---

2. A. Thomas Kirsch, *Feasting and Social Oscillation: Religion and Society in Upland Southeast Asia,* Department of Asian Studies, Cornell University, Southeast Asia Program Data Paper no. 92 (Ithaca, N.Y., 1973), pp. 24–25.

Ironworking and selling war captives into slavery also appear to have been introduced by the Lao. Maitre writes that around 1820, a Lao monk incited the highland groups on the Boloven plateau to revolt against rule by Vientiane, touching off a wave of "fire and blood" that enveloped the Halang country. The revolt was put down, and the monk sought refuge in a mountain redoubt among the Brao, an ethnic group located west of the Halang in Laos.[3]

When in June 1888 the bizarre French adventurer Mayréna was organizing his Sedang kingdom, he attempted to sign a treaty with a "Kayong" chief named Serot (on whom the Lao had conferred the title *ek,* used for local officials). Serot was unable to meet Mayréna, but he sent his cousin Khen, who bore the Laotian title Phia Keo, an honor bestowed on deputy governors. Mayréna ceremoniously presented Khen with gifts (among them a handsome percussion gun) to take back to Serot, but the Laotian governor confiscated the gifts and punished Khen for having recognized a power other than Siam.[4] The presence of the Siamese in the western part of the Halang country caused concern in the French colonial administration. In March 1891, Dugast, a military officer of the Cupet expedition (which was part of the Pavie Mission), encountered a Siamese unit in the vicinity of the San River, southwest of Kontum, and when it retreated he proceeded to the Halang village of Dak Rode, where he was joined by other officers of the Cupet expedition. On 26 April they learned that a Siamese force under the Luong Sakhon was moving on Dak Rode. Other French officers and Father Guerlach of the Kontum Mission hurried to the village. They recruited some two hundred Halang warriors, but the Luong Sakhon retreated into Laos, ending the Siamese threat to the highlands.[5]

In 1963 at Dak Rode, James and Nancy Cooper met Yop, an elderly man "who spoke with authority." He told them the following version of the late nineteenth-century events, which were transcribed from their unpublished field notes:

The Halang, Sedang, and Rengao were here. There were no Vietnamese or French. The Thai were over us. This country was taking in gold. The Thai were taxing every rice pot and sleeping room. The Laotians were servants of the Thai. The Laotians came up here every year and taxed. The children. grandchildren, brothers, and sisters could not sleep in their houses. They slept in the woods so they could look for gold to pay the taxes. There were no Vietnamese or French. And then our eyes saw these things. Lung Chokon [Luong Sakhon] and on the

3. Henri Maitre, *Les jungles Moi* (Paris: Larose, 1912), pp. 376–77.
4. Gerald Cannon Hickey, *Kingdom in the Morning Mist: Mayréna in the Highlands of Vietnam* (Philadelphia: University of Pennsylvania Press, 1988), pp. 97–99.
5. Gerald Cannon Hickey, *Sons of the Mountains: Ethnohistory of the Vietnamese Central Highlands to 1954* (New Haven: Yale University Press, 1982), pp. 244–45.

French side, Bok Bayang, a Catholic priest, came, and the French wanted to take over the Halang, Bahnar, Jarai, Rengao, but the Laotians would not let them. Lung Choken came with Laotian soldiers and thirty muzzle-loading rifles. Bok Kan, a Frenchman, came with soldiers with garand bolt-action rifles, and they built a fort on the Bobah Haliang stream. They were going to fight at the large village of Dak Rode. There were Vietnamese with the French. The French told the Laotians that they had been taking taxes from the Halang for a long time, and now it was time for the French to take taxes. "You have been taking gold and keeping half of it, giving the Thai very little." Thirty-five Laotian soldiers and fifty soldiers of Bok Kan and the priest were there. An old man from Dak Rode whose name was Bok Jogun said that if they wanted to fight they should leave the village or all would be killed. He said to the Laotians, "We will not work for you or give you gold. We are going to take care of our own village. The Thai are far away and we have not gotten anything from them. If you want to fight we will fight you tomorrow in the afternoon." The next afternoon Bok Kan, the Frenchman, and the priest brought out a rice bowl from the time of the ancestors. Lung Chokon also brought out a very old rice bowl. Lung Chokon said that the rice bowls were the same size and age, so they were brothers [Yop used the Vietnamese expression "anh-em"]. He said that this meant that as brothers they could not fight. So the Laotians let the French take over the country. We followed their religion. We followed the French, and the Vietnamese and Laotians went back to their own country.

Although the Halang, like other highlanders, came under French rule, they remained relatively isolated. Informants say that between 1945 and 1948 the Viet Minh infiltrated Halang country. During this period the Kontum Mission began working among the Halang, and in 1949, Father Beysselance took up residence at Dak Mot.[6]

Settlement Pattern

The village should be located on "cool ground" associated with a "high spirit" to bring good health, luck, and prosperity. It is also important to avoid "hot ground," devoid of a "high spirit," because it has been the scene of terrible events or the site of an abandoned tomb, which will bring sickness and misfortune. In a village plagued with an inordinate number of deaths and other misfortunes, the elders are apt to conclude that it is caused by "hot ground," and the usual recourse is to relocate. In citing an alternative, Dinh told how a section of Dak Rode was having trouble, which the residents decided was caused by "hot ground." They chose to have the shaman (*mjao*) perform a ritual to render the ground "cool," allowing the high spirit to return.

Log enclosures around villages are reminders of past warfare. Entering the village through its bamboo gate, it is easy to identify the men's

6. Société des Missions Etrangères, *Compte rendu des traveaux de 1949* (Paris: Séminaire des Missions-Etrangères, 1950), p. 110.

Photo 22. Halang village of Dak Rode (1966).

house, ritual center of the village and symbolic link with the cosmos, with its relatively high roof and large platform (Figure 20). The main entrances of all longhouses must face the men's house, signaling its importance as the physical and social center of the village. Near each longhouse is a kitchen garden (containing vegetables, fruit trees, and tobacco) surrounded by a bamboo fence to protect the crops from pigs.

The length of a longhouse (Figure 21) depends on the number of residents, and it is not unusual to have up to ten nuclear families in addition to assorted individual kin. At the main entrance is a sizable log platform on which women husk rice and dry tobacco. Just inside the entrance is the main room (*rengao*), which contains the principal open hearth near which rituals are held, family members sleep, and visitors are welcomed. On either side, corridors lead to families' compartments, each with its own hearth and small outside platform on which chicken coops often are constructed. Some longhouses also have additional compartments abutting the rear of the main room, lending the structure a rambling look.

Family

The Halang have bilateral descent, and marriage between consanguineal kin is forbidden, so kin terminology expresses proximity of relationships.

Figure 20. A Halang men's house.

Figure 21. A Halang longhouse in Dak Rode.

Nancy Cooper reports that the nuclear family is *khum*.[7] Beyond that is the *bal,* which includes "near relatives," that is, those in the direct line up to the fourth ascending generation and down to the fifth descending generation. *Kotum kotung* identifies those "distantly related," meaning collateral kin traced through the great-grandparents' siblings down to Ego's generation. Kin beyond that are simply classified as *gaŏ* or "other."

Within each generation (*chăl* or "length"), relationships to Ego are clearly defined in terminology. As Appendix B10 indicates, in Ego's generation siblings are age-graded, and sibling terms are extended to cousins who are age-graded relative to Ego. Affinal terms express polygyny. *Moŕndray* ("woman") is the first wife while *koŕnhong* is the term for additional wives with priority modifiers. In the first ascending generation, parents' siblings are age-graded relative to the parents, as are the parents' parents' siblings' children (parents' cousins). The modifier *goŕdra* is used to designate kin (other than parents) of this generation. In the second ascending generation, grandparent terms are extended to their siblings. *Bŏ koŕchĭ* and *yă koŕchĭ* are parents' parents while in the fourth ascending generation ancestral males are *bŏ kră* and females are *yă kră.* Ego's children are *koan,* and the modifiers *sèm, nay,* and *hoŕdrut* can be added to identify the firstborn, middle, and last-born respectively. A stepchild is *koan tim.* Siblings' children are *moan,* which is extended to cousins' children, spouse's sibling's children, and spouse's cousins' children. *Chau* indicates kin of the second descending generation, and only direct-line kin are recognized in the third, fourth, and fifth descending generations.

According to Nancy Cooper, combinations of kin terms are used to designate categories in the system. Grandparents, for example, are *bŏ-yă* and parents are *mĭ-bă. Miak-ma* refers to aunts while *nhò-ma* indicates aunts and uncles. Brothers and male cousins together are *'nhŏng-oh,* and sisters and female cousins are *nau-oh.* Younger children are *oh-roŕnoh* while children, children of siblings, and cousins are grouped under the designation *moan-koan.* The term *koan-chau* includes children and grandchildren, and *chau-roŕnau* is just grandchildren. Cooper reports that when Ego addresses kin of his generation he uses personal names. Ego always addresses the parents and grandparents by kin terms (it is strictly taboo to speak the father's name). Other kin in ascending generations are addressed using the kin term followed by the personal name. With nonkin, Ego uses the personal name except for an older person, who should be addressed teknonymously. Young children address older adults with the terms for grandparents. According to James Cooper, one of the few rhymes found outside of legends and sacrificial invocations is

7. Nancy Cooper, "Halang Kinship Terms," mimeograph (Saigon, 1970), pp. 1–10.

koan chaw naw oh (in the present transcription, *koan chau nau oh*), literally "child, grandchild, older sister, younger sibling." He notes that this is "use of specifics to denote a generic," in this case "village," which he feels reflects lack of formal village political organization because of "close kinship relationships."[8]

According to Dinh, young people attracted to each other begin a courtship, which often is initiated by the boy, who around midnight slips into the girl's longhouse (where he is supposed to sleep near but not with her) to remain until around four in the morning. The couple then obtains the help of two intermediaries, who give them advice enabling them to decide whether they should marry (*bŏgrăp*). Cooper reports that in marriage arrangements both parties want assurances that they will be well treated, providing another situation to use rhyme. The intermediaries embark on mediation (*troang,* a homonym of the word meaning "road"), and in their questioning of the prospective in-laws they use the rhyme *buh ?maang pŏhaang giaw* ("pound beat roast cook-on-a-stick"), which means "to treat badly." Cooper cites the contextual tale wherein Bloy, a courageous boy, is brought up in the forest by an elephant. A well-to-do man in a nearby village seeking to arrange marriage between his daughter and Bloy sends a slave into the forest to persuade him. Bloy hesitates, afraid that the rich man will "mistreat" (*buh ?maang pŏhaang giaw*) him. The slave returns to his master to express that concern and then goes back to reassure Bloy. Bloy agrees to wed the girl, and everyone is happy. Cooper notes that another question a boy may ask of the girl is, "When we are married will you divorce me if I get leprosy or go crazy or become drunk on mushrooms?" which, because divorce is relatively simple, Cooper sees as "partly persuasive and partly rhetorical."[9]

After deciding to marry, the couple prepares a jar of rice alcohol for the wedding ceremony (and may now have intercourse). The wedding can be held at either house, where kin and friends, bearing jars of alcohol, gather. The couple's parents exchange gifts of animals (the wealthy give buffalo and the poor offer chickens). Dinh noted with some disdain that the Halang, unlike the Vietnamese, "do not buy their wives," a reference to the Vietnamese bride-price. The bridal couple exchanges small hoes, a symbolic act that constitutes the marriage. While gongs play, animals are sacrificed and spirits are implored to bring the couple offspring, health, prosperity, and good crops. While the meat is

---

8. James Cooper, "An Ethnography," pp. 34–35, 37. Other specifics to denote generics are "water buffalo, cows, monkey, horse" for "animals in general"; "paddy, hulled rice, squash, squash" for vegetables; and "night, day, month (moon), star" for "all of the time."
    9. Ibid., p. 37.

being prepared for the feast, the intermediaries begin ritual drinking from the jars, followed by the bridal couple, then their parents.

After marriage, prescribed residence is matrilocal for a period of two to three years, after which the couple will move to the husband's longhouse. But permanent residence is usually guided by the expectation that a young couple must care for aging parents. Also, if there is no great need for the couple in either longhouse, with parents' consent they may build their own house nearby. When Luoi (who was from Dak Rode) married, he moved to his wife's village, Plei Khok Hnar. One neighbor was Klot, a Jarai who came to live with his wife's family (in accordance with the Jarai rule for matrilocal residence). Other neighbors included Thu and Gil, Halang from other villages. In a Dak Rode longhouse visited in 1966 there were ten compartments, two of which had been added behind the main room. The entire household numbered twenty-nine people, five of whom were of the older parental generation while their offspring had six nuclear families with a total of twelve children. A corner compartment was occupied by a widow whose husband's parents had built the house. Across the corridor were two compartments, one occupied by the widow's son, his wife, and three children, and the other by the wife's mother. Next to the widow was her daughter and her family. The daughter's husband's parents were deceased, but his father's second wife had half of the addition behind the main room, and her son and his family had another compartment. At the opposite end of the longhouse two compartments were for the daughter of the couple who built the house and her eldest son and his family. Her younger son and his wife were dead, but their son and his family had half the structure that had been added behind the main room.

A newly married couple is given its own compartment, where personal effects are stored in baskets along the wall. They sleep on mats with their heads toward the outer wall, and it is taboo to step over the head of a sleeping person (the expression "to step over one's head" is way of saying someone has committed adultery). The couple prepares meals on their own hearth but are expected to share meals with any aging parents with whom they live. Suspended from the rafters above the hearth is a bamboo shelf, a storage place for cooking utensils, maize, and salt. In the main room of the longhouse unmarried girls sleep next to the main hearth, and small boys also sleep there until they go to spend each night in the men's house. Visitors sleep on low beds by the walls. At family rituals music is provided by a large drum suspended from the rafters and gongs, the most valuable of which are of Laotian manufacture (in 1970 Luoi reported that a valuable set of gongs could be traded for fifteen buffalo). Along the walls are jars, and those of value were brought into the Halang country by Lao traders. Luoi reported that some elderly people in his village swore that during a fire in the men's house they saw one such jar emerge on its own and lower itself from the entrance platform.

Relations between a couple and in-laws are carefully prescribed. Those of the same sex may remain in a room together and talk sparingly, but those of the opposite sex should avoid each other. Joking is forbidden. Luoi and Dinh said that once away from the longhouse it is common for young people to joke about such things as "missing the mother-in-law." There is a joking relationship between grandparents and grandchildren, but once the grandchildren reach puberty, they cannot joke often. The eldest male is the household head, but this role does not give him great authority because all decisions are arrived at through discussions among all adults. Conflicts between family members are resolved through discussion.

A Halang has only one name, which is given seven or eight days after birth (*kòt* or *roñeh*). It is taboo to name a child after its deceased kin (although there is no taboo against mentioning the name). Often a child is given a name derived from nature, such as a type of local tree, a particular rock, or a watercourse, but it is forbidden to name a child after an animal or part of the human body. There is a marked preference for alliteration. Luoi's two sisters, for example, are Lep and Lum. Some parents go a step further and use a rhyming pattern. Luoi's sister's three sons are Thu, Thi, and Thong, and her daughters are Nlong, Nhom, and Nhong. Should a newborn die, the pattern is breached for the next child but continued for succeeding children. Luoi cited the case of three sons named Duong, Duot, and Diah, but the newborn daughter died. The next child was named Chieu, but when another daughter was born she was named Duoy. While discussing naming practices with Halang villagers, James Cooper observed that the names encountered did not conform to the Halang phonemic pattern.

Serious illness is caused either by a disgruntled spirit or a witch (*holeh*), who takes the form of a disembodied head floating through the night air. Most illnesses, however, are not preceded by foreboding signs, so when someone falls ill the family sends for the shaman (*mjao*) to determine which spirit is to blame and what it wants by way of propitiation. According to Dinh, the shaman is a male who learns through a dream the secret of longevity. He then experiences a period of madness, after which he has the power to communicate with spirits. Never invited to participate in village rituals, he restricts himself to meeting the needs of families and individuals. Luoi pointed out that the spirits expect the first offering to be a goat, but if the victim does not recover they want a more prestigious pig and finally a buffalo. Such sacrifices reflect social status because the rich can afford to sacrifice pigs and buffalo but most villagers do not progress beyond a pig. Upon the death of his mother, Luoi sacrificed a large male buffalo, but the village elders heartily disapproved, saying that someone of his status should have offered a small female buffalo. Luoi added that he was planning a sacrifice to mark the completion of his new house, and having once offered a prestigious animal he would have to do so again to save face. He noted that the family and close kin get the choice tenderloin and liver.

According to Dinh, a witch's power is transmitted through the female line, and it is the witch's disembodied head that seeks to "squeeze the spirit" of the victim so as to "eat his liver," causing instant death. Dinh observed that the witch's search for victims is a bad habit that cannot be changed, but, he added, neither can it be tolerated. The appearance of the disembodied head in connection with a death prompts a search for the witch, who will be banished from the village. Dinh knew a woman found guilty of witchcraft who was forced to leave her family, and later he saw her wandering around the Kontum market.

When a person dies, his family refrains from eating rice until after the funeral. Wealth is a sign of the spirits' favoritism, and the spirit of a rich person will join other spirits in the sky. The spirit of a poor person, however, will go to the forest to join spirits of rocks and trees. The eyes of the deceased are closed, and the corpse is dressed in its best clothes and laid on a mat in the main room with its head in the direction of the rising sun. The ordinary villager lies near the large open hearth, but the rich person is placed in the center of the room so that many gong players can circumambulate. A piece of red cloth and a rice bowl are tied to the head, and wads of cotton are placed on the cheeks. Kin and friends of well-to-do deceased, bearing many food dishes, gather in the main room for two nights of drinking from the jars. If the guests do not fit in the main room a temporary shelter is built outside. The body is placed on a wooden bed graced with decorative carvings. The widow, widower, or closest kin token feeds the corpse rice and alcohol, from time to time blowing smoke into its mouth. It is considered good to give away a rich man's possessions, and guests who bring elaborate offerings will receive valuable items. Luoi recalled that at one funeral some kin brought a large buffalo, and they received a set of gongs. At another funeral a guest who brought a buffalo was given the deceased's Honda motorcycle. The rich family also sacrifices more than one buffalo, and Luoi once attended a funeral at which fifteen buffalo were offered to the spirits. Tombs of the well-to-do are elaborate, with a roof (of metal in recent years) supported by four hardwood columns on which likenesses of the deceased have been carved. The coffin is placed in a shallow grave, dirt is heaped on it, and it is enclosed with a solid fence. Possessions piled on top include clothes, pipes, precious alcohol jars, and weapons. Luoi had a friend who was killed, and his family placed his expensive stereo tape recorder on his grave. Wealthy families bring cooked rice daily to the tomb, and once a month they sacrifice a pig at the site. On the first anniversary of burial, kin and friends gather to drink from the jars and play gongs while a buffalo is sacrificed. Then there is feasting, and the tomb is abandoned. The poor have simpler observances. The fare is meager with a chicken or two sacrificed and one jar of alcohol for guests. Only a few material possessions are placed on the unadorned grave. The Halang believe in reincarnation for those who die when they are very young. Upon the death of a child, the parents put a charcoal mark on a palm or bottom of a foot, and if a newborn has a similar mark it is sign of reincarnation.

When a father dies, the elder brothers and sisters receive a larger share of family goods, which include domestic animals, jars, gongs, weapons, and farm tools. Inheritance of the longhouse is usually based on who will care for the widowed mother. In recent years if there are not many gongs they are sold for cash, which is divided among the children.

Alliances

James Cooper observed in 1966 that for the Halang being an orphan is very bad, and it is not uncommon to hear a man or woman of sixty years lament, "Oh, I have no mother or father." Some Halang avoid this status by arranging a "father-child alliance (*chě koan bǎ*). This alliance most often results when an adult male or female's father dies and that person wishes to become the "child" of a man who has the same name as the father. Luoi explained that because the relationship involves mutual responsibility and support, an alliance with a wealthy man has numerous advantages for the child. If called upon, the "father" must help the child, bringing to bear his influence and wealth. The father, for example, is expected to make the child's marriage arrangements. When the father dies, if the child has an impressive pig or buffalo sacrifice for him, the child must then inherit gongs, jars, and other valuable possessions. The child must if requested provide labor in the father's fields. Periodically the father and child visit each other and sacrifice pigs. Usually the child initiates the alliance. Once the father agrees, the child convenes a gathering of both parties' kin. The child presents the father with a loincloth, a blanket, and a rice bowl, but the father is not expected to give anything. A pig or chicken is sacrificed, and blood is collected in a bowl. The child rubs some of the blood on the father's nipple and proceeds to suck the nipple. The animal's liver is offered to the spirits, after which everyone drinks from the jars and feasts. Luoi noted that following this ritual, the father and child "share with each other and take care of one another."

Luoi related that in 1968, when he was thirty-three years old, he was approached by a twenty-six-year-old Jarai girl from Plei Rolung (south of Kontum) who wanted a father-child alliance with him. Married to a Halang from Luoi's village and mother of two, she declared that her deceased father had a name similar to Luoi's, and so she wanted him as her adoptive father. Luoi at first refused, but three months later he agreed, and the girl organized the ritual. Subsequently Luoi gave her a goat that had eight kids. She attended a buffalo sacrifice in her natal village and brought Luoi the neck and some of the liver. When Luoi's mother died, the daughter sacrificed a pig for her and obtained some cement for tomb construction, and on the first death anniversary she contributed chickens and a jar of alcohol for the ritual and feasting. The daughter and her husband purchased a Honda motorcycle, and one day some Halang from Plei Khok Hnar saw him speed by the Kontum market with a Bahnar girl riding on the back. When the girl saw the villagers, she hid her face. Luoi's daughter was outraged and asked him to bring the matter before the village assembly. Because of their alliance, Luoi did so, and a public hearing was held. The Jarai girl said that she owned part of the Honda and therefore had the right to destroy it, adding that she also had the right to take Bahnar boys riding with her. The assemblage of adult villagers conferred and concluded that the fact that the Bahnar girl hid her face was proof of the husband's guilt so he was publicly reprimanded.

Jiang is an alliance between two men pledging mutual hospitality. Luoi (who had *jiang* alliances with three men) explained that it usually comes about when a person new to an area where he has no kin or friends needs entrée into local society. The person approaches a village male, most often a household head, to form an alliance. At one of their houses they sacrifice a chicken, after which the liver is rubbed around the rim of a jar of alcohol while both parties call upon the spirits to witness their alliance. Both then drink from the jar. This ritual is repeated at the other house, sealing the alliance. Luoi noted that *jiang* is not as "firm" as the father-child alliance in that the prescribed behavior is less well defined.

Economic Activities

December is the time "to look for new forest," a new swidden site. Several Halang farmers said that they look for thick, lush forest where there are large trees, a sure sign of fertile soil. They explicitly avoid a kind of elephant grass (*deya*) four or five feet high. Normally swiddens and gardens are worked cooperatively by household members, but with the parents' consent a couple can farm its own swidden, although the harvests must be shared with the parents. Although Halang plan farming activities within the annual dry-season and rainy-season cycle, they also listen to sounds emitted by eight different types of locustlike insects as signals to initiate certain activities related to clearing, planting, and harvesting. According to James Cooper, during the planting cycles there are eleven rituals, most of which are performed by the household head. The first, *moñuan ier* ("pouring out [the blood] of a chicken"), takes place in February, when men fell large trees, during which a rhyme is used in invocation to the spirits. A chicken is killed and its blood collected in a rice bowl. Next to the first tree to be felled, the household head pours some of the blood into a shallow hole while he addresses the spirits (among those Cooper names are *Ya? hopòom, Bò? Gòdre,* and *Bòr Hmeang*), "Take this, I am cutting trees. I am sacrificing a chicken. Make my ax sturdy. Don't let it get dull. I hope the trees will be hollow and full of holes. I hope they will break easily." At this point the farmer uses the rhyme, *"plèh plieu ?ngieu ?ma"* ("fall aside left right"), which Cooper translates as "Let them fall to the left and right of me." The invocation continues, "Don't let them break and fall on me. Spirit take care of me. Later on I am going to perform the *dah ?loang* sacrifice here. I will sacrifice to you (plural) here."[10]

April is the time for *chùh muuih* ("setting the field on fire"), after which debris is raked into piles on the edge of the swidden. Cooper reports that this is the time for two ritual offerings, *hùar* and *soay,* in the field. Afterward, back in the village, household members and kin gather in the main room to drink from the jars and to feast. The spirits are implored, but no offering is made. Then there is a rhyming invocation to the legendary character Grandfather Tolùum, asking him to stay out of the field because he brings weeds. Cooper explains that Grandfather Tolùum figures in many legends as one who embodies rank stupidity. He speaks in a nasal manner and cannot count beyond two. He hangs his clothes on a tree and then dives in the river after them when he sees their reflection on the surface. Grandfather Tolùum climbs down a tree head first because he sees ants descend that way. But he and his wife are kindly folk who often are taken advantage of by others. The rhyme says: *Sraay gar ?yaa, chaa kólan ik àih* ("Sow seed tobacco, eat anus"), *Sraay gar róngoang, khoang kólan ik àih* ("Sow seed bettle, burn anus"), *sraay gar hóbii, susìi kólan ik àih* ("Sow seed cabbage, rub anus"). Cooper notes that the rhyme is a threat within the context of the whole invocation, which goes, "Oh Grandfather Tolùum, don't trample down my field which is by the stream Jola. If you trample my field I will sow tobacco seed which will eat your anus, sow bettle seed which will burn your anus, sow cabbage seed which will rub your anus."[11] Normally fields are

10. Ibid., pp. 36, 38–39.
11. Ibid., pp. 38–39.

weeded two or three times, and Dinh observed that "lazy people" only weed once.

The Halang have twelve varieties of upland rain-fed rice, which mature in three to four months. *Krêng jrai, lao,* and *koʼtam* (which has a round, speckled kernel) are early three-month types. Late four-month rice includes *lŭ, boʼla,* and *blak* (the last two have long, wide grains). The remaining six—*roʼguong* (black husk), *boʼgrĭ* (black husk and speckled kernel), *ngo* (black kernel), *hoʼluoi* (long-grain), *krêng goʼlit,* and *krêng jroh* (both have small kernels)—are in between. The cropping pattern is to sow during a one-month period the early varieties, first in one section of the swidden, then in-between types in another part, and finally late rice in the remaining section. This system enables effective use of available labor at planting and harvesting when the crop must be gathered rapidly.

Maize is planted between the rows of rice plants, and along the edges of the swidden farmers plant secondary crops. Just before rice plants mature, the village has a large ritual called *phau,* honoring Yang Sri, the female Rice Spirit. Luoi said that each household is assessed cash according to its relative means to buy a sacrificial buffalo. On the day before the ritual, alcohol jars are set up in the men's house while outside villagers prepare the sacrificial stake, decorating it with festoons fashioned out of rattan and shaved bamboo. At dawn the following morning the buffalo is secured to the stake with a rattan collar and its hind legs are tied. All household heads, carrying knives and sabers, gather to implore the Rice Spirit to bring the village abundant harvests, good vegetables, robust livestock, ample clothing, health, prosperity, and wisdom. One of them steps forward to slit the buffalo's throat, and gushing blood is collected in a bucket. When the animal is dead, it is immediately dressed out. Meanwhile, everyone has gone to the men's house, where first the elderly and then the well-to-do drink from jars, after which other men take turns. A feast for all villagers follows.

Gathered rice is stored in granaries near the swiddens. Fields cleared in thick forest can be farmed for three years and then are left to fallow from seven to ten years. Fields cleared in grassy areas can be cultivated for only one year. Around the villages are coconut and mango trees, and recently papaya trees (the Halang use the Lao name) were introduced.

Halang women weave textiles using back-tension looms. Paul Guilleminet reports that in the past, Halang, who favor indigo-blue textiles, wove white cloth destined for trade with the neighboring Bahnar Jolong in the Kontum area.[12] Men hunt using crossbows, traps, and more recently firearms. Prior to leaving on a hunt they invoke Ae Rogap, a spirit

---

12. Paul Guilleminet, "La tribu Bahnar du Kontum," *BEFEO* 45 (1951–52): 524.

who is described in legends as not very bright but one who will bring success in bagging game. Women and girls go in groups to forage for wild fruits and vegetables. Nancy Cohen reports that the Jeh borrowed from the Halang a type of song called *ton* that foraging women sing.[13]

Every family produces its own rice alcohol. Unhusked rice is left to soak for several days, then hulled and placed in a mortar with bark and root of a local tree, ginger root, manioc root, and dried chili peppers. This mixture is pounded into a mash and put in a rice-alcohol jar. The bark of a tree called *yam* (which causes a burning sensation on contact with the skin) is crushed in water, then drained and added to the mash. Sealed with banana leaves, the jar is allowed to stand for at least four days.

From time to time men pan for gold in nearby watercourses. Dinh described how he did this in a stream near Dak Rode, realizing on a very good day a nugget the size of a rice kernel. Before the Vietnam War, Lao traders brought buffalo into the area to trade each one for five gold nuggets. Some men work iron using the bamboo tubes and plunges similar to those of the Sedang. A few produce such highly valued knives, sabers, spears, and bush scythes that they do it for a livelihood and do not have to farm. A few men are part-time specialists in weaving large round hats that provide protection from sun and rain. Traditionally there was intervillage barter of sets of gongs and domestic animals. Some villages also specialized in trading axes, knives, and wooden bowls.

Village Leaders

Village leaders (*ghe*), usually numbering seven or eight, attain their roles because they have special potency (*mahuol*) bestowed by the spirits. Luoi pointed out that some elderly Halang use the Bahnar term *ai* for this potency, which is manifest in physical prowess, bravery, wisdom, and wealth. The leaders are addressed as *'nhong* ("older brother") in respect for their wisdom in making decisions, but age is not a factor (Dinh knew one village leader who was twenty-seven years old). Among the leaders the headman is the wisest, richest, and bravest. Dinh related that his paternal grandfather was headman of Dak Rode. He decided to take a Rengao woman as his second wife, and while he was in her village, word spread that a herd of wild elephants was ravaging the vicinity. Searching them out, the grandfather jumped on the head of the pack leader and slew him, sending the rest fleeing into the woods. Dinh's father also was

13. Nancy Cohen, "Jeh Music," in *Notes from Indochina on Ethnic Minorities,* ed. Marilyn Gregerson and Dorothy Thomas (Dallas, Tex.: SIL Museum of Anthropology, 1980), p. 86.

headman of Dak Rode, and he displayed potency by jumping over two buffalo that had been tied together rump to rump. His potency also was demonstrated in his unfailing success at bagging game.

Despite the potency mystique attached to their roles, village leaders do not constitute an elite because leadership is embedded in kin networks that crisscross village society. The consensus of all adult villagers is needed for decisions affecting the whole community. Leaders are responsible for the well-being of the society so they handle breaches of moral order. They must cope with witchcraft, organizing the search for a witch, and meting out punishment. They also deal with conflicts (mostly stealing and lying) unresolved by family groups, convening a meeting of the parties and their respective kin and friends. Each party presents its side, after which the case is discussed by the leaders and those present. The verdict represents the consensus of the whole gathering. Luoi described a public trial that took place after a friend of his was murdered and his family accused another villager. The assembled villagers heard both sides and found the accused guilty. His family was ordered to pay the victim's family a large amount of money.

In another type of trial, called *siap,* cosmic forces intervene. Luoi gave an example in which a man accused a fellow villager of theft, which the accused denied. The conflict became bitter, and the accuser challenged his adversary to a *siap,* wherein the wrath of the spirits would be brought down on whichever party was in the wrong, resulting in his becoming crippled, blind, or inflicted with leprosy. Luoi noted that at this juncture if the accused is guilty he usually will admit it rather than face the trial. If not, the two parties come together before the leaders in a gathering of kin and friends. A jar of alcohol is tied to a stake and a pig or chicken is sacrificed. Some of the blood is poured into a bowl containing rice alcohol and blood is drawn from the fingers of both parties. Luoi interjected that up to this point either one may call off the trial by admitting that he is wrong. If the trial continues, the accuser will say, "You have wronged me, and I ask the spirits for the destruction of you, your children, and grandchildren. If you do right, you will care for me and I for you." Steadfastly refusing to admit guilt, the accused will respond, "If I really have stolen your goods may I die." Both then drink from the bowl as one of the leaders splits a bamboo tube in half. Holding both sections high, he lets them fall to the ground, and if both come up on the flat side or the round side the accused is guilty. If not, the accuser is wrong. In either case the leaders prescribe retribution, and the guilty one knows that he must face the spirits' vengeance.

In the late 1950s the Saigon government imposed upon the Halang a Vietnamese administration in which the villages had officials elected by the adults. Luoi pointed out in 1970 that regardless of who was elected, the traditional group of leaders continued to make decisions, which the elected officials had to implement. In 1966, Dinh reported that in villages they controlled, the Viet Cong named chiefs, but the people still looked to the village leaders for guidance and decisions.

Chapter 9
Sedang, Jeh, and Halang in the Vietnam War

Until 1960, the Sedang, Jeh, and Halang were able to follow traditional ways that reflected relative harmony among man, nature, and cosmic forces. Their geographic locations had removed them from the main currents of history that had swept Indochina. But everything changed when the Communists used mountain routes to infiltrate South Vietnam as part of their plan to conquer that region. A 1961 U.S. State Department report on Communist infiltration from North Vietnam tells how highlanders who had gone to North Vietnam in 1955 were trained as insurgents, and by 1959 some were in Kontum province spreading Communist propaganda in villages.[1] It describes how in October 1960 a force of a thousand Viet Cong moved against a series of South Vietnamese outposts along the Laotian border in Kontum province. One Viet Cong company made up largely of highlanders concentrated its efforts on the outpost at Dak Dru in the Sedang country. This marked the beginning of the Communist military insurgency that brought the Sedang, Jeh, and Halang into the turmoil of international warfare, which would uproot them and force wrenching readaptations that would forever alter their societies.

In August 1962 there were reported to be 13,012 refugees in Kontum province. There had been U.S. Army military advisers in Kontum town since the mid-1950s, and by the early 1960s advisers were assigned to Vietnamese military units in Dak To. A sign of growing insecurity was the arrival in April 1962 of U.S. Special Forces to open a post at Dak Pek. In

1. Information on these groups in the Vietnam War can be found in Gerald Cannon Hickey, *Free in the Forest: Ethnohistory of the Vietnamese Central Highlands, 1954–1976* (New Haven: Yale University Press, 1982), pp. 68–71, 154, 164, 188, 203, 229, 250, 308–18, 235–39, 241–47.

February 1963 a U.S. Special Forces team established a post at Dak To.[2] Beginning in 1961, when Viet Cong activities prompted the first bombings by the South Vietnamese air force, Sedang from the remote villages in the path of Communist infiltration began to move into more secure areas around Dak Sut and Dak To, where there were government military units. Jeh were abandoning villages near the Laotian border (taking with them domestic animals, gongs, jars, and artifacts, including musical instruments) to settle near Dak Sut and Dak Pek. Their traditional trade with the Lao came to a halt. Brol, Dwight Gradin's assistant, described the Dak Pek Special Forces camp, located on high ground near the Dak Pek River with a dirt airstrip nearby. A settlement nearby had refugees from Dak Gou Kram, some fifteen kilometers west of the Laotian border, and near the river was a village with 250 refugees from Dak Peng Sal Pen, twelve kilometers northwest of Dak Pek. North of the camp was a settlement with 279 refugees from Dak Gie, twenty kilometers north of Dak Pek. East of the airstrip was Plei Bom with 117 and Dak Trap with 325. Halang villagers were moving away from the border eastward, into larger villages or to the vicinity of Dak To.

Readaptations in 1964 were not drastic. The villagers dug bunkers next to their longhouses. Halang and Sedang refugees reported that nocturnal Communist theft of rice from granaries near swiddens prompted villagers to relocate these structures next to their longhouses. Brol observed that the concentration of refugees around Dak Pek forced the farmers to shorten their fallowing periods. Whereas they traditionally cleared only "old fields" (*sal kra*) that had been fallowing for at least seven years, they now had to clear *sal pok* that had been uncultivated for only four or five years. Hmou (Kenneth Smith's assistant from Kon Horing) pointed out that the movement of Sedang, Jeh, and Halang into the Dak To area caused a shortage of land for swiddening so some Sedang farmers began to follow the lead of Kon Horing farmers in arranging paddies on slopes and bottomland. Ironically, the older paddies west of Kon Horing had to be abandoned because of Communist activities. The Kontum Mission reported that in 1964 the worsening insurgency brought insecurity to thirty-four Sedang parishes (there were eight thousand Christians), some of which were abandoned when their populations fled as refugees, many going to Dak To.[3]

With the introduction in 1965 of North Vietnamese army units in

2. Francis J. Kelly, *U.S. Army Special Forces, 1961–1971* (Washington, D.C.: U.S. Department of the Army, 1973), pp. 184–85.

3. Société des Missions Etrangères de Paris, *Compte rendu de travaux de 1964* (Paris: Séminaire des Missions-Etrangères, 1965), pp. 66, 71–72; Pierre Dourisboure and Christian Simonnet, *Vietnam: Mission on the Grand Plateaus* (Maryknoll, N.Y.: Maryknoll Publications, 1967), p. 248.

Photo 23. Sedang refugees from Toumarong at Dr. Pat Smith's hospital (1965).

Kontum province, fighting intensified and involved the first use of American air power. On 1 July a combined force of Viet Cong and North Vietnamese troops attacked and captured Toumarong district town north of Kontum. Then they assaulted Dak Sut and Dak To. The fighting and bombing by U.S. warplanes sent a flood of highlander refugees southward by foot and bus on Route 14 to Kontum. Toumarong Sedang refugees bringing their wounded to Dr. Pat Smith's Minh Quy hospital related that the Communist attack began with heavy shelling of the town and nearby villages. The Sedang fled into the night, running through the thick forest so fast that they tore flesh on tree branches and brush. Some had sprains and broken ankles. One man with a strange ailment affecting his flesh had carried his grandson while his son clutched his arm, pulling him as they fled. The child and the son had held the old man so tightly that their blue handprints remained on his arm.

Dinh, James Cooper's assistant from Dak Rode, related that the Toumarong attack convinced the remaining residents of the Halang village of Dak Tang Plun that they should join the other villagers at Dak To. There, close to the South Vietnamese army's regimental headquarters they built New Dak Tang Plun. Inhabitants of Dinh's natal village of Dak Rode moved to the vicinity of Kontum, but the lack of forested land for swiddening forced them to clear grassy areas that could be farmed for only one year. The ironworkers, however, found that fragments of bombs and artillery shells and barbed wire proved excellent for forging knives and spears. At the same time, Luoi, Cooper's other assistant, and his family moved to Plei Khok Hnar, next to the Jarai village of Plei Krong west of Kontum. A wealthy family, they took along their domestic animals, gongs, and highly valued jars. Other Halang also came and farmed swiddens back in the surrounding hills. They soon learned, however, not to build the usual provisory shelters by the swiddens for those guarding the crop because these structures were now targets for jet bombers. Luoi reported that as the Halang moved westward they had more contact with Jarai Arap and intermarriages resulted.

In February 1967, while accompanying Reverend Stanley Smith (son of Gordon and Laura Smith) on a visit to his Dak To mission, a Vietnamese pastor reported that both Viet Cong and North Vietnamese army units were close to the town. Just before Christmas 1966 they had ambushed and killed two U.S. Army officers only seven hundred meters from district headquarters, prompting numerous air strikes nearby by American bombers. On the morning we visited Dak Lung, the Regional Forces had killed two Viet Cong some six hundred meters from the settlement. The pastor noted that North Vietnamese army units were camped in the nearby hills. Two French Catholic priests said that to the east and north of Dak To there were extensive swiddens, where some two hundred Sedang farmed to feed five thousand North Vietnamese troops.

The situation that existed in and around Dak Lung village in February 1967 reflected in many ways the effects of the war thus far on the Sedang, Halang, and Jeh. Since 1962 there had been a steady influx of refugees, and for miles on either side of the road from Dak To to Dak Lung stretched blackened hills, denuded of bamboo growth, a testimony to intensive swidden farming forcing farmers for the first time to mark their swidden boundaries with split sticks. Some refugees said that from time to time they would walk back to swiddens abandoned because of crumbling security to gather fruit, vegetables, and kapok that had been planted around the edges. Dak Lung had been incorporated into the South Vietnamese government's Revolutionary Development Program, which was supposed to bring security to the village along with an array of programs, such as improved sanitary conditions. One result was a completely altered settlement pattern. The village was enclosed with bamboo stakes stuck in the ground. Traditional Sedang houses (which a Vietnamese district official described as "old and filthy") were replaced by rectangular dwellings (with bamboo walls and metal roofs) built on the ground in rows. Outside the enclosure was the men's house, which villagers were in the process of dismantling in favor of a new structure

Photo 24. Not, Sedang headman of Dak Long Not (1967). Note widespread clearing for swidden as a result of the influx of refugees.

within the settlement (they noted that the shortage of men forced some villages to hire Vietnamese carpenters to help with construction of men's houses). Not far from the village a household group of four men and four women were preparing fields "that the ancestors had farmed" for the coming planting season. They had cut trees and brush some two months before and were in the process of setting dried wood ablaze (girls carried dried thatching from the old men's house to kindle the fire).

Near Dak To the large settlement of Dak Chu (whose headman was Sedang) had 325 households of Jeh and Sedang refugees. One Jeh refugee described how he and his family had fled Dak Sang not far from the Laotian border because of bombing. They initially settled at Tan Canh, close to Dak To, remaining there for eight months before moving to Dak Chu. The man was building a house (with materials brought in by the U.S. aid program) and planned to farm at least one swidden, but he was not optimistic about the prospects for a good crop because he adjudged the soil to be relatively infertile and there were too many refugees cultivating in the vicinity. He and others tried to supplement their diets by fishing in nearby rivers, but Vietnamese soldiers shot at them. A group of older Jeh complained that the larger swiddens belonged to the

Sedang, and they lamented that "there is no good soil here." This country, they added, was not the place their ancestors had farmed. Nonetheless, they had begun clearing small swiddens and planted gardens by their houses. Private voluntary organizations were distributing relief rice to each family, but everyone was short of food.

Some of the Jeh songs that Nancy Cohen recorded in refugee camps at this time reflect a nostalgia for the life they had known before the war. One woman sang a variation on the traditional si'ang (usually sung by a guest at dinner) with lyrics expressing gratitude for visitors who had come a long way to see her. But now, she sang, she was almost destitute, barely existing. Her visitors had many possessions and the blessings of the spirits, but she had nothing and no chance of improving her lot. Other women sang the traditional laments (akah), reminiscing "about past life in the village, activities of rice planting days, the abundance of food or the carefree hunting and fishing of long ago." Cohen observes that "Jeh refugees dwell on these things with great sadness and longing."[4]

By the end of 1967, the increased buildup of Communist forces around Kontum forced Luoi and his neighbors at Plei Khok Hnar to abandon their swiddens. Luoi was fortunate in having some fields belonging to a Lao friend that were low-lying and accumulated water during the rainy season so he devised a water management system that enabled him to cultivate wet rice. Around the edges he planted banana trees and sugarcane. Like many other refugees, Luoi learned that it was now important to mark the boundaries so he constructed a wire fence. In 1968 he obtained a license to open a small shop in the village (three other Halang had already opened shops). He bought his stock (tobacco, trousers, T-shirts, rubber sandals, candy, canned fish, salted fish, Vietnamese fish sauce, soy sauce, soda pop, and beer) from Chinese and Vietnamese wholesalers in the Kontum market. Luoi told how he once brought a jeepload of goods to the shop, and soon after, a detachment of Vietnamese and highlander soldiers came in and bought all the beer and many other things. Realizing an excellent profit, Luoi immediately returned to Kontum to replenish the stock. When in 1969 he decided to build a new house similar to Vietnamese houses in Kontum, he sold his Honda motorcycle, a valuable jar, and a gong to purchase cement, cinder blocks, wood, and the services of Vietnamese carpenters.

Americans used Agent Orange herbicides (containing dioxin) to deprive the Communist presence north of Kontom town them of forest cover and food crops. In 1972 interviews were conducted in several

---

4. Nancy Cohen, "Jeh Music," in *Notes from Indochina on Ethnic Minorities,* ed. Marilyn Gregerson and Dorothy Thomas (Dallas: SIL Museum of Anthropology, 1980), pp. 85, 89.

refugee camps to determine some effects of herbicide use. Sedang informants near Dak To included two young men and an elderly woman from Long Djon, an elderly man from Dak Rosa, and the headman of Dak Mot Khon. Over a period of months, aircraft sprayed swiddens around Dak Rosa and Long Djon, where the herbicide drifted into the settlement. At Long Djon "many children died," while at Dak Rosa several children died after developing abdominal cramps, diarrhea, and skin rashes that resembled burns with small blisters. At Dak Rosa there also were an "unusual number" of stillbirths. All of the villagers who been caught in the spraying complained of abdominal pains and diarrhea. In addition, at Long Djon many experienced a stinging sensation in their nasal passages, and many developed coughs that lasted more than a month. Dak Rosa villagers who went into swiddens following the spraying broke out with skin rashes that lasted for weeks. In both Long Djon and Dak Rosa all of the chickens and pigs died. Long Djon villagers noted that after the spraying there was a remarkably large number of dead fish floating in the nearby streams. Residents of Dak Mot Khon did not witness any spraying, but they did see very many dead and dying fish in the Dak Kla River. American military personnel from Tan Canh warned them not to eat the fish, and subsequently the Americans put some "medicine" in the water. Then the villagers were informed that they could eat the fish, and they did so without harmful effects. The nearby forest "dried and died," leaving them without a place to hunt and forage. Long Djon villagers reported that where the spray fell directly, all of the swidden and garden crops died. The villagers gathered wild tubers, which they washed before eating. Dak Rosa villagers dug up manioc roots but found that they were "rotten." Rice plants that continued to grow did not produce buds.

Halang refugees reported similar reactions to the herbicide. On 23 November 1972 at the Dam San refugee camp near Ban Me Thuot, a group of five men and two women from the Halang refugee village of New Dak Tang Plun described how they had farmed rain-fed rice and vegetables in swiddens several kilometers to the west. In 1968, just as the rice plants were budding and other crops were maturing, an American C-123 sprayed the area, and the herbicide blew into the settlement. Describing the spray as "medicine," the group said, "We didn't know what was happening. We didn't know what to do." Plants began to wilt; leaves on trees dried up and fell. As all vegetation began to die, most of the villagers became ill with fevers, abdominal pains, and coughing. Some broke out in skin rashes. They estimated that thirty children died. All of the chickens, most of the pigs, and many cattle and buffalo died. One woman reported that some Viet Cong who ate sprayed leaves and insects died. The group described new growth that produced small leaves strangely curled. They were reduced to surviving by foraging in un-sprayed forest.

During this period, political events involved some Sedang in national politics. In the 11 September 1966 elections for the Constitutional As-sembly, Peang, a young leader from Dak To who had served in the army since 1947, won a seat. In October 1967 he was elected to the lower house of the National Assembly and was reelected to that seat in November 1971. In May 1972, Nay Luett, minister for ethnic minorities' develop-ment, gathered a group of highland leaders at his Saigon residence to form a new bloc with the goal of "opposing Communist aggression," and one of those present was Peang. A rising young Sedang leader was Kek from Kon Horing, who had the second baccalaureate from the pres-tigious Lycée Yersin in Dalat and had been a seminarian in Kontum. In December 1969 he was named Sedang representative in the Ethnic Mi-norities Council.

By 1970 there had been an influx of American military units in the Dak To-Tan Canh area, where they built airstrips and set up fire bases. On 1 April 1970, North Vietnamese forces (a regiment and an artillery unit) attacked the Special Forces post in the Sedang country at Dak Seang. Twelve days later, the same Communist units assaulted Dak Pek, almost completely destroying the camp.[5] During this period, Dr. Pat Smith's Minh Quy hospital in Kontum was a haven for sick and wounded high-land villagers. She also launched a village health care program under the direction of former Special Forces medic Thomas Coles and his Jarai assistant, Siu Kot.[6] By the end of 1971 there were twenty-six village health workers who had been trained at the hospital and were now dispersed in villages throughout Kontum and Pleiku provinces. Between 10 October 1971 and 2 April 1972 they had treated 8,115 patients in a population totaling some 40,977. Coles's 1972 report included a summary of seasonal diseases and trauma. Diseases in the dry season included plague (harvested rice is brought into the village and rats follow), mea-sles, pneumonia (December and January are the coolest months), burns (on cold nights villagers sleep close to open hearths), snakebites (suffered by farmers preparing swiddens in heavily overgrown, snake-infested mountainsides), and traumatic injuries (military action increases in this season, and farmers clearing swiddens detonate explosives such as buried M79 grenades). The wet season brought diseases caused by waste of infected individuals carried into watering points by the rains—typhoid and a disease known locally as *cho'roh hak* characterized by sudden

5. Kelly, *U.S. Army Special Forces,* p. 154.

6. Thomas G. Coles, "Village Health Worker Program, Minh-Quy Hospital, Kontum, Vietnam," Progress Report 1, 7 June 1972, mimeograph, pp. 1–15.

Photo 25. American soldiers resting in a highland schoolyard during a military operation north of Kontum (1969).

diarrhea and vomiting, resulting in dehydration and shock, and also malaria (rains increase breeding places for mosquitoes).

Coles's reports as of March 1972 were signaling a buildup of Communist forces in Kontum province. On 25 March, for example, he and Siu Kot were treating patients in Dak Ro'man when military activity two kilometers north of the village prompted air strikes, and later that day at Dak Ri Kram there was military activity across the river. The following day there was heavy military action south of Kontum on Route 14 and northeast of Kontum. At Dak Chu on 28 March, while treating patients, Coles and Siu Kot were warned by villagers and a French priest to expect local heavy military action in the near future. On 12 April Coles and his assistant were in Dak Pek where some thirty-five hundred Jeh refugees had concentrated. Siu Kot declared, "I've seen some villages in bad shape, especially Jarai, but these people have to live in holes like animals so the VC can't kill as many when they attack. So many are sick from living like this: a lot must die." Three days later, the Communists attacked Dak Pek, and Coles reports that "over one hundred villagers were killed and only a handful of wounded were evacuated."[7]

7. Ibid., p. 7.

The main thrust of the destructive 1972 offensive began on 31 March, when the Communists launched an offensive at the Demilitarized Zone. On 2 April Sedang, Jeh, and Halang farmers paused in their task of preparing fields for planting when they heard large explosions coming from the direction of fire bases Charlie, Yankee, and Delta that the Americans had established on the ridge dominating the Dak To Valley and Route 14. The withdrawing Americans had turned the fire bases over to the South Vietnamese, and the villagers knew that the explosions indicated a rocket attack by the Communists. This time, however, the explosions lasted for days, prompting Sedang farmers to leave their fields and retreat into their houses in anticipation of a battle. On 17 April a North Vietnamese unit attacked what was now called "rocket ridge," overrunning fire base Charlie and scattering its five hundred defenders. Fire bases Yankee and Delta were immediately abandoned.

The Communists had two divisions (the 2d and 320th), in addition to two independent regiments of infantrymen, an artillery regiment, and a sapper regiment. On Saturday, 24 April, North Vietnamese Russian tanks crashed into the compound of the forward headquarters of the South Vietnamese 22d Division at Tan Canh while other units attacked nearby Dak To. The South Vietnamese made no effort to defend the post and fled at the sight of the tanks. Not long after, American bombers began to swoop over the Dak To valley as helicopters attempted to evacuate the American advisers (one helicopter with six advisers was shot down). Soldiers of the 22d Division, mixed with Vietnamese civilians from Tan Canh, began pouring southward on Route 14 to seek refuge in Kontum. As they carried the bad news that Dak To and Tan Canh had fallen, highlanders in villages along Route 14 either fled into nearby forests or joined the exodus southward. Leon Wit was at his wife's village of Dak Cho, northeast of Dak To, where on Sunday, 25 April, everyone gathered for mass said by Father Paul Renaud, but afterward they heard that North Vietnamese troops were in the vicinity. Wit had been an army interpreter so it was decided that he should leave. He made his way over trails to his own village of Dak Brao, then to Dak Lung. He heard that Communist troops had entered Kon Horing so he moved through the forest for three days to reach Kontum.

According to Father Paul Carat of the Kontum Mission, on 24 April, when refugees from Kon Horing found their escape route blocked by fighting, they returned to the village, where the Sisters of St. Vincent de Paul were treating in their dispensary hundreds of wounded and sick refugees from the fighting.[8] North Vietnamese troops entered Kon Hor-

---

8. Paul Carat, "Kontum," *Les echos de la Rue du Bac* (Paris: Séminaire des Missions-Etrangères), no. 60 (February 1973), pp. 50–53.

ing on 26 April, and on 6 May, Fathers Brice and Carat were taken prisoner by the Communists (they were held until August under harsh conditions). Sister Marie-Hélène, the sixty-three-year-old superior of the Kon Horing nuns, two highlander sisters, and Fathers Dujon and Arnould were subjected to forced marches before being released.

In Kontum, fear that the North Vietnamese would assault the city prompted people with automobiles to begin preparing to go south to Pleiku. But the flow of refugees out of Kontum ceased abruptly when the North Vietnamese 95B Regiment occupied the Mount Pao pass, cutting the only means of escape by road. Panic gripped the town, and residents hurried to the small city airport and scrambled to board military planes bringing reinforcements and supplies to the garrison. To make matters worse, the Communists began to shell Kontum and the airstrip from the surrounding hills. Dr. Pat Smith and her American staff evacuated, leaving the Minh Quy Hospital in the hands of two highland nuns, Sister Gabrielle and Sister Vincent.

Meanwhile, John Paul Vann, the senior American adviser for the II Corps area, which included the central highlands, took charge of operations in Pleiku. One of his strategies was to call in massive bombings by B-52s and other aircraft north of Kontum. In the face of this nightmare, most of the Sedang, Jeh, Halang, and Rengao fled their villages and refugee camps, either going into forests or southward to Kontum. They soon were joined by Bahnar and Jarai Arap. As large numbers of refugees poured into Kontum, all available shelters filled, forcing many to huddle under trees in school compounds. The Kontum Mission was rapidly depleting its stores of rice to keep them fed. At the beginning of May the situation worsened as fear of an impending Communist assault spread through the town. Shells and rockets struck with increased force and all semblance of order vanished.

Kek, the young Sedang leader who was serving on the Ethnic Minorities Council, arrived in Pleiku late in May and related that the increased fighting and bombing had prompted Kon Horing elders to decide to evacuate. Most villagers packed essentials, closed their longhouses, and moved eastward down the forest trail. The Catholic nuns, however, could not leave their patients in the large dispensary so they remained. Kek was one of the last to leave, and as he was departing, he was astonished to see a large group of Vietnamese civilians coming off Route 14 into the settlement. They were in a state of agitation and explained that they were trying to move south on the road when North Vietnamese tanks blocked them. The soldiers ordered them to return to Tan Canh so they turned around. But they were frightened and tired and decided to go into Kon Horing. Kek went on his way while the Vietnamese moved into some of the abandoned longhouses. On the night of 27 May the Sedang in the forest heard ear-splitting explosions from B-52 raids in the direction of Kon Horing. The following day Kek and some of the men went back to the village to find widespread devastation. The Kontum Mission later reported that around 250 had died in the raid, but miraculously the dispensary was spared and of the ten nuns only two were injured.[9]

Kek and the Kon Horing elders decided to lead the villagers over back trails in the mountains and made their way to Kontum. There they joined other Sedang refugees in a school building. The town had fallen into a state of anarchy with South Vietnamese soldiers indulging in unrestrained looting, first breaking into shuttered shops and houses and then fanning out to close-by Bahnar villages, where they took livestock. The highland refugees remained calm, lighting fires to cook, and women set up back-tension looms they had brought with them to weave.

At the Ministry for Ethnic Minorities' Development in Saigon the staff worked feverishly on plans to remove the growing number (now estimated at around fifteen thousand) of highland refugees caught in Kontum. Minister Nay Luett on 14 May consulted in Pleiku with John Paul Vann concerning assistance in removing the refugees. Vann informed him that he already had taken twenty thousand Vietnamese out of Kontum and could do nothing for the highlanders because the American senior province adviser (a colonel) and the Vietnamese province chief claimed that the highlanders did not want to leave the city. The province chief planned to organize them to defend the city against an expected North Vietnamese assault. Furious at this news, Luett went to Kontum, where he was greeted by Sedang, Jeh, Halang, Rengao, Bahnar, and Jarai Arap refugees who told him that they were very anxious to leave because of the heavy fighting and shelling. Luett returned to Pleiku to confront Vann, who agreed to arrange for aircraft to take the highland refugees to Pleiku. Unlike the Vietnamese, who stormed the planes and helicopters, highlanders lined up in orderly fashion, putting the elderly and children on the aircraft first. By 17 May some eight thousand had been airlifted to Pleiku.

Kek and his fellow Kon Horing villagers boarded an American chinook helicopter in Kontum and were flown to Pleiku, where they were housed in an abandoned supply dump. Fortunately, the highlanders remained in village groups where there was cohesion and leadership, both of which made it easier to organize refugee relief. But the panic that had seized Kontum now spread to Pleiku, sending an estimated 80 percent of the Vietnamese population down Route 19 to Qui Nhon or down Route 21 to Nhatrang. Regional Forces abandoned their weapons to flee with their families. Most of the civil servants left, and only one

9. Ibid., p. 52.

Photo 26. Sedang, Jeh, and Halang refugees in Pleiku boarding military trucks for evacuation to Ban Me Thuot (1972).

doctor was left at the province hospital. As in Kontum, Vietnamese soldiers looted the shuttered shops and houses.

Although the refugees were removed from the chaos of downtown Pleiku, they faced an increasingly dire situation because of insufficient housing, lack of firewood, and shortage of water. Then, too, there was the possibility of a Communist attack on Pleiku. This situation prompted Minister Nay Luett to plead with the American officials that the refugees be moved southward to Ban Me Thuot. The Americans responded that there were no aircraft available because the Communists had blown up the large ammunition dump near the airstrip and all of the aircraft were needed to fly in new supplies. Vann agreed to allow refugees to board empty military trucks in a large convoy going down Route 14 to Ban Me Thuot. Because the refugees in the supply dump were living under the worst conditions, it was agreed that they would be the first to leave on the convoy. Most of them, however, were reluctant to go farther south away from their villages. Nay Luett came to reassure them that when the situation improved, his ministry would arrange transportation back to their villages. Looking very confused and anxious, the refugees climbed onto the trucks to begin the arduous and perilous trip down Route 14 through territory infested with Communist troops.

The panic that had swept Kontum and Pleiku had not affected Ban Me Thuot. Word that the convoy was en route was spread among provincial authorities, the Catholic sisters, and the Protestant mission. The province chief ordered the abandoned Dam San camp just east of Ban Me Thuot (near a clear stream and thick forest) to be prepared. When the convoy arrived, the hot, dusty, and motion-sick refugees got off the trucks. They were greeted with hot food, water, and relief goods. Still, the highlanders displayed resourcefulness and self-sufficiency, women spreading out to gather wild greens and men chopping wood for fires and making fish traps. Ethnic groups separated into the various buildings.

The following morning the refugees were busy readapting to this new setting. Some were roasting fish they had trapped in the stream while others were foraging in the nearby woods. Kek explained that although they were sad to be far from their own country, the Sedang refugees were happy to be away from the bombs and shooting. He pointed out that there was grumbling about having Halang in the camp because of their powerful witchcraft, and some claimed to have seen a disembodied head floating through the night air. Leaders began discussing the possibility of farming. One elderly Sedang woman, dressed only in a dusty skirt, her breasts sagging and her eyes clouded with cataracts, was churning up earth with a hoe to plant kernels of maize.

Meanwhile, for refugees remaining in Pleiku the situation improved somewhat with the arrival of large army tents for shelter and relief goods provided by the American Women's Association in Saigon. The American aid program also brought in shipments of rice. Young highlanders, most of them Jarai and Bahnar who were associated with the FULRO movement, rendered invaluable help in distributing relief goods and in helping the refugees get settled. With their tradition of sharing, the refugees worked out equitable distributions of available goods. But they were now totally dependent upon outside agencies.

On 24 May the North Vietnamese forces attacked Kontum. The defense of the city was in the hands of elements of the South Vietnamese 23d Division. Minister Nay Luett had agreed with the prime minister to organize a force of two thousand Bahnar, Sedang, Jeh, Rengao, Halang, and Jarai Arap in the town. The Vietnamese commander, however, issued only a carbine and eight rounds of ammunition to each highlander. The attack began with heavy artillery shelling followed by a sapper ground assault on the western portion of the city, where Dr. Pat Smith's Minh Quy hospital and the Kontum Mission headquarters were located. Sister Gabrielle related that some Communist troops came into the hospital looking for Americans, but she told them there were only poor, sick highlanders in the wards and asked them to leave. They did leave, but soon after, the helicopter gunships began to swoop over the building firing rockets. Artillery shells burst nearby, and the hospital was engulfed in violence. The patients were put under beds, and Sister Gabrielle worked in the surgery, operating on wounded civilians and soldiers who were carried into the hospital. She said that when the fighting reached its peak, "We all prayed very hard," adding, "and God heard us." Every other building in the vicinity was either demolished or heavily damaged, but the hospital stood untouched.

As of 1 June 1972 the Communists still held two military compounds on the northern edge of Kontum, and Vann declared that they had lost "phase one" of their campaign. He revealed that in addition to using the B-52s, he also was deploying U.S. Navy planes that dropped "smart bombs." Vann was making daily trips from Pleiku to Kontum in his helicopter to direct operations. On 9 July the helicopter crashed and everyone on board was killed. His body was found amid highlander tombs. In early June the number of highlander refugees continued to increase as fighting and bombing around Kontum province continued. There were an estimated ten thousand still in Kontum, ten thousand in Pleiku, and seven thousand in Ban Me Thuot. In August the Communists seized the Ben Het post where Halang refugees had gathered, forcing their evacuation by helicopter.

In assessing the damage of the offensive on the Minh Quy hospital's village health program, Coles reports that in Kontum province only six of seventeen health workers (35 percent) could be located. Noting that if this reflected the broader population loss, "the present offensive has been devastating to the Montagnard population."[10] In his assessment of the offensive's effect on the mission's population, Bishop Paul Seitz reports that of the Kontum highlander population of 70,046 spread throughout 221 villages, 192 villages were abandoned, 45,000 people were accounted for as refugees and the remainder were either in the forest or dead, and seventeen new parishes were destroyed.[11] The bishop pointed out that the offensive had struck during the April–May planting period, turning the fields into battlegrounds and sending the farmers fleeing so that in the fall of 1972 there were no rice supplies. To make matters worse, on 16 September unusually torrential rains flooded the Kontum basin, washing away crops that had been planted close to the town. As a result, the entire Kontum population, highlanders and Vietnamese alike, were impoverished and facing possible famine.

As a relief measure, most of the Kontum highland refugees were moved southward to Camp Mary Lou, an abandoned American military fire base on Route 14, where they were housed in large army tents. Other refugees were grouped at Plei Don west of Kontum. At Pleiku a large

10. Coles, "Village Health Worker Program," p. 1.

11. Paul Seitz, "Dans l'espérance d'une résurrection," *Les Echos de la Rue de Bac* (Paris: Séminaire des Missions-Etrangères), no. 60 (February 1973), pp. 53–56.

number of refugees were moved into Camp Enari, the former headquarters of the U.S. Fourth Infantry Division on the Hodrung Mountain, while others occupied the former prisoner-of-war camp on the edge of town. On 28 January 1973 the cease-fire agreed upon in Paris went into effect. Before this happened, however, both sides attempted to capture or hold any positions they could. The North Vietnamese occupied the area north of Kontum and also Mount Pao pass, effectively preventing the Sedang, Rengao, or Halang refugees from returning to their territories. Louis Wiesner (who held important posts in refugee aid during the Vietnam War) reports that in mid-1973, the Vietnamese government moved some 12,000 Sedang from the Mary Lou camp to Plei M'nang, Phu Bon province, in the Jarai country.[12] In this alien, dry environment the first question the Sedang asked was "Where is our land?" Wiesner also reveals that a September 1973 survey by the American aid land reform office of 198,413 highlander refugees found that only 13.5 percent were able to grow a twelve-month rice supply and graze cattle. Some 22.5 percent gathered a six-to-twelve-month rice supply, had restricted grazing, but had some outside employment. The remaining 64 percent had less than a six-month supply of rice and little or no outside employment. This last group was, in effect, destitute.

This dire situation reflects the challenging readaptations that the refugees now faced. At the Dam San camp outside of Ban Me Thuot, the five thousand refugees planted gardens and began to farm very small swiddens. Women continued their weaving, some men worked iron, but Father Wolf of the Kontum Mission explained that most were underemployed. Also, the crowded conditions and disruption of their traditional ways gave rise to conflicts and stealing, signs of strain on the social order that had previously characterized village society. Leon Wit reported in July 1991 that some of his Sedang kin still remained in Dam San. He added that the large influx of Vietnamese around Dak To since 1975 had created a serious land shortage and the Sedang were living at near starvation levels. The refugees in the Pleiku camps had no land to farm, no forests in which to forage and hunt, and no streams to fish. They became totally dependent upon outside agencies for everything from rice to plastic sleeping mats. Under these circumstances there was little or no hope of attaining any harmony among man, nature, and cosmic forces. Soil fertility was now a concern only for their small gardens, and because everyone was impoverished, potency could not be demonstrated.

12. Louis A. Wiesner, *Victims and Survivors: Displaced Persons and Other Victims in Viet-Nam, 1954–1975* (New York: Greenwood Press, 1988), pp. 282–83.

Conclusions

The ethnographies tell us that bonds created by sheer physical adaptation and religious prescriptions for maintaining harmony among man, nature, and the cosmos have given rise to an identifiable highland world, a shared culture which is part of the common mainland Southeast Asia upland culture outlined by Kirsch.[1] The ethnographies also substantiate Kirsch's view that two primary concerns of upland mainland Southeast Asian groups are fertility and potency, constant themes that flow through highland social systems. In each ethnography the spotlight falls on leaders with manifest potency bestowed by cosmic forces, which gives them an advantage in preserving and increasing the fertility upon which survival depends. The ethnographies further support Kirsch's view that potency associated with wealth is demonstrated by lavish feasting, which for the highlanders accompanies ritual sacrifices of prestigious buffalo and pigs. Leaders with potency serve as stewards in preserving the man-nature-cosmos harmony by seeing that religious prescriptions are honored and by monitoring application of practical traditional knowledge related to physical adaptation. Finally, we see that within the context of these rituals and other observances of religious prescriptions, many aspects of material culture take on a mystical symbolism.

For the Rhadé, Yang Rong destines (*dhut*) certain individuals to grand potency in exercising authority (*knuih-koʼhuʼm*) such as that of the renowned chiefs of the pre-French period or to a lesser potency (*knuih diêt*), enabling one to become village headman. Similarly, for the Chru, Yang Ngă Poʼtao (Spirit that Bestows Leadership) inhabits a person's body at birth, creating potency (*boʼngă ayua*) manifest in external cha-

1. A. Thomas Kirsch, *Feasting and Social Oscillation: Religion and Society in Upland Southeast Asia,* Department of Asian Studies, Cornell University, Southeast Asia Program Data Paper no. 92 (Ithaca, N.Y., 1973), passim.

risma (*gonuh seri*) marking one "destined to leadership" (*lot ngă pồtao*). Potency attributed to spirits is found among the Sedang (*mohua,* which in abundance becomes *kro,* attributed to respected leaders). The Rhadé and Chru believe that potency can be increased through ritual offerings, but for them and the Sedang as well it can be lost through breaches of prescribed behavior, which for all three includes contact with females' clothing. Potency for the Halang is *mahuol* infused by spirits and manifest in wealth and luck, while the Jeh have potency of the aged *kakayh* along with a special potency that identifies a man as *yao* or "big." For the Roglai, potency (*samu vungaq*) is demonstrated in farming or hunting skills. Although no similar terms have been reported for the Katu, Bru, Pacoh, and Stieng, all of the groups identify primary stewards by their wealth (from successful farming) and "wisdom." As Grandmother of Aning, a Jeh, put it, "Wisdom and poverty do not live in the same person." Pacoh leadership potency also is demonstrated by eloquent performances in "speaking contests" and "debates." For the Katu, success in a human-blood raid demonstrates potency.

The ethnographies describe validation of stewards in rituals that implore cosmic forces while at the same time propitiating them and begging their beneficence. Within the context of these rituals, sacrificial animals, their blood (for the Katu this includes that of humans), rice, and alcohol offerings move from mundane to sublime as they become fare for the deities. Valuable sets of gongs and old, highly valued rice-alcohol jars symbolize wealth and potency. Rhadé legend says that old jars were once animals living in swamps, and Sedang villagers swore that during a fire in the men's house they saw jars emerge on their own and lower themselves to the ground. Alcohol used as an offering must be made from local rice and produced in the village (reflected in the Stieng villager's comment that Vietnamese commercial alcohol cannot be offered to spirits because they are not used to it).

Settlement patterns, house types, farming, hunting, fishing, and production of artifacts and adornment as well as rites of passage and life crises reflect stewardship of leaders and those (such as household heads, shamans, midwives, and ordinary villagers) with lesser potency.

Leaders see to it that villagers are located on well-drained ground accessible to forest and watercourses. To preserve the man-nature-cosmos harmony the Katu settlement must be oriented in relation to the rising sun as well as to the men's house and sacrificial stake (both of which reflect religious symbolism and artistic endeavor). Sedang and Halang longhouses always face the men's house (on which artistic talent is expended). The Halang must locate settlements on "hot ground," wherein live "high spirits," as opposed to "cool ground" devoid of such spirits, inviting sickness and other misfortunes.

To build a proper house the household head must draw upon traditional knowledge concerning use of available natural materials as well as architectural forms and functions attuned to ecological conditions. Adaptational efficacy of highland house types is revealed in the epidemiological research by Jacques May, who found that building houses on piling allows the residents to escape frequent contact with the malaria vector *Anopheles minimus.*[2] May also notes that abnormal hemoglobin E among the highlanders provides some protection against the worst malarial attacks. Research in 1967 conducted by the Walter Reed Army Institute of Research on malaria and hemoglobin E (summarized in Appendix C), in a sample that included Rhadé, Stieng, and Sedang, found that the highest frequencies of hemoglobin E were found among the Stieng (0.365), followed by the Rhadé (0.212) and the Sedang (0.029). The highest prevalence of glucose-6-phosphate dehydrogenase (G6PD) deficiency was in the Stieng (0.54), followed by the Rhadé (0.023) and Sedang (0.004). This finding is interesting given that the Rhadé and Sedang construct their houses on piling whereas the Stieng in the sample group have since the 1950s built theirs on the ground.

Rhadé longhouse construction reflects religious prescriptions geared to preserve the man-nature-cosmos harmony, which the household head must honor. He had best heed omens and signs and, as steward, perform prescribed rituals marking construction phases so as to gain the approval of cosmic forces for using nature while propitiating them and asking their favor. The completed longhouse (with female moon deity carvings and juxtaposing of male and female bamboo) embodies male and female themes in Rhadé adaptation. All of the ethnographies document household heads' stewardship in observing prescriptions surrounding use of the house not only as an abode but also as a reliquary for sacred symbols and a place where deities are ritually honored.

F. R. Moormann observes that dominant mountainous red and yellow podzolic and lithosolic soils "have low agricultural potential because of strong relief and predominantly poor shallow soils" and "offer only very limited possibilities for the development of a modern type of agriculture."[3] Recent studies indicate that the type of swidden farming highlanders practice is relatively well suited to the mountain ecosystem. David Harris points out that shifting (swidden) farming involves manipulation rather than transformation of the natural environment, "altering selected components without fundamentally modifying its overall struc-

2. Jacques May, "The Ecology of Human Disease," in *Studies in Human Ecology,* ed. L. Krader and A. Palerm (Washington, D.C.: Pan American Union, 1960), pp. 92, 96.

3. F. R. Moormann, *The Soils of the Republic of Vietnam* (Saigon: Republic of Vietnam, Ministry of Agriculture, 1961), pp. 17, 24.

ture." He concludes that it "comes closer to simulating the structure, functional dynamics, and equilibrium of the natural system than any other agricultural systems man has devised."[4] A. Terry Rambo observes that "so well is swidden farming adapted to the humid tropics, that, despite much effort, agricultural researchers have yet to perfect alternative systems having comparable social and ecological merits." But, Rambo warns, advantages can be lost when population increase leads to fallowing periods too short for renewal.[5]

All of the groups have ways of supervising land use. Permission of village leaders is required to clear a swidden within Bru, Pacoh, Sedang, Halang, and Stieng village territories. The female guardian of Rhadé clan land oversees farming, hunting, and fishing within the territory. She also presides over an expiation ritual for a couple guilty of incest in the territory, an affront to the ancestors, who can render the soil infertile.

Highland farmers know well what crops mountainous soils will support. Large trees and lush growth indicate soil fertility. Patches of rotting leaves packed on the earth tell the Sedang that the soil is rich. The Katu, Bru, Sedang, and Jeh look for black or brown soil, avoiding red soil, whereas the Rhadé consider local red latosols good for rice and black soil suitable for maize. The Halang avoid sites where a local high grass abounds. On the ideational side, the Jeh never clear areas dominated by large old trees, the abodes of evil earth spirits, and before clearing land, a Katu farmer performs a divination ritual to determine the spirits' will. Out of respect for the mountain-forest spirit, Roglai avoid farming near summits, and Rhadé never select a site near an abandoned tomb. A Rhadé farmer knows that disclosure of his new swidden site would draw the attention of malevolent spirits. Members of the Chru family sleep on the prospective site, and should one have a bad dream it is abandoned. At a selected swidden site the Stieng farmer performs a ritual invoking spirits (notably the spirit of unhusked rice), and he heeds unfavorable signs such as the cry of certain birds or the sound of a falling tree ("the sound of your coffin being made"), indicating cosmic disapproval.

Farmers rely on cosmic forces to make soils productive. The Pacoh, Sedang, Jeh, and Rhadé ethnographies reveal a mystical link between female fecundity and soil-rice fertility (the potency they demonstrate in farming rituals is inherent in the roles rather than in the women who play

4. David R. Harris, "Agricultural Systems, Ecosystems, and the Origin of Agriculture," in *The Domestication and Exploitation of Plants and Animals,* ed. Peter J. Ucko and G. W. Dimbley (Chicago: Aldine-Atherton, 1969), pp. 4–8.

5. A. Terry Rambo, "No Free Lunch: A Reexamination of the Energetic Efficiency of Swidden Agriculture," in *An Introduction to Human Ecology Research on Agricultural Systems in Southeast Asia,* ed. A. Terry Rambo and Percy E. Sajise (Laguna, Philippines: University of the Philippines at Los Baños Publications Program, 1984), p. 155.

the roles). The head of the Bru patrilineage maintains a cult for the Spirit of the Soil. The Rhadé look to the Lord of the Soil, the chief Spirit of Agriculture, the Rice Spirit, and brothers, Aê M'ghi and M'ghăn Tơ Làn, to ensure fertility and ample harvests. Every Chru household honors the Rice Spirit, symbolized by an egg-shaped rock kept in a special reliquary in the family rice bin where periodic offerings are made. Ties between soil fertility and ancestral spirits are common. The Rhadé female guardian of clan land performs rituals for "the backs of the ancestor," a metaphor for clan land.

Swidden sizes depend on food-consumption needs of the household group and availability of labor. One Jeh used the expression "one bed, one field," meaning that a man and wife need one field to produce enough for themselves. Practical considerations and ideational beliefs guide clearing and burning. The Bru require approval of the village headman to fell a large tree, and Sedang leave hardwood trees standing. Rhadé, Katu, and Jeh never chop down certain trees (with the Rhadé a dipterocarpus), wherein spirits dwell, and the Jeh avoid clearing areas dominated by large trees. The Halang listen to sounds emitted by eight different types of locustlike insects as signals when to initiate certain planting-cycle activities. In the first of eleven farming-cycle rituals, Halang farmers pour chicken blood next to the first tree to be felled, asking spirits to make the task easy and "let the tree fall to the left or right of me." To encounter a snake on the path to a field is for the Rhadé a good omen, but to dream of an alcohol jar or specific animals (such as a roedeer, stag, or pig) augers badly for the crop. Thunder is a sign to the Katu that further activities in the swidden are taboo for the remainder of the day, and should a Jeh farmer have a bad dream, the field is abandoned. Stieng village leaders mete out punishment for destructive burning. A Rhadé guilty of wanton burning of forest could in the past be sold into slavery or banned from the village. The Jeh first have the "big burning," followed by the "second burning." As dried wood is set ablaze, Katu observe a two-day period during which fields are taboo. Rhadé perform a postburning ritual in which three bamboo tubes of water are offered to spirits to slake thirst brought on by the fires. Afterward they observe the "prevent the wind" ritual requesting various deities to allow rain by holding back the wind, which is likened to a powerful elephant in need of restraint.

Tree roots are left in the soil, and planting is done with dibble sticks, both practices aimed at preserving topsoil structure so the lashing monsoon rains will not cause erosion, especially on the slopes where most swiddening is done. Cropping is diversified with more than one variety of rain-fed rice planted along with maize and other secondary crops. The Halang have twelve rice varieties, and the Stieng and Sedang have ten, all distinguished by the color of the husk and kernel. Circumstances determine which variety will be grown. Rhadé plant any one of their best varieties the first year in the belief that they require particularly fertile soil. Well-to-do Rhadé Kpa farmers grow a red glutinous rice for making high-quality alcohol. Halang and Rhadé Kpa divide a swidden into two or more sections, each planted in varieties with different maturation periods to allow effective use of available labor and rapid gathering of the crop. The Roglai farmer, not daunted by risk, will plant the fragrant "necklace bead" rice, a favorite food of the "tiny" bird. Each Pacoh household has its own special rice seed, which can be given, bartered, or sold for consumption but not for planting.

The Rhadé longhouse group observes a series of planting rituals, including one symbolized by the rake, and a large general planting observance by the whole village to honor Aê Diê, the supreme deity, and destroy symbolic figures of predatory birds and animals. Chru villagers carry the reliquary containing the stone symbol of the Rice Spirit to the field, where pigs and chickens are sacrificed. Before sowing rice, the head of the Bru patrilineage makes offerings to the Spirit of the Earth. The Sedang household head's wife performs a ritual sacrifice for the rice spirit, but if the crops fail for two years, she is replaced by another woman. After observing food and bathing taboos, the Jeh household Mistress of Rice Planting and Rice Harvesting makes ten holes in the field, anointing them with a secret brew as she invokes the Rice Spirit, singing a special song, after which she smears sacrificial blood on parts of the kitchen. Before planting, Katu men play gongs and women dance while a pig, chicken, and dog are offered to the spirits. To avoid angering the Rice Spirit, it is taboo for Roglai to bring children or a bush scythe into a planted field. Should weeds invade the planted field, the Halang blame it on Grandfather Tờlùum, a legendary figure, invoked in a ritual. When rice plants are one meter high, the Rhadé family performs a ritual to "call back the Rice Soul," imprisoned by other deities after the previous harvest.

When rice reaches maturity, the entire Halang village joins in to honor the Rice Spirit with a buffalo sacrifice. The Jeh Mistress of Rice Planting and Rice Harvesting is the first to gather, winnow, take rice to the granary, and cook it. Similarly, at the granary the Pacoh female ritual chief makes offerings of water and roasted sacrificial meat to the Rice Spirit, and she alone can prepare rice for meals. The wife of the Sedang household head offers an animal sacrifice to the Rice Spirit, and in the field the Roglai family places offerings, including a bead necklace, which is symbolically worn by the eldest son. A poor harvest may prompt Katu to obtain human blood to appease displeased spirits.

The highland farmer is adept at judging how long a field will produce crops. Usually swiddens are farmed for about three years. The Bru, however, use most swiddens only one year while some Rhadé fields can be cultivated from five to seven years. A Bru farmer's remark in discussing fallowing that "we do not like to cut young forest" captures the highlanders' concern for proper renewal. Most fallowing periods are between seven and ten years. But the Stieng allow fifteen to twenty years, and Sedang say that bamboo in certain areas grows rapidly enough to permit farming in alternate years.

Traditional knowledge about local fauna and aquatic life has given rise to an array of weapons, devices, and techniques. Before hunting, a Rhadé performs in the main room of his longhouse the "crossbow sacrifice" in which a young rooster is offered to the spirits to bring luck. Halang hunters invoke Aê Rogap, a spirit who will help bag game. The whole Rhadé village participates in the annual "water sacrifice," which involves offering a chicken and alcohol at the stream, after which they all join in fishing with nets and traps.

Rites of passage impart mystiques to material culture and provide occasions for stewards to demonstrate potency. Rich Stieng show potency in their ability to pay costly bride-prices for more than one wife. Various phases of a Stieng marriage are reflected in the sacrificial pigs from the "looking-for-a-wife pig," through the "stepping-on-the-mat pig," symbolizing the founding of a new household in the groom's village, to the "entering-the-bed pig," a symbol of the couple's cohabitation. Small personal knives belonging to males, pipes, ivory ear plugs, and spears take on a sacred aura after they are used in Stieng births. In a postbirth ritual household children dab rice alcohol on the Jeh newborn's chin and cheeks, and in the ritual to name a newborn, pig blood is rubbed on the newly pierced ear. Chickens figure in divination rituals at weddings of the Jeh (beak), the Roglai (beak), Katu (claw), and Chru (head, claws, and wings). The Roglai bride and groom exchange handfuls of rice; the Halang exchange small hoes used for weeding rice fields to seal the marriage. In Sedang weddings the bride drinks rice alcohol from a glass, which she then hands to the groom, who swallows the remainder to symbolize their union.

Kirsch makes the point that "death and burial provide an occasion for ostentatious feasting during which the deceased's 'social status' is reaffirmed as well as that of his heirs."[6] The ethnographies describe lavish funerals of the wealthy in which buffalo are sacrificed, whereas the poor have simple observances with chicken sacrifices. Graves of the rich

6. Kirsch, *Feasting*, p. 15.

Halang have shelters with hardwood columns on which likenesses of the deceased have been carved. Carvings of symbolic animals and timely motifs such as French and American soldiers grace tombs of rich Rhadé.

For the Rhadé, pregnancy puts a woman out of phase with the man-nature-cosmos harmony, rendering her susceptible to evil spirits, who must be dealt with by a midwife empowered to communicate with them. The most common life crisis is persisting illness, which highlanders believe is a manifestation of being out of phase with cosmic forces for such acts as breaches of a taboo. The family summons a shaman to determine which deity has been wronged and what it demands as propitiation. This procedure affords the wealthy an opportunity to demonstrate potency by making costly animal and food offerings. An ordinary Halang will not progress beyond a pig, but the ordinary Stieng is expected to move on to a buffalo sacrifice, which can force him into bondage. But though bondage seems a dire fate, it can be a means of attaining what Kirsch calls "quasi-assimilation" into a wealthier lineage that has potency.[7] Alliances provide a path for similar affiliation. A small and unstable Bru patrilineage can form an alliance (which involves mixing the parties' blood with rice alcohol to provide a symbolic drink) to become part of a larger, stronger patrilineage. The Halang "father-child" alliance (symbolized by the child sucking sacrificial blood on the father's nipple) allows an ordinary person to become the adopted child of a rich man.

Village leaders and kin-group heads deal with individuals who breach religious prescriptions. The head of a Bru patrilineage derives legal authority (symbolized by his possession of divination blocks) from the belief that should a member violate the moral code, the angered patron spirit will wreak misfortune on the whole group. Should a Pacoh girl become pregnant before marriage, out of fear that she and the boy will "meet a tiger when they go out of the village," they confess to their parents. The ethnographies cite numerous cases of punishment and propitiation imposed by leaders for adultery or more serious offenses such as theft and murder. They describe ordeal trials whose legitimacy often is validated by participation of cosmic forces.

Sorcerers and witches, shadow counterparts of the stewards, demonstrate potency bestowed by evil forces who seek disharmony among man, nature, and the cosmos, thereby threatening fertility. The ethnographies suggest that primary stewards must bring to bear superior potency when coping with them. Sickness inflicted by a Halang witch (*holeh*) is fatal, and a woman found guilty of witchcraft is banished from the village. In the past, Chru leaders executed *camo lai,* dreaded sorcerers who target

---

7. Ibid., p. 24.

their victims with special poisons (sometimes obtained from flesh-eating plants). The Stieng witch (*chaac*), when found out, could be tortured to death or sold into slavery. Sedang sorcerers (*deq*) invoke "evil ghosts" to smash a victim's bones, but tatoos symbolizing greater potency afford protection. Bru sorcery, *pan cuai*, involves shooting a metal or wood projectile through a stone tube, causing a victim to fall ill, and only a sorcerer of superior potency than that of the perpetrator can remove it.

In signaling disharmony among man, nature, and the cosmos, "bad deaths" caused by violent accidents, suicide, childbirth complications, drowning, or attacks by wild animals create an atmosphere of foreboding. Kirsch points out that abhorrence of bad deaths, which is common among Southeast Asian hill tribes, is related to the fear of sudden loss of potency.[8] Funerals for those who die bad deaths are stark and furtive, with little or no ritual observances and burial in simple isolated tombs. For the Sedang, those who die bad deaths become restless ghosts (*kia m'jiu*), while for the Pacoh and Jeh they become wandering souls, ominously manifest in rainbows. Souls of Katu who die bad deaths go to *bayo,* abode of evil spirits, while those of the Rhadé come under the sway of malevolent Yang Brieng.

Occasionally we find in the ethnographies glints of nonwealthy villagers' attitudes toward the wealthy. In a Jeh song expressing faint envy sung only by men, a lyric goes, "There is someone rich and able to acquire possessions; we follow him but we're not able to acquire possessions." At the same time, the Jeh believe that the soul of a deceased wealthy person must remain earth-bound, an undesirable state, until the inheritance is settled. The Jeh, too, fear accumulation of large amounts of such items as rice, maize, and firewood, which become *kayh* ("to have an evil power radiating out from"). The Halang also display mixed feelings about wealth. As a sign of potency, it commands respect, but wealth invites chiding intended to goad the well-to-do into giving many rituals and feasts or to show disdain for worldly goods.

Historical Changes

Sons of the Mountains and the ethnographies tell us that although the highlanders stood aloof from the Chinese and Indian great traditions that molded civilizations of the Vietnamese, Cham, Khmer, and Lao, they were never isolated from lowland influences.[9] Mon Khmer–speaking

8. Ibid., p. 15.
9. Gerald Cannon Hickey, *Sons of the Mountains: Ethnohistory of the Vietnamese Central Highlands to 1954* (New Haven: Yale University Press, 1982), passim.

highland groups still share swiddening, the levirate (with the exception of the Jeh), and deities associated with agriculture along with crossbows, all traits associated with the Mon Khmer–speaking antecedents of the Vietnamese. Some groups still retain other such traits, including tatooing (Bru and Katu), teeth-blackening (Bru and Stieng), areca-betel chewing (Bru, Hre, Cua, and Stieng), and communal or men's houses on piling (Sedang, Halang, Jeh, Rengao, and Bahnar). Historical and ethnographic data suggest that patrilineal descent found among the Vietnamese, Katu, Bru, Pacoh, and Stieng (as well as the Hre, Cua, and Maa) and swidden farming might also have been shared by all of the Mon Khmer–speaking groups.

The primary outside source of historical change was the Cham, who had matrilineal descent and sophisticated wet-rice farming. Chru ethnography reveals that Cham refugees intermarried with the Roglai (who have matrilineal descent and swidden farming) to create the Chru ethnic group and introduced sophisticated wet-rice farming and family-owned fields transmitted through the female line. This readaptation diminished the importance of the female clan land guardian, altered the division of labor, and necessitated village "water chiefs." It appears that the Cham also brought similar paddy farming to the neighboring Mon Khmer–speaking Sre, Lat, and Mnong Rlam. It is conceivable that introduction of family-owned land led to borrowing of Cham matrilineal descent as a means of transmitting family-owned land from one generation to another. Rhadé ethnography does not suggest that Cham introduced wet-rice farming among the Bih and Kpa but raises the possibility that it was borrowed from the neighboring Mnong Rlam.

The ethnographies reveal that some aspects of religious beliefs and practices reflect a pattern strongly suggesting further widespread Cham- and/or Austronesian-speakers' influence. Henri Maitre believes the role of shamans called *pajao* (or a cognate word thereof) was borrowed from the Cham.[10] According to Antoine Cabaton, the Cham had priestesses called *pajau* or *paja*.[11] Such cognate designations are found among the Austronesian-speaking Rhadé (*mojao,* who are males or females), Chru (*po juru,* males), Roglai (*vijou,* males), and Jarai (*pojao,* male or female). Interestingly, there are cognates among the Mon Khmer–speaking Sedang (*pojao,* females), Halang (*m'jao,* males), and Jeh (*m'jao,* males). There also are cognates among the Mnong (*njao*), Sre (*bojao*), and Maa (*bijou*). No cognates, however, are found among the Bru (*mo,* male), the Pacoh (*mo ramon,* male, and *curu,* female), Katu (*abo,* female), and

---

10. Henri Maitre, *Les jungles Moi* (Paris: Larose, 1912), p. 443.

11. Antoine Cabaton, *Nouvelle recherches sur les Chams* (Paris: Ernest Leroux, 1901), pp. 28–36.

Stieng (*mê bra,* female, and *chondrong,* male). (Interestingly, the Muong have shamans called *po mo.*)

More widespread is diffusion of deities called *yang* or a cognate thereof. It is the word for "spirit" in the Cham language, and cognates are found in some languages in Indonesia, Malaysia, and Malagasy, indicating that it is of Austronesian origin.[12] Most commonly, *yang* are conceived of as spirits intrinsic to features of the physical environment, and in some groups they are important special deities such as those associated with fertility and rice. The Katu appear to be unique in not having a category of spirits called *yang.* There is only I Yaang, who laid down the taboos which the Katu must respect. Another Cham word widespread among highland groups is *potao,* which connotes potency of leadership, such as among the Rhadé and Chru (powerful shaman leaders among the Jarai are Potao Apui [King of Fire], Potao Ea [King of Water], and Potao Angin [King of Wind]). Among the Sedang the terms *yang* and *potao* appear to be Bahnar terms introduced via Catholic catechisms. Less widespread is the Cham word *bia* (or a cognate thereof), the term for "queen, princess, or goddess," which is associated with the Kon Klor Cham vestige near Kontum. Various Rhadé female deities carry the title H'bia. *Apea* is a very beautiful woman in Sedang legends. Stieng, Katu, Bru, and Pacoh have neither term.

Interestingly, the Stieng, Katu, Bru, and Pacoh all are located outside the zone of Cham hegemony marked by their vestiges. These groups have swidden farming, patrilineal descent, and display no borrowing of Cham terms for shamans or leaders, but they do have the term *yang.*

Lao contact with the Sedang, Jeh, and Halang is evident in their ironworking (which among the Jeh is linked with shamanism). The Halang, who in the nineteenth century were under Lao hegemony, also borrowed gold panning. Both Lao and Khmer also were involved in slave trading with these groups and the Bahnar. Paul Guilleminet, who conducted considerable research on Bahnar customs, observes that well before the twentieth century direct or indirect influences of the Khmer and others

12. The Cham word *yang* is listed as meaning "spirit" in Gerard Moussay, *Dictionnaire Čam-Vietnamien-Français,* s.v. *yang, ésprit,* and *génie.* In a discussion, Mathew Charles, an authority on Austronesian languages in Southeast Asia, explained that the old Javanese word *hyang,* meaning "godhead," is listed in H. N. Van der Tuuk, *Kawi-Balineesch-Nederlandsch woordenboek,* 4 vols. (Batavia: Landsdrukkerij, 1897) 1: s.v. *hyang.* In R. J. Wilkinson, *A Malay-English Dictionary* (romanized), s.v. *yang,* the word *yang* is translated as "divinity," or "godhead," usually being used in compounds such as *sangyang* (to indicate a major Hindu divinity) and *sembahyang* (prayer). In Gabriel Ferrand, "La langue malgache," in *Feestbundel uitgegeven door het Koninklijk Bataviaasch Genootschap van Kunsten en Wetenschappen,* 2 vols. (Weltevreden: G. Kolff & Co., 1929), 1:182, 186, it is noted that in Arabic-Malagasy manuscripts the Old Malagasy word *yang* is used to mean "divinity."

wrought changes in Bahnar traditions.[13] Both the Lao and Khmer have bilateral descent systems so it is conceivable that their prolonged contact with the Sedang, Jeh, Halang, and Bahnar resulted in these highlanders shifting from patrilineal to bilateral descent systems. It also is possible that some Bahnar Jolong borrowed paddy-farming techniques from the Lao.

Gauging French influence, which varies from group to group, gives some indication of how each group might be classified in Kirsch's "democratic"-"autocratic" framework.[14] The ethnographies suggest that the French presence had the effect of autocratic groups rather than democratic. With their impressive appearance and firearms, the French demonstrated greater potency, thereby gaining the cooperation of the chiefs. Establishment of a colonial administration with appointed headmen ended autocratic rule for Rhadé and Chru chiefs with "grand potency," but their lineages or clans nonetheless retained their wealth and continued to be recognized as elites through their ability to demonstrate potency by their wealth and elaborate rituals with copious feasting. Kirsch observes that the British colonial administration's establishment of "tribal courts" tended to "democratize" in that disputes over ritual status, which would ordinarily have been determined by village leaders (those with potency), were now treated as "legal" by the British court.[15] This also was the case when the French organized "customs courts" among the Rhadé, Chru, and other groups. When a Chru tribunal found a sorcerer guilty of poisoning a fellow villager, he was duly executed, but when a guilty sorcerer confessed his crime to French authorities, his poisons were confiscated and he was jailed.

Armed resistance against French rule by the Stieng and Sedang suggests that there were among them chiefs with autocratic authority who organized military forces. These chiefs also possessed slaves, a sign of wealth and potency also found among the Halang. There is the suggestion in the ethnographies that after the French restricted slavery at the end of the nineteenth century, Sedang, Stieng, and Halang societies moved in the direction of democracy. Sedang and Stieng war chiefs disappeared, as did slaveholding in all groups, although wealth (potency) still determines leadership. Still, all Sedang and Halang males participate in men's house activities and adults have a voice in making decisions and resolving conflicts. The Jeh have democratic institutions such as the communal house, accessible to all adults including women, who not only

13. Paul Guilleminet, *Coutumier de la tribu Bahnar des Sedang et des Jarai de la province de Kontum*, 2 vols. (Paris: Ecole Française d'Extrême-Orient, 1952), 1:18.

14. Kirsch, *Feasting*, pp. 23–29.

15. Ibid., p. 32.

can become household heads but serve among the village elders as well. More removed from French influence, the Katu have relatively democratic characteristics, including lack of village territories, egalitarian potency through human blood raids that any adult male can conduct, the men's house, no slavery or bondage, and bride-prices adjusted to the family's means. Neither the Bru nor Pacoh had war chiefs or slavery, but both have village territories, and marriages are relatively costly. Well-to-do Bru patrilineages function as elites, but lesser patrilineages can affiliate with them. There is the suggestion that although patrilineal affiliation among the Katu, Bru, and Pacoh is important, it is somewhat diffused by kindreds, which extend social and economic ties to a network of non-patrilineal fictive kin.

The forced assimilation policy of the Diem government in the late 1950s reflected not only Vietnamese ethnocentrism and nationalism but also the notion, prevalent in the capitals of many post–World War II Southeast Asian new states, that to attain national integration, ties to kin groups, villages, religious sects, and ethnic groups (particularly ethnic minorities) must be replaced by loyalty to the state. Clifford Geertz observes that "considered as societies, the new states are abnormally susceptible to serious disaffection based on primordial attachments." He adds that these "primordial attachments" (a term he borrowed from Edward Shils) have come to be regarded as competing with civil attachments to the state. Neither Geertz nor Shils feels that the two loyalties are intrinsically antithetical. They see primordial attachments as part of the fabric of the society and also part of the fabric of the new state. In Geertz's view, what is required is an "integrative revolution" to bring about an adjustment of primordial and civil attachments, making them compatible. Ethnicity would be legitimized so that solidarity and "consciousness of kind" associated with it are extended into the "developing social order" of the new state. The individual, in effect, would retain his ethnic identity and come to develop loyalty to the state. Without this integration, Geertz warns, there can be disaffection leading to political disintegration, partition, or irredentism.[16]

The Diem administration's failure to attempt an integrative revolution led to disaffection of highlanders and the rise of the Bajaraka and FULRO movements. These developments signaled the emergence of a new pan-highlander leadership made up for the most part of members of an intergroup elite descended from the great chiefs. They were educated

---

16. Clifford Geertz, "The Integrative Revolution: Primordial Sentiments and Civil Politics in the New States," in *Old Societies and New States,* ed. Clifford Geertz (New York: Free Press, 1963), pp. 105–57; Edward Shils, "Primordial, Personal, Sacred and Civil Ties," *British Journal of Sociology* 8, no. 2 (1957): 130–45.

in French schools and began in the 1950s to intermarry, forming the intergroup elite described in *Sons of the Mountains* and *Free in the Forest*.[17] Potency was demonstrated in Bajaraka's standing up in 1958 to the Diem government and in FULRO's 1964 takeover of five Special Forces camps. Interestingly, among the leaders were Christians, some of whom pointed out that the French priests and American Protestants had imbued them with the idea that in the eyes of God, all people are equal, and so they believed that the highlanders should be treated as equals of the Vietnamese. These Christian leaders dutifully attended rituals at which animals were sacrificed and joined in the feasting, although the Protestants avoided drinking alcohol from the jars.

The spread of a pan-highlander ethnic identity carried with it recognition that the highland people shared a common culture, which the leaders sought to preserve. Between 1965 and 1975, attempts by the Saigon government (with the encouragement of the Americans) to make an accommodation with the FULRO and non-FULRO highland leaders were in the spirit of Geertz's integrative revolution. Efforts forcibly to assimilate the highlanders ceased when programs were designed to give the highlanders a place within the national framework that would preserve their ethnic identity. The new Ministry of Ethnic Minorities' Development signaled greater highlander participation in national politics. To preserve the highlanders' common culture, indigenous law courts were reinstated, highland languages and cultures were given a place in school curriculums, and programs for granting land titles were begun.

Minister Nay Luett and his staff discussed at length what the highlanders should preserve and what they would have to change so as to hold their own in the modern world with its emphasis on "progress." This tradition/change dilemma was also being faced at local levels by some groups such as the Chru, for whom outside influences were causing considerable change. Chru leaders advocated preservation of traditional customs such as favoring houses on piling (previously they had preferred Cham-style "low houses" built on the ground). But many young Chru leaders, who had been exposed to French and Vietnamese ways, opposed reinforcing the matrilineal descent system, which was beginning to disintegrate (matrilineal descent and the matrilocal residence rule had already been breached by some older Chru leaders). These young leaders had accumulated land, houses, and furnishings, which they claimed as their own possessions and wanted their sons to inherit.

The ethnographies tell us that by the early 1960s, changes had pro-

---

17. Gerald Cannon Hickey, *Free in the Forest: Ethnohistory of the Vietnamese Central Highland, 1954–1976* (New Haven: Yale University Press, 1982), passim.

duced an interesting spectrum in adaptations. At one end the Katu (particularly the High Katu) were still deeply embedded in nature and very dependent upon cosmic forces for sustaining their relatively precarious traditional adaptation to a harsh physical environment. One might speculate that given the uncertainty (perhaps even fear) engendered by their adaptational situation, coupled with their heavy reliance on cosmic forces for survival, the Katu were prompted at some time in the distant past to move beyond sacrificing buffalo to demonstrate potency and maximize fertility by offering human blood. One also might speculate that the precarious Katu adaptation and lack of wherewithal (ample buffalo and pigs) for demonstrating potency through lavish rituals and feasting led to offerings of human blood. At the other end of the spectrum, the Chru had a relatively comfortable adaptation to the fertile Danhim Valley, where they long had a sophisticated irrigation system with reliable sources of water. By the early 1960s they were making many farming innovations using modern technology greatly to expand cash cropping. As traditional economic activities diminished, they began to rely on the Roglai for textiles, baskets, and even some shamanistic services. Their increasing control over farming resources rendered the Chru less embedded in nature than other highland groups. Their sudden sweeping acceptance of Christianity in 1962 suggests that the Chru may have felt sufficiently secure to abandon (to a great extent if not completely) traditional deities.

The Vietnam War

The ethnographies reveal how, as the Vietnam War unfolded, spread, and intensified, it drew an ever-growing number of highland villagers into its vortex. Forced to abandon villages, Katu, Bru, Pacoh, Sedang, Jeh, Halang, Stieng, Roglai, and many Rhadé devised strategies to preserve what they could of the man-nature-cosmos harmony. Kin groups stayed together and followed village leaders. Initially adaptations were relatively easy as refugees went into other villages, where they usually had kin and land for swiddening. More difficult was the later readaptation to refugee settlements near district towns away from familiar soils, where population concentrations began to create land shortages. Rhadé refugees abandoned clan lands so land guardians were shorn of their traditional social and religious functions. Jeh, Halang, and Sedang left village territories, thereby depriving headmen of certain responsibilities and prerogatives. It was difficult for them to leave tombs, particularly ones that had not been ritually abandoned, an unfulfilled duty toward ancestors. Still, as long as they could bring their domestic animals, some jars and gongs, and basic artifacts, they could have rituals to preserve harmony with nature and cosmic forces, to maximize fertility, and to demonstrate potency.

But as the war intensified, use of bombers, rockets, and long-range artillery created precipitous situations, and the war could come crashing in anywhere without warning. Even where there was no fighting, disruption was spreading as villages were emptied by the Communists, who needed labor, and by American and South Vietnamese commanders, who in a war without front lines sought to create them with free-fire zones. In the face of a worsening situation, refugees flowed into the relatively secure enclaves already filled with those who had earlier left their villages. As new arrivals built shelters, crowded settlements took on a shantytown look. Lack of security beyond the immediate vicinity severely restricted hunting, fishing, foraging, and swidden farming. To cope with the lack of land for swiddening, farmers shortened fallowing periods and prolonged use of swiddens with organic and, in the case of the Rhadé, chemical fertilizers. A small group of Bru adopted paddy farming in bottomland near a coffee estate, Sedang farmers increased wet-rice farming they had learned from Vietnamese settlers in the late 1950s, and Chru taught some Roglai refugees how to farm paddy fields in the Danhim Valley. Stieng farmers cleared fallowing areas, and some in desperation returned to farm in Communist-controlled zones. Rhadé Kpa villagers and refugees began to produce more cash crops in gardens and swiddens for the Ban Me Thuot markets, and some started small enterprises as alternatives to farming. Stieng opened small shops to supplement their diminished incomes. Despite their efforts, a great many refugees found themselves becoming impoverished, increasingly relying on rice supplied by the government and American aid. The refugees' sadness was expressed by a Jeh woman in a song of longing for the "past life in the village with its rice-planting days, abundance of food, and carefree hunting and fishing."

The highland group that appears to have suffered most during this period was the Katu, whose territory in 1964 became a free-strike zone for the South Vietnamese air force. Subsequently, American air strikes and herbicide spraying drove the Katu westward, where they were forced to survive in forest redoubts, a grueling readaptation. In the man-nature-cosmos triad the forest is associated with nature, domain of cosmic forces. Although highlanders had the farming, hunting, fishing, and foraging skills to survive, the woods are not a place where man lives (Rhadé mythology depicts forest dwellers as brutish creatures who do not know how to eat rice). In addition to the threat of bombing, even for the experienced highlanders the woods hold constant physical danger, not only from wild creatures but also from falling branches and trees (particularly during storms) and treacherous rivers. In their readaptation, Katu refugees built lean-tos, hunted, fished, planted small plots of manioc, bananas, and pineapples (the same forest crops grown by the Viet Cong insurgents), and foraged. Impoverished, they could retain only the most basic social practices, unable to have animal sacrifices or blood raids to meet concerns for fertility and to demonstrate potency. The harmony they had known with nature and cosmic forces fell into disarray, creating the possibility that they would in time come to resemble backwoods Katu whom Le Pichon described as "true savages, living in rude shelters, surviving as hunters-gatherers wearing animal skins."[18]

In every war it is inevitable that as the fighting continues and intensifies, both sides resort to harsher strategies. The ethnographies tell us that around 1967 Katu, Halang, and Sedang refugees were among the highlanders subjected to herbicides sprayed from American and South Vietnamese aircraft in a direct assault on the ecosystem. The dioxin killed infants, crops, livestock, fish, and wildlife and caused general sickness. Fear prevented the refugees from farming, fishing, hunting, or foraging, which led to malnourishment, sickness, and death. In December 1967, North Vietnamese forces launched an attack on the Stieng refugee village of Dak Son, where, using Russian grenades and flamethrowers, they killed over two hundred, most of them women, children, and elderly.

Caught in some of the bloodiest battles of the late 1960s and early 1970s, the Bru, Pacoh, Sedang, Jeh, Halang, and Stieng had their readaptations torn asunder. On the alien hot, dry coastal plain the Bru and Pacoh were unable to farm, forage, hunt, or fish, and they died in large numbers. In a desperate attempt to restore harmony, they obtained a chicken to offer the Spirit of the Earth. Sedang, Jeh, and Halang ended up in refugee camps far from their villages, totally dependent on outside agencies for everything. Many Stieng sought refuge in An Loc, only to be victims of the Communists' two-month siege. Thievery, interpersonal conflicts, and infractions of sex taboos signaled eroding moral order among the refugees. Most of them were now impoverished, none could demonstrate potency, and religious prescriptions were neglected. Man-nature-cosmos harmony was in shambles.

The Vietnam War exacted its toll, and one of the most tragic and little-known consequences was the decimation and destruction it brought to the highland people. By war's end in 1975 around 85 percent of their villages were either in ruins or abandoned. Not one Bru, Pacoh, or Katu house was left standing. Of the estimated one million highlanders, between 200,000 and 220,000 had died. But a great many were not killed by bullets or bombs. They perished because their world was shattered.

18. J. Le Pichon, "Les chasseurs du sang," *Bulletin des Amis du Vieux Hué* 24, no. 4 (1938): 366.

Epilogue

The end of the Vietnam War did not bring any morning light to end the surviving highlanders' long night of horror. Since 1975 the Vietnamese government has been implementing programs aimed at abolishing the highlanders' adaptation and common culture, replacing them with a Vietnamese lowland adaptation and culture, both alien to the mountain country. Like that of the Diem government, this policy has strains of Vietnamese ethnocentrism and nationalism, but now cloaked in dogmatic Marxism-Leninism ideology. Neil Jamieson points out that Marxism-Leninism in Vietnam is distinctive in its unique combination of borrowing and rejecting elements from Vietnamese tradition and from the West. There are traces of traditional culture, such as the value for harmony with nature in the Taoist yin-yang framework and Neo-Confucianism, which defines that harmony in the human body, in families, in villages, and in nations. With the French conquest, Western enlightenment precepts of a natural order based on a Newtonian worldview began to displace Neo-Confucianism. Both cosmological systems "depicted the world as orderly hence predictable, and therefore improvable." But it was Marxism-Leninism that provided the most suitable replacement for Neo-Confucianism as a dominant cosmology. Both were "highly moralist ethical systems firmly based on a bedrock of metaphysical justification," and "both claimed to possess unalterable universal principles that provided them with a deserved monopoly of wisdom, power, and legitimacy." Imbued with this ideology, Hanoi leaders have a deep-seated belief in techno-scientific planning and top-down social engineering that they brought to bear after 1975 to "develop" what they perceived to be the underpopulated and underutilized central highlands.[1]

1. Neil L. Jamieson, *Culture and Development in Vietnam,* East-West Center Indochina

Within this framework, highland cultures are judged on the basis of what must be eliminated "in the transition to socialism," one way of describing Vietnamization. This bodes badly for the highlanders' religious prescriptions for preserving man-nature-cosmos harmony. In a 1984 article Dang Nghiem Van of the Institute of Ethnology writes that in the "pre-liberation" highland societies, "every act, whether by the community or individual, was understood to be controlled by supernatural forces. Every year, the process of production was also that of worshipping divinities and begging them for a bumper crop." And "the people's wealth, the larger part of the food produced, nearly all of the fowl and domestic animals, were spent on rituals for the village, family or for oneself."[2] It also bodes badly for highlanders' primordial ties to kin, villages, and ethnic groups. Luu Hung of the Institute of Ethnology declared in a 1985 Hanoi conference that "in socialist society, the communal relations must be expanded beyond the ties among kinfolk and villagers, and manifestations of sectionalism stemming from the old communal relations must be overcome."[3]

Since 1975 central planners have been implementing two major programs to realize development of the central highlands. One involves massive resettlement of Vietnamese, carriers of lowland culture and adaptation. On 2 March 1989, Radio Hanoi announced that since 1981 two million settlers had been sent to New Economic Zones, most to the central highlands, the China border, or the Red River delta, and that 250,000 would be sent annually.[4] The ethnographies document that some groups are experiencing vast influxes of Vietnamese, thereby creating land shortages. By 1989, for example, with well over 400,000 settlers in Dak Lak province, the Rhadé accounted for less than one-third of the population. This influx is credited by officials with having helped bring about the final defeat of FULRO, yet on 10 May 1991 *Quân Đội Nhân Dân* (People's Army) reported that the guerrillas had split "into small groups implanted in villages," and "set up sanctuaries in the forests."[5] In late August 1992, Nate Thayer reported in the *Far Eastern Economic Review* that he visited a redoubt of FULRO troops deep in the forest of the Cambodian province of Mondolkiri.[6] The troops were living in five

Initiative Working Paper Series, Working Paper No. 1 (Honolulu: East-West Center, 1991), pp. 7–9, 14–15, 18–20, 26–33.

2. Dang Nghiem Van, "Glimpses of Tay Nguyen on the Road to Socialism," *Vietnam Social Sciences,* no. 2 (1984): 43, 46.

3. Vietnam Committee for Social Science, "Vietnam's Central Highlands: A Number of Socio-Economic Problems," *Vietnam Social Science,* nos. 1 and 2 (1986): 167.

4. Translated in FBIS-EAS 89–141.

5. Translated in FBIS-EAS 91–92.

6. Nate Thayer, "The Forgotten Army," and "Trail of Tears: 'Lost' Montagnard Army Vows to Fight On," *Far Eastern Economic Review* (10 September 1992): 16–22.

riverine villages, and their adaptation was based on hunting and gathering supplemented by maize, pumpkins, cucumbers, and chili peppers grown in small gardens. The commander told Thayer that 400 FULRO troops operated along the border and another 1,500 were active in the Vietnamese central highlands.

The other "development" program can be traced to the 1968 creation (Decree No.38) of the Department of Fixed Cultivation and Sedentarization in the Ministry of Forestry. Expressed in the Vietnamese term *định canh định cu* ("fixed field, fixed residence"), commonly known as "sedentarization," this policy reflects erroneous notions that the highlanders are nomads and that swidden farming is wanton and destructive. This program has resulted in the forced resettlement of highlanders into new Vietnamese-style communities where swidden farming and traditional ways are forbidden. In a 1986 edition of the *Vietnam Courier,* Vu Can explained that forbidding swidden farming was intended "to turn nomads into sedentary workers" in agricultural cooperatives, state farms, and logging camps, enabling them to "join the advance to socialism."[7] The Rhadé ethnography describes how extended families are being forced from their longhouses, then split up to live in Vietnamese settlements. Rhadé refugees in the United States describe how those resettled are prevented from observing traditional ways, notably religious practices (such as animal sacrifices) and rites of passage. Communist sources claim that these programs have had success in abolishing "backward customs and habits," as well as "superstitions."[8]

One result of development programs is that deforestation is taking place at an alarming rate. In 1985, Dang Thu of the Ministry of Labor reported that between 1975 and 1985, one-fourth of the central highlands forests had been destroyed.[9] The government's banning of swidden farming reflects its belief that highlanders are responsible for much deforestation, but no mention is made of forest destruction by the vast number of Vietnamese settlers or by widespread illegal logging. The dire effects of similar development programs are apparent in the highlands of northern Vietnam. A recent study by a team composed of scientists from Vietnam, the East-West Center in Honolulu, the University of Hawaii, and the Southeast Asian Agroecosystem Network in the northern uplands describes how in the post-1954 government-sponsored resettlement program, forest was cleared for farming and watercourses were dammed

7. Vu Can, "Farewell to Primitive Life," *Vietnam Courier,* no. 10 (1986): 17–19.

8. A May 1985 article (translated in JPRS-SEA, 19 July 1985) in *Quân Đội Nhân Dân* (People's army) hails the "decline in superstition in the highlands, citing the disappearance of traditional birth, marriage, and burial customs and the "many sorcerers and soothsayers" who have "promised to earn an honest living."

9. Vietnam Committee for Social Science," Vietnam's Central Highlands," pp. 158–59.

to irrigate valley-bottom paddies. As a result, the habitat for malaria-carrying mosquitoes was greatly reduced, making the midlands a relatively safe place for Vietnamese settlement. But "the deforestation led to serious environmental degradation, including deep gully erosion, loss of top soil, humus, and soil fertility, and drying up of water sources during the dry season." This in turn caused an almost total loss of production in downstream agriculture and also disastrous consequences resulting from flash floods and siltation of dams, reservoirs, and irrigation canals. The study concluded that "the Kinh [Vietnamese] people have, therefore, simply brought their lowland production technology to the uplands which has exacerbated soil loss and destruction of the natural habitat."[10]

There is a ray of hope in a 1991 report prepared by a team of scientists from the Vietnamese Ministry of Forestry and international agencies. It notes that although some highland people (the Hmong are cited) in Vietnam migrate periodically in search of land for swidden farming, there are others (numbering "some two million") that "live in fixed settlements but rely mainly on shifting cultivation of surrounding hillsides." The report points out that although shifting cultivation "was mostly in equilibrium with the local conditions," population increases have created problems. But sedentarization has produced "mixed results," and "an over-centralized, non specific, top-down approach was probably responsible for some negative results." One was the failure to give the swidden farmers any new options so that "some continued their shifting cultivation practices. Some even left the settlements." With the founding in 1990 of the office for Ethnic Minorities and Mountainous Areas (the "Mountain Office") came a new policy calling for a sustainable food production system that is "superior to shifting cultivation in the view of the people concerned." This would involve irrigated rice fields whenever possible and "different types of upland farming techniques." In sum, "the main theme is variation, depending upon local circumstances such as soil capability, markets, tradition, interest and competence among the shifting cultivators."[11]

The Ministry of Forestry report stands as the first indication of any official awareness that the highlanders' physical adaptation is relatively well suited to the mountain country. The report unfortunately does not include anything about the paddy-swidden farming adaptation found among many highlanders (and described in the Rhadé, Chru, and Sedang

10. Le Trong Cuc, Kathleen Gillogly, and A. Terry Rambo, eds., *Agroecosystems of the Midlands of Northern Vietnam: A Report on a Preliminary Human Ecology Field Study of Three Districts in Vinh Phu Province,* Occasional Paper No. 12, Environment and Policy Institute, East-West Center (Honolulu, 1990), pp. 12–14, 47–52.

11. Ministry of Forestry, Socialist Republic of Vietnam, *Vietnam: Forestry Sector Review, Tropical Forestry Action Programme, Main Report* (Hanoi: 1991), pp. 9, 21, 25, 94.

ethnographies), which should be included in the "variation theme" of the new policy. It also should be recognized that the highlanders' adaptation derives from their man-nature-cosmos harmony cosmology, just as the Vietnamese settlers' lowland adaptation rests on the concept of harmony rooted in their animist-Taoist-Confucianist-Buddhist cosmology.

But time is running out. Jamieson observes that "population growth, poverty, and environmental degradation have formed an interactive, self-amplifying system. Further increase in any of these areas promotes further increase in the others, threatening the viability of the resources upon which Vietnamese depend for life." He concludes, "Vietnam is on the brink of an abyss."[12]

Meanwhile, continued threats to the highlanders' adaptational and cultural bonds may well force them to seek haven in the more remote, rugged reaches of the mountain country. There, to survive, they will no doubt readapt, drawing upon the resilience and courage they displayed during the Vietnam War to preserve harmony with nature and cosmic forces. There they will live with unflagging dignity, working unceasingly from day to day to salvage the remaining pieces of their shattered world.

12. Jamieson, *Culture and Development,* p. 3.

Appendix A: Highland Population Figures

Ethnic differentiation in the present work and two companion works, *Sons of the Mountains* and *Free in the Forest*, is based on fieldwork conducted between 1956 and 1973. *Free in the Forest* also has population figures for highland groups collected during 1965 to 1967 in collaboration with SIL researchers, missionaries, local authorities, and highland leaders. Also reported were population estimates of the Special Commission for Highland Affairs (a forerunner of the Ministry for Ethnic Minorities' Development) and the FULRO movement.[1] The 1967 totals were 877,000 (SIL, Hickey, et al.), 610,314 (Special Commission), and 792,635 (FULRO). In 1970 the Ministry for Ethnic Minorities' Development estimated the total at 848,174. Because there were some ill-defined ethnic groups and inaccessible populations (such as the High Katu), it was generally agreed in 1967 that the highland population was close to one million. The 1967 estimates of SIL, Hickey, et al. for the groups in the present study are as follows: Rhadé, 100,000; Roglai, 57,000; Chru, 15,000; Stieng, 30,000; Katu, 40,000; Bru, 40,000; Pacoh, 15,000; Sedang, 40,000; Jeh, 10,000; Halang, 10,000. In *Free in the Forest* it is noted that in 1972 Nay Luett, minister of ethnic minorities, estimated that some 200,000 highlanders had died since 1965.[2] By the end of the war in 1975 that figure was estimated by ministry staff at around 220,000, including military personnel on both sides. The wartime pattern suggests that the heaviest civilian losses were among the Bru, Pacoh, Katu, Sedang, Halang, Jeh, Stieng, and Roglai. The Rhadé Kpa and Bih were less

1. Gerald Cannon Hickey, *Sons of the Mountains: Ethnohistory of the Vietnamese Central Highlands to 1954* (New Haven: Yale University Press, 1982), pp. 4–19, 439–40; Hickey, *Free in the Forest: Ethnohistory of the Vietnamese Central Highlands, 1954–1976* (New Haven: Yale University Press, 1982), pp. 300–303.

2. Hickey, *Free in the Forest*, pp. 252–53, 290–91.

affected than Rhadé in more remote areas, and the Chru were the least affected of all groups.

The 1989 national census in Vietnam reports figures for highland groups.[3] Ethnic differentiation therein appears to be the same as that contained in a 1984 Vietnamese work, *Ethnic Minorities in Vietnam* by Dang Nghiem Van, Chu Thai Son, and Luu Hung, which also has population figures.[4] Only the Rhadé (Ê-dê), Roglai (Ra-glai), Chru (Chu Ru), Stieng (Xtiêng), and Jeh (Gié-Triêng) appear to be identified similarly in the present work and the census. Population figures in the census are Ê-dê, 194,000; Ra-glai, 71,696; Chu-ru, 10,746; Xtiêng, 50,194; and Gié-Triêng, 26,924.

In the 1989 census the Cơ Tu (Katu) number 36,967, but the 1984 work subgroups include the "Phuong," another designation for Phuang, whose ethnic status (noted in Chapter 5) is not clear. Bru-Vân Kiều has 40,132 and includes the Bru and Pacoh. The Xơ-dăng (Sedang) population is 96,766 and includes among its subgroups the Halang. Included also are the "To-drah" and "Ca-rong" (Kayong), whose statuses are discussed in Chapters 6 and 8.

In *Sons of the Mountains* it is reported that a 1921 census of the French protectorate of Annam revealed that there were around 8,100 Vietnamese in the highlands, and by 1943 this number had risen to 42,267.[5] In 1970 the Ministry for Ethnic Minorities' Development estimated that the Vietnamese numbered 448,349.[6] This figure was at the time considered too low because there was a steady influx of Vietnamese (Pleiku town was estimated at 50,000 in 1966, but it was thought to be more like 100,000 in the early 1970s). Large numbers of Vietnamese fleeing the highlands in 1975 perished when the withdrawal became a rout. Resettlement programs since 1975 have brought about vast increases in the Vietnamese population, but no figures are available.

3. Central Census Steering Committee, *Vietnam Population Census, 1989: Completed Census Results,* vol. 1 (Hanoi, 1991), p. 66.

4. Dang Nghiem Van, Chu Thai Son, and Luu Hung, *The Ethnic Minorities in Vietnam* (Hanoi: Foreign Language Publishing House, 1984), pp. 51–57, 73–94, 224–49.

5. Hickey, *Sons of the Mountains,* pp. 441–42.

6. Hickey, *Free in the Forest,* pp. 303–4.

Appendix B: Basic Kin Terminology

1. Rhadé

Ancestors
Ayang Aduôn Aê Dum   (distant ancestors)
Ayang Atâo or Ayang Tâo (deceased grandparents)

Second Ascending Generation
Aê   (parents' fathers)
Aduôn   (parents' mothers)

First Ascending	*Matrilineal*	*Nonmatrilineal*
Ama		F
Amĭ	M	
Awa	MoB	
Amiêt	MyB	
Amĭ aprŏng	MoSi	
Amĭ neh	MySi	FySi
Aprŏng êkei		FoB
M'neh		FyB
Aprŏng m'niê		FoSi

Ego's Generation		*Collateral*	*Affinal*
Ayŏng	oB	(PSbS older than Ego)	
Amai	oSi	(PSbD older than Ego)	
+ khua = eldest sibling			
Adei êkei	yB	(PSbS younger than Ego)	

Adei m'niê ySi	(PSbD younger than Ego)	
Dăm knai	(MBS, FSiS for male Ego)	
Juk or Juk tô	(MBD, FSiD for female Ego)	
Knai		YSiH
Iê êkei		WB
Iê m'niê		WSi

First Descending	*Matrilineal*	*Nonmatrilineal*
Anak	Ch	(BCh, MBChCh, MSiSCh, FSbChCh)
+ êkei (S) m'niê (D)		
+ khua = eldest		
+ kluč = youngest		
Amuôn	SiCh, MSiDCh	

Second Descending		
Čô		SCh
+ gap djuê	DCh	

Third Descending		
Čě		(DSCh, SChCh)
+ găp djuê	DDCh	

Fourth Descending		
Rông rê rông rai	DDDCh	

2. Roglai

Fourth Ascending Generation

Acơi Canau	PPPF
Amoq Canau	PPPM

Third Ascending

Acơi Coq	PPF
Amoq Coq	PPM

Second Ascending

| Acơi | PF | + Vamah Ama = FF, FM |
| Amoq | PM | + Jơc = MF, MM |

First Ascending

Ama	F, FB	Ghơng (older than parent)
Awơi	M, PSi	+
Miaq	MB	Ben (younger than parent)

Ego's Generation — *Collateral* — *Affinal*

| Sa-Ai | oSb | PSbS (older than Ego) | + matou = HoSb, WoSb |
| Adơi | ySb | PSbS (younger than Ego) | + Matou = HySb, WySb |

+ Lacơi = oB,yB
+ Cumơi = oSi, ySi
+ Kachua = eldest

Awơi

PSbD + Ghong = Older than Ego
+ Ben = Younger than Ego
+ Gơq cumơi preh = MSiD
+ Gơq cumơi lingao = FSbD
+ Timiha = HM, WM

Sidiuq	W
Pisac	H
Ama timiha	HF, WF

First Descending

Anaq

+ Lacơi = S
+ Cumơi = D
+ Kachua = eldest
+ Khrah = middle
+ Taluiq = youngest

| Camuon | SbCh |

Second Descending

| Ticho | ChCh |

Third Descending

| Ticheq | ChChCh |

Fourth Descending
Laneq   ChChChCh

Fifth Descending
Laniau   ChChChChCh

Sixth Descending
Iau   ChChChChChCh

Seventh Descending
Hanoaq   ChChChChChChCh

3. Chru

Fourth Ascending Generation
Akây Amo Phun   Ancestors

Third Ascending
Amo Pang   MMM
Akây Pang   MMF
Akây Pô Pang or Ơn   FFF
   Pô Pang
Amo Pô Pang   FFM

Second Ascending
Amo   MM
Akây or Ơn   MF
Amo Pô   FM
Akay Pô or Ơn Pô   FF

First Ascending		*Affinal*
Ama	F	
Ame	M	FBW
Ame Dơng	MoSi	
Ame Tét	MySi	
Miăh Dong	MoB	Miah = (FSiH, WF, HF)
Miăh Tét	MyB	
Ama Dơng or Wa Dơng	FoB	Wa = (MSiH)
Ama Tét or Wa Tét	FyB	
Ame Dơng or Pò Dong	FoSi	

| Ame Tét or Pò Tét | FySi | |
| Tamahama | FSi | (MBW, HM, WM) |

Ego's Generation	*Collateral*	*Affinal*
Saay oSb + Kochua = 1st + Lơkây = oB + Kơmây = oSi	(FBS, MSiS, FSiD, MBD older than Ego)	(BW, FBSW, FSIDH, MBDH, WSi)
Adây ySb + Tolui = last	(FBS, MSiS, FSiD, MBD younger than Ego)	(BW, FBSW, MSiSW, FSiDH, MBDH, WSi)
Gơ Lơkây (female Ego) = B	(FBS, MSiS)	
Gơ Kơmây (male Ego) = Si	(FBD, MSiD)	(FSiSW, MBSW)
Prui	(FSiS, MBS)	(SiH, FBDH, MSiDH)

First Descending		
+ Lơkay = S		(SiDH, SiSW, WSiS, WSiD, WBDH, WBSW)
Ana Ch	BCh	
+ Kơmây = D		
Kơmoăn	SiCh	
+ Lơkây =		DH
Mơrtơu		(WSiDH, WSiSW)
+ Kơmây =		SW

Second Descending	
Acho	ChCh

Third Descending	
Aché	ChChCh

Fourth Descending	
Achít	ChChChCh

4. Stieng

Third Ascending Generation
Yi   Parents' Parents' Parents

Second Ascending
Yau   Parents' Parents

First Ascending		*Affinal*	
Bươp	F		= WF
		+ Pô	
Mê	M		= WM
+ Oh Nur	MSi		
+ Rôh Bươp	FSi		
Côônh	MB		
Moom	FB		

Ego's		*Collateral*		
Bi	OSb	(PSbS older than Ego)	+ Porsa =	(WOSi, WOBW)
+ Rôh = OSi				
Oh	YSb	(PSbS younger than Ego)	+ Porsa =	(WYSi, WYBW)
Rôh		PSbD		
Sai				H
			+ Urbaang =	W
Côônh				WB
Clay				WSiH

First Descending			
Coon	Ch	BCh	
+ Bi = eldest			
+ Phôt = youngest			
+ Oh = second to youngest			
+ Taal = in between			
Moom		SiCh	

Second Descending
Sau   (all kin)

Third Descending
Sê   (all kin)

5. Katu

Third Ascending Generation

Abuôp bleeh	FFF, MFF
Ayêq (or Amoq) bleeh	FFM, MFM

Second Ascending

Abuôp	FF, MF
Ayêq (or Amoq)	FM, MM

First Ascending

Ama (or Konh)	F
Amêq (or Akan)	M
Ava	FoB, MoB, FoSi, MoSi
Ayâi	FyB, MyB
Angah	FySi, MySi

Ego's Generation		*Collateral*	*Affinal*
+ N'druih = oB		(FBS, MSbS older than Ego)	
Anó			
+ N'dil = oSi		(MSiD older than Ego)	
Voq (or Adi)	yB	(FBS, MSbS younger than Ego)	
Amoq	ySi	(MSiD younger than Ego)	
Mamooq		FBD	
Cha Chaau		FSiCh	
Shuya		MBD	
Kayik			H
Kadial			W
Ava			(WoB, WoBW, WoSI, WoSiH)
Kalâi			WyB
Yaya			WM

First Descending

+ N'druih = S	Tahar = Eldest

Second Descending
Chi Chau   ChCh

Third Descending
Chi Chau Ache   ChChCh

Fourth Descending
Cha Chau Achar   ChChChCh

6. Bru

Fifth Ascending Generation
Achiac   FFFFF

Fourth Ascending
Achúc   FFFF

Third Ascending
Achêh   FFF

Second Ascending		*Patrilineal*	*Nonpatrilineal*
Achuaih	FFB	+ Ỗng = (FF)	+ Muq = MF
Ayoaq	FFSi	+ Ỗng = (FM)	+ Muq = MM

First Ascending		*Patrilineal Collateral*	*Affinal*
M'poaq	F		
M'piq	M		
Bac	FoB, FOSi, MoSi	(FFBS, FFBD older than Ego's father)	(FoBW, FoSiH, MoSiH)
Anhi	FyB	(FFBS, yr than F)	FySiH, MySiH
Avia	FySi, MySi	(FFBD, yr than F)	FyBW
Cũq	MB		MBW

Ego's Generation		*Collateral*	*Affinal*
Ai	oB	(PSbS, older than Ego)	
Ơĩ	oSi	(PSD, older than Ego)	(oBW, WoSi, HoBW, HoSi)
	+ Mansễn = yB	PSbS, younger than Ego	
A−Ễm	+ Semieng = ySI	PSbD, younger than Ego	

For female		YBW, HyBW
Ego =		
Semai	(male cousins)	
Semaui	(female cousins)	
Lacuoi		W
Alêp		WySi
Mpual		WSiH
Cayac		H
Alơi Bac		HoB
Rlep		HyB
Lŏh		HySi
Plơi Ai		HoSiH
Plơi Yaih		HySiH
Kumân Êm		yBW
Mahai		SiH, WB
Yasai (female Ego)		oSiH
Aplai (female Ego)		ySiH

First Descending	*Collateral*	*Affinal*
Con	Ch	
Ramon	SbCh, PSbChCh	
Kumân		SW
Partiam (or Aplai)		DH

Second Descending		
Châu	ChCh	SbChCh, PSbChChCh

Third Descending	
Chẽ	SSCh

Fourth Descending	
Cho	SSSCh

7. Pacoh

Fourth Ascending Generation	
Achoh	FFFF, FFFM

Third Ascending	*Patrilineal*	*Nonpatrilineal*
+ Choanh =	FFF	
Achaih		
+ Preng =		MFF

	+ Choanh or	FFM	
	Yaq =		
Acheh			
	+ Preng =		MFM

Second Ascending

	+ Choanh =	FF	
Avoq			
	+ Preng =		MF
	+ Choanh or	FM	
	Yaq =		
Acaq			
	+ Preng =		MM

First Ascending

A-Am	F
+ Put =	FoB
+ Ket =	FyB
Ai	M
+ Put =	FoSi
+ Ket =	FySi
Anhi	MB
Ama	MSi

Ego's Generation		*Collateral*
Ačhai	oB	(FBS, FSiS, MBS, MSiS older than Ego)
Amoq	oSI	(FBD, FSiD, MSiD older than Ego)
+ Cŏnh = yB		(FBS, FSiS, MBS, MSiS younger than Ego)
A-Em		
+ Cám = YSi		(FBD, FSiD, MSiD younger than Ego)
Lu Lep		MBD

First Descending

+ Cŏnh = S	
Acay	
+ Cám = D	
Amon	SbCh

Second Descending

Ache	SCh

Third Descending

Achĕ	SSCh

8. Sedang

Third Ascending Generation

Nôa	FFF, FMF, MFF, MMF
Vóng	FFM, FMM, MFM, MMM

Second Ascending

Pôa	FF, MF, FFB, FMB, MFB, MMB
Ja	FM, MM, FFSi, FMSi, MFSi, MMSi

First Ascending		*Collateral*	*Affinal*
Pa	F, FoB	FFoBS, MMoSiS	MoSiH
Nôu	M, MoSi	FFoBD, MMoSiD	FoBW
Meh	Fosi, MoB	FFoSiCh	FoSiH, MoBW
Mie	FySi, MyB	FFySiCh	FySiH, MoBW
Tăm	FyB, StepF	FFyBS	MySiH
Sáng or Să	MySi, StepM	FFyBD	FyBW

Ego's Generation			
Ngoh	oB	PSbS older than Ego	WoSiH, HoSiH
Na	oSi	PSbD older than Ego	WoBW, HoBW
	+ konốu = yB		(WyB, WySiH, HySiH)
O		PSCh younger than Ego	
	+ kodrai = ySi		(WyBW, HySi, HyBW)
	+ ki reng ta = 1		
	+ ki reng dế = 2		
	+ pai = 3		
	+ pun = 4		
	+ hodrui = 5		
Konốu			H
Kodrai			W
Vá			HF, WF
Sa			HM, WM
Mai			(OBW, OSiH, WSi, male Ego = yBW female Ego = ySiH)
Meh			WoB, HoSi

Mé   (female Ego = yBW)
ŏ   (male Ego = ySiH)
Roi   SWP, DHP

First Descending
Kuĕ   Ch   + môjiang = Ch
                  + tobo = StepCh
Muán   SbCh, PSbCh, Ch
Dôh   (DH, SbDH,
                                        PSbDH)
Mé   (SW, SbSW, PSbSW)

Second Descending
Cháu   ChCh
Mé cháu   ChChW
Dôh cháu   ChChH

Third Descending
Chéi (or Hei)   ChChCh

Fourth Descending
Chá   ChChChCh

Fifth Descending
Chía   ChChChChCh

9. Jeh

Third Ascending Generation
Boŏ ka baă   FFF

Second Ascending
Boŏ   FF, MF
Yă   FM, MM

First Ascending
Baă   F
Uŭ   M
Mih   FoB, FoSi, MoB, MoSi
Nhu   FyB, MyB
Ma   FySi, MySi

Ego's Generation			*Collateral*
Mĕe	oSb	= oB	PSbS older than Ego
		= oSi	PSbD older than Ego
	+ loulou		
	+ dridri		
Oh	ySb	= yB	PSbS younger than Ego
		= ySi	PSbD younger than Ego

First Descending					*Affinal*
		+ paseem	= eldest		
Kon	Ch	+ sut	= youngest		
		+ nay	= in between		
Mon	SbCh				
Mai					SW
Ong					DH

Second Descending

Chau	ChCh		
			SbChCh

Third Descending

Chau chek	ChChCh

Fourth Descending

Chau Chi	ChChChCh

10. Halang

Fourth Ascending Generation

Bŏ kră	Male ancestors
Yă kră	Female ancestors

Third Ascending

Bŏ kơchĭ	FFF, FMF, MFF, MMF
Yă Kơchĭ	FFM, FMM, MFM, MMM

Second Ascending

Bŏ	FF, MF, FFB, FMB, MFB, MMB
Yă	FM, MM, FFSi, FMSi, MFSi, MMSi

First Ascending	*Collateral*	*Affinal*
Bă	F	

Mĭ	M		
Mih	PoB, PoSi	(PPSbCh older than parents)	POSbH/W
Nhò	PyB	(PPSbS younger than parents PPSbD)	
Ma	PySi		
Miak			PYSbH/W

Ego's Generation

'Nhŏng	oB	(PSbS older than Ego)	
Nau	oSi	(PSbD older than Ego)	
Oh	yB, ySi	(PSbCh younger than Ego)	
Bơnklo			H
Mơndray			W
Kơnhŏng	+ nay =		2d W
	+ hodrut =		3d W
Mì			(oBW, oSiH)
Mai			yBW
Ŏng			ySiH
Braih băn			(WBW, WSiH, HBW, HSiH)
Ruy			SWP, DHP

First Descending

Koan	Ch		
+ tim = Step Ch			
Moan	SbCh	PSbChCh	H/WSbCh

Second Descending

Chau	ChCh	SbChCh

Third Descending

Chau chĕk	ChChCh

Fourth Descending

Chau chi	ChChChCh

Fifth Descending

Chau kơni blak	ChChChChCh

Appendix C: Epidemiological Research on the Rhadé, Stieng, and Sedang

Between 24 June and 4 July 1967 a Walter Reed Army Institute of Research team headed by Captain Andrew Cottingham, M.D., conducted thick blood film examination for malaria and filariasis in the Stieng village of Bu Kroai. Of the fifty-three villagers examined, the Plasmodium vivax was found in seventeen (32.08 prevalence ratio), Plasmodium falciparum was diagnosed in one (1.89), a mixture of the two was found in one (1.89), and Microfilaria was detected in ten (18.87). Findings by household are summarized in the table below.[1] In addition, fifty-seven Stieng militiamen in the Bu Dop Special Forces camp were examined. The positive numbered: P. vivax, six (10.53); P. falciparum, one (1.75); mixed, zero; and Microfilaria, eight (14.04). The totals for Bu Kroai and Bu Dop were P. vivax, twenty-three (20.91); P. falciparum, two (1.82); mixed, one (0.91); and Microfilaria, eighteen (16.36).

In 1967, a Walter Reed Army Institute of Research team gathered blood samples of Vietnamese, Khmer, Cham, Rhadé, Stieng, and Sedang.[2] Among the highland samples the highest frequencies of hemo-

1. Walter Reed Army Institute of Research Team, Table 1, "Results of Thick Blood Film Examination for Malaria and Filariasis Accomplished on Stieng Villagers of Bu Kroai Village, 24 June 1967"; Table 4, "Results of Malaria and Filariasis Prevalence Survey Accomplished in Phuoc Long Province, Republic of Vietnam, 24 June–4 July, 1967," mimeograph (Saigon, 1967).

2. James E. Bowman, Paul E. Carson, Henri Frischer, Robin D. Powell, Edward J. Colwell, Llewellyn J. Legters, Andrew J. Cottingham, Stephen C. Boone, and Wesley W. Hiser, "Hemoglobin and Red Cell Enzyme Variation in Some Populations of the Republic of Vietnam with Comments on the Malaria Hypothesis," *American Journal of Physical Anthropology* 34, no. 3 (1971): 313–24.

Results of thick blood film examination for malaria and filariasis accomplished on Stieng villagers of Bu Kroai village, 24 June 1967, by the Walter Reed Army Institute of Research team

House	Name	Sex	Malaria	Filariasis
#1	Nhooch	M	Vivax 500/cmm	Positive
	Nhiem	M	Vivax 150/cmm	Negative
	Thuoc	M	Vivax 2/400F	Negative
	Ti Thuoc	F	Vivax 2/400F	Positive
#2	Brao	F	Vivax 3/400F	Negative
	Ot	F	Vivax 10/400F	Positive
	Luom	F	Vivax 8/400F	Negative
#3	Hu	M	Vivax 2/400F	Negative
	Luom	F	Vivax 2/400F	Negative
#4	Lghe	F	Vivax 5/400F	Negative
	Khul	F	Vivax 2/400F	Negative
#5	Moom	F	Vivax 300/cmm	Negative
	Mooch	F	Vivax 500/cm	Negative
#6	Dung	M	Negative	Positive
	Wil	F	Falciparium 2/400F	Positive
	Chhong	M	Vivax 500/cmm	Negative
	Phoq	F	Vivax and Falciparum 1000/cmm	Positive
#7	Yuong	M	Negative	Positive
	Branh	M	Vivax 1/400F	Negative
	Kli	M	Vivax 3/400F	Positive
#8	Bim	F	Vivax 1/400F	Positive

globin E were found among the Stieng (0.365), followed by the Rhadé (0.212) and the Sedang (0.029). The highest prevalence of glucose-6-phosphate dehydrogenase (G6PD) deficiency was in the Stieng (0.54), followed by the Rhadé (0.023) and Sedang (0.004).

A Note on Bibliography

A general ethnolinguistic work on mainland Southeast Asia that includes information on the central highlands is Frank M. Lebar, Gerald C. Hickey, and John K. Musgrave, *Ethnic Groups of Mainland Southeast Asia* (New Haven: Human Relations Area Files Press, 1964). Dang Nghiem Van, Chu Thai Son, and Luu Hung, *The Ethnic Minorities in Vietnam* (Hanoi: Foreign Languages Publishing House, 1984), presents a Vietnamese view of highland groups. A source on highland music is Georges de Gironcourt, "Recherches de géographie musicale en Indochine," *BSEI* 7, no. 4 (1942): 7–174. Staff members of the Summer Institute of Linguistics (SIL) focused their linguistic and ethnographic research primarily on the Mon Khmer–speaking groups. Articles presenting results of comparative linguistics and lexocostatistical research are David Thomas and R. K. Headley, Jr., "More on Mon-Khmer Subgroupings," *Lingua* 25, no. 4 (1970): 398–418; and David Thomas, "A Note on the Branches of Mon Khmer," *Mon Khmer Studies IV*, Language Series no. 2, Center for Vietnamese Studies and Summer School of Linguistics (Saigon, 1973), pp. 138–41.

Earlier articles on the Mon Khmer–speaking groups are by French investigators, while more recent ones are by members of the SIL. In his "Les chasseurs de sang," published in the *Bulletin des Amis du Vieux Hué* 25, no. 4 (1938): 257–409, J. Le Pichon gives us a broad ethnographic picture of this group. Nancy Costello details Katu human blood sacrifices in "Socially Approved Homicide Among the Katu," *SA* 2, no. 1 (1972): 77–87, and she describes Katu burial practices and concepts of death in "Death and Burial in Katu Culture," in *Notes from Indochina on Ethnic Minority Cultures*, ed. Marilyn Gregerson and Dorothy Thomas (Dallas: SIL Museum of Anthropology, 1980), pp. 99–106. John Miller reports on Bru kinship, religious beliefs, and village political organization in "Bru Kinship," *SA* 2, no. 1 (1972): 62–70, and on Bru vowels in "An Acoustical Study of Brou Vowels," *Phonetica* 17 (1967): 149–77. In his "Reduplication in Pacoh" (M.A. thesis, Hartford Seminary Foundation,

1966), Richard L. Watson treats the various kinds of reduplication that occur in the Pacoh language. His illustrative texts contain information on Pacoh proverbs, prayers, and the feast of the tombs. A brief article containing information on Sedang villages and households is Georges Devereux, "Functioning Units in Ha(rh)ndea(ng) Society," *Primitive Man* 10 (1937): 1–7. Two articles on the Sedang language by Kenneth Smith are "Sedang Dialects," *BSEI* 42, no. 3 (1967): 196–255; and "More on Sedang Ethnodialects," *Mon Khmer Studies IV,* Language Series no. 2, Center for Vietnamese Studies and Summer Institute of Linguistics (Saigon, 1973), pp. 43–51. The function of music in Jeh culture is discussed in Nancy Cohen, "Jeh Music," in *Notes from Indochina on Ethnic Minorities,* ed. Marilyn Gregerson and Dorothy Thomas (Dallas: SIL Museum of Anthropology, 1980), pp. 85–98. Jeh marriage, birth, and funeral practices are described in Dwight Gradin, "Rites of Passage Among the Jeh," *SA* 2, no. 1 (1972): 53–61. James Cooper analyzes some Halang rhymes within a cultural context in "An Ethnography of Halang Rhymes," *Mon-Khmer Studies IV,* Language Series no. 2, Center for Vietnamese Studies and Summer Institute of Linguistics (Saigon, 1973), pp. 33–42. Théophile Gerber, a French administrator, produced two works on the Stieng. One is *Lexique Française-Stieng* (Saigon: Imprimerie du Théâtre, 1937), a French-Stieng dictionary, and the other is "Coutumier Stieng," *BEFEO* 45 (1951): 228–69, a codification of Stieng customs. Lorraine Haupers presents a wide range of ethnographic data in "Notes on Stieng Life," *Notes from Indochina on Ethnic Minority Cultures,* ed. Marilyn Gregerson and Dorothy Thomas (Dallas: SIL Museum of Anthropology, 1980), pp. 143–76.

A work dealing with Austronesian (Malayopolynesian) languages is Isador Dyen, "The Chamic Languages," in *Current Trends in Linguistics,* ed. E. Sebeok (The Hague: Mouton, 1971), 8:200–210. More has been written about the Rhadé than any other highland group. A depth study of Rhadé kinship within the context of village society is Anne de Hauteclocque-Howe, *Les Rhadés: Une société de droit maternal* (Paris: Editions du Centre National de la Recherche Scientifique, 1987). Bernard Y. Jouin practiced medicine for many years in Ban Me Thuot and wrote numerous articles. The most comprehensive is "Grossesse et naissance en pays Rhadé," *BSEI* 34, no. 3 (1959): 1–84, which concerns birth practices. Albert Maurice and Georges Marie Proux's article, "L'âme du riz," *BSEI* 29, nos. 2–3 (1954): 1–134, describes swidden farming and associated rituals. Albert Maurice's article, "L'habitation Rhadé: Rites et techniques," *IIEH* 5, fasc. 1 (1942): 87–106, describes longhouse-construction techniques and related religious beliefs and practices. Léopold Sabatier, *Recueil de coutumes Rhadées du Darlac* (Hanoi: Imprimerie d'Extrême-Orient, 1940), is a codification of Rhadé customs.

Two focused articles on the Roglai are Vurnell Cobbey, "Some Northern Roglai Beliefs About the Supernatural," *SA* 2, no. 1 (1972): 125–29; and Lois Lee, "Pregnancy and Childbirth Practices of the Northern Roglai," *SA* 2, no. 1 (1972): 49–50. Aspects of Chru kinship are discussed in Eugene E. Fuller, "Cross-Cousin Marriage and Chru Kinship Terminology," in *Notes from Indochina on Ethnic Minority Cultures,* ed. Marilyn Gregerson and Dorothy Thomas (Dallas: SIL Museum of Anthropology, 1980), pp. 113–19.

Information on the role of highlanders in the U.S. Special Forces Program is contained in Francis J. Kelly, *U.S. Army Special Forces, 1961–1971* (Washington, D.C.: U.S. Department of the Army, 1973). A treatment of highlander refugees within the context of Vietnam War dislocations is found in Louis A. Wiesner, *Victims and Survivors: Displaced Persons and Other Victims in Viet-Nam, 1954–1975* (New York: Greenwood Press, 1988).

Highland soils are described in F. R. Moormann, *The Soils of the Republic of South Vietnam* (Saigon: Ministry of Agriculture, 1961), and forests are discussed in R. Champsoloix, *Rapport sur les forêts de P.M.S., République du Viet-Nam* (Saigon: Ministère de la Réforme Agraire et de Développment en Agriculture et Pêcherie, 1952). A work on big game and hunting in the central highlands is Henri de Monestrol, *Chasses et faune d'Indochine* (Saigon: Editions A. Portail, 1952); and highland ornithology is reported in Philip Wildash, *Birds of South Vietnam* (Rutland, Vt.: Charles E. Tuttle Co., 1968).

Index

Adornment, xxi; as symbolic gift, 60, 66, 89, 91, 155, 162, 183; beads, xxi, xxvii, 156, 183, 250; ear plugs, xxi, xxvii, 91, 93, 104; mystique, xxvii, 251; production of, xxi, 156

Age-grading: and kin-group leadership, 19, 27, 57; in kin terminology, 17, 55, 64–66, 82, 124, 147, 150, 160, 182, 196, 217

Alcohol: as wedding symbol, 20, 57, 66–67, 89, 156, 184, 197–98, 251; birth, 21, 203, 251; mystique, xxvii, 246, 251; origin legend, 7; preparation of, 23–24, 33, 47, 64, 68, 132, 157, 164, 172, 226, 246, 250

Alliances: and blood raids, 119–20; fictive kinship, 59, 142, 151, 211, 222–23, 252, 257; friendship, 59; mutual aid, 59, 223; rituals, 59, 120, 222–23, 252

Ancestors: and descendants, 2, 19, 20, 25, 53, 66, 73–74, 82, 86, 93, 117, 118, 123, 128, 134, 142, 151, 159, 199, 204, 259; and incest, xxvii, 6, 20; and soil fertility, xxvi–xxvii, 27, 29–30, 142, 248, 249; common, of ethnic group, 1, 79, 194; malevolent, 53–54; ritual offerings to, xxvii, 10, 20, 21, 25, 27, 29–30, 34, 35, 53, 57–59, 67, 69, 71, 89, 95, 124, 129, 153, 160, 162, 199, 200, 204, 209

Animals, xix, xxi, xxiv, 2; domestic, xix, xxvii, xxx; dream omens, 8–9, 31, 118; dressing out of, 37, 116, 125, 153, 163, 225; in bride-price, 57, 86, 87, 125, 155; in dowry, 20; mystique, xxvii, 246, 251; symbolic, 26, 32, 35, 71, 89, 252; taboos, 199; wild, xx–xxi, 37–38, 61, 73, 93, 101, 107, 118, 126, 132, 143, 153, 158, 165, 172. *See also* Buffalos; Elephants

Architecture: and Communist policy, 46, 140, 264; and malaria exposure, xxi, xxiv, 246; ideational aspects, xiv, xxxvii, 8–17, 54, 62, 80, 122–23, 245–46; innovations, 8, 64; of abodes, xxi, 54, 62, 80, 147, 246; Vietnam War, 232–33, 234, 260, 261. *See also* Longhouse

Austronesian languages, xiii, xv, xxviii, 254

Bahnar, xxviii, xxix, xxx; Khmer influence, 254

Bajaraka movement, xxx, 4, 30, 40; potency, 255

Ban Me Thuot: 1975 Communist capture of, 45, 140; education center, xxix, 3–4; in 1968 Tet Offensive, 44, 45; market center, 3

Baskets, xx, xxx, 16, 23; as offerings, 32, 47, 128, 199; mystique, xxvii, 27, 29; types/uses of, 17, 64, 73, 89, 92, 111, 117, 120–21, 123, 126, 131, 132, 188, 189, 196, 207; weaving, xxi, 54, 89, 126, 156, 193

Betel (leaves) and areca (nuts), 71; chewing, 55, 157, 254; in early Vietnam, xxvii; offerings, 48, 57, 100; trade items, 109, 111

Bilateral descent, xix, xxviii, 181–83, 192, 196, 210–11, 214, 256; and house types, 180; and marriage, 181–83, 196, 214–15; inheritance, 203–4, 222, 253; residence, 199, 219

Birds, xx, 53, 107, 132; as omens, 11, 22, 48, 71, 99, 128; crop predators, 34, 72, 100, 165, 187; devices to scare, xxi, 34, 100, 187–88; symbolic, 33

This book was set in Times and Eras typefaces. Times is a modified book version of the original Times New Roman, a newspaper typeface, commissioned in 1931 to be designed under the supervision of Stanley Morison for the London *Times*.

Eras was designed in 1969 by Studio Hollenstein in Paris for the Wagner Typefoundry. A contemporary script-like version of a sans-serif typeface, the letters of Eras have a monotone stroke and are slightly inclined.

Printed on acid-free paper.